SOUTHERN AND POSTCOLONIAL PERSPECTIVES ON POLICING, SECURITY AND SOCIAL ORDER

Edited by
Roxana Pessoa Cavalcanti, Peter Squires
and Zoha Waseem

First published in Great Britain in 2025 by

Bristol University Press
University of Bristol
1-9 Old Park Hill
Bristol
BS2 8BB
UK
t: +44 (0)117 374 6645
e: bup-info@bristol.ac.uk

Details of international sales and distribution partners are available at bristoluniversitypress.co.uk

© Bristol University Press 2025

British Library Cataloguing in Publication Data
A catalogue record for this book is available from the British Library

ISBN 978-1-5292-2366-8 hardcover
ISBN 978-1-5292-2367-5 paperback
ISBN 978-1-5292-2368-2 ePub
ISBN 978-1-5292-2369-9 ePdf

The right of Roxana Pessoa Cavalcanti, Peter Squires and Zoha Waseem to be identified as editors of this work has been asserted by them in accordance with the Copyright, Designs and Patents Act 1988.

All rights reserved: no part of this publication may be reproduced, stored in a retrieval system, or transmitted in any form or by any means, electronic, mechanical, photocopying, recording, or otherwise without the prior permission of Bristol University Press.

Every reasonable effort has been made to obtain permission to reproduce copyrighted material. If, however, anyone knows of an oversight, please contact the publisher.

The statements and opinions contained within this publication are solely those of the contributors and editors and not of the University of Bristol or Bristol University Press. The University of Bristol and Bristol University Press disclaim responsibility for any injury to persons or property resulting from any material published in this publication.

Bristol University Press works to counter discrimination on grounds of gender, race, disability, age and sexuality.

Cover design: Nicky Borowiec
Front cover image: istock/jacoblund

Contents

List of Figures and Tables		v
Notes on Contributors		vi
Acknowledgements		xi
1	Introduction: Southern and Postcolonial Perspectives on Policing, Security and Social Order *Peter Squires, Roxana Pessoa Cavalcanti and Zoha Waseem*	1

PART I Policing, Law and Violent Legacies

2	Asymmetric Policing at a Distance? Frontiers, Law and Disorder in the Weaponized South *Peter Squires*	23
3	From Overseer to Officer: A Brief History of British Policing through Afro-Diasporic Music Culture *Lambros Fatsis*	45
4	Police Violence, Anti-Police Protest Movements and the Challenge of Decolonialism *Chris Cunneen*	62
5	Crossing Red Lines: Exploring the Criminalization and Policing of Sedition and Dissent in Pakistan *Ammar Ali Jan and Zoha Waseem*	82

PART II Southern Institutions and Criminal Justice Politics

6	Reform, Restructure and Rebrand: Cursory Solutions to Historically Entrenched Policing Problems *Danielle Watson, Nathan W. Pino and Casandra Harry*	105
7	Democratic Policing in Authoritarian Structures: Policing Models and the Exercise of Authority in São Paulo, Brazil *Viviane de Oliveira Cubas, Frederico Castelo Branco and André Rodrigues Oliveira*	119
8	Rioting Struggles in Brazil: Prison Gangs, Staff and Criminal Justice Hegemony *Vitor Dieter*	143

| 9 | The Political Economy of Punishment in the Global Periphery: Incarceration and Discipline in Brazilian Prisons | 169 |
| | *Luiz Dal Santo* | |

PART III Southern Narratives and Experiences: Culture, Resistance and Justice

10	Colonial Violence, Contemporary Conflict and Socio-Ecological Renewal: Analysis from Bougainville	191
	Blaise Iruinu and Kristian Lasslett	
11	Exploring the Moving Lines of the 'Global South': Citizenship and Political Participation in a Rio de Janeiro *Favela*	211
	Elizabete Ribeiro Albernaz	
12	Social Mobilization and Victims of Violence: Emotional Responses to Justice in an Urban Periphery	232
	Valéria Cristina de Oliveira and Jaqueline Garza Placencia	
13	Women, Peace, Security and Justice: A Postcolonial Feminist Critical Review	251
	Giovana Esther Zucatto	

PART IV Conflicts, Criminalization and Protest in the New Neoliberal Internationalism

14	The Contemporary Criminalization of Activists: Insights from Latin America	269
	Roxana Pessoa Cavalcanti, Israel Celi and Simone Gomes	
15	Framing Human Insecurity between Dispossession and Difference	286
	Guilherme Benzaquen and Pedro Borba	
16	Private Military Force in the Global South: Mozambique and Southern Africa	304
	John Lea	
17	Distant Conflicts, Southern Deaths: The Trials of Neoliberal Internationalism in 'Southern Nowhere'	322
	Peter Squires	
18	Conclusion/Afterword	346
	Roxana Pessoa Cavalcanti, Zoha Waseem and Peter Squires	

| Index | | 354 |

List of Figures and Tables

Figures

7.1	Theoretical model of police perceptions of organizational and distributive justice in support of 'democratic policing'	130
7.2	Police perceptions: research results	132
8.1	Paraná riots in prisons and jails (1998–2017) and total state prison population (2003–2014)	157
11.1	Morro do Palácio and the ethnic distribution in the surrounding neighbourhoods	213
11.2	Morro do Palácio and the income distribution in the surrounding neighbourhoods	214
12.1	Writings of memory on walls in Parque Santana	244
14.1	Protests led by women in October 2018, Recife, Brazil, against the presidential campaign of Jair Bolsonaro	272

Tables

7.1	Sample descriptive statistics	131
A.1	Constructs and measures	136
A.2	Structural model	138
A.3	Indirect effects	139

Notes on Contributors

Guilherme Benzaquen is Postdoctoral Fellow in Sociology at Federal University of Pernambuco, Brazil. He holds a PhD in sociology from the same institution. His research focuses on political sociology and economic sociology, with an emphasis on collective violence, social movements and financialization.

Pedro Borba is Lecturer in Political Science at Federal University of Rio de Janeiro, Brazil. He holds a PhD in political science from State University of Rio de Janeiro. His research interests are Latin American politics, sociology of the state, critical theory and world-system analysis.

Frederico Castelo Branco is a researcher at the Centre for the Study of Violence, University of São Paulo (USP), Brazil. He has a PhD in political science from USP. His work has focused on citizen–police contact and its consequences for attitudes towards police agencies, governments and democracy in Brazil.

Israel Celi is Director of the Constitutional Law Programme at the Universidad Técnica Particular de Loja, Ecuador. He is the author of the book *Neoconstitucionalismo en Ecuador: ¿Judicialización de la política o politización de la justicia?* (Universidad Andina Simón Bolívar, 2017). His earlier work has focused on participatory democracy, criminalization of activism and social movements. Israel is pursuing a PhD in political science at Universidade Federal do Rio Grande do Sul in Brazil. He also works in popular education as Executive Director of Dolores Cacuango Foundation.

Chris Cunneen is Professor of Criminology at the University of New South Wales (UNSW) Arts and Social Sciences and UNSW Law, Australia. He has an international reputation as a leading criminologist specializing in juvenile justice, restorative justice, policing, prison issues, human rights and Indigenous people and the law. He is the author of several books including, with Juan Tauri, *Indigenous Criminology* (Policy Press, 2016), and *Conflict, Politics and Crime: Aboriginal Communities and the Police* (Allen & Unwin, 2020).

NOTES ON CONTRIBUTORS

Luiz Dal Santo is a DPhil candidate and Graduate Teaching Assistant in Criminology at the Oxford Law Faculty, UK. He is co-founder and co-convenor of the Oxford Southernising Criminology Discussion Group. Luiz has previously been Visiting Lecturer in Criminology at the University of Roehampton, and Research Assistant at the Oxford Centre for Criminology and at the University of Hull. He has published papers on punishment, penal populism, prison, policing, racism and criminal justice, Southern criminology and criminal law. He is currently working, in collaboration with other scholars, on four edited volumes – on Southern criminology, punishment in global peripheries, punishment in Latin America, and local dimensions of the Brazilian mass incarceration.

Valéria Cristina de Oliveira is Professor at Faculdade de Educação (Faculty of Education, FaE) at the Universidade Federal de Minas Gerais (Federal University of Minas Gerais, UFMG), Brazil. Oliveira is also a researcher at Centro de Estudos em Criminalidade e Segurança Pública (Center for Crime and Public Safety Studies, CRISP) and at Núcleo de Estudos em Desigualdades Escolares (Research Center on School Inequalities, NUPEDE). She has a BA in social sciences (2006) and a master's (2012) and PhD (2016) in sociology from UFMG. She has prior experience in state public administration of public safety policies (2007–2010) and social development in the Brazilian federal government (2010–2012).

Viviane de Oliveira Cubas is a researcher at the Centre for the Study of Violence, University of São Paulo (USP), Brazil. She has a PhD in Sociology from USP, and her research interests include security and policing, specifically police violence, community policing, private security, the police ombudsmen, security in university campuses and police training. Currently, her research focuses on police, legitimacy and democracy, a project developed in the city of São Paulo.

Vitor Dieter has a PhD at the Doctorate in Global and Cultural Criminology (DCGC, Eramus+) from the University of Kent, UK. He is a lecturer in applied criminology at the University of San Carlos de Guatemala, Guatemala, and a postgraduate lecturer at the Institute for Criminology and Criminal Policy, Brazil. His main topics of research are prison order, prison gangs and Southern criminology.

Lambros Fatsis is Senior Lecturer in Criminology at the University of Brighton, UK. His research interests revolve around police racism and the criminalization of Black music (sub)culture(s), fusing cultural criminology with Black radical thought. His writing on the policing of UK drill music won the first-ever Blogger of the Year Award from the British Society of

Criminology and an Outstanding Research & Enterprise Impact Award from the University of Brighton. When he doesn't teach or write, he continues to exist as a never-recovering vinyl junkie and purveyor of Afro-diasporic music. His book, *Policing the Pandemic*, co-authored with Melayna Lamb, was published in 2022.

Jaqueline Garza Placencia is a full-time lecturer-researcher at El Colegio de Jalisco, Mexico, and responsible for research in the rule of law, security and justice, at the same institution. She holds a degree in communication sciences from the Autonomous University of San Luis Potosí in Mexico; a master's degree in communication of science and culture from ITESO, and a PhD in anthropology from the Regional University Ciudad de México. She is a member of the National System of Researchers (SNI) Level 1 and Associate Researcher at the Latin American Forum of Anthropology. She is associated to the Latin American Forum for the Anthropology of Law, Mexico, and is also the coordinator of the Permanent Seminar on the Anthropology of Law at El Colegio de Jalisco.

Simone Gomes is Assistant Professor in Social Sciences at the University of Pelotas (UFPel), Brazil. She holds a PhD in Sociology from the Institute of Social Studies and Politics of the State University of Rio de Janeiro and an MSc in Sociology from Université Paris 7 – Denis Diderot, France. She conducts research on narcotrafficking, violence and social movements. She has published on gender theory, crime and social movements in Brazil and Latin America.

Casandra Harry is Assistant Professor at the University of Trinidad and Tobago. Her research interests are multidisciplinary in scope, spanning criminology, sociology, gender studies and international relations. She conducts research on plural policing and police reform with a focus on developing countries.

Blaise Iruinu is a respected village elder, peace-builder, knowledge custodian, chief and political activist from Bougainville. Born in Onove village in 1950, Iruinu was a key intellectual figure of the Bougainville revolution. He has also coordinated a range of grassroots peacebuilding initiatives following the subsequent conflict.

Ammar Ali Jan is a scholar and activist based in Pakistan. He obtained his PhD in history from the University of Cambridge, UK. He researches the formation of communist thought in colonial India. He is also the founder and president of the Haqooq-e-Khalq Movement, which advocates for democracy in Pakistan, and a member of Progressive International.

NOTES ON CONTRIBUTORS

Kristian Lasslett is Professor of Criminology at Ulster University, Northern Ireland. His areas of research interest include state crime, corporate crime, decolonization and political economy. He has been conducting research on the Bougainville conflict since 2005, and has published widely on crisis. He is producer of the feature documentary film *Ophir* and the co-director of the web documentary, *The Colonial Syndrome*.

John Lea is a visiting professor at Goldsmiths, University of London, UK. His previous books include *Crime and Modernity* (2002) and *Privatising Justice: The Security Industry, War and Crime Control* (2020) (with Wendy Fitzgibbon)

Roxana Pessoa Cavalcanti is a critical criminologist and author of the book *A Southern Criminology of Violence, Youth and Policing* (Routledge). She is a member of the British Society of Criminology and the European Group for the Study of Deviance and Social Control, and is co-leader of the Cities Injustices and Resistance research group at the University of Brighton, UK. Roxana conducts research that examines and contests the criminalization of intersecting inequalities. She has written about urban violence in Brazil, insecurity, feminism, cities, criminology, police violence and the criminalization of dissent in Latin America.

Nathan W. Pino is Professor of Sociology and Honorary Professor of International Studies at Texas State University, USA. His primary research area focuses on the linkages between globalization, development, crime and crime control. He is co-author of *Unraveling the Crime Development Nexus: Modernization, Underdevelopment, Austerity, and the Post-Neoliberal Development Agenda* (Rowman & Littlefield, 2022); *Globalization, Police Reform and Development: Doing it the Western Way* (Palgrave Macmillan, 2012); and co-editor of *The Emerald Handbook of Crime, Justice, and Sustainable Development* (Emerald Publishing, 2021).

Elizabete Ribeiro Albernaz holds a PhD in anthropology. She is Visiting Researcher at Wits University, South Africa and Vice-coordinator of the Laboratory of Studies on Conflict, Citizenship and Public Security (LAESP) at Universidade Federal Fluminense (UFF), Niterói, Brazil.

André Rodrigues Oliveira is a researcher at the Centre for the Study of Violence, University of São Paulo (USP), Brazil. He has an MSc in geography from USP. His research focuses on attitudes towards the police, fear of crime, and socio-spatial heterogeneity through quantitative surveys and spatial analyses.

Peter Squires is Professor Emeritus of Criminology and Public Policy at the University of Brighton, UK. His work covers a wide range of issues, including community safety, policing, youth crime, gangs, violence and anti-social behaviour management, as well as firearm-related crime. He was President of the British Society for Criminology (2015–2019). He is the author of several books, which directly examine gun-enabled crime and police armed response: *Gun Culture or Gun Control?* (Routledge, 2000), *Shooting to Kill?* (Wiley/Blackwell, 2010) and *Gun Crime in Global Contexts* (Routledge, 2014). His most recent book, *Rethinking Knife Crime* (Palgrave) was published in November 2021.

Zoha Waseem is Assistant Professor in Criminology at the Department of Sociology, University of Warwick, UK. She obtained her PhD in security studies from King's College London in 2018. She researches policing and security in Pakistan and is interested in critical criminology, security studies and urban conflict broadly. She is also a co-coordinator for the Urban Violence Research Network. Her latest book is *Insecure Guardians: Enforcement, Encounters and Everyday Policing in Postcolonial Karachi* (Hurst & Co. and Oxford University Press, 2022).

Danielle Watson is Senior Lecturer at the Queensland University of Technology, Australia. She conducts research on police/civilian relations on the margins with particular interests in hotspot policing, police recruitment and training as well as many other areas specific to policing in small-island developing country contexts.

Giovana Esther Zucatto is Assistant Professor at the Institute of International Relations and Defense of the Federal University of Rio de Janeiro and PhD student in sociology at the Institute of Social and Political Studies (IESP) of the State University of Rio de Janeiro, Brazil. She has a degree in international relations from the Federal University of Rio Grande do Sul, Brazil, and works as a researcher at the Center for Studies of Social Theory and Latin America (NETSAL) and the South American Political Observatory (OPSA). Her work focuses upon issues related to international relations and sociology, especially with a gender focus.

Acknowledgements

The editors would like to thank the British Society for Criminology for sponsoring and supporting the summer 2019 research day conference, from which this book was developed, through its 'innovation funding'. The University of Brighton also provided administrative support, facilities and resources for the event. Thanks to all our contributors for sticking with the project over the intervening, pandemic-impacted years. A number of colleagues contributed to the original research day but chose, for various reasons, not to write for the book, we thank them also for their contributions and their support: Dr Jyoti Belur, Dr Sacha Darke, Professor Bill Dixon, Professor Alison Wakefield and Philip Wane.

Roxana Pessoa Cavalcanti thanks the British Academy for supporting her research (2020-2022/grant number KFSBSF\100004) and providing the opportunity to meet some of the other authors in this book, including Simone da Silva Ribeiro Gomes, Valeria Cristina de Oliveira and Elizabete Albernaz in Rio de Janeiro at the Urban Violence Symposium in 2020. She also thanks the University of Brighton for the Sabbatical awarded in 2021 and the Rising Stars Award in 2020, which facilitated the completion of this project and enabled her to work with Guilherme Benzaquen and Giovana Zucatto in, amongst other things, producing one of the chapters for the book. Roxana is indebted to too many friends for helping to look after her children so she could undertake fieldwork, write and attend conferences, including Karen, Grace Iara, Gilly, Nicoletta, Clare and Emilia. She thanks her friends Stacey, Deanna, Marias, Nic, Raph and her children for providing welcome distractions and is grateful to her partner for patiently sharing the childcare duties that enable her to focus on her research.

Zoha Waseem would like to thank her colleagues at the Urban Violence Research Network, King's College London, and the University of Warwick. She would also like to thank Ammar Ali Jan, Asad Jamal and a host of scholars, journalists and activists from Pakistan who have contributed to and inspired the research that informs her writing for this volume. She is also grateful to her partner Yasser Kureshi and her parents Waseem and Talat for their generous support and understanding.

1

Introduction: Southern and Postcolonial Perspectives on Policing, Security and Social Order

Peter Squires, Roxana Pessoa Cavalcanti and Zoha Waseem

Southern perspectives in criminology: an agenda

Several chapters that make up a large part of this book began life as papers presented at a 'Southern Perspectives' one-day research seminar at the University of Brighton in the early summer of 2019. The purpose of the day was to draw together several academic/theoretical research and network connections to explore a range of emerging concerns relating to 'Southern Perspectives' in criminology and existing scholarship on colonialism and the decolonization of the criminological imagination – or, in Agozino's terms – developing a critique of 'imperialist reason' (Agozino, 2003).

In pursuing this agenda, the distance we might have to travel from the familiar assumptions of academic criminology was, at this early stage, less than absolutely clear to us, but we were hopeful and keen to explore. In any event, Carrington et al's remarkably concise, but wonderfully coherent and challenging, introduction to *Southern Criminology* (2019) had recently appeared – preceded by the enormous, free-ranging *Palgrave Handbook of Criminology and the Global South* (Carrington et al, 2018). These texts convinced us of the viability of criminology, a 'rendezvous discipline' like no other, as an appropriate vehicle for these developing enquiries. As such, the present volume builds on established and growing efforts to examine the ongoing legacies of colonialism on institutions of control and practices of ordering (Agozino, 2003; Aliverti et al, 2021). This is a book looking to facilitate dialogue between multiple critical and interdisciplinary perspectives, in particular Southern and postcolonial perspectives, through collaborations between activists, academics and intellectuals across the globe. Some years ago, Jock Young had likewise remarked that the 'very liveliness of criminology and, at its best, its intellectual interest' derived its place from the busy crossroads of social theory, concerned especially with order and regulation, political economy, and the state (Young, 2003: 97). Given our current concerns with postcolonial legacies, policing and violence, and the distinctive, frequently racialized, character of (in)security, (in)justice and (dis)order in Southern contexts, these seem like indispensable themes. For, as Carrington et al have noted:

> [C]rime problems in the Global North ... generally pale in scale and significance alongside the violence (including armed conflicts, military coups and grave human rights abuses) and other crimes that seriously threaten human security in many Global South countries ... the countries with the highest rates of homicide, violence against women, corruption and drug trafficking in the world are located in the South ... [while] a large proportion of the world's police and half the world's 10.2 million prisoners are also to be found in the South. (Carrington et al, 2019: 2)

Of course, in situating our project, it is important to be clear that any reference to 'the global South' or 'Southern perspective' is far more than a simple geographical descriptor. On the contrary, the idea of 'Southern-ness' is intended to refer both to a dynamic relationship and a social division. The division concerns the way in which 'Southern-ness' defines a distinct space – or series of spaces. Here, key assumptions regarding the nature of order, the role and capacity of the state and political authorities, the purpose of law, the nature and infrastructure of security, the formation of 'civil society' (and the norms, relations and values found there), and the character of 'justice', rest upon foundations often quite different than those prevailing in the 'North'. To take a specific example relevant to our present project, the role, character and functions of the police in many Southern or postcolonial areas (Cole, 1999; Thomas, 2012; Owen, 2016), despite later convergences and the now widespread practice of international policy transfer, can still reveal significant differences, deriving from their imperial histories, in comparison with the police in many Northern jurisdictions. Taking up these themes, Watson, Pino and Harry (Chapter 6, this volume), describe the difficulties entailed in reforming a postcolonial policing system in Trinidad and Tobago, noting especially the problems of policy transfer in a still resistant policing culture. Cubas, Branco and Oliveira (Chapter 7, this volume) raise similar questions in respect of the dual (civil and military) policing systems in Brazil and, in particular, the potential of a model of police 'due process' to act as a catalyst for police reform. However, the distance to be travelled here, as regards police reform, is starkly depicted in Evans et al's work, *Equal Subjects, Unequal Rights* (2003), wherein the primary purpose asserted for a law to govern the dispossessed Indigenous peoples of the colonies was boldly stated as to 'deter them from attacking colonists', and for that reason, martial law and a brutal summary justice exercised by local police were especially recommended (Evans, 2005: 57). Many of the chapters in this volume explore similar contrasting perceptions of values and practices (order making, justice and due process, rights and liberties, and notions of security) that differentiate the 'Northern' and 'Southern' experiences. In this light, Dal Santo (Chapter 9, this volume) explores the applicability of a 'political economy of punishment' explanatory framework to account for the particular shape and functioning of Brazilian penal policy, and the role and nature of prisons and penal discipline.

Sustaining legacies

Already, in accounting for such differences and the divisions upon which they were based, the vital dynamic producing and sustaining the legacies of North and South is emphatically revealed: imperial conquest followed by political subordination, economic exploitation, juridical subjection, racial discrimination and persecution, and, on some occasions, genocidal annihilation (Gott, 2011). In this way the 'South' is constituted as the space where these multiple imperial and colonizing practices were played out and where the abused, marginalized and dispossessed were construed as inferior 'races'. And there began the process of economic underdevelopment (Frank, 1966; Rodney, 2018 [1972]) by which kleptocratic Northern states and corporations both enslaved and later indentured and transported Indigenous workforces to serve a range of Northern commercial interests (Williams, 2021 [1944]). As Carrington et al remark, 'being "under-developed" or economically backward was not the normal or natural condition of countries so labelled, but commonly a consequence of their subordinate place in the global economic and political order' (2019: 4). Northern/ European colonist settlers dispossessed Indigenous people of their historic homelands (often relocating them to reservations and work camps – or simple banishment), ravaged their flora and fauna (creating plantations, ranches and cash crops in their place) and extracted raw materials (Lasslett and McManus, 2018; Williams 2021 [1944]). Later, Southern lands became (legal and illegal) dumping destinations for global waste, hazardous products and processes (Pearce and Tombs, 1998; Lasslett, 2017). Indigenous peoples who protested or resisted these infractions were in turn harassed, killed or criminalized. Chapters in this volume by Benzaquen and Borba (Chapter 15), and Cavalcanti, Celi and Gomes (Chapter 14), detail several contemporary aspects – struggles around mineral extraction, deforestation and the commercialization of agriculture, and the criminalization of protest – of these historical realities of Southern experience. Similarly, in a highly original contribution curated by Lasslett (Chapter 10), Chief Blaise Iruinu from Bougainville, a respected tribal elder, activist and knowledge custodian, narrates an Indigenous experience of cultural disruption associated with colonization that led to alienation, impoverishment and marginalization for Indigenous peoples. From the 1960s, a commercial mining development further dispossessed people of traditional landholdings, culminating in a conflict in which some 20,000 people were killed, although, in turn, this laid the foundations of an independence movement capable of breaking free from colonial legacies. Iruinu's account reiterates the argument that 'the reasons that a certain story matters to a specific people are themselves historical' (Trouillot, 1995: 13). Such narratives draw essential cultural connections with the past, 'reinterpreting what it is to be human' (Satia, 2020) in the face of oppression and ideological conditioning. Iruinu and Lasslett's chapter in this collection is a recognition of the many subjugated Southern and Indigenous narratives that have been lost, forgotten or which remain still yet undiscovered.

It is precisely the experience of marginalization and persecution which leads Cunneen and Tauri (2017) to insist that any Southern or postcolonial criminology should position the construction of indigeneity at its centre. This would include localized intersectional hierarchies and identities of rural/urban, class, race, religion, gender and sexuality, including the consequences of imperialism for each. In this regard, West (2003) narrates an astonishing account of the gender-targeted tax collection practices developed in colonial Mozambique in the 1890s. The Portuguese authorities had effectively subcontracted tax collection to a private company who administered a 'hut tax' (essentially the same as that established by the British in Kenya [Elkins, 2005]). However, when news of the impending arrival of the tax collectors reached the villagers, the men would abscond. Frustrated by the disappearance of the men, the company changed tactics, now targeting the women as tax subjects. They began kidnapping the women, taking them to jails where they were held until their tax/ransoms were paid. 'Captive women were forced to work, until ransomed, were often denied sufficient food, and were sometimes beaten and/or raped. One report indicated two or three deaths per day of women held at a particular company post' (West, 2003: 99). Women who had been paid for were given tokens to prove that payment had been made, so that they would not be taken again – at least until the next taxes were due.

Dynamics of 'dependency-producing and dependency-experiencing', the combined legacies of global capitalism, neoliberal imperialism and coercive policy transfer, remain vital to contemporary Southern and postcolonial perspectives. Drawing out these kinds of issues in a concrete case study in this volume, Albernaz (Chapter 11) depicts the cross-cutting solidarities, alliances, divisions and tensions impacting the life and work of a community activist/entrepreneur in a marginalized urban *favela* in Rio de Janeiro. Her illustration reveals how governmental actions can frustrate rather than promote the establishment of welfare, social justice and order. These are certainly not issues exclusive to the global South, but the *favela* context represents such divisions as especially stark contrasted realities.

So much of the rhetoric of empire, the accumulated common sense of imperialism, has internalized many of the fabricated 'truths' of colonialism including, for example, the imputed character and behavioural traits of various subjugated peoples as 'savage', 'lazy', 'untrustworthy' or 'violent' (Gilroy, 1982; Nigam, 1990; Kumar, 2018; Carrington et al, 2019: 18–19) although sometimes also 'intelligent' (but often translated as 'calculating'). In so doing, the importance of context and social determinism in the shaping of adaptive and coping behaviours was entirely overlooked, somewhat akin to blaming the victim. Connell (2007) has shown how such selective misunderstandings of race and difference, now elevated to the level of science, reinforced a modernist metropolitan racism at precisely the time that social science was first taking recognizable shape. For our particular purposes, this was when criminology, allied with anthropology and eugenics, was positing the existence of a savage and atavistic 'criminal man' (Pasquino, 1980), doomed to supposed extinction in the face of 'progress', although there were undoubtedly many European imperialists and frontier settlers happy to assist the process (Lindqvist, 1997; Wolfe, 2006). Furthermore, while criminology looked southwards to describe a savage, uncivilized criminality to be found in that hemisphere for many years, it largely overlooked 'the use of violence as a tool of states and nation-building and its role in war, conquest and colonisation' (Carrington et al, 2019: 21). When developing our critique of these ideological formulations it is important, as Trouillot (1995) has noted, to write against the prevailing discourses of power. In the 18th century, he notes:

> Colonization provided the most potent impetus for the transformation of European ethnocentrism into scientific racism ... the more European merchants and mercenaries bought and conquered other men and women, the more European philosophers wrote and talked about Man ... [yet] non-European groups were forced to enter various philosophical, ideological, and practical schemes ... ultimately some humans were more so than others. ... Blacks were inferior and therefore enslaved; black slaves behaved badly and were therefore inferior. In short, the practice of slavery in the Americas secured the blacks' position at the bottom of the human world ... culturally destined to be slaves. (Trouillot, 1995: 75–77)

Further compounding the transnational inequality that is such a potent legacy of Europe's history of imperialism and more contemporary neoliberal globalization are yet further examples of the Southern legacy of postcolonial disruption and conflict. War (and weaponization), political and economic insecurity (poverty), religious persecution and strife, as well as rising sea levels, drought and land degradation, resulting from climate change, have mobilized many hundreds of thousands of new refugees and asylum seekers exiting Southeast Asia, sub-Saharan Africa and Latin America,[1] seeking new hope in the global North (McAdam, 2012; Welzer, 2012). Their reception, either in refugee relief camps run by international aid agencies, or confronting the reluctant, discriminatingly litigious and 'hostile' immigration environments of 'fortress' destination countries (Goodfellow, 2019) and their Immigration Removal Centres (their naming already predicated on the assumption of 'removal'), both echo and reinforce a divisive racism (Anderson, 2013). They add a new layer to the dependency/racial vilification dynamic we have already alluded to. The work of police, security and borders agency institutions – agents or contractors of the state – routinely, sometimes violently, reinforcing postcolonial boundaries, are still diligently performing the legacy work of empire (Aliverti, 2013; Elliott-Cooper, 2021; Trafford, 2021).

Welzer (2012) makes the point that climate change, in and of itself, may not always be sufficient to mobilize widespread migration. Invariably climate change catalyses other regional tensions and localized resentments, conflicts and divisions, destabilizing economic relationships and social orders, fomenting protest, corrupting states and weakening the rule of law as elites (both governments and corporations) increasingly come to disrespect the due processes that sustain democracy (persecuting trade unions, restricting rights to protest, weakening protections for accused persons and 'unleashing' the police, disrupting electoral procedures, cultivating hostilities). Civil wars, a major producer of refugees, can result. Many conditions can trigger a civil war, but a plentiful supply of weapons and ammunition (through licit and illicit channels) can both exacerbate and prolong the killing (Greene and Marsh, 2012). It follows that attempting to intercept, disrupt and prevent illegal weapon trafficking to 'outlaw' states and non-state groups (militia, insurgencies, terror cells and organized criminal networks) is a major priority of international law enforcement agencies including the United Nations (UN) (Squires, 2014, 2022). The Arms Trade Treaty adopted by the UN General Assembly in April 2013 has been a significant vehicle for that ambition.

Later European imperial centres tended to look upon Southern and colonial societies and their compromised political regimes with a patronisingly superior mixture of avarice, contempt and irritation, carefully balancing 'settler economic interests', a measure of administrative legitimacy, with an effective hegemony, even 'winning hearts and minds' (Weiner, 2009). Earlier empires had been rather less discerning. These were lands, and peoples, for conquest and exploitation. Governance arrived by gunboat and was violently imposed by whip and rifle butt, the mundane regularity of everyday colonial violence (Fanon, 2005 [1963]; Muschalek, 2019), for these 'uncivilized and inferior savages' could, it was implied, appreciate nothing else. There were many manifestations of resistance to these logics, not least the struggles for decolonization. As Fanon wrote:

> Decolonization is the encounter between two congenially antagonistic forces that in fact owe their singularity to the kind of reification secreted and nurtured by the colonial situation. Their first confrontation was colored by violence and their cohabitation – or rather the exploitation of the colonized by the colonizer – continued at the point of the bayonet and under cannon fire. ... Decolonization is truly the creation of new men. ... Decolonization ... implies the urgent need to challenge the colonial situation. (Fanon, 2005 [1963]: 2)

Koram (2022) narrates an account of how in 1920 – significantly, only a year following the Amritsar massacre in India – delegates of the National Congress of British West Africa arrived in London to press for legal and political emancipation. Although things appeared to be progressing well initially, they were soon met with increasing political resistance. Lloyd George refused to meet with them and the final blow to their ambitions came from colonial governors in Nigeria and the Gold Coast. They warned the government 'not [to] take these over-educated elites, dressed up in the clothes and vocabulary of English gentlemen as representative of the West African masses. Real Africans, they insisted, were primitive, fiercely tribal, and nowhere near ready to handle the modern pressures of statecraft' (Koram, 2022: 21). In the event, Churchill determined that there was 'no prospect' of African self-government any time soon. The matter was closed.

Yet just as dispossessed peoples were criticized for their own 'backwardness' and lack of 'civilization', so 'failed' and 'failing' states (militarily destabilized, politically dominated, economically exploited) were likewise castigated for their own 'failure'. Unable to exercise competent governance, secure their own borders, uphold the law, or keep the peace, or – tellingly – regulate the supply of military hardware (small arms and light weapons), such states became prone to coercive policy interventions, sanctions, arms and trade embargoes intended to police their own failing governance. Anna Stavrianakis (discussed in the chapter by Squires, Chapter 2, this volume) suggests this is why international arms control efforts can represent the latest version of imperialist reason, or global neoliberalism. She argues that arms control itself 'contributes to the reproduction of imperial relations' while the problems of armed conflict, interethnic division, corruption and organized crime are perceived to be strictly *internal* to Southern states (rooted in their failure to establish a monopoly of legitimate violence, in the classic Westphalian mode of statecraft). Defining the problem in this fashion leaves contemporary Northern imperial influences, colonial legacies and the global relations of armed violence (the arms trade itself, still dominated by Northern and European states) conspicuous by their absence (Stavrianakis, 2011: 195, 205).

'Boomerang effects'

In the global neoliberal order, failed states are 'bad states' which need to be policed, order restored, authority re-established, and consent – well, maybe consent – and the rule of law can wait. Analysing recent counterinsurgency doctrine and the activities of international partners fighting the 'war on terror' after 9/11, Caroline Holmqvist argues that recent liberal interventionism has collapsed a distinction between war and policing (Holmqvist, 2014). While some of the chapters in this volume might take issue with some aspects of this characterization, there is a substantial historical literature on the conflation of military force and policing activities within the realm of empire (Elkins, 2005; Newsinger, 2006; Gott, 2011; Thomas, 2012; Walter, 2017; Dwyer and Nettelbeck, 2018). The assessment rests in part upon contrasts between the 'formal' and 'linear' large-scale European wars of the 18th–20th centuries, where troops fought in regular regimental ranks or squares, line-abreast and later in trenches, firing coordinated volleys and advancing (although not retreating) in parade-ground order. This way of fighting contrasts markedly with the irregular, asymmetric, 'risk-transfer', 'new' insurgent or 'policing wars' of the later 20th century and beyond (Kaldor, 1999; Shaw, 2005) which, as Lea (Chapter 16, this volume) shows, now rely extensively upon private military companies in all aspects of battle logistics, except actual fighting (although sometimes, often covertly, that too). And yet, as Walter (2017) clearly demonstrates, there was nothing quite so asymmetric as the old colonial wars (modern firepower versus tribal weapons, with predictably disproportionate casualty rates) and often mercenaries of various kinds were centrally involved. And yet, in the guerrilla insurgencies, suicide bombings, ambush tactics, and improvised explosive devices of recent conflicts, we have a colonial violence 'boomerang effect' like no other. Even the low-tech 'terrorist knife attacks' of recent times have their colonial precedent in the 'amok killers' of colonial Malaya, which contemporary authorities viewed as the result of weak and primitive masculine 'natures' exercising an indiscriminate, impotent and frustrated, undercivilized violence (Wu, 2018).

Koram (2022) draws upon Cesaire's colonial 'boomerang effect' in which 'all experiments carried out in the peripheries of the empire eventually come flying back to its very heartland' (2022: 5). This idea entails several dimensions. In the first place, the re-importation of policing techniques originally deployed in overseas trouble-spots around the empire, for example the practices of surveillance, public order management, interrogation and internment deployed in Kenya in the 1950s (Elkins, 2005), found ready application in Northern Ireland in the early 1970s, some of which, as described by Hillyard in 'From Belfast to Britain' (1981) and *Suspect Community* (1993), eventually found their way into mainland policing practices. Lambros Fatsis (Chapter 3, this volume) describes similar efforts at cultural and musical suppression in Afro-diasporic communities now being employed to close Black music venues and prevent 'drill' music performances. Another version of the effect, termed 'blowback' in arms control circles, refers to the way that weapons, originally manufactured in Northern and European factories, from whence they are exported around the world before, in due course, make their way, albeit illicitly, back home to arm gangs and organized criminal groups (Squires, 2014: 237, 244). The boomerang effect is also reflected in patterns of immigration – *we are here because you were there* – prompting destination countries to resurrect, at home, the discriminatory orders that prevailed abroad. In this sense, as both Trafford (2021) and Sanghera (2021), in their own ways relate, *Empireland* comes home too.

And finally, the boomerang effect turns full circle when modern postcolonial armies are required to fight modern insurgencies that bear striking resemblance to the 'small wars' (Callwell, 1996 [1896]) fought by their predecessors in the period of imperial conquest many years earlier. The context is still empire, but everything has changed, not least a strong preference to see these new wars for democracy, or 'regime change' – wars to create order – as primarily 'policing operations' or 'peacekeeping' exercises (Holmqvist, 2014). In Holmqvist's case the notion of 'policing war' serves as a narrative of legitimation, reiterating that both the *ends* for which the war is fought are themselves just and that the *conduct* of military intervention (fighting) corresponds to the rules of war, the international neoliberal order, for example, the Geneva Conventions. In her analysis, the thinking about war has changed 'as a result of the ideological quests of liberal interventionism and liberal internationalism' (2014: 3).

For Neocleous (2014), by contrast, taking inspiration from Foucault's depiction of liberal modernity founded upon a 'military dream of society' (Foucault, 1977: 169), both war and policing are already closely intertwined 'as *processes* working in conjunction as state power' (Neocleous, 2014: 13, emphasis in original). The goals of such processes are revealed as security, order and accumulation. Here, Neocleous connects his earlier analysis of the origins of 'policing' in *The Fabrication of Social Order* (2000) with the wider imperatives of colonial accumulation and global pacification which at first produced and now sustain neoliberal internationalism. While domestic policing confronts the enduring *internal* 'enemies of order', an external police power, in constant search of new opportunities for accumulation, similarly confronts the permanent global enemies of *international* order. In this way, Neocleous offers a reinterpretation, consistent with much recent revisionist historiography of both empire-building and imperial policing, of 'Empire' as a form of war power and of capitalism as violence. He continues by insisting that 'far from outlawing violence, liberalism seeks to regulate it and see that it is exercised for just reasons, offering an argument not against war, but *for* war conducted in the right manner and the right reasons' (Neocleous, 2014: 42, emphasis in original). And, we might add, against the right persons, associations or states. It follows that 'the history of liberal thought needs to be read in terms of the history of capitalist violence' (Neocleous, 2014: 45), while liberal empire's presumed greatest achievement, international law, although disguised as a means to 'peace and security, law and order – even civilisation', a commitment to ending violence and oppression, is nothing more than 'international war in action' (Neocleous, 2014: 46). In these respects, the contemporary rule of neoliberal internationalism follows closely in the paradoxical footsteps of its European and Northern forerunners, exploiting and killing, obscuring and colluding, all beneath an ideological veneer of justice, civilization and peace, although seeking 'hearts and minds' once again. Where once the enemies may have been Indigenous peoples, nomadic tribes and peasants, today such groups are joined by 'rogue states', protestors, dissenters and resisters, insurgents and terrorists, militias and cartels. And in this 'new world order' as Carrington et al (2019: 13) remark, remnants of older empires return in new roles and forms. Carrington et al refer specifically to the role of British overseas territories now serving as tax havens, but one might also refer to contemporary practices of incarceration rendition and interrogation, the tactics of gang surveillance and disruption (Nijjar, 2018), the selectivity applied to immigration/refugee status and the differing rights accruing thereto (Aliverti, 2013), and even the policing of the pandemic (Fatsis and Lamb, 2022) and protest movements (Jan and Waseem, Chapter 5, this volume; Cunneen, Chapter 4, this volume).

With specific reference to constructions of gender and ethnicity one might cite the deplorable practice of 'virginity testing' of would-be immigrant South Asian women (Smith and Marmo, 2011) in the 1970s, a scrutiny reflecting a wide range of intersecting subordinations of gender, race, identity, class, identity and labour market value. As Carrington et al remark, 'gendered violence ... is a much bigger problem in the global South' (2019: 39), with commentators addressing intimate partner violence, femicide, rape, honour killings, emotional abuse and coercive control, sexual trafficking, female infanticide and genital mutilation (DeKeseredy and Hall-Sanchez, 2018; Miedema and Fulu, 2018). As DeKeseredy and Hall-Sanchez note, however, recognizing the disproportionate concentration of violence against women in the global South is not to pathologize the region or its inhabitants, nor to minimize the victimization faced by women in Northern developed cultures; rather, it is to recognize the importance of contexts: rural living, poverty, a lack of support services or alternative opportunities, asymmetrical gender relations and 'traditional' value systems (2018: 885). And as Giovana Zucatto describes in this volume (Chapter 13), women from the global South have organized for many years to press for change and an emancipatory feminist politics that recognizes the specific nature of the legacies of a colonial patriarchy.

Yet even culturally significant killings recycle tensions powerfully inflected by Southern and postcolonial racial divisions. The three examples which follow all represent what Carrington et al (2019: 12) refer to as illustrations of 'the South in the North' or what we have also referred to as the 'boomerang effect' or cultural 'blowback' in which ideas, practices and values taking their first shape in a Southern colonial context migrate to the urban metropolitan north. Here one might cite both the judgement of 'institutional racism' imposed upon the Metropolitan Police in 1999 as well as the self-justificatory 'explanations' offered by officers for their apparent investigative failures (Foster, 2008). In a first case, the shooting of Trayvon Martin in Florida in 2012, by an 'armed citizen' protected by the state's 'stand your ground' law, a delegated racialized power to kill with impunity (Gray et al, 2014), which symbolically energized the #BlackLivesMatter movement and showed how legacies of racism, fear and mistrust persist. In this volume, Cunneen (Chapter 4) takes up the account of how the #BLM protests fed into a broader global challenge, often rooted in Southern experiences, regarding discriminatory police use of force against Black and/or Indigenous peoples, including police killings of Aboriginal people in Australia, police shootings in the United States and violence and extrajudicial killings and excessive use of police force in Kenya and Nigeria. In India, Belur (2010) and Jauregui (2016) have similarly described how armed police 'encounters', or a form of extrajudicial ambush killings observed across South Asia, have existed in a cultural landscape bordered by denial, tolerance and impunity, defining a particularly robust approach to policing gangs and organized crime with rather familiar colonial antecedents. In respect of Brazil, Chevigny (1995) and Willis (2015) relate similarly 'exceptional' policing practices.

In a second case, Razack (2020) has explored the 2014 killing of a 27-year-old Navajo woman by a White police officer following a suspected offence of shoplifting in Winslow, Arizona. She argues that both the shooting itself, and the way that it is narrated in official and media accounts, as a *'justifiable* use of force' (emphasis added), reveal and recycle the

> psychic and material underpinnings of a settler state ... that continually imagines itself as a community of whites imperilled by Indians. ...

White settler violence directed at those imagined as threats lives just beneath the surface of everyday life, and flows through institutions such as policing, embedding itself in everyday professional routines. (Razack, 2020: 1)

In similar fashion Stevenson's detailed account in the *Contested Murder of Latasha Harlins* (2013) excavates the class and ethnic tensions entailed when a Korean shopkeeper shot and killed a 15-year-old African-American girl in Los Angeles in 1991, importantly prefiguring the patterns of urban conflict reflected in the following year's LA riots as African-American rioters targeted Korean-owned businesses. Other writers have developed conceptions of aggressive and hostile 'frontier' or 'Southern masculinity' emboldened by weapon ownership (Farr et al, 2009) and gendered oppression reflected especially in rates of intimate violence, rape and femicide in northern Mexico and South Africa (Olivera, 2006; Staudt, 2008; Abrahams et al, 2012).

The scale and resilience of contemporary criminal, terrorist or insurgent groupings has certainly facilitated the discursive slippage from policing to warfare (Steinert, 2003). Northern 'policing wars' are rhetorically waged on 'crime', on drugs, even on 'poverty' and, most recently, on 'terror'. Policing – and societies themselves – are said to have become increasingly militarized (Kraska, 2001; Balko, 2014), criminal justice agencies subsumed within the wider goals of social and political security and economic ordering. And yet in many Southern jurisdictions, dual policing systems comprising civil and state or military police (as in Brazil, Mexico and Pakistan) continue to perform differentiated crime control and security functions, while differentiations between 'high' and 'low' policing undertake similar responsibilities on a more global scale (Andreas and Nadelmann, 2006: 61). Low policing addresses everyday violence and criminality, and as Carrington et al (2019) make clear, the Global South has more than its fair share:

[A]lmost all, (42 out of 43) of the countries ranked by the WHO as having the highest rates of death by violence in the world are in the global South [and] … of the 50 most violent cities in the world, 46 are in the global South [furthermore] … the distribution of violence, especially lethal violence, is highly racialised in the world today. (Carrington et al, 2019: 34–35)

By contrast, high policing engages with more elevated security risks including threats to the political and economic order, and to states (such as from terrorism and insurgencies). Neocleous (2014) has noted the tendency of commentators to refer to the increasing paramilitarization of policing without acknowledging the profound militarism of high policing, its evident departure from familiar notions of accountability, just as military interventions have tended to cloak themselves in a narrative of 'peace-building', 'regime change' and security governance (Holmqvist, 2014) – or, as Neocleous would put it, war for international order, or violence for peace and prosperity. In such contexts Neocleous (2016) depicts various 'universal adversaries' against which we might pit our forces; George W. Bush was undoubtedly targeting terrorists in his post-9/11 'war on terror' announcement, but the neoliberal imagination construes many others, from the trade union 'enemies within', to protesters and resisters of all kinds, 'enemies of progress' or of property rights. The line runs from the victims (or survivors) of empires, slavery or genocide, those caught up in the surrogate conflicts of the Cold War (Grandin, 2011), many of them originally located in the South, to those still trapped in their contemporary legacies of race, gender and class, many of them *of* the South, even if no longer resident there: refugees, migrants, disenfranchised guest workers, the poor. Studying police violence in Guyana, Mars (2002: xiv) argues that the issue 'cannot be adequately addressed without an understanding of the enduring legacy of colonialism and its role in the definition of the police function'. Similarly, discussing the ongoing persecution and criminalization of Indigenous and Black land activists in Honduras, Loperena (2017: 801) points to a 'lack of political will to resolve long-standing issues of racial inequality ... because it is important to understand the [contemporary] development model as a continuation and expansion of economic practices from earlier historical periods'. To these examples we might add the failure to address inequalities of class and gender, of poverty, disease and climate change, in the face of which, especially in the postcolonial South, policing, security and the forces of political and economic order too often stand as reinforcements to social exclusion rather than pathways to social justice. These 'Southern Perspectives' are the core themes of our book, and the chapters which follow.

Structure of the book

We have arranged the chapters in parts. In Part I chapters by Squires, Fatsis, Cunneen, Dal Santo, and Jan and Waseem explore different aspects of the postcolonial legacies in the global South. These include the weaponized and especially violent forms of paramilitary policing as 'pacification' characteristic of Southern postcolonial policing, and the inseparable connections between policing and imperial dominance, as discussed in the chapter by Squires. Next, Fatsis considers the hostile and racially discriminatory policing of Black Afro-diasporic cultures, explored via a case study of the regulation of Black music styles in the United Kingdom. Cunneen explores the violent policing legacies which, under the impetus of the #BlackLivesMatter activism, coalesced globally as a series of protest campaigns against racist police violence. And finally, Jan and Waseem explore the enduring legacies of colonial laws, in particular the laws of sedition, and how such frameworks are retained by postcolonial states to police and control activism and civil society resistance, as in Pakistan.

Part II specifically addresses aspects of Southern policing and in particular the apparent difficulties of penal reform in Southern contexts. Cubas, Branco and Oliveira examine how the organization and structure of Brazilian policing challenges perceptions of legitimacy and due process, by assessing the support among police officers themselves for procedural justice practices. Watson, Pino and Harry assess the prospects for the adoption of community-centred policing strategies in Trinidad and Tobago, especially considering a seemingly non-receptive police culture. Dal Santo discusses the distinct political economy of punishment which has significantly shaped the nature and role of Brazilian penal policy and the character of its penal discipline. Also drawing upon research in Brazil, Dieter explores how prison riots are borne out of the hegemonic nature of the prison apparatus and may be caused by struggles for hegemony and control between authorities and inmates.

Part III engages with Indigenous and Southern experiences by tracing, first, the narrative of an Indigenous historian, Chief Blaise Iruinu, from Bougainville (curated by Lasslett) as he relates a cultural history of colonial dispossession, marginalization, war and resistance, in so doing reconnecting with a potent alternative cultural history. A second case study, by Albernaz, centres upon the boundaries, tensions and relationships negotiated by a community activist/entrepreneur working in a *favela* in Rio de Janeiro. Relatedly, Oliveira and Placencia explore the collective narratives regarding young victims of violence in São Paulo, Brazil, showing how they express a powerful sense of community loss and empathy. Finally, Zucatto's chapter in this part describes the efforts of feminist activists to articulate and campaign for a progressive feminist politics to challenge the continued exclusion of women and the explicit acknowledgement of women's rights in international security, peacebuilding and reconstruction projects and agreements.

We acknowledge mainstream criminology's complicity in generating knowledge that is used to legitimize and maintain the oppression of marginalized, Black and Indigenous people around the globe (Agozino, 2003; Cavalcanti, 2020), and use this book as a critical intervention, a platform to dissent and turn our gaze to the legacies of colonialism, crimes of the powerful, and political and environmental harms. Accordingly, in our final part, Benzaquen and Borba begin by outlining the forms of colonial expropriation and exploitation, which, in contemporary neoliberal imperialism, have continued to generate deepening forms of human insecurity because of land grabs, enforced population displacement, primitive and extractive accumulation, and coerced and exploitative labour contracts. Complementing and developing this analysis is a chapter by Cavalcanti, Celi and Gomes, who draw upon findings from Mexico, Brazil and Ecuador to explore how new laws, the police and criminal justice agencies have been employed to crush dissent, deter and criminalize activists and campaigners, stigmatizing trade unionists, environmental and human rights advocates as criminals, terrorists and insurgents to delegitimize and disrupt social movements. Recognizing the increasing involvement of private security agencies, corporate military logistics enterprises and even private military companies in security work, surveillance, police work and war work, Lea examines the issues arising when states engage private forces to engage in state-sanctioned conflict or protect the interests of transnational corporations – sometimes against citizens themselves. Finally, Squires explores a number of war crimes and abuses that have taken place across conflict zones, including Iraq and Afghanistan, in the aftermath of colonial rule, and discusses how violence, pacification and military and police power remain as relevant to contemporary neoliberal imperialism as they were to empire's past.

Collectively, these chapters also contribute to the growing range of perspectives that address both inequalities and divisions within our academic scholarship and practice, especially in mainstream criminology that has had an overwhelming focus on the 'metropolis'. Often this has come at the risk of marginalizing postcolonial states and peripheral societies in terms of the epistemic value they add to the study of crime (and criminalization), justice, policing, security and social order. As such, the contributions in this volume collectively speak to decolonial, postcolonial, Southern and critical perspectives, contributing to debates that are still developing and evolving, and furthering them with the ultimate aim of amplifying the voices, experiences and epistemologies of those on the margins (Connell, 2007; Aliverti et al, 2021).

Note

[1] By 2050 World Bank predictions suggest there are likely to be in excess of 140 million 'climate migrants' moving to more hospitable environments (Walter, 2022: 76).

References

Abrahams, N., Mathews, M., Jewkes, R., Martin, L.J. and Lombard, C. (2012) Every eight hours: Intimate femicide in South Africa 10 years later. *South African Medical Research Council: Research Brief*, August.

Agozino, B. (2003) *Counter-Colonial Criminology: A Critique of Imperialist Reason*. London: Pluto Press.

Aliverti, A. (2013) *Crimes of Mobility: Criminal Law and the Regulation of Immigration*. Abingdon: Routledge.

Aliverti, A., Carvalho, H., Chamberlen, A. and Sozzo, M. (2021) Decolonizing the criminal question. *Punishment & Society*, 23(3): 297–316. doi:10.1177/14624745211020585

Anderson, B. (2013) *Us & Them: The Dangerous Politics of Immigration Control.* Oxford: Oxford University Press.

Andreas, P. and Nadelmann, E. (2006) *Policing the Globe: Criminalization and Crime Control in International Relations.* Oxford: Oxford University Press.

Balko, R. (2014) *The Rise of the Warrior Cop.* New York: Public Affairs Books.

Belur, J. (2010) *Permission to Shoot: Police Use of Deadly Force in Democracies.* New York: Springer.

Callwell, C.F. (1996 [1896]) *Small Wars: Their Principles and Practice* (4th edition). Lincoln: University of Nebraska Press.

Carrington, K., Hogg, R., Scott, J., Sozzo, M. and Walters, R. (2019) *Southern Criminology.* Abingdon: Routledge.

Cavalcanti, R.P. (2020) *A Southern Criminology of Violence, Youth and Policing: Governing Insecurity in Urban Brazil.* London and New York: Routledge.

Chevigny, P. (1995) *Edge of the Knife: Police Violence in the Americas.* New York: New Press.

Cole, B. (1999) Post-colonial systems, in R. Mawby (ed) *Policing Across the World: Issues for the Twenty-first Century.* London: UCL Press, pp 88–108.

Connell, R. (2007) *Southern Theory: The Global Dynamics of Knowledge in Social Science.* Cambridge: Polity.

Cunneen, C. and Tauri, J. (2017) *Indigenous Criminology.* Bristol: Policy Press.

DeKeseredy, W. and Hall-Sanchez, A. (2018) Male violence against women in the global south: What we know and what we don't know, in K. Carrington, R. Hogg, J. Scott and M. Sozzo (eds) *The Palgrave Handbook of Criminology and the Global South.* Cham: Palgrave Macmillan, pp 883–901.

Dwyer, P. and Nettelbeck, A. (eds) (2018) *Violence, Colonialism and Empire in the Modern World.* Cham: Palgrave Macmillan.

Elkins, C. (2005) *Imperial Reckoning: The Untold Story of Britain's Gulag in Kenya.* New York: Henry Holt/Owl Books.

Elliott-Cooper, A. (2021) *Black Resistance to British Policing.* Manchester: Manchester University Press.

Evans, J. (2005) Colonialism and the rule of law: The case of South Australia. In B. Godfrey and G. Dunstall (eds) *Crime and Empire: 1840–1940.* Cullompton: Willan, pp 57–75.

Evans, J., Grimshaw, P., Philips, D. and Swain, S. (2003) *Equal Subjects, Unequal Rights: Indigenous Peoples in British Settler Colonies: 1830–1910.* Manchester: Manchester University Press.

Fanon, F. (2005 [1963]) *The Wretched of the Earth.* New York: Grove Press.

Farr, V., Myrttinen, H. and Schnabel, A. (2009) *Sexed Pistols: The Gendered Impact of Small Arms and Light Weapons.* Geneva: United Nations University Press.

Fatsis, L. and Lamb, M. (2022) *Policing the Pandemic: How Public Health becomes Public Order.* Bristol: Policy Press.

Foster, J. (2008) 'It might have been incompetent, but it wasn't racist': Murder detectives' perceptions of the Lawrence Inquiry and its impact on homicide investigation in London. *Policing and Society*, 18(2): 89–112.

Foucault, M. (1977) *Discipline and Punish: The Birth of the Prison*. London: Allen Lane, Penguin Books.

Frank, A.G. (1966) *The Development of Underdevelopment*. Boston: New England Free Press.

Gilroy, P. (1982) The myth of Black criminality. *Socialist Register*, 47–56.

Goodfellow, M. (2019) *Hostile Environment: How Migrants became Scapegoats*. London: Verso.

Gott, R. (2011) *Britain's Empire: Resistance, Repression and Revolt*. London: Verso.

Grandin, G. (2011) *The Last Colonial Massacre: Latin America in the Cold War* (updated edition). Chicago: University of Chicago Press.

Gray, K.A., St. Clair, J. and Wypijewski, J. (2014) *Killing Trayvons: An Anthology of American Violence*. Petrolia: CounterPunch Books.

Greene, O. and Marsh, N. (eds) (2012) *Small Arms, Crime and Conflict: Global Governance and the Threat of Armed Violence*. London: Routledge.

Hillyard, P. (1981) From Belfast to Britain: Some critical comments on the Royal Commission for Criminal Procedure, in D. Adlam (ed) *Politics and Power #4*. London: Routledge, pp 131–145.

Hillyard, P. (1993) *Suspect Community: People's Experience of the Prevention of Terrorism Acts in Britain*. London: Pluto Press in association with Liberty/NCCL.

Holmqvist, C. (2014) *Policing Wars: On Military Intervention in the 21st Century*. Basingstoke: Palgrave Macmillan.

Jauregui, B. (2016) *Provisional Authority: Police, Order, and Security in India*. Chicago: Chicago University Press.

Kaldor, M. (1999) *New and Old Wars: Organised Violence in a Global Era*. Stanford University Press.

Koram, K. (2022) *Uncommon Wealth: Britain and the Aftermath of Empire*. London: John Murray Publishers.

Kraska, P. (2001) *Militarizing the American Criminal Justice System*. Boston: Northeastern University Press.

Kumar, R. (2018) Seeing like a policeman: Everyday violence in British India, c. 1900–1950, in P. Dwyer and A. Nettelbeck (eds) *Violence, Colonialism and Empire in the Modern World*. Cham: Palgrave Macmillan, pp 131–149.

Lasslett, K. (2017) *Uncovering the Crimes of Urbanisation: Researching Corruption, State Crime and Urban Conflict*. Abingdon: Routledge.

Lasslett, K. and McManus, T. (2018) Crimes of the powerful in the global south: State failure as elite success, in K. Carrington, R. Hogg, J. Scott and M. Sozzo (eds) *The Palgrave Handbook of Criminology and the Global South*. Cham: Palgrave Macmillan, pp 633–656.

Lindqvist, S. (1997) *Exterminate all the Brutes*. London: Granta Books.

Loperena, C.A. (2017) Settler violence? Race and emergent frontiers of progress in Honduras. *American Quarterly*, 69(4): 901–907.

Mars, J.R. (2002) *Deadly Force, Colonialism and the Rule of Law: Police Violence in Guyana*. Westport: Greenwood Press.

McAdam, J. (2012) *Climate Change, Forced Migration and International Law*. Oxford: Oxford University Press.

Miedema, S.S. and Fulu, E. (2018) Globalization and theorizing intimate partner violence, in K. Carrington, R. Hogg, J. Scott and M. Sozzo (eds) *The Palgrave Handbook of Criminology and the Global South*. Cham: Palgrave Macmillan, pp 867–882.

Muschalek, M. (2019) *Violence as Usual: Policing and the Colonial State in German Southwest Africa*. Ithaca: Cornell University Press.

Neocleous, M. (2000) *The Fabrication of Social Order: A Critical Theory of Police Power*. London: Pluto Press.

Neocleous, M. (2014) *War Power, Police Power*. Edinburgh: Edinburgh University Press.

Neocleous, M. (2016) *The Universal Adversary: Security Capital and 'The Enemies of All Mankind'*. Abingdon: Routledge.

Newsinger, J. (2006) *And the Blood Never Dried: A People's History of the British Empire*. London: Bookmarks Publications.

Nigam, S. (1990) Disciplining and policing the 'criminals by birth', part 1: The making of a colonial stereotype – the criminal tribes and castes of North India. *The Indian Economic & Social History Review*, 27(2): 131–164.

Nijjar, J. (2018) Echoes of empire: Excavating the colonial roots of Britain's 'war on gangs'. *Social Justice*, 45(2/3): 147–161.

Olivera, M. (2006) Violencia femicida: Violence against women and Mexico's structural crisis. *Latin American Perspectives*, 33(2): 104–114.

Owen, O. (2016) Policing after colonialism, in B. Bradford, B. Jauregui, I. Loader and J. Steinberg (eds) *The SAGE Handbook of Global Policing*. London: SAGE.

Pasquino, P. (1980) Criminology: The birth of a special savoir. *Ideology & Consciousness*, 7: 17–32.

Pearce, F. and Tombs, S. (1998) *Toxic Capitalism: Corporate Crime and the Chemical Industry*. London: Routledge.

Razack, S.H. (2020) Settler colonialism, policing and racial terror: The police shooting of Loreal Tsingine. *Feminist Legal Studies*, 28: 1–20.

Rodney, W. (2018 [1972]) *How Europe Underdeveloped Africa*. London and New York: Verso.

Sanghera, S. (2021) *Empireland: How Imperialism has Shaped Modern Britain*. Dublin: Penguin Books.

Satia, P. (2020) *Time's Monster: History, Conscience and Britain's Empire*. London: Penguin, Random House.

Shaw, M. (2005) *The New Western Way of War: Risk Transfer War and its Crisis in Iraq*. Cambridge: Polity.

Smith, E. and Marmo, M. (2011) Uncovering the 'virginity testing' controversy in the national archives: The intersectionality of discrimination in British immigration history. *Gender & History*, 23(1): 147–165.

Squires, P. (2014) *Gun Crime in Global Contexts*. Abingdon: Routledge.

Squires, P. (2022) Illegal firearms, illicit markets and weapon trafficking, in H. Poole and S. Sneddon (eds) *Firearms: Global Perspectives on Consequences, Crime and Control*. Abingdon: Routledge, pp 51–72.

Staudt, K. (2008) *Violence and Activism at the Border: Gender, Fear and Everyday Life in Ciudad Juarez*. Austin: University of Texas Press.

Stavrianakis, A. (2011) Small arms control and the reproduction of imperial relations. *Contemporary Security Policy*, 32(1): 193–214.

Steinert, H. (2003) The indispensable metaphor of war: On populist politics and the contradictions of the state's monopoly of force. *Theoretical Criminology*, 7(3): 265–291.

Stevenson, B. (2013) *The Contested Murder of Latasha Harlins: Justice, Gender and the Origins of the LA Riots*. Oxford: Oxford University Press.

Thomas, M. (2012) *Violence and Colonial Order: Police, Workers and Protest in the European Colonial Empires: 1918–1940*. Cambridge: Cambridge University Press.

Trafford, J. (2021) *The Empire at Home: Internal Colonies and the End of Britain*. London: Pluto Press.

Trouillot, M.-R. (1995) *Silencing the Past: Power and the Production of History*. Boston: Beacon Press.

Walter, B. (2022) *How Civil Wars Start: And How to Stop Them*. London: Penguin, Random House.

Walter, D. (2017) *Colonial Violence: Colonial Empires and the Use of Force*. London: Hurst & Co.

Weiner, M.J. (2009) *An Empire on Trial: Race, Murder and Justice under British Rule: 1870–1935*. Cambridge: Cambridge University Press.

Welzer, H. (2012) *Climate Wars: Why People will be Killed in the 21st Century*. Cambridge: Polity.

West, H.G. (2003) 'Who rules us now?' Identity tokens, sorcery and other metaphors in the 1994 Mozambique elections, in H.G. West and T. Sanders (eds) *Transparency and Conspiracy: Ethnographies of Suspicion in the New World Order*. Durham, NC: Duke University Press, chapter 3.

Williams, E. (2021 [1944]) *Capitalism & Slavery* (3rd edition). Chapel Hill: The University of North Carolina Press.

Willis, G.D. (2015) *The Killing Consensus: Police, Organised Crime and the Regulation of Life and Death in Urban Brazil*. Oakland: University of California Press.

Wolfe, P. (2006) Settler colonialism and the elimination of the native. *Journal of Genocide Research*, 8(4): 387–409.

Wu, J.C. (2018) Disciplining native masculinities: Colonial violence in Malaya, 'land of the pirate and the amok', in P. Dwyer and A. Nettelbeck (eds) *Violence, Colonialism and Empire in the Modern World*. Cham: Palgrave Macmillan, pp 175–196.

Young, J. (2003) In praise of dangerous thoughts. *Punishment & Society*, 5(1): 97–107.

PART I

Policing, Law and Violent Legacies

2

Asymmetric Policing at a Distance? Frontiers, Law and Disorder in the Weaponized South

Peter Squires

Introduction

Discussing the development of law and order in a global context, Comaroff and Comaroff (2012) have argued that our understanding of the nature and development of policing would be better informed by more fully incorporating perspectives on the operation of policing systems in the 'global South'. They make this argument in marked contrast to what they refer to as a central assumption of *Euromodernity* that invariably sees the 'global South' as forever tracking behind the North, 'behind the curve of universal history, always in deficit, playing catch up' (2012: 12; Connell, 2007). Instead, they argue, 'there is good reason to think the opposite', for '[g]iven the unpredictable ... dialectic of capitalism and modernity in the here and now, it is the south in which radically new assemblages of capital and labour are taking shape [prefiguring] the future of the global North' (Comaroff and Comaroff, 2012: 12). And of course, where capitalism, governance and refashioned social orders lead, policing systems are likely to be thoroughly implicated, a sharp reminder, discussed later in this chapter, that 'Southern' and colonial (weaponized, unaccountable, asymmetric) policing and security systems, far from being reformed are, in fact, lying in wait. As Bell (2013) has also argued, it is important not to see policing policy transfers as 'uni-directional': for often, supposedly 'exceptional' police practices more usually deployed in the colonies and typically 'seen as having been particularly marked by paramilitarism' and intensive surveillance (especially 'widespread during the period of decolonisation as local forces sought to deal with political insurgency' and 'suspect populations') have also come to be increasingly normalized within Britain itself (Bell, 2013; see also Nigam, 1990a, 1990b; Elkins, 2005; Fekete, 2013; Silvestri, 2019; Elliott-Cooper, 2021 for imperial examples). Cole also notes that one of the difficulties in assessing colonial *policing* resides 'in the lack of a clear distinction between policing and military action' and in any event, 'most of the colonial senior police officers in Africa and Latin America were recruited directly from the imperial armies ... and the majority of the police forces ... were paramilitary units' (Cole, 1999: 89).

These questions, the blurred distinctions between policing and quasi-military force and the legacies they represent, form a central concern of the chapter. In addition, I draw upon a number of Southern and postcolonial contributions to global policing development, an issue which has already accumulated a substantial literature (Arnold, 1986; Brogden, 1987; Anderson and Killingray, 1991, 1992; Cole, 1999; Emsley, 2014; Owen, 2016). The discussion is developed via a commentary upon two closely related aspects of the legacy of empire in the global South and, therefore, two characteristics fundamental to 'Southern' policing traditions and related practices of security making and social ordering: firstly the proliferation of firearms and, secondly, the development and persistence of armed and (quasi-)militarized forms of policing.[1] In some respects, these issues are addressed, in part, to try to answer some of the further questions posed by Comaroff and Comaroff in 2006. How are we to account for the seemingly violent and disorderly character of postcolonial (Southern) societies and their apparently corrupt and ungovernable, frequently authoritarian, often unequal and highly racialized, cultures of security and order maintenance, persisting – even growing – in an era of democratization (Comaroff and Comaroff, 2008; Collier, 2009)? As they suggest, there is indeed 'something deeper' at issue here, and the story of imperial conquest, the weaponization it entailed and the punitive authoritarianism by which it was sustained, are part of that answer. Central to both are questions about what policing did, what it represented and how it evolved.

Weaponizing the world

Recent publications by, respectively, the United Nations Office of Drugs and Crime (UNODC, 2020) and the Small Arms Survey reveal important patterns regarding the prevalence of lethal violence around the world and the proliferation of firearms. In 2018, the Small Arms Survey estimated that there were just over one billion firearms on the planet, an increase of some 32 per cent (or some 200 million firearms) over the decade, and a doubling since 1995 (Karp, 2014, 2018). Roughly 85 per cent of these weapons were in civilian hands (13 per cent held by the military and the remaining 2 per cent by law enforcement agencies), although only 12 per cent are recorded as legally registered or licensed within the jurisdictions in which they are held. Discussing the collection of data on global firearms, Karp has noted that firearms 'can be hardest to find in many of the places where armed violence is worst', or, conversely, 'where they are needed most' (Karp, 2018: 10). In light of these estimates (notwithstanding questions regarding the reliability of the data) firearm proliferation has been recognized as a significant independent (although not isolated) variable in the production of armed violence, conflict and insecurity (Greene and Marsh, 2012: 250). Weaponization undoubtedly features as both cause and consequence of regional violence and insecurity, including racialized inequalities, economic dislocations and political divisions ('regime' factors), fomenting an aggressive individualism and accelerating social breakdown (Currie, 2005). This is likely to be especially acute particularly where a preponderance of angry young, lower-class men (the foot-soldiers of gangs, cartels, militias, warlords, organized crime, insurgencies and terrorist groups – and not overlooking armies and private military contractors) see weapon use and ownership as a much sought-after form of empowerment and opportunity (Squires, 2014: 249). Reflecting this regional distribution of weapon proliferation, the UNODC *Global Homicide Report* (volume 3) reveals that, in 54 per cent of global homicides, firearms are the means of killing, and this is especially so in Southern and postcolonial regions – the Americas (in particular Central and Southern America), Africa and, although rather less so, Asia (UNODC, 2019: 75–77).

Accounting for this historic patterning of firearm proliferation, Headrick (1981) sought to explore what he called the largely uncharted relationship between technology and imperialism, although he wrote at a time prior to the widespread recognition of a distinctly 'Southern' epistemology and related perspectives on issues of development, governance, race and social order. His complaint was that, with a few notable exceptions (although, in the 19th century, the invention of the breech-loading rifle and, later, the Maxim gun, were certainly among them), historians of empire and of technology had seldom drawn together their findings, in order to help develop a fuller understanding of conquest and subordination, or the legacies of violence and racism thereby established. However, the account requires rather more than a technologically determinist account of the 'hardware of imperialism', for just as various technologies played their part, so did a willingness to use those technologies to exterminate, expropriate and institutionalize racial hierarchies, shaping for posterity the social relations between colonial interlopers and Indigenous peoples.

One of the most obvious legacies of the imbalance of weaponry was the slave trade itself, 'at the time of the slave trade, imported guns had been one of the main commodities for which slaves were exchanged, and in turn these guns were used to capture more slaves' (Headrick, 1981: 106). Satia (2018), likewise, describes how a gun-making industry centred on Birmingham, the 'workshop of the world and the arsenal of the empire', distributed firearms across four continents. She writes:

> [B]y 1815 the British empire owed its existence to the Midlands' ability to produce guns ... a talent [developed] through the long competitive patronage of the East India Company and the Ordnance office ... and strong demand for guns on the Western frontier ... whilst in Africa where they were bartered, as currency, for slaves, enabling slave gatherers to capture more slaves. (Satia, 2018: 145, 193)

Chew (2012) likewise describes a three-stage process of direct relevance to weapon proliferation, globalization and 'Southern' security. The first stage involved the industrialization which modernized and mass produced firearms; the second stage involved the 'tentacles of empire and indigenous crisis through which arms procurement was first "globalised"'. Finally, there is a third stage, which we will encounter later, associated with the 'crescendo of violence augmented by arms proliferation [through] which arms control was first internationalised' (Chew, 2012: 2–3).

Firearms were dispersed into Indigenous Southern and colonized regions in many ways; in the course of formal trading, as we have seen, and following military encounters where firearms were lost, surrendered or stolen. Firearms were widely distributed throughout settler communities, often as a delegated or (semi-)official arm of colonial policies intended to subjugate Indigenous peoples or consolidate landownership in frontier regions (Dunbar-Ortiz, 2018) so as to act as buffer zones for centres of colonial administration (Gott, 2011; Horne, 2017). Firearms were also sold, as contraband, by gunrunners seeking to exploit Indigenous demand for new weapons. Indigenous peoples, for example tribes in North America, sometimes engaged in games of 'brinkmanship', allying themselves with different colonial powers, the English or the French, in order to obtain supplies of firearms (Schilz and Worcester, 1987). Recent scholarship has revealed how firearm proliferation – or cultural weaponization – effectively *remade* many Southern and colonial societies (Squires, 2014). Likewise, Storey argues that 'the proliferation of firearms in South Africa ... was a decisive factor in constituting the new society' (Storey, 2008: 17). In many Southern cultures, the right to own a gun became closely connected to one's status and position in the social and racial hierarchy of the colonized society. While firearms 'served as vital tools in wild country for harvesting animal capital: for subsistence, sport and soldiering' not to mention personal defence, they were 'also invested with a set of cultural codes ... signifiers of colonial might, masculine prowess, elitist adventuring and ritualised control over space, the firearm conferred a power far beyond its ballistics range' (Jones et al, 2013: 2). One feature of this power was the genocidal licence granted to European colonizers and their agents to treat Indigenous peoples as part of the very wilderness to be tamed by firepower as reflected in the bounties to be claimed for scalps, heads and other souvenirs of conquest throughout the empire (Brown, 1972 [1970]; Gott, 2011; Lindqvist, 2018). According to Dunbar-Ortiz (2018: 46), on the US frontier 'scalp-hunting became a lucrative commercial practice from the early 18th century onwards ... the authorities had hit upon a way to encourage settlers to take off on their own ... to gather scalps, at random, for the reward money' in so doing they 'established the large-scale privatisation of war within American frontier communities' (Grenier, 2005: 39–43). This turning of genocide into souvenir hunting was by no means confined to North America; Sir Joseph Banks the renowned botanist and president of the Royal Society who had accompanied James Cook on his voyage to Botany Bay in 1768–1771 and, later, was largely responsible for laying out Kew Gardens, was sent a consignment of pickled heads – for his private collection – of Aboriginals killed in Australia (Gott, 2011: 90).

Conceptions of race and masculinity constructed around gun ownership were later reflected in the efforts made by many authorities (the southern US states being perhaps the best known) to regulate the ownership of firearms (in the name of 'gun control') by Indigenous peoples or 'subordinate' races (Wendt, 2007; Storey, 2008: 52–53; Johnson, 2014). Muschalek (2019) similarly details a prohibition imposed in German South-West Africa on Africans and other non-Europeans owning firearms. As Shear et al (2003) have noted, in South Africa, these concerns extended to the question of the arming of Black police officers, even as the regime relied upon Black officers policing the majority dispossessed populations. From 1890 onwards, international efforts began to 'bring the thriving global trade in small arms under control', while the disarming of colonial subjects was seen as a 'precondition for asserting the authority of the [colonial] state' (Jones et al, 2013: 9). In this, a powerfully imperialist, and still continuing, imperative in arms control can be seen to have its roots.

In a series of important articles, Anna Stavrianakis (2011, 2016, 2019) has criticized the core assumptions of a 'conceptual Eurocentrism', which, she argues, has continued to reproduce key assumptions about the global South as the problematic, but fortunate, beneficiary of benevolent Northern interventions, a viewpoint which substantially obscures and exonerates the continuing political, economic and military preponderance of Northern states. In short, she argues, 'small arms control contributes to the reproduction of imperial relations' while 'the problem of small arms and armed violence is ultimately deemed to be *internal* to Southern states and regions, [and] the international relations of armed violence remain conspicuous by their absence' (Stavrianakis, 2011: 195, 206, emphasis added). This perspective, she argues, consistently 'obscures the role of the legal, state-sanctioned trade, and the uneven development of capitalist globalization that creates the conditions for the violence conducted with a variety of categories of arms' largely procured from the global North (2011: 207) and ultimately legitimizing liberal forms of militarism (Stavrianakis, 2016). She continues, arguing that arms control processes often marginalize both historical and structural forces operating throughout international governance processes and that the resulting *asymmetry* in small arms control treaties reproduces a perception that the supposedly 'weak', 'failing' or 'corrupt' nations of the South are unable to exercise control over the means of violence and the conflicts these provoke. She concludes that the implied requirement for 'guidance, support, and other forms of intervention by a coalition of actors led by Northern agencies, is what makes this an imperial relation' (2011: 195). Ultimately, this perspective recycles and reproduces older Northern imperialist notions about the bringing of order, civilization and religion to the uncivilized and heathen wildernesses of the South.

In a later article exploring the tensions 'between arms transfer control and militarism' and exposing the Northern imperial legacies persisting in weapons control processes, Stavrianakis insists that whether 'expressed in terms of sovereignty, political economy, or human security' contemporary arms control processes still evidence competing modes of militarism, and 'are underpinned by ongoing imperial relations: racial, gendered and classed relations of asymmetry and hierarchy that persist despite formal sovereign equality' (Stavrianakis, 2019: 58), thereby reiterating the need for feminist, postcolonial anti-militarist critiques of the arms control process (Stavrianakis, 2019: 58). Having stripped away much of the supposedly 'civilizing' ethic, attached to many attempts to control the proliferation of firearms in Southern postcolonial and frontier cultures, it is important to recognize that many such efforts were undoubtedly motivated (then, as now), in part, by the willingness and ability of many Indigenous peoples to acquire firearms in order to fight back against their White imperial overlords and oppressors, or otherwise, as insurgents, terrorists, militias or drug cartels, to destabilize the existing neoliberal order.

The liberal myth of imperial policing

A directly parallel ambition, largely entangled in the same 'liberal paradox of empire' (Dwyer and Nettelbeck, 2018; Andrews, 2021), or of liberal militarism (Stavrianakis, 2016; Stavrianakis and Stern, 2018), and equally struggling for compelling evidence, has concerned the much heralded civilianization of policing (or, in a wider sense, the misleadingly labelled 'winning of hearts and minds' strategy),[2] to which we turn in the next section. As has been noted, a particular irony of this empire *policing* story has been the fact that police reform and, even then, an especially *paramilitary* version of policing with frequent resort to martial law, has only been deemed possible in the wake of punitive colonial campaigns to quell rebellions, insurgency and unrest. The argument here draws upon and extends important conclusions deriving from the work of I.D. Balbus (1973), which offered an analysis of public order policing (the US race riots in Los Angeles, Detroit, and Chicago) in the mid-1960s. US police public order management practices very much reflected the forceful (and legally questionable) police practices of colonial population control (Neocleous, 2014). Balbus likewise argued that the imposition of order invariably preceded the application of the law. Order served as its own axiomatic justification; justice often followed as a distant second. In his impressive study of inter-racial murder cases around the British Empire in the late 19th century, Martin Weiner (2009) shows, in similar fashion, how justice and due process only gradually replaced arbitrary private violence (the beating of servants and employees, or random brutality towards 'natives') that had been deemed necessary to preserve the racialized colonial order. Similar strategies – order first/justice later – have continued to characterize the policing of large-scale industrial disputes (Christian, 1985) or 'gang' cultures (Nijjar, 2018).

As Dwyer and Nettelbeck conclude, it becomes impossible to reconcile the disjuncture 'between imperial self image and colonial realities' (2018: 5). Actually *policing* Indigenous communities (as opposed to repressing or controlling them) was not something that many colonial police agencies were equipped, or much interested, in performing. In any event, any such policing often proceeded largely upon the basis of deep-rooted suspicions about the criminal inclinations or violent temperaments of the subject ethnic groups involved, rather than any notions of due process or evidence gathering (Chemery, 2017; Nigam, 1990a, 1990b). Whether in the French, British or Dutch empires, 'race was the primary variable ordering colonial life' (Anderson, 2017: 106) and forceful armed policing was largely a consequence of a perceived need to ensure security and order in empires riven by racial difference, dispossession, injustice and punitive cruelty, but in which a spirit of insurgent resistance, buoyed up by access to the weapons of the oppressor, was becoming increasingly possible. Hill (2018), drawing upon a range of research collated by O'Reilly (2018), details similar tensions and relations in the policing of the Lusophone (Portuguese) Empire. Kumar (2018) describes a constant tension between 'the rule of law and the rule of force' in rural India, where 'state coercion was continuous and subtle, and woven into the warp and weft of everyday life, in the form of policing' and able to respond to trouble very quickly 'with spectacular use of violence' (2018: 131, 134–135) or 'exemplary punitive force' (Bennett, 2013). Furthermore, as Newsinger has argued, 'once a country was conquered, imperial rule was maintained by force. Whatever the particular architecture of imperial rule, it always rested in the end on the back of a policeman torturing a suspect' (Newsinger, 2006: 17). As Dwyer and Nettelbeck add, 'policing was not only essential to the maintenance of imperial rule [it] was often its most visible symbol' (2018: 12).

Revisionist histories of policing have long ago dispelled many of the myths associated with the development of policing systems around the world. In Britain, the much vaunted 'Peelian Principles', which have for far too long been held to embody the spirit and philosophy of British policing, have largely been exposed as a post-hoc fabrication (Loader, 2016), a 20th century and chiefly decorative addition to the process of police self-understanding and legitimation (Emsley, 2013). Whether they might yet serve to assist in a fundamental recalibration of policing, establishing 'a police service that listens closely to the demands of all citizens while directing scarce resources towards meeting needs of the most vulnerable' (Loader, 2016: 437) remains to be seen. In any event, even in mainland Britain, where notions of 'policing by consent' have had perhaps the deepest roots, these have faced substantial challenge and criticism for over four decades (Gilroy, 1982; Elliott-Cooper, 2021), allied with the idea that recent years have seen a decisive shift towards a more forceful (paramilitary style) enforcement-led policing (Fekete, 2013). If 'domestic' policing systems have faced mounting academic and political criticism, especially in the wake of the Black Lives Matter protests, imperial models of policing the empire have fared even worse. As Anderson and Killingray (1991) have noted, while the differences can be overstated and local practices varied considerably, the model of policing adopted for mainland Britain was noticeably more cognisant of 'local sensibilities' than that which British administrators inflicted on the rest of the world. Although, as they remark, 'whether the East End of London was policed with any more consent than were the poorer areas of Bombay, Durban or Melbourne is to be doubted' (Anderson and Killingray, 1991: 10). For policing was experienced in profoundly different ways according to class, race and nationality and it was the armed, paramilitary, discriminatory and substantially unaccountable policing that the British had imposed on Ireland which was to be the model for the greater part of the British Empire.

That there were two versions of 'British policing' is now generally accepted and a great deal of writing (including both scholarship and memoir: Gwynn, 1934; Jeffries, 1952; Hawkins, 1991; Sinclair, 2016) testifies to this. However, Hawkins (1991) and Anderson and Killingray (1991) caution against too literal an adoption of these 'models', for, although there is much reference to the 'Irish' or 'Ulster' models of colonial policing, underpinned by the fact that Phoenix Park (Dublin) and, later, Newtownards (near Belfast) were important training centres for colonial police officers, colonial policing institutions were often much differentiated according to local circumstances: 'the colonial reality was much more complex ... no colonial force was quite like the Irish or Ulster Constabularies, whatever claims were made for the influence of any model' (Anderson and Killingray,

1991: 2, 4). In due course, however, 'a steady stream of former officers of the Royal Irish Constabulary moved into the Indian and Colonial Police forces ... valued for their experience in the difficult circumstances of Ireland ... and for their stern discipline ... RIC men "stiffened" the ranks of many colonial police forces' (Killingray and Anderson, 1992: 8). What Irish and colonial officers did have in common, however, was that they were armed and organized along military lines, were controlled centrally (rather than accountable locally), and they lived separately, in barracks, rather than among the communities they policed. This implied that, throughout the empire, such policing forces primarily served the interests of the state and the local propertied classes and 'paid scant regard to any ideal of the need to cultivate a community of consent' (Killingray and Anderson, 1992: 9). As Lehning (2018) notes, French colonial efforts to suppress opposition continued to be seen as 'policing rather than military operations', although, especially as the end of the age of empires approached, such distinctions continued to blur and overlap. As Fanon argued in 1961:

> The colonized world is a world divided in two. The dividing line, the border, is represented by the barracks and the police stations. In the colonies, the official, the legitimate agent, the spokesman for the colonizer and the regime of oppression, is the police officer or soldier. ... In colonial regions ... the colonized are kept under close scrutiny, and contained by rifle butts and napalm ... the government's agent uses a language of pure violence. (Fanon, 2001: 38)

These degrees of separation undoubtedly facilitated violent actions while also, given the frequent resort to martial law during periods of local disturbance, shielding the involvement of police agencies engaging in punitive acts of brutality, oppression and genocide under the pretext of law-and-order maintenance (Newsinger, 2006; Gott, 2011; Ryan, 2018). As Thomas (2012) has noted, imperial governments relied heavily upon police institutions in all of their major economic activities, from tax collection and land appropriation to disciplining workers and suppressing popular dissent. Yet both national policing traditions and local circumstances shaped the form and character of direct policing practices even as 'intra-imperial borrowings' and, not least, the circulation of career officers, steeped in certain attitudes, experiences, training and cultures, exerted their own influences. Scholars working in different traditions and drawing their evidence from different empires have drawn a range of similar conclusions about the varieties of colonial policing – although largely agreeing that violence formed an essential element of all modern empires (McCulloch, 2007). For example, Muschalek details the mundane regularity of everyday normalized violence – the 'quotidian practices of colonial life' – which complemented the genocidal violence of conquest; 'the slaps in the face, kicks, beatings, painful cuffing, shoving and forceful dragging' which formed the repertoire of authority in German South-West Africa at the beginning of the 20th century (Muschalek, 2019). Violence was the oil that greased the wheels of a delegated authoritarianism. It was, in Muschalek's terms, echoing Arendt (1970), 'a compensation for a perceived or actual lack of state power', practised by the dominant in lieu of legitimate authority, and by the subaltern in order to maintain precarious advantages in a racialized status hierarchy. The point resonates throughout Blanchard et al's (2017) volume of studies on French Algeria, the Belgian Congo, Portuguese Mozambique and Danish Greenland. While economic and imperial interests provided the broad outlines for the work of these colonial 'police states', policing authorities also 'policed' in a more conventional 'European' sense (Neocleous, 2000), supervising roads and the movement of vehicles, dealing with vagrants, prostitutes and beggars, licensing street traders and collecting fees, addressing public health risks, ensuring the prompt payment of taxes, breaking strikes and supervising industrial disputes and guarding important public buildings (Blanchard et al, 2017). Thomas (2012) concurs, 'colonial governments assigned police to help maintain order on plantations, in processing plants, factories, mines and other European controlled workplaces', they managed labour quotas, passport controls, travel permits and other aspects of worker movement and internal migration. 'At the personal level as well as at the structural one, the political priorities and security practices of colonial rule were ... attuned to its *economic* organisation' (Thomas, 2012: 4–5, emphasis added).

And yet, even among this catalogue of domestic policing responsibilities, colonial police agencies remained especially 'closely linked to labor regulations and workforce management', including recruiting indentured labourers and forcing the unemployed to work, thereby often resembling the 'slave patrol' aspects of local policing (tracking and returning escapees and augmenting plantation discipline) that had characterized the American South, the Caribbean, Central and South America (Walker, 1980; Reichel, 1988; Hadden, 2003; Durr, 2015). Not unlike the labour policing duties described by Blanchard et al (2017), the role of the slave patrols included breaking up slave organized meetings, keeping slaves 'in their place' on plantations and searching their homes and lodges for contraband, such as potential weapons or anything stolen from their owners. By 1837, apparently, the Charleston Police Department had 100 officers, whose chief responsibility consisted in patrolling slaves, free Blacks and, later, indentured labourers; regulating their movement, checking passes, enforcing slave codes; protecting against slave revolts and catching runaways (Barlow and Barlow, 1999). Renowned for their cruelty and mercilessness, these White vigilante patrollers helped to control slave populations throughout the antebellum years, although they were never entirely disbanded, even after slavery ended. Following the collapse of Southern Reconstruction in the 1870s (Lane, 2008), these patrol and vigilante arrangements, often including the Ku Klux Klan (KKK), were absorbed into the policing systems of the 'Jim Crow South'. Their core function remained the maintenance of segregation and a reign of terror over the now supposedly 'free' Black underclass by supporting the discipline of exploitative labour markets. Southern police departments and the KKK often had overlapping personnel (Wendt, 2007; Johnson, 2014) while the coexistence of racist criminal justice and widespread lynching evidenced the extent of a common heritage. Post-Civil War concerns about miscegenation and a violent preoccupation with stigmatized Black masculinity contributed to racialized fears that fed into a style of violently oppressive, firearm heavy policing of African-Americans which has persisted to the present day (Weissinger and Mack, 2018; Von Robertson and Chaney, 2019).

Policing, violence and the decolonial struggle

The tensions and contradictions at the heart of different models of colonial policing became especially strained and stretched in the final years of empire when, facing increasing economic and political crisis, war, trade union mobilization, popular nationalist pressures and radical insurgencies, policing organizations became increasingly paramilitary in both form and content. 'Police forces were caught in a cleft stick, notionally obligated to serve the public, but called upon to uphold elite interests and the hierarchies of difference on which they rested' (Thomas, 2012: 9). Even as police forces were expected to continue their performance of 'general civil duties' and uphold the law, they also took on increasing security and surveillance functions and combating civil unrest. This often led to the re-equipping and repurposing of police units: the provision of new weaponry, armoured vehicles, water cannon and riot training, and the recruitment of specialist new units and the adoption of new tactics (Killingray and Anderson, 1992: 5), which often brought policing agencies into conflict with the law. Although running to differing timescales across the various European empires, continents and regions, processes of transition were often marked by violence and conflict, and in the British Empire what Thomas calls a 'repressive consensus' prevailed: 'a broad agreement about the merits of coercion as pre-emption ... the calculation that coercive capacity rapidly deployed, sustained colonial authority cheaply and efficiently. Policemen, soldiers and, increasingly, military aircraft were the key instruments in this strategy' (Thomas, 2012: 65). The irony, of course, a lesson for the future, was that repressive policing represented weakness rather than strength: for 'greater use of violence pointed to a crisis of authority rather than its ultimate incontestability' (Thomas, 2012: 65). Even as moves towards 'police reform' asserted themselves they were confronted ever more by growing trade union mobilization and rising nationalist pressures. In India, the Caribbean and Africa police were called to suppress labour unrest and nationalist protest. As Killingray and Anderson note, when police opened fire on striking miners in Nigeria, in 1949, 'the ineptitude of the colonial police in handling such matters was only matched by their ferocity' (Killingray and Anderson, 1992: 11), they were not well suited to dealing with political protest and communal resistance. A prescient warning to the future, no doubt, as (British) 'police ... of all ranks displayed strong racial prejudice' in their dealings with subject populations (Killingray and Anderson, 1992: 14).

Many examples might suffice to illustrate this 'end of empire' repression, Newsinger (2006) and Gott (2011) catalogue many instances of grotesque police brutality employed to suppress resistance and opposition in a range of locations, India, China, Palestine, Egypt and South Africa. Likewise, Elkins' disturbing study of 'Britain's Gulag' in Kenya (Elkins, 2005) and, not least the departing administration's efforts to burn all the files, expunging from the historical record the killings, torture and human rights abuses detailed there. Few single incidents might rival the horror of the 1919 Amritsar massacre, in the Punjab, when troops opened fire, without warning, upon a prohibited rally of some 25,000 people, killing several hundred (Wagner, 2019), yet this incident captures the essence of the punitive pre-emption. Volleys of rifle fire into the crowd continued for over ten minutes, a ceasefire being ordered only when the supply of ammunition was running low. The officer commanding the shooting, General Dyer, was unrepentant, he explained in his report that he continued the shooting 'until the crowd dispersed ... [but] it was no longer a question of merely dispersing the crowd, but one of producing a sufficient moral effect' (General Dyer, quoted in Newsinger, 2006: 120). The use of pre-emptive lethal force as a means of supplying 'moral effect' to discipline, intimidate and control populations has come to define what French has called, somewhat ironically, 'the British way in counter-insurgency' and which often comprised 'considerable ruthlessness ... [such as] search and destroy operations which were both ineffective and conducted with considerable brutality' (French, 2011: 6).[3]

However, perhaps one of the most instructive (and disturbingly prescient) applications of repressive asymmetric policing for moral effect concerned the almost forgotten deployment of 'air control' or 'police bombing' as practised by the Royal Air Force (RAF) over the skies of Afghanistan, Iraq and Somalia in the years after the First World War (Lindqvist, 2001; Renfrew, 2015). Neocleous (2014: 149) argues that 'moral effect', later rendered as 'morale' and most recently as the modern doctrine of 'shock and awe', was specifically intended to shatter the morale and disrupt the lives of its Indigenous victims. This may *seem* a rather contradictory legacy for the supposed 'liberal empire of the sky', but wholly consistent with centuries of imperial raiding to facilitate primitive accumulation and correctly anticipating contemporary drone governance.

While other empires certainly adopted aerial bombing tactics of civilian targets, for example Italy in its conquest of Turkish-controlled Libya, these methods were developed furthest by Britain. Satia contends that the explanation for the adoption of 'aerial policing' by bombing in Iraq and the Middle East, 'lies in the realm of cultural history', as this was a place particularly suited to aerial surveillance and 'far enough beyond the pale of bourgeois "convention" to [raise] concerns about inhumanity' (Satia, 2008: 240). Others stressed more directly 'economic' advantages, such as Clayton (1986), who argued that in the wake of the economic disaster of the First World War, large areas of an increasingly turbulent empire might have to be abandoned were it not for modern technologies: armoured motor vehicles, wireless but above all aircraft, and a new concept of 'control without occupation' (Clayton, 1986). 'Air control assisted colonial population control at minimal cost' (Thomas, 2013: 69), and estimates suggested that the RAF could carry out 'colonial operations' for just 5 per cent of what it would cost to deploy forces on the ground. Keen to retain its role as a single service – at a time when politicians and civil servants were planning to scrap the service to save money – the RAF enthusiastically committed to the policy (Smith, 1984). Several operations, such as the dropping of 16 20-pound bombs on Kabul, the bombing and machine-gunning of demonstrators in the Punjab (killing at least 12 people) and a month-long bombing campaign on the northwest frontier of India which saw 20 planes drop over five tons of bombs on 'rebellious tribesmen' unwilling to submit to British rule, convinced British authorities 'that air power would prove most valuable to the Empire in a policing role' (Omissi, 1990: 11–12).

Air control, a force multiplier, could be employed to efficiently police huge, largely unknown and featureless, expanses of the Middle East, Asia and North Africa, crucial but sparsely populated territories (Satia, 2008), over great distances as a form of flying 'gun boat diplomacy'. Even though, to be most effective, bombing operations had to be targeted against centres of population. Later, reading a report of a raid on Baghdad, Churchill took exception to reading of the way pilots had machine-gunned fleeing civilians, including women and children (Lindqvist, 2001: 103). Yet this was precisely the way to deliver a 'cheaper means of pacification' (Omissi, 1990). Police bombing could be used to deliver punishment to resistant tribesmen, put down revolts, pursue bandits, target small wars and regional skirmishes and even leverage the enforcement of tax collection (Renfrew, 2015: 11). As Neocleous explains, air power was an ideal educative method to compel distant rebellious tribes to succumb to a system of taxation, thereby compelling engagement in a monetary economy and markets in place of subsistence agriculture. In this fashion, air power extended the liberal capitalist regime, doing its work of exploiting, pacifying and 'civilising' (Neocleous, 2014: 143–147). Aircraft could truly 'rule the desert' (Satia, 2008: 241), exercising constant surveillance, delivering bombs and bullets, but also dropping propaganda leaflets. Although, as Lindqvist (2001) notes, later ordnance also included timed bombs, phosphorous bombs, oil and liquid fire – a forerunner to napalm. According to Omissi (1990: 28), however, here (and contra Neocleous) lay the inherent limits of the strategy: air policing could only serve as a means of propaganda or an 'instrument of terror'. Real *governance* required rather more. Even so, according to Blanchard, 'aerial bombing and machine-gunning operations were not seen as acts of war' but rather as 'modes of [police] enforcement action' (Blanchard et al, 2017: 22). Officials mounted what Satia has termed a 'defence of inhumanity' to justify the practice, perceiving little wrong in the bombing of 'semi-civilised and uncivilised tribes … what was permissible only in wartime in advanced countries turned out to be *always* permissible in Iraq', and it was suggested that 'an air bomb in Iraq was, more or less, the equivalent of a policeman's truncheon at home' (in Satia, 2008: 246–250, emphasis in original).

Air control and the practice of police bombing continued across the region throughout the 1920s, venturing also into Transjordan, Egypt, the Sudan, Aden (Yemen) and Somalia, clinging on to the fringes of empire without prohibitive rates of military expenditure. Omissi discusses in great detail the deployment of British air power in a wide range of settings, acknowledging a growing recognition of its strengths and weaknesses as a policing strategy. There was ready acknowledgement of air power's 'moral effect', its ability to terrorize and intimidate, but, at the same time, recognition that the bombing and strafing of urban or built-up areas was a pretty blunt and indiscriminate tactic, frequently killing women and children. Indeed, because air actions were 'cheap, quick and often effective', there was increasing concern that punitive sorties might be too frequently and hastily deployed (Omissi, 1990: 94). And in any event, as Omissi shows, the subjects or air attacks also gradually came to learn how to hide, avoid, limit the impact of, or even repel, air attacks. Populations would construct bomb-shelters or vacate targeted areas during day-time (bombing and navigating at night were very imprecise) while 'British aeroplanes on policing missions were frequently damaged and occasionally destroyed by intense and accurate rifle fire from the ground' (Omissi, 1990: 123). In any event, over time, even the sought-after terrifying 'moral effect' of air policing began to diminish as its subjects came to realize how limited in impact it could be. In Britain too, and across the international community, opinions regarding colonial policing by bombing began to turn. By the early 1930s the issue of aerial bombing of non-military targets had become an issue for the Geneva disarmament conference, challenging British assertions that aerial bombing was a 'humane and economical' form of territorial control (Omissi, 1990: 163).

At the 1933 Geneva disarmament conference, British diplomats tabled a proposal calling for 'the complete abolition of bombing from the air, except for police purposes in outlying regions' (quoted in Kiernan, 1982: 200). Although anxious 'to prevent the future bombing of Britain, the government and the great majority of people did not see any connection between bombing "backward" tribes and their opposition to air attacks on "civilized" countries'. Yet as the RAF leadership put it, 'if villages are not to be bombed, our capacity to control semi-civilised countries will be jeopardised' (Renfrew, 2015: 234). Foreign Office delegates concurred with this assessment, arguing that:

> [I]t was absurd to compare the bombing of an Iraqi village with an attack on a European town ... the term 'civilian population' has a very different meaning in Iraq from what it has in Europe ... it is far the most humane as well as inexpensive method of punishment that can be employed in these regions. (Renfrew, 2015: 234)

In line with the original justifications, the unfettered right to retain 'air bombing for police purposes, to carry out our Empire and mandatory obligations ... is not only an unusually effective deterrent but also the most expeditious, economical and human method of maintaining law and order' (cited in Renfrew, 2015: 235–236). Of course, this is far from being the end of the bombing story, as Guernica, the London Blitz, Dresden, Hiroshima, Nagasaki and Vietnam all testify. For Neocleous (2014), the vital development heralded by air power was the erasure of a distinction between civilian and combatant, although, as we have already argued, colonial military and policing operations across the global South acknowledged no such distinctions anyway. The augmentation of imperial violence by air power and police bombing may have established a new technique of 'paradoxical liberalism' whereby bombing might be a civilizing force and 'to be bombed is to experience civilisation' (Neocleous, 2014: 150). Henceforth, air power as police power would become central to the construction of neoliberal internationalism, the New World Order, finding widespread application in recent counterinsurgency 'policing wars' (Holmqvist, 2014).

Conclusion

The 1933 Geneva disarmament conference had produced no agreement on the bombing of civilians, frustrated, according to Lloyd George, by a stubborn reluctance on the part of Britain 'insist[ing] on the right to bomb niggers (sic.)' (in Kiernan, 1982: 200). Hitler withdrew the German delegation, bombing's future was assured and the threadbare justifications of imperial violence, 'the British way in counter-insurgency', were exposed for all to see, although still to be repeated ad infinitum in very similar places. In the wake of the Second World War, no doubt anticipating the 'doublethink' of *1984*, George Orwell had launched a critical attack on the brutal euphemism of much contemporaneous political discourse. 'Defenceless villages are bombarded from the air', he complained, 'the inhabitants driven out into the countryside, the cattle machine-gunned, the huts set on fire with incendiary bullets: this is called *pacification*' (Orwell, 2021 [1946]: 7, original emphasis). His words spoke to a future we have all since witnessed, but describe a past often forgotten, sometimes purposely erased, as Elkins (2005) has shown. But what this hypocrisy – in Thomas' words a 'bitter proof of Europeans' inhuman practices and alien beliefs' (2013: 69) – has rested on, indeed, what has obscured the vital asymmetry in our fictions of accountability, 'minimum force' and 'policing by consent' in the British way of policing writ large, have been fundamental divisions of 'otherness' established by inequality, racism and postcoloniality: the *Southern* as both other and metaphor. In effect, just another 'myth of black criminality' (Gilroy, 1982), with which to police the continuing political crisis. At a time when government in the United Kingdom is forcing through legislation further chipping away these supposed virtues of 'the British way', and when certain 'Southern practices' are returning home, as it were – for example recent proposals within the Police, Crime, Sentencing and Courts Bill restricting the right to political protest (Siddique, 2021), it is essential to remain alert to these connections.

Notes

[1] This is intended to refer to both militarized civilian policing systems and combined or 'hybrid' systems where the military shared substantial domestic policing responsibilities such as in Brazil, West Africa (Cole, 1999) and Pakistan (Waseem, 2019), although the picture has become more complicated given the accretion of 'high-policing' (Brodeur, 1983) responsibilities, the involvement of military agencies in 'peacekeeping' activities (Harig, 2020) and the development of specialist counterterrorist or special weapons and tactics units in many police jurisdictions (Kraska, 2001; Balko, 2014; Wood, 2014). Combined civil/military policing systems are not restricted to Southern jurisdictions, but are also found, for example, in France, Italy and Portugal.

[2] The subject of a substantial outpouring of literature over recent years, but which, for all its apparently democratic and accountable credentials, remains highly contested (Dixon, 2009) even though the writings of a range of end-of-empire police administrators have, in their various ways, sought to prolong the police reform project (see, for example, Gwynn, 1934; Jeffries, 1952; and for commentaries see Clayton and Killingray, 1989; Sinclair, 2017).

[3] French's observations are of more than just historical interest for, looking forwards to the British engagement in Iraq and Afghanistan, he notes that much British counterinsurgency doctrine had been 'based upon historical arguments that are at best ill-informed, and at worst almost the opposite of what actually happened' (French, 2011: 7).

References

Anderson, D.M. and Killingray, D. (1991) *Policing the Empire: Government, Authority and Control*. Manchester: Manchester University Press.

Anderson, D.M. and Killingray, D. (1992) *Policing and Decolonisation: Nationalism, Politics and the Police 1917–65*. Manchester: Manchester University Press.

Anderson, M.L. (2017) Race, violence and white crime: French assimilationism and its limits in the Saigon colonial police, in E. Blanchard, M. Bloembergen and A. Lauro (eds) *Policing in Colonial Empires: Cases, Connections, Boundaries*. Brussels: Peter Lang, pp 105–118.

Andrews, K. (2021) *The New Age of Empire: How Racism and Colonialism still Rule the World*. Dublin: Penguin Books.

Arendt, H. (1970) *On Violence*. New York: Harcourt Books.

Arnold, D. (1986) *Police Power and Colonial Rule: Madras 1859–1947*. Delhi: Oxford University Press.

Balbus, I.D. (1973) *The Dialectics of Legal Repression: Black Rebels before the American Courts*. New York: SAGE.

Balko, R. (2014) *The Rise of the Warrior Cop*. New York: Public Affairs Books.

Barlow, D.E. and Barlow, M.H. (1999) A political economy of community policing. *Policing: An International Journal of Police Strategies & Management*, 22(4): 646–674.

Bell, E. (2013) Normalising the exceptional: British colonial policing cultures come home. *Mémoire(s), Identité(s), Marginalité(s) dans le monde occidental contemporain*, 10: np.

Bennett, H. (2013) *Fighting the Mau Mau: The British Army and Counter-Insurgency in the Kenya Emergency*. Cambridge: Cambridge University Press.

Blanchard, E., Bloembergen, M. and Lauro, A. (2017) Tensions of policing in colonial situations, in E. Blanchard, M. Bloembergen and A. Lauro (eds) *Policing in Colonial Empires: Cases, Connections, Boundaries*. Brussels: Peter Lang, pp 11–38.

Brodeur, J.P. (1983) High policing and low policing: Remarks about the policing of political activities. *Social Problems*, 30(5): 507–520.

Brogden, M. (1987) The emergence of the police: The colonial dimension. *British Journal of Criminology*, 27(1): 4–14.

Brown, D. (1972 [1970]) *Bury My Heart at Wounded Knee*. London: Pan Books.

Chemery, V. (2017) Policing and the problem of crime in local communities in colonial Algeria: 1850–1890. In E. Blanchard, M. Bloembergen and A. Lauro (eds) *Policing in Colonial Empires: Cases, Connections, Boundaries*. Brussels: Peter Lang, pp 119–136.

Chew, E. (2012) *Arming the Periphery: The Arms Trade in the Indian Ocean during the Age of Global Empire*. Basingstoke: Palgrave Macmillan.

Christian, L. (1985) Restriction without conviction: The role of the courts in legitimising police control in Nottinghamshire, in B. Fine and R. Millar (eds) *Policing the Miners' Strike*. London: Lawrence & Wishart, pp 120–137.

Clayton, A. (1986) *The British Empire as a Superpower: 1919–1939.* Athens, GA: University of Georgia Press.

Clayton, A. and Killingray, D. (1989) *Khaki and Blue: Military and Police in British Colonial Africa.* Athens, OH: Ohio University Press.

Cole, B. (1999) Post-colonial systems, in R. Mawby (ed) *Policing Across the World: Issues for the Twenty-first Century.* London: UCL Press, pp 88–108.

Collier, P. (2009) *Wars, Guns and Votes: Democracy in Dangerous Places.* London: Vintage Books.

Comaroff, J. and Comaroff, J.L. (eds) (2008) *Law and Disorder in the Post-Colony.* Chicago: University of Chicago Press.

Comaroff, J. and Comaroff, J.L. (2012) *Theory from the South: Or, How Euro-America is Evolving Toward Africa.* Abingdon: Routledge.

Connell, R. (2007) *Southern Theory: The Global Dynamics of Knowledge in Social Science.* Cambridge: Polity.

Currie, E. (2005) *The Roots of Danger: Violent Crime in Global Perspective.* Columbus: Prentice-Hall.

Dixon, P. (2009) 'Hearts and minds'? British counter-insurgency from Malaya to Iraq. *Journal of Strategic Studies,* 32(3): 353–381.

Dunbar-Ortiz, R. (2018) *Loaded: A Disarming History of the Second Amendment.* San Francisco: City Lights Books.

Durr, M. (2015) What is the difference between slave patrols and modern day policing? Institutional violence in a community of color. *Critical Sociology,* 41(6): 873–879.

Dwyer, P. and Nettelbeck, A. (2018) 'Savage wars of peace': Violence, colonialism and empire in the modern world, in P. Dwyer and A. Nettelbeck (eds) *Violence, Colonialism and Empire in the Modern World.* Cham: Palgrave Macmillan, pp 1–23.

Elkins, C. (2005) *Imperial Reckoning: The Untold Story of Britain's Gulag in Kenya.* New York: Henry Holt/Owl Books.

Elliott-Cooper, A. (2021) *Black Resistance to British Policing.* Manchester: Manchester University Press.

Emsley, C. (2013) Peel's principles: Police principles, in J. Brown (ed) *The Future of Policing.* Abingdon: Routledge, pp 41–52.

Emsley, C. (2014) Policing the empire/policing the metropole: Some thoughts on models and types. *Crime, History & Societies,* 18(2): 5–25.

Fanon, F. (2001) *The Wretched of the Earth.* London: Penguin.

Fekete, L. (2013) Total policing: Reflections from the frontline. *Race & Class,* 54(3): 65–76.

French, D. (2011) *The British Way in Counter-Insurgency: 1945–1967.* Oxford: Oxford University Press.

Gilroy, P. (1982) The Myth of Black Criminality, *Socialist Register,* 47–56.

Gott, R. (2011) *Britain's Empire: Resistance, Repression and Revolt.* London: Verso.

Greene, O. and Marsh, N. (eds) (2012) *Small Arms, Crime and Conflict: Global Governance and the Threat of Armed Violence*. London: Routledge.

Grenier, J. (2005) *The First Way of War: American War Making on the Frontier*. Cambridge: Cambridge University Press.

Gwynn, C.W. (1934) *Imperial Policing*. London: Macmillan.

Hadden, S.E. (2003) *Slave Patrols: Law and Violence in Virginia and the Carolinas*. Cambridge, MA: Harvard University Press.

Harig, C. (2020) Soldiers in police roles. *Policing and Society*, 30(9): 1097–1114. DOI: 10.1080/10439463.2019.1650745

Hawkins, R. (1991) The 'Irish model' and the empire: A case for reassessment, in D.M. Anderson and D. Killingray (eds) *Policing the Empire: Government, Authority and Control*. Manchester: Manchester University Press, pp 18–32.

Headrick, D.R. (1981) *The Tools of Empire: Technology and European Imperialism in the Nineteenth Century*. Oxford: Oxford University Press.

Hill, R.S. (2018) Comment: The Portuguese colonial policing mission in comparative perspective, in C. O'Reilly (ed) *Colonial Policing and the Transnational Legacy: The Global Dynamics of Policing across the Lusophone Community*. Abingdon: Routledge, pp 67–88.

Holmqvist, C. (2014) *Policing Wars: On Military Intervention in the 21st Century*. Basingstoke: Palgrave Macmillan.

Horne, G. (2017) *The Apocalypse of Settler Colonialism: The Roots of Slavery, White Supremacy and Capitalism in 17th Century North America*. New York: Monthly Review Press.

Jeffries, C. (1952) *The Colonial Police*. London: Max Parrish.

Johnson, N. (2014) *Negroes and the Gun*. New York: Prometheus Books.

Jones, K. Macola, G. and Welch, D. (eds) (2013) *A Cultural History of Firearms in the Age of Empire*. Farnham: Ashgate.

Karp, A. (2014) Stockpiles: The global geography of small arms numbers, in P. Batchelor and K.M. Kenkel (eds) *Controlling Small Arms: Consolidation, Innovation and Relevance in Research and Policy*. Abingdon: Routledge, pp 64–82.

Karp, A. (2018) Estimating global civilian-held firearms numbers. *Small Arms Survey, Briefing Paper*, June.

Kiernan, V.G. (1982) *Colonial Empires and Armies: 1815–1960*. Stroud: Fontana Paperbacks.

Killingray, D. and Anderson, D.M. (1992) An orderly retreat: Policing the end of empire, in D.M. Anderson and D. Killingray (eds) *Policing and Decolonisation: Nationalism, Politics and the Police 1917–65*. Manchester: Manchester University Press, pp 1–21.

Kraska, P. (2001) *Militarizing the American Criminal Justice System*. Boston: Northeastern University Press.

Kumar, R. (2018) Seeing like a policeman: Everyday violence in British India, c. 1900–1950, in P. Dwyer and A. Nettelbeck (eds) *Violence, Colonialism and Empire in the Modern World*. Cham: Palgrave Macmillan, pp 131–149.

Lane, C. (2008) *The Day Freedom Died: The Colfax Massacre, the Supreme Court and the Betrayal of Reconstruction*. New York: Holt Paperbacks.

Lehning, J.R. (2018) Categories of conquest and colonial control: The French in Tonkin, 1884–1914, in P. Dwyer and A. Nettelbeck (eds) *Violence, Colonialism and Empire in the Modern World*. Cham: Palgrave Macmillan, pp 73–90.

Lindqvist, S. (2001) *A History of Bombing*. London: Granta Books.

Lindqvist, S. (2018) *Exterminate all the Brutes*. London: Granta Books.

Loader, I. (2016) In search of civic policing: Recasting the 'Peelian principles', *Crime, Law and Philosophy*, 10(3): 427–440.

McCulloch, J. (2007) Empire and violence: 1900–1939, in P. Levine (ed) *Gender and Empire*. Oxford: Oxford University Press, pp 220–239.

Muschalek, M. (2019) *Violence as Usual: Policing and the Colonial State in German South-West Africa*. Ithaca, NY: Cornell University Press.

Neocleous, M. (2000) *The Fabrication of Order: A Critical Theory of Police Power*. London: Pluto Press.

Neocleous, M. (2014) *War Power, Police Power*. Edinburgh: University of Edinburgh Press.

Newsinger, J. (2006) *And the Blood Never Dried: A People's History of the British Empire*. London: Bookmarks Publications.

Nigam, S. (1990a) Disciplining and policing the 'criminals by birth', part 1: The making of a colonial stereotype – the criminal tribes and castes of North India. *The Indian Economic & Social History Review*, 27(2): 131–164.

Nigam, S. (1990b) Disciplining and policing the 'criminals by birth', part 2: The development of a disciplinary system, 1871–1900. *The Indian Economic & Social History Review*, 27(3): 257–287.

Nijjar, J. (2018) Echoes of empire: Excavating the colonial roots of Britain's 'war on gangs'. *Social Justice*, 45(2/3): 147–161.

Omissi, D.E. (1990) *Air Power and Colonial Control*. Manchester: Manchester University Press.

O'Reilly, C. (2018) *Colonial Policing and the Transnational Legacy: The Global Dynamics of Policing across the Lusophone Community*. Abingdon: Routledge.

Orwell, G. (2021 [1946]) *Politics and the English Language*. London: Renard Press.

Owen, O. (2016) Policing after colonialism, in B. Bradford, B. Jauregui, I. Loader and J. Steinberg (eds) *The SAGE Handbook of Global Policing*. London: SAGE, pp 303–319.

Reichel, P.L. (1988) Southern slave patrols as a transitional police type. *American Journal of Police*, 51(7): np.

Renfrew, B. (2015) *Wings of Empire: The Forgotten Wars of the RAF: 1919–1939*. Stroud: The History Press.

Ryan, L. (2018) Martial law in the British empire, in P. Dwyer and A. Nettelbeck (eds) *Violence, Colonialism and Empire in the Modern World*. Cham: Palgrave Macmillan, pp 93–109.

Satia, P. (2008) *Spies in Arabia: The Great War and the Cultural Foundations of Britain's Covert Empire in the Middle East*. Oxford: Oxford University Press.

Satia, P. (2018) *Empire of Guns: The Violent Making of the Industrial Revolution*. Richmond: Duckworth.

Schilz, T.F. and Worcester, D.E. (1987) The spread of firearms among the Indian tribes on the northern frontier of New Spain. *American Indian Quarterly*, 11(1): 1–10.

Shear, K., Lindsay, L. and Miescher, S. (2003) 'Taken as boys': The politics of black police employment and experience in early twentieth-century South Africa, in L.A. Lindsay and S. Miescher (eds) *Men and Masculinities in Modern Africa*. London: Heinemann, np.

Siddique, H. (2021) Curb on protest in policing bill breach human rights laws, MPs and peers say. *The Guardian*, 22 June.

Silvestri, M. (2019) *Policing 'Bengali Terrorism' in India and the World: Imperial Intelligence and Revolutionary Nationalism 1905–1939*. Cham: Palgrave Macmillan.

Sinclair, G. (2016) The 'Irish' policeman and the Empire: Influencing the policing of the British Empire–Commonwealth. *Irish Historical Studies*, 36(142): 173–187.

Sinclair, G. (2017) *At the End of the Line: Colonial Policing and the Imperial Endgame*. Manchester: Manchester University Press.

Smith, A. (1984) *British Air Strategy between the Wars*. Oxford: Clarendon Press.

Squires, P. (2014) *Gun Crime in Global Contexts*. Abingdon: Routledge.

Stavrianakis, A. (2011) Small arms control and the reproduction of imperial relations. *Contemporary Security Policy*, 32(1): 193–214.

Stavrianakis, A. (2016) Legitimising liberal militarism: Politics, law and war in the Arms Trade Treaty. *Third World Quarterly*, 37(5): 340–365.

Stavrianakis, A. (2019) Controlling weapons circulation in a postcolonial militarised world. *Review of International Studies*, 45(1): 57–76.

Stavrianakis, A. and Stern, M. (2018) Militarism and security: Dialogue, possibilities and limits. *Security Dialogue*, 49(1–2): 3–18.

Storey, W.K. (2008) *Guns, Race, Power in Colonial South Africa*. Cambridge: Cambridge University Press.

Thomas, M. (2012) *Violence and Colonial Order: Police, Workers and Protest in the European Colonial Empires, 1918–1940*. Cambridge: Cambridge University Press.

Thomas, M. (2013) Markers of modernity or agents of terror? Air policing and colonial revolt after World War I, in C. Baxter, M.L. Dockrill, K. Hamilton, J.W. Young, E.G.H. Pedaliu and M.D. Kandiah (eds) *Britain in Global Politics: Volume 1*. London: Palgrave Macmillan, pp 68–98.

UNODC (United Nations Office of Drugs and Crime) (2019) *Global Study on Homicide: Booklet 3: Understanding Homicide*. Vienna: UNODC.

UNODC (United Nations Office of Drugs and Crime) (2020) *UNODC Study on Firearm Trafficking*. Vienna: UNODC.

Von Robertson, R. and Chaney, C.D. (2019) *Police Use of Excessive Force against African Americans: Historical Antecedents and Community Perceptions*. Lexington: Lexington Books.

Wagner, K. (2019) *Amritsar, 1919: An Empire of Fear and the Making of a Massacre*. New Haven: Yale University Press.

Walker, S. (1980) *Popular Justice*. New York: Oxford University Press.

Waseem, Z. (2019) Brothers in arms: A police paramilitary partnership in Karachi. *Policing and Society*, 31(2): 131–147.

Weiner, M.J. (2009) *An Empire on Trial: Race, Murder and Justice under British Rule: 1870–1935*. Cambridge: Cambridge University Press.

Weissinger S.E. and Mack, D.A. (eds) (2018) *Law Enforcement in the Age of Black Lives Matter: Policing Black and Brown Bodies*. Lexington: Lexington Books.

Wendt, S. (2007) *The Spirit and the Shotgun: Armed Resistance and the Struggle for Civil Rights*. Gainesville: University Press of Florida.

Wood, L.J. (2014) *Crisis and Control: The Militarization of Protest Policing*. London: Pluto Press.

3

From Overseer to Officer: A Brief History of British Policing through Afro-Diasporic Music Culture

Lambros Fatsis

Introduction

In the aftermath of the 2020 #BlackLivesMatter protests, renewed calls to decolonize university curricula and abolish the police became hot topics within UK academia. This is certainly not the first time that such debates have captured the criminological imagination.[1] The sheer energy of such mass mobilizations, however, compels criminologists to think decolonization and police abolition anew; as inextricably intertwined demands that ought to be brought together. Alas, discussing decolonization and police abolition in the same breath reveals a dearth of criminological literature on the links between colonialism and policing[2] and a profound lack of non-Eurocentric approaches to knowledge production. In an attempt to address such a lacuna in the 'white'[3] mainstream criminological canon, this chapter narrates a brief history of British policing by excavating its colonial roots and unearthing Black or Afro-diasporic music[4] as an undermined resource for decolonial scholarship. Drawing on the policing of UK drill music as a contemporary example that illustrates historical continuities in how 'race' is policed through the policing of Black music(s), British policing will be reintroduced as colonially configured and therefore racist by design – if not by default (Owusu-Bempah, 2017; Elliot-Cooper, 2021; Chowdhury in Duff, 2021: 85–94; Fatsis, 2021a, 2021b; Fatsis and Lamb, 2021). Black music, therefore, features here as an instrument of scholarship with which to trace the origins of British policing in the colonial militias that patrolled, captured and controlled the enslaved through suppressing their cultural expression (Fatsis, 2021b: 35–37). Documenting or 'phonograph[ing]' (Moten, 2003: 68) the history of policing Black forms of creative expression, however, doesn't just help us place British policing in its proper historical – that is to say, imperial-colonial context (Brogden, 1987; Emsley, 2014; Elliott-Cooper, 2021; esp 23–30; Chowdhury in Duff, 2021; Fatsis and Lamb, 2021: 23–8). It also enables us to embrace Black music as a decolonial 'Black method' (McKittrick, 2021: 5, 9, 41), which disrupts and subverts modes of knowledge production that reproduce (neo)colonial(ist) ways of seeing, thinking about, acting towards and being in the world. In so doing, this chapter aims at ridding criminology of its 'Occidentosis' (Al-i Ahmad, 1984) – while also ushering Black music in; as an alternative scholarly praxis (Fatsis, 2021b: 42–5; Lee, 2021) that offers arresting insights on how the '*overseer* who rode in the plantation' becomes the '*officer* who patrols the nation' (KRS-One, 1993, emphasis added).

Beat(s) for blame: policing against UK drill music

UK drill music is a contemporary and popular rap subgenre – boasting number one hits in the UK charts, while simultaneously featuring as public enemy number one; due to lurid media imagery and legal penal system[5] tactics that represent and pursue it as such (Fatsis, 2019b). Originating in Chicago in the mid-2000s, it rippled across the Atlantic and took root in the UK rap music scene soon after. Unlike other forms of rap music, UK drill is decidedly darker in sound and more graphic in its violent imagery. It is unabashedly edgy and violent in its posture, lyrics, imagery and sonic qualities – depicting fictional larger-than-life personas, who tell their story in the first person and pose as violent. As such, drill lyrics are often (mis)taken for real-life descriptions of crimes committed, rather than as first-person narratives that may be partly or purely performative, fictional, hyperbolic or fabricated even, as is the case with many other music lyrics or literary works. Crucially, drill rappers consciously exploit stereotypes of violence, 'gangsterism' and 'ghetto life' as a sought-after commodity to be consumed online by followers whose clicks, views, likes and shares can and *do* yield material rewards (Stuart, 2020). Rather than offering a simple or 'authentic' voice, rappers are highly attuned to the commercial relations of their work and deploy themes of violent crime that they know to be very marketable (Quinn, 2005). A central impetus and theme of the music, therefore, is the desire to become a successful rapper to escape poverty and the violence in drill is part of the genre's conventions and part of its commercial appeal too. UK drill enjoys a huge following among young listeners of all ethnic backgrounds. The main audience of UK drill music, however, is young Black people who can relate to the themes of marginalization and social exclusion, as well as consume and produce it as an outlet for creative expression – in line with the artistic conventions of the genre and without conflating the literary with the literal (Dennis, 2007; Stoia et al, 2018; Lutes et al, 2019; Nielson and Dennis, 2019; Owusu-Bempah, 2020).

Lacking the cultural literacy (Ilan, 2020) to distinguish between performative and actual violence, the police, prosecutors and judges energetically criminalize UK drill through various discriminatory and unjust interventions that turn Black cultural activity into a legally punishable offence. These include Criminal Behaviour Orders, gang injunctions, suspended prison sentences and the monitoring and removal of drill music videos from video-sharing platforms such as YouTube. The Metropolitan Police even formed a Drill Music Translation Cadre, consisting of police officers who act as 'rap expert' witnesses; decoding lyrics and translating them into evidence for the prosecution (Quinn, 2018). Similarly, the Crown Prosecution Service has published decision-making guidance which makes direct references to drill music as 'evidence' of gang-affiliation and 'bad character' to establish joint enterprise convictions (CPS, 2021). Recent amendments to the government's Police, Crime, Sentencing and Courts Bill (Liberty, 2021) also increase the likelihood of subjecting drill rappers to expanded suspicion-less stop and search (Fatsis, 2019b: 1304; Fatsis, 2021c; Fatsis et al, 2021) – as does the introduction of Serious Violence Reduction Orders and Knife Crime Prevention Orders, which accompany existing stop and search powers that already disproportionately affect young, Black Britons (Shiner et al, 2018; HMICFRS, 2021).

So far so good (at least for the punitively-minded), provided that hard, tangible evidence could connect drill to criminal wrongdoing (Fatsis, 2019b; Ilan, 2020; Lynes et al, 2020). Alas, where drill lyrics or videos are adduced as evidence in court, they often have no direct connection to the offence charged – as case law evidence reveals (Owusu-Bempah, 2022). Such measures, therefore, are only justified because drill music is pursued as dangerous by legal penal system functionaries, without being able to substantiate what amounts to little more than pure suspicion. In the absence of any real evidential weight that would lend some credence to such penal hysteria, the only evidence that exists points to the discriminatory, illiberal and unjust logic, nature and outcomes of such legal penal tactics (Paul, 2021). This is not to deny, justify or condone any violence in (*some* but not *all*) drill music – which rarely amounts to anything more than isolated incidents anyway (Fatsis, 2019b; Ilan, 2020). Rather, it is to note that this is not what all drill is (and indeed, that this is all that drill is) – while also stressing that it is *selectively* criminalized in ways that prompt more questions about policing and racialized state-sanctioned violence, than they do about the danger that drill music ostensibly poses. To do justice to such a provocative assertion, this section aims at pointing out that what may be thought of as an unusual stigmatization of an entire genre actually shows what is typical about policing in the way it chooses its targets from (racially and otherwise) minoritized 'suspect communit[ies]' (Hillyard, 1993). The British state's 'war against drill', therefore, is not seen here as a deviation from what policing is and does. It is approached instead as a normal and normalized feature of policing as an instrument of discriminatory suppression, with a long history of targeting Black music(s) and other forms of Black cultural expression – dating back to the era of colonial slavery (Fatsis, 2021b: 35–37).

Beat cops now and then

Placing the birth of British policing in the context of colonial rule, this section will demonstrate how pre-professional slave-catching militias are the forgotten precursors of the 'new' or modern police that was established in 19th-century England (Taylor, 1997). This neglected 'colonial dimension' (Brogden, 1987) in the history of British policing situates its origins in the policing of Black music culture(s) in Britain's colonial outposts – pointing at the necessity of its formation to clamp down on activities that would encourage resistance to the violent domination, subjugation and exploitation of the enslaved. Anchored in this alternative conceptualization and periodization of policing (building on Fatsis, 2021b: 35–7 and Fatsis and Lamb, 2021: 23–8), what follows restores policing to its imperial-colonial historical context and reintroduces policing as a fundamentally cultural and political institution, rather than a (purely) crime-fighting one. To achieve this, the remainder of this section draws on the historical suppression of Afro-diasporic music(s) and culture – as the keynote through which colonial overseers kept the enslaved and their expressive activities in check. An exhaustive account of how the music of the enslaved was targeted, monitored, disciplined and censored goes beyond what could be achievable in the space of a book chapter. What follows nevertheless offers a potted history of the racist logic and legislation that made the prohibition of Black music possible, out of fear for the danger it poses as the soundtrack to revolt and resistance to racial oppression; colonial and postcolonial alike.

Let us begin at the beginning with the banning of African drumming and dancing in Britain's colonies in the Caribbean, in Africa and that other former British colony, the United States, where slave patrol legislation was introduced to 'prevent all caballings amongst negroes, by dispersing of them when drumming or playing' (McCord, 1841: 640). Such statutes were of a piece with similar ordinances that targeted 'the tumultuous gatherings of the Negroes' (Du Bois, 2007: 166) and banned 'Negro Frolicks' (Whitfield, 2016: 27). Further south, British colonial rule in the Caribbean became almost synonymous with 'police regulations' that 'lay at the very heart of the slave system' – so much so that 'without them, the system became impossible to maintain' (Goveia, 1960: 82). Such police regulations were aimed at 'the pursuit, capture, suppression and punishment' of the enslaved – who were 'forbidden to beat drums and blow horns, since these were means of communication which might be used to help runaways. All such activities were dangerous, too, as means of concerting uprisings – another reason for the existence of these laws' (Goveia, 1960: 84). A characteristic example is the 1787 Consolidated Act[6] (especially Clause 21), which was introduced to enable the 'government of slaves' and prevent 'rebellions concerted at negro dance' (Wynter, nd: 84). Similar legislation across the Caribbean outlawed religious rites and ceremonies like *obeah*, prohibited drum dances like Calenda/Kalinda, Belaire and Bongo – and suppressed cultural festivals like Jonkonnu parades in Jamaica and Carnival/*canboulay* processions in Trinidad (Quevedo, 1983: 55–56; Cowley, 1996; Robinson, 2021: 246), for their potential to function as 'mechanisms of rebellion … sited in culture' (Wynter, nd: 411–412[7]). Such regulatory measures were also enforced under colonial rule in Africa (Drewett and Cloonan, 2006) through bans on 'drums of African origin in all types of public meetings' (Moore, 1997: 69) and prohibitions on 'playing objectionable native tunes' (Collins, 2006: 172–173). Banning drumming, dancing and musical performance that accompanied religious rites and cultural festivals, however, did not end with the abolition of colonial slavery. It continued apace but morphed into police harassment of Trinidadian calypso/*kaiso* (Quevedo, 1983) and West African Àsìkò music (Collins, 2006). In Britain, Carnival celebrations (APC, 1989; Gutzmore, 1993; Blagrove Jr, 2014: 123–159), reggae soundsystems (Bradley, 2001: 427–428; Gilroy, 2002: 95–104, 115–116; Campbell, 2007: 5, 191–195, 200, 428; Gilroy, 2007: 152; Tebbutt and Bourne, 2014; *Transpontine*, 2015; Ward, 2018), garage, bashment and grime music (Fatsis, 2019a) faced similar suppression – bringing echoes of the colonial, 'plantation archipelago' (Wynter, nd: 372) closer to Britain's postcolonial shores. The policing of Carnival in colonial Trinidad (Quevedo, 1983), for example, was hardly different from the policing of Carnival in postcolonial Britain as a site of 'criminality' and disorder (Chowdhury, 2019). To further emphasize such continuity today, it is worth comparing the policing of calypso/*kaiso* in 1930s Trinidad with the policing of UK drill today – in ways that reintroduce policing as an ideology and technology of racial rule; colonial and postcolonial alike. At first glance, the two genres could not be more different. While calypso is celebrated for its jolly, jump-up rhythmic feel, as well as for its imaginative and risqué wordplay and picong, drill is feared for its haunting beats, menacing pose and graphic lyrics. Yet, a closer look at the negative police attention they both have received should make us pause and think about whether policing Black music serves any other purpose; beyond enforcing an unequal social order through oppressive and discriminatory social control.

The year is 1934 in sun-kissed Trinidad and as calypsonians sharpen their minds, flex their muscles and ready their tongues to showcase their musical poetry in calypso tents during the Carnival season, a new Theatre and Dance Halls Ordinance came into force, setting up the 'benighted police force and alien high-ranking [colonial] officers as the supreme authority over the kaiso'[8] with powers to 'ban records' and forbid calsypsonians to 'sing in [calypso] tents without a license duly signed by the police officer superintending the district' (Quevedo, 1983: 57–58), on the grounds that the characteristic 'barbed wit, biting satire and ridicule' (Quevedo, 1983: 27) – that are essential characteristics of the genre – can be 'insulting' to individuals and certain sections of the community, 'whether referred to by name or otherwise' (Quevedo, 1983: 61). Attempting to 'cleanse' Carnival festivities from what the authorities perceived as lowly, vulgar and perverse lyrics, the police and the Colonial Secretary – who had the power to enforce such regulations – could effectively determine who could sing and what they could sing about, while also imposing sanctions that put calypsonians in a position of legal and economic disadvantage – through the banning of their live performances and records. Worse still, such judgements were made by people with a questionable understanding of 'the subtleties, innuendos, insinuations and nuances connected with this art medium' (Quevedo, 1983: 58). Raymond Quevedo, who is quoted here as an authority on calypso and a renowned calypsonian to boot (Atilla [sic] the Hun), spoke against such police regulations in the Trinidad Legislative Council, lambasting amendments to the original Theatre and Dance Halls Ordinance as 'wicked', 'nefarious', 'perverse', 'pernicious' and 'dictatorial' (Quevedo, 1983: 60, 63), on the grounds that: 'the police arrogated to themselves the right to decide what calypsos should or should not be sung – a responsibility for which they lack the necessary ability and even appreciation', in an attempt to 'suppress the calypsonian from expressing his views' (Quevedo, 1983: 62). In his speech, Quevedo also referred to calypso as a 'form of West Indian art' – insisting on the word ' "art" despite whatever some of my friends around this table may think' (Quevedo, 1983: 60). Nearly nine decades later, in the British Isles – where sunshine is a rare sight, the police target drill rappers with Criminal Behaviour Orders that require artists to inform the police before publishing their music online and warn them before any planned live performance, as was the case with drill group 1011 and drill rapper Digga D (Browne and Hudson, 2018; Mohamed, 2020). Such restrictions essentially amount to banning drillers from sharing their music with their audience (Evans, 2018) at the discretion of police officers, who routinely use drill music videos as evidence of criminal wrongdoing in court proceedings, act as expert witnesses and even question the artistic merit of drill – despite their own lack of formal qualifications or sufficient knowledge with which to judge such matters, if they ever should (Dennis, 2007; Lutes et al, 2019; Nielson and Dennis, 2019; Garden Court Chambers, 2020; Owusu-Bempah, 2020; Lerner and Kubrin, 2021; Paul, 2021; Ward and Fouladvand, 2021: 6–8).

As this snapshot into the policing of calypso and drill reveals, colonial and postcolonial police officers act as arbiters of aesthetic judgement and cultural taste: through regulating the creative output of calypsonians and drillers, by restricting what they can say and limiting their means for doing so – through a criminalizing process, which converts artistic expression into a legally punishable offence, on the grounds that it offends the state and its dutiful subjects. As such, what connects the 'oppressively restrictive measure[s]' (Quevedo, 1983: 57) against calypso in 1930s Trinidad to the discriminatory suppression of drill in 2020s Britain, is their racialized state-sanctioned criminalization. Such comparisons, however, don't simply highlight how and why Black music is policed. They also invite questions about the very nature of policing, as an institution that is imbued with a cultural and political role – rather than a strictly crime-fighting one. This is an important consideration, which illuminates how and why the aesthetic, the cultural and the political merge in the policing against Black music – which is treated as 'as aesthetically "out of tune", culturally "out of place" and politically "out of order"' (Fatsis, 2021b: 38). The policing of Black music(s), therefore, shows that policing has less to do with what is 'criminal' and more to do with what is (racially) 'criminal*ized*' – owing to a political ideology (racism) which sorts human difference (biological or cultural) in a rank order, to establish hierarchies of belonging according to social status. Such power relations are not accidental but inscribed on policing at birth; due to the imperial-colonial origins of policing, as an order maintenance institution which was *instituted* to suppress the enslaved through their cultural activities (in similar ways to how young Black Britons are policed through their music today). Thinking *with* Black music about British policing and its long colonial history – which is ignored as it is erased in criminological research and teaching alike (Moore, 2016, 2020) – attunes us to insights that encourage a different approach to criminological scholarship itself. The final section of this chapter weaves those observations together through a discussion of policing as an intrinsically cultural and political institution and Black music as an instrument for the sharpening of the decolonial criminological imagination.

Decolonizing criminology and thinking with our ears, one beat at a time

The preceding discussion on the policing of Black music(s) across time strikes a jarring note in the conventional portraiture of what policing is and does – swimming, as it does, against the current of the criminological mainstream. Instead of taking policing to be the democratic, kindly, benevolent institution that it is usually mistaken for (Fatsis and Lamb, 2021: 31), this chapter has offered a different interpretation of policing as a *cultural* institution. Such a 'deviant take' on police scholarship involves an understanding of policing that goes beyond common and unfortunately false conceptions of it as a 'crime-fighting' institution.[9] What is offered here, instead, is a deep reckoning with the role of policing as a governing logic that rationalizes, normalizes, legitimizes, serves and protects hierarchies of power through enforcing laws that uphold a sociopolitical order that does not police 'crime', but cultural belonging. Simply put, when Black music is policed what is *actually* being policed is 'blackness' as a signifier of cultural (un)belonging and the very embodiment of political disorder (Fatsis, 2021a). Dismissed on aesthetic grounds by having their artistic status denied, Black music cultures are policed as noisy violations of 'normative, respectable, cultural codes' (McKittrick, 2021: 162). Their 'subterraneally subversive' (Wynter, nd: 218) character, however, does not simply pose a threat as cacophonous noise to be eliminated. Their sonic presence also features as an assault to a social and political order that is racialized as 'white'. Indeed, in what Charles Mills terms the 'racial contract' – to describe the colonial origins and contemporary afterlives of the modern state – disorder is embodied by people who are not racialized as 'white', but who can be 'conceptualized in part as carrying the state of nature around with them, incarnating wildness and wilderness in their person' (Mills, 1999: 87). This racist ideology is what allowed colonial overseers to target 'any slaves [that] assemble together and beat their military drums or blow horns' that 'every white person [finds] so offending' (Wynter, nd: 84; quoting pro-slavery legislation) and metropolitan officers to deny drill its status as music (see, for example, Hurley, 2021).

Viewing policing as a cultural institution by focusing on how Black music has *always* been policed, therefore, rejects racist fantasies about how Black music endangers public safety. Rather, what becomes obvious is the ideological justification for such policing – whose colonial legacy is laid bare: as a worldview which imagines Black cultural presence to be an affront to a social and political order that is protected through law and order. While none of this suggests a linear progression from colonial to metropolitan policing (Elliott-Cooper, 2021: 148), the (colonial) history of policing against Black music nevertheless points to the legacy of racist logics and tactics that remain unchanged. In narrating the colonial history of British policing in the light of the history of policing against Black music(s), the latter is enlisted as decolonial, Black epistemology that brings to view what is otherwise omitted in dominant, Eurocentric criminological scholarship. Doing so has not only allowed a proper historicization of policing as an instrument of political rule from the era of colonial slavery to the present day. Black music also features here as a generative force that enables a different kind of criminological scholarship: a 'musicriminology' (Lee, 2021) that is sensitive to the sonic and the sensory as modes for thinking and knowing (Fatsis, 2021b: 42–45; Herrity et al, 2021). By listening carefully to what insights Black music can offer as sonic testimony and a 'sonic critiqu[e] of colonialism, racism, structural inequalities, and other forms of violence' (McKittrick, 2021: 50–51), police historiography and policing itself have both been remixed, producing different versions to standard, conventional and 'white' hegemonic scholarship.

With Black music as our guide, this chapter sounds a note of caution against any interpretation that fails to see policing and legal penal institutions as a cultural ensemble of state institutions that orchestrate social, cultural and political life through regulation and social control – punishing those who do not, could not and should not belong *here* socioculturally and politically too. Dismissed though such an approach might be as an oddball rumination beyond the perimeter of acceptable scholarly conventions, no other medium could have illuminated better the tactics and rationales that would explain how and why Black music genres continue to be policed the way they are. Equally, by virtue of its Afro-diasporic nature, no better medium than Black music could have been drawn on to question the very scholarly norms we have come to accept and uncritically inherit as neutral, natural givens. Might they also have a colonial history that we neglect and ignore? Could there be a historical connection between forms of colonial rule (discipline) and modes of knowledge (disciplines)? Could it even be that such histories of knowing and governing *police* who can know and who needs to be governed as police property? Legendary rapper, KRS-One – who inspired this chapter – may have the answer, rhyming, as he did, about how: 'I'm stolen property, kicking the flavor to society. Police be clocking me, but logically they got to be. Cause they were taught that serious poetry would come from Socrates. But that ain't it, in '94 I'll kick the hit' (KRS-One, 1993). Finishing this chapter at the tail end of 2021, I am inclined to believe that rappers like KRS-One once again hit the right note. Will criminologists listen and learn?

Notes

[1] For indicative discussions on decolonization within criminology, see: Cain (2000), Agozino (2003), Cunneen (2011), Carrington et al (2016) Cunneen and Tauri (2016), Moore (2016), Carrington and Hogg (2017), Moosavi (2018), Unnever and Owusu-Bempah (2019), Cavalcanti (2020), Moore (2020), Phillips et al (2020), Dimou (2021) and Fatsis (2021d). There is also a dedicated criminology journal on decolonization, *Decolonization of Criminology and Justice*, which was launched in 2018. Unfortunately, debates on police abolition remain marginal(ized) in mainstream criminological discourse, textbooks, conferences and curricula in the UK – notable exceptions notwithstanding (Hope, 2014). The 2020 #BlackLivesMatter protests gave new impetus to discussing the issue – however timidly – but the relevant literature on police abolition continues to be

led by US scholars, or UK-based academics; most of whom are not criminologists (see, for example, *Critical Resistance* (nd), Williams (2015), Vitale (2017), Correia and Wall (2018), Maynard (2020), Elliott-Cooper (2021), Purnell (2021), Duff (2021), Maher (2021), Fatsis and Lamb (2021)).

2   Not unlike police abolition (see previous note), criminological literature on colonialism and policing also features as an absent presence, with the exception of Brogden (1987) and Emsley (2014). Other relevant texts include: Arnold (1986), Das and Verma (1998), Brown (2002), Williams (2003), Bell (2013), Jackson (2016) and Trafford (2021).

3   'Whiteness' here and throughout the text, does not refer to skin colour or physiological traits. Rather, whiteness is understood as a political term that describes ways of being *structurally* 'white'; a social identity *and* a social structure that upholds it. 'Whiteness' is therefore approached here as an ontology (a way of *being*), a racist ideology (a way of *seeing*) and a power relation (a way of *doing*) that enables the domination, authority and perceived humanity of those who are racialized and identify themselves as 'white'. As Olsen (2004: 43) aptly puts it: whiteness has historically been 'not a biological status but a political color that distinguished the free from the unfree, the equal from inferior, the citizen from the slave'. This echoes similar perspectives on 'race' and racialization that approach 'whiteness' and 'blackness' as 'the colour of [people's] politics and not the colour of [their] skins' (Sivanandan, 2008: xviii).

4   References to 'Afro-diasporic' or 'Black' music, culture(s) and politics throughout this chapter, are limited to the strict Afro-diasporic sense and meaning of the word 'Black' – to refer to the people and cultures of the African diaspora. This is not to strip the term of its coalitional potential, by including other visible minority ethnic communities who are also oppressed by racism, but to stress the specific usage adopted here.

5   The neologism 'legal penal system' – not unlike the abolitionist catchphrase 'criminal legal system' – is coined here to problematize, refute and refuse the term 'criminal justice system'; insisting that the latter is a system of laws that (literally) *creates* 'crime' – both as a concept and a reality – through turning certain activities into punishable offences. This is not to deny that violence and harm exist, or that there are people who commit violent acts that cause harm. Rather, it is to stress that 'crime' is a political category that condemns, stigmatizes, marginalizes and racializes violence as the inherent trait, individual anomaly, cultural pathology and personal responsibility of 'deviant' individuals and groups. Notions like 'law' and 'justice', therefore, are not understood here as interchangeable or synonymous. As Ben Quigley (2007: 15) argues, '[w]e must never confuse law and justice. What is legal is often not just. And what is just is often not at all legal'. Legal practitioners, therefore, do not (necessarily) observe principles and ideas of 'justice', but enforce 'the law'; the technical and legal(istic) restrictions on the behaviour, actions and activities of 'the public'. While 'justice' denotes and embodies notions and ethical standards of fairness, 'the law' is 'the technical embodiment of attempts to order society' (Williams, 1993: 139). What we refer to or think as 'the law', therefore, simply refers to 'written law, codes, [and] systems of obedience' (Williams, 1993: 138), *not* that higher, 'just' ethical plane that we think that the law signifies, or stands for. For that reason, the term 'legal penal system' is used throughout this chapter to stress that the state's juridical infrastructure delivers punishments, not justice – using 'the law' as an instrument of political (mis)rule.

6   This Act legislated for the treatment and punishment of the enslaved people in Jamaica. A digital copy is available at the Wellcome Collection's online archive and can be retrieved from: https://wellcomecollection.org/works/azdsb5wh

7   This citation has no date, coming as it does from Sylvia Wynter's *Black Metamorphosis*: a highly influential, but hitherto unpublished text from the 1970s by foremost Caribbean

scholar Sylvia Wynter. The full text is housed in the Institute of the Black World papers at the Schomburg Center for Research in Black Culture at the New York Public Library.
8   Calypso is also often referred to as '*kaiso*', a word whose origins are unclear. As such the word's etymology is thought to derive from the Hausa language of West Africa (*kaico*), or creolized versions of the French word 'carrousseaux' (*cariso*) and the Spanish word 'caliso'. It eventually became established as 'calypso' owing to the growing dominance of the English language in Trinidad (Hill, 1967; Quevedo, 1983: 4).
9   For good critical discussions that challenge established mythologies of policing as a crime-fighting institution, see: Bayley (1996: 3, 10), Reiner (2010: 19), Vitale (2017: 36) and Loader (2020: 10–11).

References

Agozino, B. (2003) *Counter-Colonial Criminology: A Critique of Imperialist Reason*. London: Pluto Press.

Al-i Ahmad, J. (1984) *Occidentosis: A Plague from the West*. Berkeley: Mizan Press.

APC (Association for a People's Carnival) (1989) *'Police Carnival' 1989: A Report on the Notting Hill Carnival*. London: APC.

Arnold, D. (1986) *Police Power and Colonial Rule, Madras, 1859–1947*. New York: Oxford University Press.

Bayley, D.H. (1996) *Police for the Future*. Oxford: Oxford University Press.

Bell, E. (2013) Normalising the exceptional: British colonial policing cultures come home, *Mémoire(s), identité(s), marginalité(s) dans le monde occidental contemporain, Cahiers du MIMMOC*. Available from: https://journals.openedition.org/mimmoc/1286 [Accessed 23 April 2021].

Blagrove, Jr, I. (2014) *Carnival: A Photographic and Testimonial History of the Notting Hill Carnival*. London: Ricenpeas.

Bradley, L. (2001) *Bass Culture: When Reggae was King*. London: Seprent's Tail.

Brogden, M. (1987) The emergence of the police: The colonial dimension. *British Journal of Criminology*, 27(1): 4–14.

Brown, M. (2002) The politics of penal excess and the echo of colonial penality. *Punishment and Society*, 4(4): 403–423.

Browne, S. and Hudson, A. (2018) Kill drill: The death of freedom of expression? *Index on Censorship*. Available from: www.indexoncensorship.org/2018/06/kill-drill-the-death-of-freedom-of-expression/#1 [Accessed 21 December 2021].

Cain, M. (2000) Orientalism, occidentalism and the sociology of crime. *British Journal of Criminology*, 40(2): 239–260.

Campbell, H. (2007) *Rasta and Resistance: From Marcus Garvey to Walter Rodney*. London: Hansib.

Carrington, K. and Hogg, R. (2017) Deconstructing criminology's origin stories. *Asian Journal of Criminology*, 12(3): 181–197.

Carrington, K., Hogg, R. and Sozzo, M. (2016) Southern criminology. *British Journal of Criminology*, 56(1): 1–20.

Cavalcanti, R. (2020) *A Southern Criminology of Violence, Youth and Policing: Governing Insecurity in Urban Brazil*. London: Routledge.

Chowdhury, T. (2019) Policing the 'Black party': Racialized drugs policing at festivals in the UK, in K. Koram (ed) *The War on Drugs and the Global Colour Line*. London: Pluto Press, pp 48–65.

Collins, J. (2006) One hundred years of censorship in Ghanaian popular performance, in M. Drewett and M. Cloonan (eds) *Popular Music Censorship in Africa*. Farnham: Ashgate, pp 171–186.

Correia, D. and Wall, T. (2018) *Police: A Field Guide*. London: Verso.

Cowley, J. (1996) *Carnival, Canboulay and Calypso: Traditions in the Making*. New York: Cambridge University Press.

CPS (Crown Prosecution Service) (2021) *Decision Making in Gang Related Offences*. Available from: https://www.cps.gov.uk/legal-guidance/gang-related-offences-decision-making [Accessed 20 July 2021].

Critical Resistance (nd) Abolish Policing. Available from: http://criticalresistance.org/abolish-policing/ [Accessed 21 December 2021].

Cunneen, C. (2011) Postcolonial perspectives for criminology, in M. Bosworth and C. Hoyle (eds) *What is Criminology?* Oxford: Oxford University Press, pp 249–266.

Cunneen, C. and Tauri, J. (2016) *Indigenous Criminology*. Bristol: Policy Press.

Das, D. and Verma, A. (1998) The armed police in the British colonial tradition. *Policing: An International Journal of Police Strategies & Management*, 21(2): 354–367.

Dennis, A.L. (2007) Poetic (in)justice? Rap music lyrics as art, life, and criminal evidence. *The Columbia Journal of Law & the Arts*, 31: 1–41.

Dimou, E. (2021) Decolonizing southern criminology: What can the 'decolonial option' tell us about challenging the modern/colonial foundations of criminology? *Critical Criminology*, 29: 431–450.

Drewett, M. and Cloonan, M. (2006) *Popular Music Censorship in Africa*. Farnham: Ashgate.

Du Bois, W.E.B. (2007) *The Philadelphia Negro: A Social Study*. Oxford: Oxford University Press.

Duff, K. (2021) *Abolish the Police*. London: Dog Section Press.

Elliott-Cooper, A. (2021) *Black Resistance to British Policing*. Manchester: Manchester University Press.

Emsley, C. (2014) Policing the empire/policing the metropole: Some thoughts on models and types. *Crime, Histoire & Sociétés/ Crime, History & Societies*, 8(2): 5–25.

Evans, C. (2018) Court says drill music group banned from sharing songs without police permission. *RightsInfo*. Available from: https://rightsinfo.org/court-says-drill-music-group-banned-from-sharing-music-with-police-permission/ [Accessed 21 December 2021].

Fatsis, L. (2019a) Grime: Criminal subculture or public counterculture? A critical investigation into the criminalization of Black musical subcultures in the UK. *Crime Media Culture*, 15(3): 447–461.

Fatsis, L. (2019b) Policing the beats: The criminalisation of UK drill and grime music by the London Metropolitan Police. *The Sociological Review*, 67(6): 1300–1316.

Fatsis, L. (2021a) Policing the union's black: The racial politics of law and order in contemporary Britain, in F. Gordon and D. Newman (eds) *Leading Works in Law and Social Justice*. London: Routledge, pp 137–150.

Fatsis, L. (2021b) Sounds dangerous: Black music subcultures as victims of state regulation and social control, in N. Peršak and A. Di Ronco (eds) *Harm and Disorder in the Urban Space: Social Control, Sense and Sensibility*. London: Routledge, pp 30–51.

Fatsis, L. (2021c) Stop blaming drill for making people kill. *The British Society of Criminology Blog*. Available from: https://thebscblog.wordpress.com/2021/10/18/stop-blaming-drill-for-making-people-kill/ [Accessed 21 December 2021].

Fatsis, L. (2021d) Black tools for white schools?, in *Decolonising the Curriculum: Teaching and Learning about Race Equality*. Brighton: Centre for Learning and Teaching, University of Brighton, pp 4–6.

Fatsis, L. and Lamb, M. (2021) *Policing the Pandemic: How Public Health Becomes Public Order*. Bristol: Policy Press.

Fatsis, L., Ilan, J., Kadiri, H., Owusu-Bempah, A., Quinn, E., Shiner, M. and Squires, P. (2021) Missing the point: How policy exchange misunderstands knife crime in the capital. *Identities Blog*. Available from: https://www.identitiesjournal.com/blog-collection/missing-the-point-how-policy-exchange-misunderstands-knife-crime-in-the-capital [Accessed 21 December 2021].

Garden Court Chambers (2020) Drill music, gangs and prosecutions: Challenging racist stereotypes in the criminal justice system. Webinar Series. Available from: https://www.gardencourtchambers.co.uk/events/drill-music-gangs-and-prosecutions-challenging-racist-stereotypes-in-the-criminal-justice-system [Accessed 21 December 2021].

Gilroy, P. (2002) *There Ain't No Black in the Union Jack*. London: Routledge.

Gilroy, P. (2007) *Black Britain: A Photographic History*. London: Saqi Books.

Goveia, E.V. (1960) The West Indian slave laws of the eighteenth century. *Revista de Ciencias Sociales*, 4: 75–105.

Gutzmore, C. (1993) Carnival, the state and the black masses in the United Kingdom, in C. Harris and W. James (eds) *Inside Babylon: The Caribbean Diaspora in Britain*. London: Verso, pp 207–230.

Herrity, K., Schmidt, B. and Warr, J. (2021) *Sensory Penalities: Exploring the Senses in Spaces of Punishment and Social Control*. Bingley: Emerald Publishing.

Hill, E. (1967) On the origin of the term calypso. *Ethnomusicology*, 11(3): 359–367.

Hillyard, P. (1993) *Suspect Community: People's Experience of the Prevention of Terrorism Acts in Britain*. London: Pluto Press.

HMICFRS (Her Majesty's Inspectorate of Constabulary, Fire & Rescue Services) (2021) *Disproportionate Use of Police Powers: A Spotlight on Stop and Search and the Use of Force*. February. London: HMICFRS. Available from: https://www.justiceinspectorates.gov.uk/hmicfrs/wp-content/uploads/disproportionate-use-of-police-powers-spotlight-on-stop-search-and-use-of-force.pdf [Accessed 21 December 2021].

Hope, T. (2014) What are the alternatives to policing. *Centre for Crime and Justice*. Available from: https://www.crimeandjustice.org.uk/sites/crimeandjustice.org.uk/files/alternatives%20to%20policing%20slides.pdf [Accessed 5 January 2021].

Hurley, K. (2021) Police are absolutely right to target drill rappers … their toxic words are responsible for far too many deaths in Britain. *RT*. Available from: https://www.rt.com/op-ed/511838-uk-police-drill-rap/ [Accessed 21 December 2021].

Ilan, J. (2020) Digital street culture decoded: Why criminalizing drill music is street illiterate and counterproductive. *British Journal of Criminology*, 60(4): 994–1013.

Jackson, N. (2016) Imperial suspect: Policing colonies within 'post'-imperial England. *Callaloo*, 39(1): 203–215.

KRS-One (1993) *Sound of Da Police*. New York: Jive Records.

Lee, M. (2021) This is not a drill: Towards a sonic and sensorial musicriminology. *Crime Media Culture*, 18(3): 446–45.

Lerner, J.I. and Kubrin, C.E. (2021) Rap on trial: A legal guide for attorneys. *UC Irvine School of Law Research Paper*, No 2021–35.

Liberty (2021) *Policing Bill Amendments are a Dangerous Power-Grab*. Available from: https://www.libertyhumanrights.org.uk/issue/policing-bill-amendments-are-a-dangerous-power-grab/ [Accessed 21 December 2021].

Loader, I. (2020) Revisiting the police mission: Policing insight paper 2, the strategic review of policing in England and Wales. *The Police Foundation*. Available from: https://policingreview.org.uk/ wp-content/uploads/insight_paper_2.pdf [Accessed 21 December 2021].

Lutes, E., Purdon, J. and Fradella, H.F. (2019) When music takes the stand: A content analysis of how courts use and misuse rap lyrics in criminal cases. *American Journal of Criminal Law*, 46(1): 77–132.

Lynes, A., Kelly, C. and Kelly, E. (2020) Thug life: Drill music as periscope into urban violence in the consumer age. *British Journal of Criminology*, 60(5): 1201–1219.

Maher, G. (2021) *A World Without Police: How Strong Communities Make Cops Obsolete*. London: Verso.

Maynard, R. (2020) Police abolition/black revolt. *Topia: Canadian Journal of Cultural Studies*, 41: 70–78.

McCord, D.J. (1841) *Statutes at Large of South Carolina*, vol 9, part 2. Columbia, SC: A.S. Johnston.

McKittrick, K. (2021) *Dear Science and Other Stories*. Durham, NC: Duke University Press.

Mills, C.W. (1999) *The Racial Contract*. London: Cornell University Press.

Mohamed, M. (2020) Defending Digga D. *BBC One*. Available from: https://www.bbc.co.uk/programmes/p08xkspf [Accessed 21 December 2021].

Moore, J.M. (2016) Built for inequality in a diverse world: The historic origins of criminal justice. *Papers from the British Criminology Conference*, 16: 38–56.

Moore, J.M. (2020) 'Law', 'order', 'justice', 'crime': Disrupting key concepts in criminology through the study of colonial history. *The Law Teacher*, 54(4): 489–502.

Moore, R.D. (1997) *Nationalizing Blackness: Afrocubanismo and Artistic Revolution in Havana, 1920–1940*. Pittsburgh: University of Pittsburgh Press.

Moosavi, L. (2018) Decolonising criminology: Syed Hussein Alatas on crimes of the powerful. *Critical Criminology: An International Journal*, 27(2): 229–242.

Moten, F. (2003) *In the Break: The Aesthetics of the Black Radical Tradition*. London: University of Minnesota Press.

Nielson, E. and Dennis, A.L. (2019) *Rap on Trial Race, Lyrics, and Guilt in America*. New York: New Press.

Olsen, J. (2004) *The Abolition of White Democracy*. London: University of Minnesota Press.

Owusu-Bempah, A. (2017) Race and policing in historical context: Dehumanization and the policing of Black people in the 21st century. *Theoretical Criminology*, 21(1): 23–34.

Owusu-Bempah, A. (2020) Part of art or part of life? Rap lyrics in criminal trials. *LSE Blogs*. Available from: https://blogs.lse.ac.uk/politicsandpolicy/rap-lyrics-in-criminal-trials/ [Accessed 24 July 2021].

Owusu-Bempah, A. (2022) The irrelevance of rap. *Criminal Law Review*, 2: 130–151.

Paul, S. (2021) *Tackling Racial Injustice: Children and the Youth Justice System: A Report by JUSTICE*. London: Justice.

Phillips, C., Earle, R., Parmar, A. and Smith, D. (2020) Dear British criminology: Where has all the race and racism gone? *Theoretical Criminology*, 24(3): 427–446.

Purnell, D. (2021) *Becoming Abolitionists: Police, Protests, and the Pursuit of Freedom*. Beijing: Astra House.

Quevedo, R. (1983) *Atilla's Kaiso: A Short History of Trinidad Calypso*. St. Augustine: University of West Indies Press.

Quigley, B. (2007) Letter to a law student interested in social justice. *Depaul Journal for Social Sciences*, 1(1): 7–28.

Quinn, E. (2005) *Nuthin' but a G Thang: The Culture and Commerce of Gangsta Rap*. New York: Columbia University Press.

Quinn, E. (2018) Lost in translation? Rap music and racial bias in the courtroom. *Policy@Manchester Blogs*. Available from: http://blog.policy.manchester.ac.uk/posts/2018/10/lost-in-translation-rap-music-and-racial-bias-in-the-courtroom/ [Accessed 24 July 2021].

Reiner, R. (2010) *The Politics of the Police*. Oxford: Oxford University Press.

Robinson, C.J. (2021) *Black Marxism: The Making of the Black Radical Tradition*. Chapel Hill: The University of North Carolina Press.

Shiner, M., Carre, Z., Delson, R. and Eastwood, N. (2018) *The Colour of Injustice: 'Race', Drugs and Law Enforcement in England and Wales*. Available from: www.stop-watch.org/uploads/documents/The_Colour_of_Injustice.pdf [Accessed 17 June 2020].

Sivanandan, A. (2008) *Catching History on its Wing: Race, Culture and Globalisation*. London: Pluto Press.

Stoia, N., Adams, K. and Drakulich, K. (2018) Rap lyrics as evidence: What can music theory tell us? *Race and Justice*, 8(4): 330–365.

Stuart, F. (2020) *Ballad of the Bullet: Gangs, Drill Music and the Power of Online Infamy*. Princeton: Princeton University Press.

Taylor, D. (1997) *The New Police in Nineteenth-Century England: Crime, Conflict and Control*. Manchester: Manchester University Press.

Tebbutt, M. and Bourne, D. (2014) Shebeens and black music culture in Moss Side, Manchester, in the 1950s and 1960s. *Manchester Region History Review*, 25: 21–34.

Trafford, J. (2021) *The Empire At Home: Internal Colonies and the End of Britain*. London: Pluto Press.

Transpontine (2015) 'Mek' it blow: Police raid New Cross Jah Shaka blues dance. *Transpontine Blog*. Available from: http://transpont.blogspot.com/2015/10/mek-it-blow-police-raid-new-cross-jah.html [Accessed 18 August 2021].

Unnever, J.D. and Owusu-Bempah, A. (2019) A black criminology matters, in J.D. Unnever, S.L. Gabbidon and C. Chouhy (eds) *Building a Black Criminology: Race, Theory, and Crime*. London: Routledge, pp 3–28.

Vitale, A.S. (2017) *The End of Policing*. London: Verso.

Ward, P. (2018) Sound system culture: Place, space and identity in the United Kingdom, 1960–1989. *Historia Contemporánea*, 2(57): 349–376.

Ward, T. and Fouladvand, S. (2021) Bodies of knowledge and robes of expertise: Expert evidence about drugs, gangs and human trafficking. *Criminal Law Review*, 6: 442–460.

Whitfield, H.A. (2016) *North to Bondage: Loyalist Slavery in the Maritimes*. Vancouver and Toronto: University of British Columbia Press.

Williams, K. (2015) *Our Enemies in Blue: Police and Power in America*. Edinburgh: AK Press.

Williams, P.J. (1993) *The Alchemy of Race and Rights*. London: Virago.

Williams, R. (2003) A state of permanent exception: The birth of modern policing in colonial capitalism. *Interventions*, 5(3): 322–344.

Wynter, S. (nd) *Black Metamorphosis: New Natives in a New World* (unpublished manuscript).

4

Police Violence, Anti-Police Protest Movements and the Challenge of Decolonialism

Chris Cunneen

Introduction

A starting point for the chapter involves the theoretical argument that the concepts of the 'global North' and 'South' are not simply separable geographic terms. I prefer to tie the idea of a 'Southern perspective' directly to understanding colonialism and decoloniality and, following Mignolo (2011), consider modernity and coloniality as two sides of the colonial matrix of power. Modernity is celebrated as development and progress and its institutions (including police) are promoted globally. Meanwhile, modernity's effects (dispossession, poverty, inequality) are marked as modernity's absence – its 'dark side' where repression rules. Colonialism (as a series of historical events) and coloniality (as relations of power) are global narratives. The idea of a 'Southern perspective' only makes sense if it is decoupled from its strictly geographical connotations and in its place 'the South' is understood as a relational space where the dispossessed and marginalized dwell. The colonial matrix of power provides a way of understanding the multiple sites of marginalization (including by way of class, race, ethnicity/religion, Indigeneity, gender, sexuality and ableism) through which modern state institutions of repression (police, military and various security forces) routinely and violently enforce social, economic and political boundaries within state borders – indeed endemic police violence against marginalized communities unites the geographic north and south, and what becomes central are questions of power, inequality and exploitation. Further, the colonial matrix of power links these 'internal' state strategies with the broader dynamics of global capitalism and imperialism.

Although this chapter focuses primarily on the police, it recognizes, as Neocleous has argued, that police power and what he terms 'war power' are intertwined, that police power and military power are not two distinct forces and institutions, and further that the technologies of state violence are shared across the police and military (Neocleous, 2021a: 10–11). Thus, when we talk of the militarization of police, it is important to recognize this is neither a new nor unique phenomena – it is an *ongoing process* that reproduces police power (Neocleous, 2021b). It is argued here, selectively joining the insights of Mignolo and Neocleous, that the connections between police, military and war have a history which is intertwined with coloniality: that police power and war power find their perfected convergence during the colonial periods of occupation, control, exploitation, genocide, enslavement and dispossession of colonized peoples; and further that the contemporary instances of police power reproduce this coloniality – a matrix of 'modern' institutions engaged in unaccountable repressive violence from Lagos, Nigeria to Portland, Oregon. So, for the purposes of this chapter, a 'Southern perspective' emphasizes the coloniality of police power which can be found in both the geographic north and south. It can be seen equally in the police killings of Aboriginal people in Australia and in the police torture of Adivasi and Dalit peoples in India.

Contextualizing the anti-police uprisings of 2020 also enables us to understand more clearly the symbiotic link between police and penal power. Much has been written about the long-term increases in imprisonment, hyper-incarceration and the rise of the carceral state. Attention has been directed at punitive penal policies: for example, the more extensive use of imprisonment, the increased use of pre-trial detention, more punitive approaches to community corrections, and the tightening of access to parole (Cunneen et al, 2013). Increased punishment and imprisonment are focused on those seen as high risk, dangerous and marginalized, which translates to the targeting of well-known groups defined by race, gender, ableism, class and other social characteristics. While penal policy has played an important role in creating this 'new punitiveness', a central and perhaps neglected player in this reorientation is the police. Although other functionaries both within and outside the legal system are involved in criminal/risk surveillance (from prosecutors, judges and correctional officers to social workers, teachers and health workers), the police are the frontline troops of penal governance. They are the public symbol and the visceral presence of state violence; they are the operatives of criminalization which assist in making the penal state an historic possibility. The anti-police protest movements highlighted the violence of carceral systems at the point where people often have the most immediate contact with state force: the police and security forces.

The global movement against state violence

The uprisings of 2020 brought to the fore the extensive nature of state violence and the depth of public resistance. In Africa, protest movements in support of Black Lives Matter (BLM) occurred for example in Kenya, South Africa, Ghana and Nigeria. However, the protesters were not only there in support of the American BLM movement. They were also there to express their opposition and outrage at police brutality within these African nations. For example, in Nairobi, Kenya, protesters drew attention to domestic police violence and extrajudicial killings, while in Lagos, Nigeria, protest against police violence continued throughout 2020 particularly aimed at the Special Anti-Robbery Squad (SARS) police unit that has been responsible for multiple killings of citizens over recent years. Indeed, in late October 2020 army and police forces opened fire on a demonstration in Lagos which was protesting police brutality. At least 12 people were killed and hundreds severely injured (Amnesty International, 2020). In addition, violent policing intensified in many African countries during the COVID-19 pandemic where police enforced curfews in poor neighbourhoods with beatings, tear gas and shootings – leading to dozens of deaths within the first few weeks of lockdowns. In fact, the National Human Rights Commission, Nigeria (2020) reported more people killed by police than COVID-19 in the first few months of the lockdown. Similarly the police in Kenya 'shot and beat people … even before the daily start of the curfew. Police also broke into homes and shops, extorted money from residents or looted food … across the country' (Human Rights Watch, 2021: 390).

In parts of Asia, including India, Malaysia, Japan, the Philippines, Korea, Indonesia, Hong Kong and Taiwan, demonstrators came out in protest after the killing of George Floyd. Police violence and racism were dominant themes in these protests. Yet, like African nations, each country had its own history and contemporary experience of police brutality and the use of lethal violence. In the Philippines, solidarity with BLM was shown while demonstrating against new restrictive anti-terror laws and the more than 27,000 deaths by police and vigilantes since the government's war on drugs began in 2016 (International Criminal Court [ICC], 2021). In India, there is a long history of police torturing and killing people in custody and police torture is seen as routine (National Human Rights Commission, India, 2018: 44). As in other countries, lockdowns to counter the COVID-19 pandemic exacerbated police brutality against the urban poor and the tens of thousands of homeless migrant workers attempting to return to their communities (Kalhan et al, 2020). In mid-2020, the deaths of a father and son, Jeyeraj and Benicks, in Tamil Nadu sparked a broader debate about police killings in India in the context of the BLM movement. The pair were taken into police custody for breaching lockdown restrictions on trading and held overnight. Both were tortured and died two days later (Human Rights Watch, 2021: 319).

The death of George Floyd also coincided with protests across Latin America and the Caribbean, stretching from Jamaica, Trinidad and Tobago, to Mexico, Colombia and Brazil. The sheer volume of police killings in the region meant there were ongoing protests against police violence independent of the events in the United States. In Brazil, for example, police kill nearly six times the number of people compared to the United States, and 75 per cent of the people killed are Black (Carvalho, 2020). Similar to the Philippines, much of the police violence in Brazil is related to the war on drugs, increased militarization and indiscriminate state violence against poor and Black communities. Like the situation in South Asia and Africa, the COVID-19 pandemic increased poverty and inequality, impacted social unrest and intensified police violence.

Across Europe, the UK, Canada, Australia and Aotearoa-New Zealand the protest movement was equally extensive. In Canada, the death of George Floyd reignited an ongoing concern over the large number of Black and Indigenous people killed by police (Marcoux and Nicholson, nd). In Aotearoa-New Zealand it was observed that over the past decade, two-thirds of all victims of fatal police shootings have been Māori or Pasifika (Thom and Quince, 2020). In Australia, attention was drawn to the more than 400 First Nations deaths in custody since the landmark report of the Royal Commission into Aboriginal Deaths in Custody (RCADIC) in 1991 and the fact that not one police or prison officer has been convicted for any criminal offences relating to these deaths (Whittaker, 2020). In French, German and UK cities tens of thousands of protesters drew attention to police violence and racism, the lack of police accountability, and the deaths of Black and other minority groups, refugees and asylum seekers while in police custody (France 24, 2020; Perrigo and Godin, 2020: Elliott-Cooper, 2021: 4–5).

Shared themes in the global protests

Unaccountable state violence, bloated police budgets, corruption and repression became the subject of public protest on a global scale. There were many shared themes across these anti-police protest movements. Despite the sheer scale of police violence against the poor, marginalized and racialized, one common denominator was that police violence and abuse goes largely unpunished – there is a lack of any effective accountability for police violence and police can kill with apparent impunity. Another frequent premise to protests was that the vast majority of people killed by police are Black, Brown, Indigenous or from other minoritized or disempowered groups. In many countries attention was also drawn to police violence against women, people with disabilities and people from lesbian, gay, bisexual, transgender, queer and intersex (LGBTQI) communities. The collective experience of police violence provided opportunities for building solidarity across various groups, including, for example, abolitionists, feminists, and human rights, LGBTQI, Black, Indigenous and disability activists.

The hypocrisy of local elites was also a focus of protests. In African nations like South Africa, Kenya and Nigeria, state officials were held to be hypocritical for comments condemning the death of George Floyd, while consistently ignoring the hundreds of police killings in their own countries (Egwu, 2020). The same hypocrisy was noted by activists and in social media in India where egregious killings by police typically attracted far less outrage than a single death in the United States (for example, Ravi, 2020). Similarly, in Australia and Aotearoa-New Zealand, First Nations activists drew attention to the apparent lack of popular (non-Indigenous) mobilization against local Black deaths in custody prior to the events in the United States (Thom and Quince, 2020; Whittaker, 2020).

Another recurrent theme across the geographic north and south was that the histories of colonialism, slavery, racism and dispossession were fundamental to understanding the targets of policing and violence, as well as the way police are organized as a state institution of repression. Understanding the coloniality of state power and the requirement for a decolonial politics was a recurrent refrain. There was thus an international dimension to the protests against the police that linked to the longer histories of imperialism and colonialism, and an important part of the critique of policing was the call to decolonize policing institutions.[1] In Africa, there was acknowledgement that police forces were established by colonial rulers to conquer, repress and dominate the population and were never there to protect their citizens or respect human rights. The widespread use of police violence during the COVID-19 pandemic lockdowns reinforced the view that governments had failed to reform the structures of colonial policing (Dahir et al, 2020). In India, the basic structure of the criminal law and police date from the time of British colonialism and attempts to decolonize the criminal law have been limited (Sekhri, 2020). In Australia and Canada, police were instrumental in the colonial dispossession and repression of Indigenous peoples – and Indigenous peoples today are more likely than others to be killed by police (Cunneen and Tauri, 2017).

The remainder of this chapter will elaborate some of the key issues already noted to explore the parameters of a critical decolonial perspective on policing – a perspective in large degree informed by the global praxis of various activist groups. In this context, it is also worth noting that protest movements against police violence and killings are often built on multiple demands from opposition to austerity measures and the ravages of neoliberal capitalism to, for example, demands for racial justice, for First Nations sovereignty and an end to violence against women. That these broad-ranging demands should coalesce around opposition to police violence is hardly surprising when we consider the structural position of police in protecting the interests of ruling elites and international capital through state systems of control.

The colonial roots of policing

The historical context of colonial policing is integral to understanding contemporary resistance to policing. The core element of colonial policing was the defence of the colony – which was true of both 'extractive' colonies (as in parts of Africa and Asia) as well as 'settler colonies' (such as in parts of the Americas and Australasia). The legal order enforced by the police was the law of a colonial state – a legal system which largely excluded colonized peoples from protection. The order that the police maintained was an order aimed at protecting the few, while ensuring the ruthless exploitation of the many. The exercise of police power did not involve the consent of the colonized. The racist ideologies underpinning imperialism and the motive of ruthless economic exploitation meant that the idea of political legitimacy and popular consent was largely irrelevant. The aims of policing were to ensure colonial efficiency, stability and profitability for capitalism. As Tankebe notes, 'to speak of colonial policing and "policing by consent" – and for that matter legitimacy – is therefore a contradiction in terms; it is oxymoronic' (Tankebe, 2008: 74). Colonial policing never achieved legitimacy beyond the few who directly benefited from it – as an exercise of power it remained exogenous (Blanchard, 2014: 1838). Thus, in the colonial setting we see police power and violence in its most naked form – through the gaze of the colonized we see that power stripped bare of all its niceties. For example, in Ghana, no legal and disciplinary procedures controlled the police exercise of power or dealt with widespread police abuses. The police were 'hated as unaccountable representatives of an alien colonial power imposing a range of new laws and measures of social control which lacked any semblance of popular consent' (Killingray, 1991: 119).

The use of military weaponry and training, the military style uniforms and ranks of the commanding European officers were fundamental to the colonial structure of policing and were required to violently quell resistance to colonial rule. Although the idea of bringing the superior European rule of law to inferior races had been used as a justification for colonialism, in fact arbitrariness, violence and impunity were prevalent. The intensity of war-like police operations was influenced by the inherent level of resistance by colonized peoples. People do not give up everything – their lands, homes, families and livelihoods – without some level of resistance, which, depending on the intensity, could threaten the viability and prosperity of the colony. Establishing police legitimacy was not a motivating factor for colonial power; ensuring governance and stability for the extraction of wealth was. Blanchard, for example, comments that French colonial police forces 'were never known to put a strong emphasis on disciplining and educating their personnel' and that the 'French empire was marked by the permanence of this logic consisting of slaughtering protesting crowds of colonised people' (Blanchard, 2014: 1842–1843).

Police also had the role of managing the colony through administrative functions which variously aimed at suppressing, controlling, exploiting and at times civilizing and assimilating colonized peoples. There were extensive regulatory regimes which often sought complete control of the Native and which, when it suited colonial authorities, also effectively criminalized the culture, beliefs and practices of the colonized. In many places, police were the face of colonial power and fulfilled regulatory and administrative tasks in the interests of a functioning colonial government. Some were directly aimed at ensuring the colony's profitability, such as reporting on the conditions of roads or crops (Sinclair, 2006: 26); others aimed at assimilation/genocide such as removing Indigenous children from their families (Cunneen, 2001: 66–79). In either case, 'a distinctive feature of colonial policing was the exercise of wide-ranging discretionary powers without accountability' (Tankebe, 2008: 75).

The final point to note in this discussion is the intersection between the developments of policing in the colonies and in the metropolitan centres of colonial power. The intersection occurs through at least three processes. First, metropolitan centres developed modes of policing for the colonies which were different to the domestic versions: the so-called 'colonial model of policing' which was exported and adapted across the colonies (for example, Sinclair, 2008: 173–187). The domestic model was less militaristic and sought legitimacy. However, like colonial policing, domestic policing also had an extensive role well beyond any narrow concept of crime control. It was engaged in regulatory activities from managing public hygiene and public behaviour to policing 'lunacy' legislation, child welfare and school truancy. Police were integral to mechanisms of carcerality which included both prisons and asylums. Periods of social unrest and industrial disputes also showed that domestic policing could quickly transform into more military-style responses. A second process in the intersection between the colonies and metropolitan centres was the influence of colonial modes of policing within metropolitan centres. Various anthropometric and identification techniques, communication technologies, transportation and control methods which became more widely adopted were developed as part of colonial policing from British Ghana (Tankebe, 2008) to French Indochina (Blanchard, 2014) to the American Philippines (Go, 2020). Indeed, policing in the colonies acted as 'veritable laboratories of modernity' (Hönke and Müller, 2016: 8).

Third, these two processes continued in the post-1945 period of colonial independence when centres of global power continued to directly influence developments in policing in the periphery, and developments in the periphery were introduced back into policing within metropolitan centres (Harcourt, 2018: Schrader, 2019). This process relates to policing techniques and technologies, but also to the targets of policing and the nature of resistance. The origins of policing colonized peoples is key to understanding racialized policing today within metropolitan centres of power, from the use of deadly force to the routine racial profiling underlying stop and searches, identity checks and so on. Resistance to these forms of policing is ongoing, and in recent decades in the UK, France, the United States and Australia, for example, anti-police uprisings and protests have been mostly associated with police racism and lethal violence against racialized, colonized and formerly enslaved peoples (for example, Fassin, 2013; Elliott-Cooper, 2021; Maher, 2021).

Police violence: the current contagion

The global protest movement highlighted the extent, nature and targeting of police violence – indeed police killing civilians was the catalyst for the protest movements. Although police violence is experienced at a local level, it is pervasive to the institution and has global reach. It directly costs the lives of at least tens of thousands of people annually, and many more if we include the estimates of enforced disappearances. It leaves incalculable numbers of people with permanent injuries and disabilities. The victims are overwhelmingly from the most marginalized communities whether defined by race, religion, class, Indigenous status, gender, sexual orientation, disability, citizenship and immigration status and their various and compounding intersections. A defining feature of policing is state legitimacy for the use of force, including lethal violence, against citizens. Notwithstanding the fundamental importance of a state-sanctioned decision to end someone's life or seriously maim them, it is difficult to get a handle on the overall size of the problem of police violence, killings or police custodial deaths. Most countries do not publish comprehensive national information, so the estimates are left to media, human rights and other non-government organizations. A further problem is that even where governments do provide data there are widely inconsistent reporting and definitions that make international comparisons difficult.[2]

In the United States, according to the *Washington Post* data, police fatal shootings remain steady at around 1,000 per year. More than half the people fatally shot by police are White. However, given their population size, Black Americans are fatally shot at more than twice the rate and Hispanic people at slightly less than twice the rate of White Americans (*Washington Post*, nd). In England and Wales, the community-based organization INQUEST maintains a database on deaths in police custody. Analysis of decades of data found that 'Black, Asian and Minoritised Ethnicities die disproportionately as a result of use of force or restraint by the police, raising serious questions of institutional racism as a contributory factor in their deaths' (INQUEST, 2022). In Australia, Indigenous people are more than five times more likely to die in police custody than non-Indigenous people (Doherty and Sullivan, 2021). The Canadian Broadcasting Commission's (CBC) *Deadly Force* database shows that, based on their population, Indigenous people are nearly four times and Black people nearly three times more likely to die in police 'fatal encounters'. The majority of these fatal encounters involve a police shooting (CBC, nd). The Prison Policy Initiative compared police killings (primarily based on fatal shootings) across ten 'wealthy' countries and found that the United States is an outlier. Compared to those countries with next highest rates, the United States has a rate over three times higher than Canada and four times higher than Australia (Jones and Sawyer, 2020). Despite the different rates, the targets are similar: Black, Brown and First Nations peoples.

The incidence of police violence against civilians takes on qualitatively different dimensions when we consider the experiences of parts of the geographic global South. The Philippines and Brazil provide a window on the effect of the war on drugs on policing and violence, and both further highlight the problem of police acting as vigilantes in conducting state-condoned and/or encouraged extrajudicial killings. In September 2021, the ICC ordered an investigation into the killings associated with the war on drugs in the Philippines. It found the initial evidence indicated the killings were not the result of legitimate law enforcement operations and that a widespread and systematic attack against the civilian population had taken place. The prosecutor's preliminary investigation found a reasonable basis to believe that crimes against humanity had been committed in the Philippines (ICC, 2021).

Like the Philippines, the broader context for police killings in Brazil is the war on drugs, which has continued to blur distinctions between police and military roles. For example, in Rio de Janeiro in May 2021 some 200 heavily armed police supported by armed helicopters moved into a poor, densely populated *favela* and engaged in a firefight with alleged drug traffickers that killed at least 25 people. The UN High Commissioner for Human Rights called for an independent investigation of the incident (Neuman, 2021). In recent years, President Bolsonaro has openly promoted the police use of deadly force. Across Brazil police killings have been rising and the official figures do not include extrajudicial killings by vigilante death squads, which often also involve police (Human Rights Watch, 2021: 105–108). Police killings have sparked various movements since the late 1970s, including the Unified Black Movement Against Racial Discrimination (MNU-CDR, later the MNU), and the Reaja ou Será Mortx (React or Die) who are active against police violence and share similar messages to the BLM movement. The war on drugs was introduced into Latin America as a result of international pressure and in many countries in the region as a condition for US economic assistance and trade. Highly punitive drug laws, more heavily militarized policing and growing prison numbers were the result. As has been commented upon frequently, the 'war' has fallen most heavily on poor Black and Indigenous communities (Metaal and Youngers, 2011: 5–7).

Another feature of police violence underlined by protest movements and human rights organizations is the use of torture by the police to extract confessions, bribes, and impose summary punishment. The major South Asian countries of India, Bangladesh and Pakistan provide examples. In India the National Human Rights Commission (2018: 4) found that the police practice of torturing suspects was common and the primary cause of deaths in police custody. In addition, the National Campaign Against Torture (NCAT) indicated that armed security forces (the Indian Army and the Central Armed Police Forces) who are deployed in insurgency affected areas and the border areas and have the power to take persons into custody were the subject of many reported cases of torture and sexual violence. Further, Forest Department officials were also responsible for torture, sexual violence and killing, particularly of Adivasi peoples (NCAT, 2021: 131–136). The majority of torture victims come from poor and marginalized communities, including Dalit, Adivasi and Muslim minorities. The Chief Justice of India publicly named the nation's police stations as the most significant threat to human rights and bodily integrity. According to the Chief Justice, 'custodial torture and other police atrocities are problems which still prevail' and fall disproportionately on the poor (Dhillon, 2021). A national survey of Indian police personnel indicated commonly held views which justified torture and violence: four in five police believed 'there was nothing wrong with beating up criminals to extract a confession' and three in four police felt that 'police violence towards criminals was justified' (Common Cause and CSDS, 2019: 131).

In neighbouring Bangladesh, deaths in police custody from torture, the frequency of extrajudicial killings, and enforced disappearances by police have been widely criticized including by the UN Committee against Torture. The UN Committee recognized the allegations of widespread and routine use of torture and ill-treatment by police for the purpose of obtaining confessions or soliciting bribes. The Committee also noted numerous, consistent reports that law enforcement agencies have 'arbitrarily deprived persons of their liberty, subsequently killed many of them and failed to disclose their whereabouts or fate' (Committee Against Torture, 2019: para 14). Killings and disappearances are committed with impunity. In Pakistan there are numerous reports by human rights groups of police extrajudicial killings, enforced disappearances, detention without charge, torture of detainees to obtain confessions, biased investigations, failure to investigate crimes, corruption, harassment and extortion of individuals, incompetence and lack of professionalism (Human Rights Watch, 2016; National Commission on Human Rights, Pakistan, 2019). Public surveys and reports show that the police are among the most feared, complained against, and 'least trusted government institutions in Pakistan', lacking accountability and 'plagued by corruption at the highest levels' (Human Rights Watch, 2016: 1). Waseem (2021) notes that police violence, excesses and corruption have led to 'social movements and civil society resistance borne out of public grievances with publicly punitive and authoritarian styles of policing', such as the Pashtun Tahafuz Movement (PTM) that has grown out of opposition to the violence of law enforcement and security forces against the Pashtuns and has been fuelled by extrajudicial killings.

A death sentence for being poor, marginalized or disabled

One of the aggravating features of deaths in police custody is that in many cases the initial police intervention might often be for a trivial matter or where there is no criminal offence at all. Reviews of deaths in police custody in England and Wales over the last two decades have found that more than half of the deaths involved custody for public order, public drunkenness, driving and theft offences (Independent Police Complaints Commission, UK, 2010: 14; Lindon and Roe, 2017: 30). The RCADIC in Australia investigated 99 First Nations deaths (two-thirds of whom were in police custody at the time) and noted that most of those deaths involved custody for public drunkenness, minor public order offences (such as offensive language) or being unable to pay fines (Johnston, 1991). A review of police fatal shootings of 135 unarmed Black men and women in the United States found many of the deaths arose from police interventions for minor offences or from interventions where there was no legal reason for arrest. Of the 135 fatal shootings of unarmed citizens, two police were found guilty of murder and two were found guilty of manslaughter (Thompson, 2021).

The apparent senselessness of these deaths adds to the public outrage globally. In the United States, George Floyd was arrested for an alleged counterfeit $20 note, and Eric Garner for selling single cigarettes. Police killings often involve innocent bystanders: in Brazil, children have been killed in *favelas* as collateral damage in police shoot-outs; children and adults are dead in Africa, Asia and Latin America as a result of the violent policing of COVID-19 public health regulations (see Cunneen, forthcoming). In the UK, police use of force has increased against Black and racially minoritized communities during the COVID-19 pandemic, even while crime rates have been dropping (Harris et al, 2022).

The over-representation of people with disabilities among those killed by police is also evident, and intersects with other social categories of race, class, gender and sexuality to magnify marginalization and to increase the risk of police violence. In countries where there is some level of aggregate data on disability and deaths in police custody (such as the United States, the United Kingdom, Australia and Canada), the evidence reveals that Black, Indigenous and other racialized communities are over-represented among those killed who have a cognitive disability or are in a mental health crisis. In England and Wales, for instance, Black and minority ethnic people are twice more likely to feature in mental health-related deaths in police custody compared to others, and particularly so among those deaths involving restraint by police officers (Runnymede Trust, 2021: 21). Many deaths occur during police 'welfare checks'. For example, in Canada in the three months prior to the June–July 2020 mass protests over police killings, six people died during mental health-related welfare checks by police. Four were shot by police. All were Black, Indigenous, or people of colour. Police violence also causes permanent disabilities among victims from beatings, non-fatal shootings and torture. In addition, women with disabilities fail to receive police support when they report violence, particularly sexual violence (for example, in India, see Human Rights Watch, 2018: 33–38, and Australia, see Murray and Heenan, 2012: 280). Globally, police also play a role in defining, regulating and funnelling people with disabilities into various carceral systems – prison, private and state-based institutions and faith-based centres – where people are kept in abusive, overcrowded situations for prolonged periods (Human Rights Watch, 2014).

The failure to protect women

The global protest movement also emphasized the gendered nature of policing. The failure to protect women, the complicity in violence and indeed direct police participation in violence against women were all evident themes in protests from London to Lahore (Dodd and Grierson, 2021; Human Rights Watch, 2021: 520). The World Health Organization (2021) estimates that 30 per cent of women globally have been physically or sexually assaulted and the likelihood and incidence of physical and sexual violence is increased for Black, Brown, Indigenous, disabled and poor women. Yet very few women report violence and sexual assault to police – the International Violence Against Women Survey (IVAWS) found that less than one-third of women reported experiences of physical and sexual violence (Johnson et al, 2008). According to IVAWS many women choose not to report violence because they are afraid of the 'negative attitudes' of police. For the minority of women who do report to police, there is no guarantee that their complaint will be taken seriously and progress through the justice system. The IVAWS notes that less than half of reported cases of violence against women are referred to prosecution and, in some instances, less than one-quarter.

A further problem in relying on the police for protection in matters of violence against women is that police officers frequently commit domestic and sexual violence themselves, and regularly use their authority to ensure immunity from sanctions and prosecution. For example, North American research points to a higher incidence of domestic violence by police officers – some estimates suggest 15 times greater than the general population – and the various problems that women face when police are central to accessing legal protections (Goodmark, 2015). Further, police engage in abusive practices particularly against minoritized women. For instance, in Canada, Human Rights Watch (2013: 50–65) has reported on abusive policing practices against First Nations women and girls including the use of excessive force, assaults, inappropriate use of police dogs, pepper spray and tasers, and rape and sexual assault by police officers (2013: 50–65); and in India the NCAT (2021) and the National Human Rights Commission (2018) have detailed the killing, torture and rape of women, including minors, by police.

The protest movements reignited the question of how and why more policing, criminalization and incarceration have become the primary answer to the problem of violence against women. The protest movements brought to the fore the contradictions between carceral feminism and decolonial/abolitionist feminists (Davis et al, 2022); that is, between those advocating for greater police and carceral intervention to protect women and those who argue this not a solution because it is ineffective and compounds the oppression of Black, Indigenous, poor and minoritized women (and men of colour who are most heavily criminalized).

Conclusion

In drawing the threads of this chapter together, it is important to go back to the foundational questions of coloniality and how that intersects with the nature, intensity and targets of police violence and killings. At the most obvious level, we see the influence of a range of factors impacting police violence including: the effect of the war on drugs on penal policies and the militarization of police; the collapsing of police and military functions in the name of protecting internal (or national) security and fighting crime; the role of specialist police squads in conducting disappearances and state-sanctioned extrajudicial killings either in the interests of a crime control enforcement policy or as a direct political tool of authoritarian regimes; the extent to which police torture is routinized; and the extent to which police play a direct role in controlling and/or dispossessing workers, local landholders, villagers and communities who, for whatever reasons, threaten capitalist economic development and its projects.

What this chapter also repeatedly demonstrates is that the targets of law enforcement violence are inevitably poor and marginalized communities, whether by way of class, caste, race, gender, Indigeneity, ability, sexual orientation, religion and ethnicity or other status. The targets of repression represent both ongoing legacies and contemporary manifestations of colonialism, imperialism and slavery – and they intersect *across* the geographic divisions between the global North and South. The histories of colonialism, slavery, racism, and dispossession are fundamental to understanding both the targets of policing and violence, as well as the colonial origins of policing as a state institution of repression.

Police violence against women and people with disabilities also raises questions of coloniality. Decolonial feminists have been critical of a policing and carceral approach because reliance on criminalization furthers the colonial and patriarchal continuities of punishment within countries of the global South and North. In other words, policing further entrenches violent and oppressive carceral systems which were founded in colonialism and have been used against colonized and enslaved women ever since – there is a continuum in the violent treatment of Black, Indigenous and women of colour (Baldry and Cunneen, 2014; Ritchie, 2017: 21). As the colonial project impacted on the culture, language and beliefs of the colonized, so too did it reframe gender, sexuality and disability in the interests of the colonizers. Colonialism both created disability through its violent treatment of the colonized and enslaved, as well as definitions of disability (such as lunacy, feeble-mindedness and specific mental illnesses attributable to the colonized and slaves, for example 'drapetomania'). Policing and carceral systems were normalized as part of the colonial response – what Grech (2015) refers to more broadly as a colonial normativity.

The politics of decoloniality are reflected in the broad-ranging demands that coalesce around opposition to police violence, and this is hardly surprising when we consider the structural position of police and their immediate physical presence in protecting the interests of ruling elites and international capital – interests that reflect not only money and political power but also social relations of racism, patriarchy and ableism. The collective experience of police violence has provided motivation for building solidarity across various groups. Not surprisingly, there are a variety of political strategies emerging through the protest movements including, as examples, strategies to disarm and demilitarize the police; the need for social-democratic reforms to ensure police accountability; the need for decriminalization of various policies, particularly drugs; and the reduction of police budgets and reinvestment in alternative, community-driven approaches to safety. What is common to these demands and connects them to decolonial strategies is the demand for a reimagining of safety and governance. It urges us to reflect on 'the many and rich possibilities of governance' that are open to the people outside of the current state which has been forged through the processes of colonialism (Mignolo, 2011: 15).

Notes

[1] As well as the intellectual supports such as criminology (for example, Sadiki and Steyn, 2022).

[2] A death in police custody is variously defined by agencies to include deaths arising from police pursuits, road traffic incidents, fatal shootings, fatalities caused during police restraint, deaths arising from torture and beatings, medical conditions, suicides or other causes while in custody. In the UK such incidents are collectively referred to as 'deaths after police contact' (Baker, 2016).

References

Amnesty International (2020) Nigeria: Killing of #EndSARS protesters by the military must be investigated. [online] 21 October. Available from: www.amnesty.org/en/latest/news/2020/10/killing-of-endsars-protesters-by-the-military-must-be-investigated/ [Accessed 15 November 2022].

Baker, D. (2016) *Deaths after Police Contact: Constructing Accountability in the 21st Century*. London: Palgrave Macmillan.

Baldry, E. and Cunneen, C. (2014) Imprisoned Indigenous women and the shadow of colonial patriarchy. *Australian and New Zealand Journal of Criminology*, 47(2): 276–298.

Blanchard, E. (2014) French colonial police, in G. Bruinsma and D. Weisburd (eds) *Encyclopedia of Criminology and Criminal Justice*. New York: Springer, pp 1836–1846.

Carvalho, B. (2020) Latin America is ready for its Black Lives Matter reckoning. *New York Times*, 29 June. Available from: www.nytimes.com/2020/06/29/opinion/latin-america-racism-police.html [Accessed 15 November 2022].

CBC (Canadian Broadcasting Commission) (nd) *Deadly Force*. Available from: https://www.cbc.ca/news/canada/manitoba/iteam/deadly-force-cbc-analysis-1.4603696 [Accessed 15 November 2022].

Committee Against Torture (2019) *Concluding Observations on the Initial Report of Bangladesh*, CAT/C/BGD/CO/1. Geneva: United Nations.

Common Cause and CSDS (2019) *Status of Policing in India Report 2019*. New Delhi: Common Cause and Lokniti (CSDS).

Cunneen, C. (2001) *Conflict, Politics and Crime: Aboriginal Communities and the Police*. Abingdon: Routledge.

Cunneen, C. (forthcoming) *Defunding the Police*. Bristol: Bristol University Press.

Cunneen, C. and Tauri, J. (2017) *Indigenous Criminology*. Bristol: Policy Press.

Cunneen, C., Baldry, E., Brown, D., Schwartz, M., Steel, A. and Brown, M. (2013) *Penal Culture and Hyperincarceration*. Farnham: Ashgate.

Dahir, A.L., Maclean, R. and Chutel, L. (2020) George Floyd's killing prompts Africans to call for police reform at home. *New York Times*, 8 July. Available from: www.nytimes.com/2020/07/03/world/africa/george-floyd-protests-police-africa.html [Accessed 15 November 2022].

Davis, A.Y., Dent, G., Meiners, E. and Richie, B. (2022) *Abolition. Feminism. Now.* London: Penguin.

Dhillon, A. (2021) India's police stations are human rights threat, says chief justice. *The Guardian*, 10 August. Available from: www.theguardian.com/world/2021/aug/10/india-police-stations-human-rights-threat-chief-justice [Accessed 15 November 2022].

Dodd, V. and Grierson, J. (2021) Sarah Everard vigil report strongly defends police's use of force. *The Guardian*, 31 March. Available from: www.theguardian.com/uk-news/2021/mar/30/police-handling-of-sarah-everard-vigil-appropriate-says-watchdog [Accessed 15 November 2022].

Doherty, L. and Sullivan, T. (2021) *Deaths in Custody Australia 2019–20*. Canberra: Australian Institute of Criminology.

Egwu, P. (2020) As the world marches for American victims, police brutality in Africa goes unnoticed. *Foreign Policy*, 17 June. Available from: www.foreignpolicy.com/2020/06/17/black-lives-matter-protests-africa-police-brutality/ [Accessed 15 November 2022].

Elliott-Cooper, A. (2021) *Black Resistance to British Policing*. Manchester: Manchester University Press.

Fassin, D. (2013) *Enforcing Order: An Ethnography of Urban Policing*. Cambridge: Polity.

France 24 (2020) Thousands rally in fresh Paris protest against racism and police brutality. *France 24*, 13 June. Available from: www.france24.com/en/20200613-protesters-gather-in-paris-for-fresh-march-against-racism-and-police-brutality [Accessed 15 November 2022].

Go, J. (2020) The imperial origins of American policing: Militarization and imperial feedback in the early 20th century. *American Journal of Sociology*, 125(5): 1193–1254.

Goodmark, L. (2015) Hands up at home: Militarized masculinity and police officers who commit intimate partner abuse. *Brigham Young University Law Review*, 5: 1183–1246.

Grech, S. (2015) Decolonising Eurocentric disability studies: Why colonialism matters in the disability and Global South debate. *Social Identities*, 21(1): 6–21.

Harcourt, B. (2018) *The Counterrevolution: How Our Government Went to War Against Its Own Citizens*. New York: Basic Books.

Harris, S., Joseph-Salisbury, R., Williams, P. and White, L. (2022) Notes on policing, racism and the Covid-19 pandemic in the UK. *Race and Class*, 63(2): 92–102.

Hönke, J. and Müller, M.M. (eds) (2016) *The Global Making of Policing*. Milton Park: Routledge.

Human Rights Watch (2013) *'Those who take us away': Abusive Policing and Failures in Protection of Indigenous Women and Girls in Northern British Columbia, Canada*. New York: Human Rights Watch.

Human Rights Watch (2014) *One Billion Forgotten: Protecting the Human Rights of Persons with Disabilities*. New York: Human Rights Watch.

Human Rights Watch (2016) *'This Crooked System': Police Abuse and Reform in Pakistan*. New York: Human Rights Watch.

Human Rights Watch (2018) *Invisible Victims of Sexual Violence: Access to Justice for Women and Girls with Disabilities in India*. New York: Human Rights Watch.

Human Rights Watch (2021) *World Report 2021: Events of 2020*. New York: Human Rights Watch.

Independent Police Complaints Commission, UK (2010) *Deaths in or Following Police Custody: An Examination of the Cases 1998/99 – 2008/09*. London: IPCC.

ICC (International Criminal Court) (2021) *Decision on the Prosecutor's Request for Authorisation of an Investigation Pursuant to Article 15(3) of the Statute, Situation in the Republic of the Philippines*. Pre-Trial Chamber 1, 15 September 2021, No. ICC-01/21

INQUEST (2022) *BAME Deaths in Police Custody*. Available from: www.inquest.org.uk/bame-deaths-in-police-custody [Accessed 25 February 2022].

Johnson, H., Ollus, N. and Nevalla, S. (2008) *Violence Against Women: An International Perspective*. New York: Springer.

Johnston, E. (1991) *National Report*. Canberra: Royal Commission into Aboriginal Deaths in Custody.

Jones, A. and Sawyer, W. (2020) Not just a few bad apples: US police kill civilians at a much higher rate that other countries. *Prison Policy Initiative*. Available from: www.prisonpolicy.org/blog/2020/06/05/policekillings/ [Accessed 15 November 2022].

Kalhan, A., Singh, S. and Moghe, K. (2020) Locked down, trapped and abandoned migrant workers in Pune City. *Economic and Political Weekly*, 27 June.

Killingray, D. (1991) Guarding the extended frontier: Policing the Gold Coast, 1865–1913, in D.M. Anderson and D. Killingray (eds) *Policing the Empire: Government, Authority and Control 1830–1940*. Manchester: Manchester University Press, pp 106–125.

Lindon, G. and Roe, R. (2017) *Deaths in Police Custody: A Review of the International Literature*. London: Home Office.

Maher, G. (2021) *A World Without Police*. New York: Verso.

Marcoux, J. and Nicholson, K. (nd) Deadly force: Fatal encounters with police in Canada 2000–2017. *CBC News*. Available from: www.newsinteractives.cbc.ca/longform-custom/deadly-force [Accessed 15 November 2022].

Metaal, P. and Youngers, C. (2011) *Systems Overload: Drug Laws and Prisons in Latin America*. Amsterdam and Washington, DC: Transnational Institute and Washington Office on Latin America.

Mignolo, W. (2011) *The Darker Side of Western Modernity*. Durham, NC: Duke University Press.

Murray, S. and Heenan, M. (2012) Reported rapes in Victoria: Police responses to victims with a psychiatric disability or mental health issue. *Current Issues in Criminal Justice*, 23(3): 353–368.

National Commission on Human Rights (NCHR), Pakistan (2019) *Report on Enforced Disappearances*. Islamabad: NCHR.

National Human Rights Commission, India (2018) *Annual Report 2017–2018*. Available from: www.nhrc.nic.in/annualreports/2017-2018 [Accessed 15 November 2022].

National Human Rights Commission, Nigeria (2020) Press release. 15 April. Available from: www.nigeriarights.gov.ng/nhrc-media/press-release/100-national-human-rights-commission-press-release-on-covid-19-enforcement-so-far-report-on-incidents-of-violation-of-human-rights.html [Accessed 15 November 2022].

NCAT (National Campaign Against Torture) (2021) *India: National Report on Torture 2020*. New Delhi: National Campaign Against Torture.

Neocleous, M. (2021a) 'Original, absolute, indefeasible': Or, what we talk about when we talk about police power. *Social Justice*, 47(3–4): 9–32.

Neocleous, M. (2021b) Kettle logic. *Critical Criminology*, 29: 183–197.

Neuman, S. (2021) UN calls for investigation as police in Brazil kill at least 24 in Rio drug raid. *National Public Radio*, 7 May. Available from: www.npr.org/2021/05/07/994588467/u-n-calls-for-investigation-as-police-in-brazil-kill-at-least-24-in-rio-drug-rai [Accessed 15 November 2022].

Perrigo, B. and Godin, M. (2020) Racism is surging in Germany: Tens of thousands are taking to the streets to call for justice. *Time*, 11 June. Available from: www.time.com/5851165/germany-anti-racism-protests/ [Accessed 15 November 2022].

Ravi, P. (2020) Unnamed George Floyds of India: The episodic police brutality in 2019–20. *Feminism in India*, 17 June. Available from: www.feminisminindia.com/2020/06/17/unnamed-george-floyds-india-episodic-police-brutality-2019-20/ [Accessed 15 November 2022].

Ritchie, A.J. (2017) *Invisible No More: Police Violence Against Black Women and Women of Color*. Boston: Beacon Press.

Runnymede Trust (2021) *England Civil Society Submission to the United Nations Committee on the Elimination of Racial Discrimination*. London: Runnymede Trust.

Sadiki, L. and Steyn, F. (2022) Decolonising the criminology curriculum in South Africa: Views and experiences of lecturers and postgraduate students. *Transformation in Higher Education*. www.doi.org/10.4102/the. v7i0.150

Schrader, S. (2019) *Badges Without Borders: How Global Counterinsurgency Transformed American Policing*. Berkeley: University of California Press.

Sekhri, A. (2020) The criminal law reform committee. *The India Forum*, 6 November. Available from: www.theindiaforum.in/article/criminal-law-reform-committee [Accessed 15 November 2022].

Sinclair, G. (2006) *At the End of the Line: Colonial Policing and the Imperial Endgame*. Manchester: Manchester University Press.

Sinclair, G. (2008) The 'Irish' policeman and the Empire: Influencing the policing of the British Empire–Commonwealth. *Irish Historical Studies*, 36(142): 173–187.

Tankebe, J. (2008) Colonialism, legitimation and policing in Ghana. *International Journal of Law, Crime and Justice*, 36: 67–84.

Thom, K. and Quince, K. (2020) Black lives outrage must drive police reform in Aotearoa-New Zealand too. *The Conversation*, 9 June. Available from: www.theconversation.com/black-lives-matter-outrage-must-drive-police-reform-in-aotearoa-new-zealand-too-139965 [Accessed 15 November 2022].

Thompson, C. (2021) Fatal police shootings of unarmed black people reveal troubling patterns. *National Public Radio*, 25 January. Available from: www.npr.org/2021/01/25/956177021/fatal-police-shootings-of-unarmed-black-people-reveal-troubling-patterns [Accessed 15 November 2022].

Waseem, Z. (2021) A post-colonial condition of policing: A comparative look at Pakistan and Nigeria. Presented at Decolonising the Criminal Question Workshop, University of Warwick, 17 September 2021.

Washington Post (nd) *Police Shootings Database*. Available from: www.washingtonpost.com/graphics/investigations/police-shootings-database/?itid=lk_interstitial_manual_10 [Accessed 27 February 2022].

Watson, K. (2020) Brazil's racial reckoning: 'Black lives matter here, too'. *BBC News*, 25 July. Available from: www.bbc.com/news/world-latin-america-53484698 [Accessed 15 November 2022].

Whittaker, A. (2020) Despite 432 Indigenous deaths in custody since 1991, no one has ever been convicted: Racist silence and complicity are to blame. *The Conversation*, 3 June. Available from: www.theconversation.com/despite-432-indigenous-deaths-in-custody-since-1991-no-one-has-ever-been-convicted-racist-silence-and-complicity-are-to-blame-139873 [Accessed 15 November 2022].

World Health Organization (2021) *Violence Against Women: Fact Sheet.* 21 March. Available from: www.who.int/news-room/fact-sheets/detail/violence-against-women [Accessed 15 November 2022].

5

Crossing Red Lines: Exploring the Criminalization and Policing of Sedition and Dissent in Pakistan

Ammar Ali Jan and Zoha Waseem

Introduction

From the Crown to the colony

> There are certain red lines that cannot be crossed. There are some things that cannot be spoken about because it may be construed as a national security threat. Your speech may first be seen as a 'law and order problem,' and then a threat to the nation. Then, the law may be applied on a whim. (Interview 02, lawyer, Lahore, 21 December 2021)

> Whosoever by words, either spoken or intended to be read, or by signs, or by visible representation or otherwise, excites or attempts to excite feelings of disaffection to the Government established by law in British India, shall be punished. (Act XXVII of 1870 in Section V of the Indian Penal Code, 1870)

The law of sedition has been in place in South Asia since the mid-19th century and continues to be applied by states in the region more than seven decades after independence from colonial rule. Indeed, beyond South Asia, sedition laws remain in place in other former colonies too, including but not limited to, Nigeria, where the post-independence state readily accepted the law, and the courts restrained themselves from challenging it (Okonkwor, 1983); Malaysia, where it has been used by the government in its campaigns against human rights and anti-corruption activists (Kanna,

2020); and Hong Kong, where the once-dormant colonial law has been resurrected to criminalize 'seditious publications' and squeeze fundamental rights, particularly in the aftermath of protests against new national security legislations (Davis, 2022). Due to its continued designation as a political crime, and its undermining of fundamental rights and civil liberties, the criminalization of sedition and dissent at large demands further investigation through a critical criminological gaze.

We suggest that the growing application of the law of sedition, in conjunction with other legal frameworks and the extra-legal use of state force (through the police, paramilitary and other institutions), to suppress protests and social movements, a vibrant and critical media, and an active civil society, is symptomatic of persisting regime insecurity in postcolonial Pakistan, where successive governments have neither protected the interests of the masses nor ensured harmonious relations between state actors (such as civilian and military institutions), resulting in excessive reliance upon a broad range of legal instruments for curbing opposition from multiple platforms and power centres. In the process, we see these instruments and technologies applied most severely to voices of critical resistance and activism, to create fear, paranoia, uncertainty and manipulation, or 'rule by fear' (Jan, 2021), and deter criticism against an insecure regime that can further compromise its already weak legitimacy. The increasing use of the sedition law in Pakistan, and the accompanied criminalization of dissent and activism, must be understood in these historical and political contexts.

Here, we explore the application and effects of the law of sedition and how it constricts freedoms of speech, press, collective action and civil liberties at large. The criminalization of sedition in Pakistan remains ill-documented and underexplored. In undertaking this investigation, we also contribute to emerging works on the criminalization of activism (Weis, 2022; Cavalcanti et al, Chapter 14, this volume) and the policing of street-level dissent and activism in the global South broadly (Curtice and Behlendorf, 2021), strengthening critical activist-scholar conversations around the law of sedition in South Asia (Bakhle, 2010; Singh, 2018; Sinha, 2019; Mishra, 2020), as well as critical and postcolonial perspectives on crime and criminality in the global South.

At the time of writing, state clampdowns – often violent and spectacular – have been witnessed across the world, from Hong Kong to Bolivia, from Colombia to Iraq, to France, Nigeria, Lebanon, the United States and the United Kingdom. While reactive and overt repression came at the hands of the police and other law enforcement and security agencies against disgruntled and aggrieved protesters, much of the repression has happened in legal, judicial and bureaucratic corridors, using legal tools in addition to varieties of security technologies designed to frustrate resistance against state oppression. Laws prohibiting criticism of the state, and state policies, such as sedition are part of this 'lawfare' found most prominently in postcolonial environments (Comaroff, 2001), especially under regimes that have remained insecure in the aftermath of independence from colonial rule.[1] Exploring their impact further, on the ground, on individuals most vulnerable to such forms of state violence is imperative.

Dissent in the world of 'terrorism', fear and paranoia

In early 2020, an international non-governmental organization on human rights noted a persisting 'climate of fear' in Pakistan due to the unjust application of sedition and counterterrorism laws that were stifling dissent, regulating civil society activism and enabling authorities to 'crack down on members and supporters of opposition political parties' (Hashim, 2022). While a number of former colonies, especially India, have seen frequent applications and abuses of sedition laws, Pakistan has witnessed a surge in how the law is weaponized to criminalize dissent and censor free speech. In this chapter, we focus specifically on the use of sedition laws to suppress human rights, dissent and civil resistance in Pakistan.

Sedition has been described as a 'form of political speech, an expression against the authority of the government and state' that the state forbids on the grounds that it exceeds 'the limit of legitimate criticism', a limit that remains undefined and unclear, and 'therefore, not protected by the right to freedom of speech and expression' (Singh, 2018: 3). As a political crime, sedition was defined in 16th-century England due to perceived threats to 'public order' and 'social stability', but more importantly for the suppression of 'political discussion or criticism of the government' that did not invoke the same penalty as treason but was still punishable as a 'lesser offense' (Manning, 1980). By the end of the 16th century, the idea of 'dissatisfaction towards the state' or authority became central to the concept of sedition and its criminalization (Manning, 1980). While it remained in place for several centuries in Britain (abolished only in 2009), it criminalized 'disaffection' against the Crown, the government or the justice system, which was punishable by life imprisonment, fines or both. But while it largely abandoned the use of the law against its own citizens in the metropole in the 20th century, the British administration in colonial India strengthened the framework through political and judicial moves, due to fears of revolutionary plots and movements that, the government believed, necessitated intense surveillance of its Indian subjects both in the subcontinent as well as in England (Bakhle, 2010).

In colonial contexts, sedition laws were noted for their 'oppressive application', where they 'assumed their most draconian form' and were weaponized for suppressing nationalism and anti-colonial resistance (Kanna, 2020). In the aftermath of colonial rule, these criminal laws and other codes put into place by the British remained largely intact in postcolonial South Asia where, regardless of the form of governance, military or civilian, the retention of the law has been justified on grounds of maintaining state security (Singh, 2018). Furthermore, post-partition from India, Pakistan adopted a range of colonial laws and criminal justice institutions and their institutional processes. The law of sedition was integrated into Section 124-A of the Pakistan Penal Code (PPC). As it stands, at the time of writing, the law echoes the code introduced in 1870 and reads as follows:

> Whosoever by words, either spoken or written, or by signs, or by visible representation, or otherwise, brings or attempts to bring into hatred or contempt, or excited or attempts to excite disaffection towards, the federal or provincial government established by law shall be punished with imprisonment for life to which fine may be added. (Section 124-A, PPC)

In the colonial period, such laws were accompanied by surveillance as a 'technology of state control that placed an increasingly large number of revolutionaries under systematic monitoring' (Bakhle, 2010: 53). In postcolonial South Asia, especially since the 1990s, sedition charges have been applied in conjunction with charges of terrorism. In India, for instance, these were applied alongside the Unlawful Activities Prevention Act (1967) and, for a brief period, under the 2002 Prevention of Terrorism Act (that was repealed in 2004) (Singh, 2018). In Pakistan, they have been applied alongside the 1975 Suppression of Terrorist Activities Act, the Anti-Terrorism Act (1997) (ATA), as well as the Maintenance of Public Order Ordinate (MPO, 1960). In applying the law of sedition in conjunction with terrorism charges, government authorities have been able to ensure that the offence has the potential to be tried in special (anti-terrorism) courts, where, according to lawyers, the judges take a stricter approach to the alleged 'criminal'. Furthermore, applying the ATA reduces the chances for the 'offender' to get bail. It also ensures that, under the ATA, a confessional statement in the presence of the police is admissible during judicial proceedings.

While sedition laws have been applied more frequently in postcolonial India after the end of the British raj, Pakistan has seen an increased application of the law of sedition in the aftermath of the 'war on terror'. As Jan (2021) has noted, 'while increasing paranoia of the "hybrid regime"[2] unleashes violent repression by the coercive state apparatus, the state is also intensifying its focus on controlling the thoughts of its citizenry' by instilling fear, paranoia, and by undermining and delegitimizing dissenting voices. Dissidents are framed as 'working on a hostile agenda controlled by external enemies of Pakistan', a reference to India, Afghanistan and other potentially hostile states (Jan, 2021).

Attempts were made in 2020 to abolish Section 124-A, but these were blocked by the government of Pakistan Tehreek-e-Insaaf, which was in power at the time of writing. A federal minister justified this reluctance on the part of the state on the grounds that the 'law protects the security and sanctity of the country' (Malik, 2020). Indeed, Pakistan has seen not just such draconian and problematic laws as existing to protect the 'sanctity and security' of the state, by arresting dissenters and opposition members, but also the coexistence of extrajudicial and extra-legal practices that dissenters and critics frequently highlight in their 'seditious' speeches and opinions, including extrajudicial killings and enforced disappearances.

Methods and limitations

Our chapter draws especially upon the personal experiences and observations of the first author, whose own activism and ongoing pursuit for justice for Pakistan's minoritized and marginalized communities has led to his own victimization under problematic sedition laws. These first-hand observations are supplemented by the second author's interviews with those who have been directly involved in such cases or targeted by similar forms of criminalization. These interviews were conducted predominantly in the cities of Lahore and Karachi between 2020 and 2021 and have been anonymized to protect the identities and personal security of each interviewee.

We first situate this chapter and our discussion within the developing fields of Southern criminology, conversing especially with calls for decolonizing the discipline and incorporating postcolonial perspectives. We explore how the law of sedition, and the criminalization of political dissent more generally, are essential objects of study for these academic agendas. Thereafter, we explore how sedition has come to be criminalized and applied in colonial South Asia, before empirically demonstrating its contemporary impact in the case of post-9/11 Pakistan, focusing on two key nonviolent social movements that centre around student activism and an ethnic movement geared towards the protection of Pashtun rights.

We acknowledge that beyond these two examples, such laws have been used for repressing journalists and opposition political parties, among other social and political groups. Due to time and space constraints, we are unable to analyse these cases in detail, nor do we seek to present a complete historical account of the criminalization of dissent in the subcontinent. Instead, we aim to provide a snapshot of the contemporary, deteriorating state of dissent and dissidence, and growing censorship, in South Asia with potential for further research in criminology.

Decolonial and Southern perspectives on crime and criminology

Calls to decolonize criminology and criminal justice are gaining traction, coming on the heels of critical and counter-colonial perspectives on crime and criminal justice that question and challenge traditional and conventional approaches to crime that have inadequately considered the role of the state, political and historical processes in the commission of injustice and insecurity (Agozino, 2003). Counter-colonial criminology seeks to interrogate and challenge criminalization processes, including labelling and penal responses, that find their origin in colonialism and empire (Agozino, 2003). Similarly, decolonizing the discipline, as an agenda, asks us to 'interrogate critically the impact of colonialism in the past and present of institutions and practices of crime control' (Aliverti et al, 2021). Given that the empire and colonial governmentality most strongly shaped and influenced criminal justice structures and institutions, and the impacts of this reverberate decades after the fall of the empire, a decolonizing agenda seeks to 'identify, explain and assess the effects of colonialism in crime and crime control policies, institutions, and practices, as well as its impact in framing and shaping dominant criminological theories and methodologies' (Aliverti et al, 2021: 299).

Furthermore, these approaches help us bring into our criminological analysis the importance of race and racism, which is gradually finding its space in British criminology (Parmar, 2017; Phillips et al, 2020). Recognizing the racist foundations of criminal law, justice and penal systems helps us connect how racial stereotyping (such as of Indian people) led to the criminalization and marginalization of communities around the world (Aliverti et al, 2021). In the case of Pakistan, the marginalization of ethnic Pashtuns, and Baloch, among other minority groups who remain vulnerable to punitive penal policies and extra-legal state violence, are cases in point, but the lack of criminological interest in Pakistan has meant that racialized violence against these communities by the postcolonial state and its authorities remains unexplored.

Within this broader push for decolonizing criminology and criminal justice, scholars have also drawn upon Southern perspectives that ask us to look beyond the over-researched spaces in the global North, an encouragement to which this volume and chapter respond (Cunneen, 2011; Carrington et al, 2016, 2018). Employing these perspectives and responding to calls for both decolonizing and Southernizing the discipline, allows us to investigate the 'historical role of state violence in nation-building, the expansion of colonialism across the global South and the neglect of contemporary violent phenomena, like armed conflict, drug wars and ethnic cleansing, that are more common in the Global South' (Carrington et al, 2016: 3). Equally common is the continued application, weaponization and exploitation of colonial frameworks designed to secure and sustain the power and authority of postcolonial states, such as the law of sedition.

Moreover, South Asian criminology is in its preliminary stage of development. While there is a steady interest generated on research on policing in postcolonial South Asia (Jackson et al, 2014; Jauregui, 2016; Lokaneeta, 2021, Waseem, 2021), and early conversations around creating separate academic space for South Asian criminology (Jaishanker, 2021), these works are not directly engaged with Southern and decolonizing perspectives, at least not theoretically, but have paved the road for distinct contributions. An exploration of the criminalization of dissent, activism and civilian resistance cuts across the region spatially, but also the theoretical and conceptual grounds briefly outlined here. In examining these questions we connect underexplored geographies and jurisdictions with developing areas within criminology.

Situating dissent and resistance within criminology

While legal and political scholars have looked at the formulation and legacies of the law of sedition, the criminalization of sedition and activism at large remains underinvestigated. Indeed, as scholars point out, this mirrors the shortcomings of the criminal justice systems at large, one of which is the 'under-criminalisation of the powerful' and the 'over-criminalisation of activism' (Weis, 2022), a discrepancy that is reflected within the discipline of criminology. Recent works such as Weis' (2022) collection of scholarship on the criminalization of resistance and activism, Manuel (2014) on the criminalization of environmental activism, Yonucu (2018) on the policing of oppositional politics, and border or migrant activism (Fernandez-Bessa, 2019), are gradually pushing the boundaries of sociological, criminological and political analyses of political dissent, protests and more. Much of this literature has emerged over the past decade, indicating that it is an area developing interest – particularly on scholarship leaning towards critical criminology.

Criminology can therefore look towards how postcolonial criminal law and criminal justice systems have been studied in their historical and structural contexts beyond its own domain, and how British colonial governance, policing and security practices have persisted after independence (Kalhan et al, 2006). Furthermore, Southern, counter-colonial and postcolonial perspectives overlap in how they ask us to look at the injustices and violences of states against their own people, or the enduring legacies of colonialism on contemporary state crime and human rights (Cunneen, 2011). Here, the criminalization of dissent, opinion and resistance (in addition to works that explore extrajudicial killings and enforced disappearances, also prevalent in Pakistan) makes a crucial empirical contribution. As Cunneen explains, 'a postcolonial perspective sees crime as a category contextualized through the material practices and ideologies of colonial states and by the resistances of colonized peoples' (Cunneen, 2011: 250). Combined, therefore, these perspectives help establish colonial continuities in South

Asian law, criminology and human rights (Kalhan et al, 2006), but also how these legacies have evolved and aged in postcolonial contexts where dissent and disagreement has been disciplined and policed through a variety of institutions designed to serve political interests and stifle dissent, as seen historically in Nigeria (Daly, 2019) and India (Heath, 2021), and in non-democratic contexts at large where such policing and suppression not only delegitimizes these institutions but can also fuel civilian action and ignite future protests (Curtice and Behlendorf, 2021).

Constructions and continuities: a brief history of sedition in South Asia

In 2020, shortly after being slapped with sedition charges for participating in student protests, the first author wrote that '[t]he subcontinent is witnessing a strange rebirth of nationalism' (Jan, 2020). Under colonial rule, nationalism was viewed as a form of resistance to colonial governance, and charges of sedition came to be viewed as a 'rite of passage' (Jan, 2020). Postcolonial India and Pakistan are going through a period in which a skewed sense of nationalism and loyalty to the nation is now used to justify the criminalization and suppression of dissent. As Jan wrote elsewhere, 'the nation is being defined not by the people, but by majoritarian groups or lifeless state "institutions," and dissenting voices are the primary targets of sedition laws' (Jan, 2020). In this section, we provide a rather brief historical introduction to the colonial and postcolonial trajectories of this 'crime', before focusing on our contemporary findings from Pakistan.

In the aftermath of the 1857 revolt to its authority, and the first major challenge to British rule in India, there were intense and rushed efforts to prevent repeat attempts at Indigenous resistance. The late 19th century saw sedition trials against journalists and editors of local newspapers. As Singh writes, in some of these cases, 'disaffection came to be identified with disloyalty to the government' (Singh, 2018: 142). Furthermore, disaffection could be seen as being promoted through speeches, newspaper articles, songs, poetry and other revolutionary literature (Morton, 2012). In subsequent amendments to the Indian Penal Code (a colonial criminal legislation), in 1898, the law stated that disaffection could include 'disloyalty and all feelings of enmity' (Singh, 2018). In Singh's words, the amendment 'secured the criminalisation of the illocutionary effect of any expression' (2018: 146). Furthermore, the 'crime' of sedition did not need to be committed by an act; even the harbouring of *feelings* 'such as "hatred", "contempt", and so on, was construed as performance of the act of sedition' (Singh, 2018: 146).

The application of the law increased in momentum in the early 20th century, after nationalist movements and radical thought (particularly, leftist revolutionary thought) in British India threatened the colonial state and the law of sedition became one of the many problematic legal tools at the colonial regime's disposal to suppress resistance to its authority and rule. The law was extended not just to violent forms of resistance to the empire, and applied to freedom movement leaders such as Bhagat Singh, but also criminalized nonviolent dissent and incriminated opposition leaders, such as Mohandas Gandhi. Gandhi's sedition trial took place in 1922 and he was charged with 'inciting "disaffection" against [the colonial regime]' (Bakhle, 2010: 72). But Gandhi, and others, interpreted such incrimination as a form of 'privilege' given that 'some of the most loved of India's patriots [were] convicted under it' (Morton, 2012: 187).

In these years, the deployment of sedition accompanied the 'emergency measures' that the colonial regime had adopted (for example, extra-legal violence, as seen most obviously during the 1919 Amritsar/Jallianwala Bagh massacre) to maintain colonial power, and police and oppress the 'Indian seditionist' and the 'revolutionary terrorists' (Morton, 2012: 187). This joint application of sedition and terrorism charges and framings have shaped the policing and surveillance of dissidents, activists and critics in post-9/11 Pakistan.

Post-1947, both India and Pakistan prioritized the security of the newly independent postcolonial states over the security of the public, thus retaining most of the criminal laws, procedures and criminal justice mechanisms, including the law of sedition, despite concerns about these laws compromising the freedom of speech and opinion (Narrain, 2011). In the early years, legal and political opponents of the law challenged it and found it to conflict with new discourses of democracy and in contradiction to constitutional protections of fundamental freedoms, such as the right to freedom of expression (Singh, 2018: 182–183). Although, in India, for example, initial sedition trials found the framework to be unconstitutional, later judgements of the supreme court maintained that it was constitutional (for example, the trial of Kedar Nath in the 1960s). This was due to the conflation of national security and public order maintenance, a conflation that persists to this date. Because of this, where the 'security of state' was seen as being dependent on 'the maintenance of law and order', as seen in the landmark judgement of the 1962 case of Kedar Nath, disaffection shown towards an organ of the government (in this case, a political party) was translated as amounting to a threat to the security of the state (Singh, 2018: 201). In other words, in the trial of Kedar Nath, the court found that due to Nath's vilification of the government, 'incitement to revolution', the speech he made was seditious (Narrain, 2011). In contemporary Pakistan, the 'crime' of sedition similarly remains connected to the conflation of state security, national security (and national interest) and the maintenance of public order, which is often interpreted loosely.

In the following section, drawing specifically upon findings from Pakistan, we evidence the impacts of the criminalization of dissent and activism, and the 'chilling effects' (Narrain, 2011) of the law of sedition, as it affects two areas: student activism and a protest movement for Pashtun rights.

Criminalizing resistance in postcolonial Pakistan

Pakistan's participation in the 'war on terror' has exacerbated and empowered the utilization of the legal frameworks that seek to curb dissent and resistance against the Pakistani state, conflating criticism and critical thought with terrorism and existential threats to national security and cohesion. These frameworks continue to be applied to sentiments and speeches critical of the 'state', even though such criticism is directed towards particular forms of governments (such as military regimes) and types of governmentalities (such as authoritarian rule) and not the 'nation' of Pakistan. In recent years, the targets of such draconian laws have included politicians such as Javed Hashmi, who was sentenced to 23 years[3] on sedition charges and 'incitement to mutiny' after he distributed a letter written by members of the armed forces who criticized the then President-General Pervez Musharraf. Such criminalization has frequently occurred alongside extra-legal and illegal state practices, such as extrajudicial killings, custodial torture, illegal detentions and enforced disappearances, that have impacted activists, journalists and political party workers (Hussain, 2018). While these methods have been justified as essential for the 'elimination of terrorism', they have extended to the civilian and military governments' efforts to curb political dissent, leading several activists, academics and minorities to flee their persecution (Hussain, 2018). Here, we focus on select cases to exemplify the ongoing criminalization of political dissent, particularly that which is tied to social movements in Pakistan.

Student activism: the Student Solidarity March

Student activism and campus politics have long shaped political dissent in Pakistan, generating new political parties, protesting military rule, and fighting for civilian supremacy and democratic rights, through peaceful protest but also violence when faced with fierce state clampdowns (Mullick, 2008). In the 1980s, under a military dictatorship, Pakistan banned student unions and campus politics. In 2018, the country witnessed a revival of student politics led by left-wing organizations such as the Progressive Students Collective and the Students Action Committee. These groups managed to organize the 2019 Student Solidarity March (SSM) with mass rallies held across more than 50 cities in the country on 29 November. The SSM demanded democratic rights for students, such as the right to unionize, and better education budgets. The event generated broad sympathy for the demands of these protestors and the revival of student politics appeared imminent.

The following day, however, student leaders heard about the abduction of Alamgir Wazir, a student who had spoken at the SSM rally (Gabol, 2019). Wazir had been detained from his hostel at the University of Punjab, an example of high-handed state response. After a day of being arbitrarily detained, it was revealed that five individuals, including the first author and Alamgir, had been slapped with sedition charges. The first author was also accused and termed as 'an enemy of the state for voicing dissent over the disastrous conditions of higher learning in the country' (Jan, 2020). It was alleged that the student marches were a 'foreign conspiracy' aimed at destabilizing Pakistan in the name of human rights. The organizers of the SSM were left stunned at this abrupt government decision to repress the movement.

Three issues stood out in the sedition trial against these student leaders. First, the conflation of popular protests with 'foreign conspiracies' has turned into a regular motif invoked by the state to delegitimize and eventually suppress dissent. In Pakistan, the state had developed an elaborate vocabulary to target political opponents including calling them 'RAW agents' (that is, those working on behalf of Indian intelligence agencies). Such allegations substitute any serious attempts to nominate or even understand the social and economic roots of popular rage, turning the country's political crisis into a linguistic crisis. A similar pattern is observed across the border, in India, where student activists from the Jawaharlal Nehru University (JNU) protested the high-handedness of the Modi regime in 2016. Sedition was used as a weapon against JNU students, and a case was also registered for 'sedition and conspiracy against "unknown persons" for allegedly raising anti-India slogans at an event organised by some students' (Singh and Dasgupta, 2019: 66). As a result, student leaders were charged with sedition and accused of being 'ISI agents' (that is, on the payroll of Pakistan's premier intelligence agency). The equation of dissent with a foreign conspiracy allows the state to evict opponents from the legitimate political community and transform them from citizens into enemies. It has the further effect of suspending constitutional protections of dissidents by terming the situation an 'exceptional circumstance' that threatens national security and necessitates excessive forms of violence (Agamben, 2005). Suspension of legal rights and demonization of opponents as 'outsiders' is a crucial technique of discipline and governance in South Asia that facilitates the use of sedition charges against activists.

Second, the movements that are being targeted as 'sedition' are often those that claim legitimacy by invoking the constitution of Pakistan. For example, the SSM demanded the restoration of student unions by invoking the right to unionize, a right protected by the constitution. The Pashtun

Tahaffuz Movement (PTM; discussed in the next section) also premises its demands for accountability of security forces by laying claim to constitutional guarantees for the protection of life and liberty. However, leaders of both these movements have faced sedition charges, demonstrating the spectacular erasure of legal protections for those who are presented as threatening the status quo. In these circumstances, constitutional republicanism has made a comeback with dissidents defending their actions in the name of the constitutions, turning the state's foremost legal document into subversive literature. Therefore, applications of the laws of sedition in South Asia have led many to call into question their constitutionality.

Finally, the question of identity has also emerged as central to accusations of sedition. The postcolonial state has tried to build a homogenous identity, out of an otherwise heterogenous population, premised on state-sanctioned Islam, a move that has threatened the cultural and linguistic identities of ethnic minorities. This anxiety and insecurity of the state from minority groups was evident in the aftermath of the SSM protests as many students from Pakistan's peripheral regions participated in the rallies and demanded respect for their cultural and linguistic rights. At the Senate hearing on the sedition cases against student organizers, it was fascinating to note that senior senators were not as outraged about Alamgir Wazir's criticisms of the military (undoubtedly the strongest state institution in Pakistan) as they were about his claims that Urdu was imposed upon Pashtuns in the country. Under normal circumstances, this claim could at best generate a polite intellectual disagreement. However, some legislators claimed that this statement was tantamount to undermining the ideological boundaries of the nation as it questioned the country's national identity.

What this case revealed was that the ambit of sedition law is being widened to criminalize debates on history, culture and identity. Such paranoia fits into a larger state narrative by officials claiming that foreign powers are using 'subversive' ideas to undermine state sovereignty. As a result, universities, streets and the media have become symbolic battlegrounds for security agencies that often use censorship (such as the Pakistan Electronic Crimes Act 2016) and extra-legal violence to control these spaces. It is no surprise, therefore, that student leaders, activists and journalists have faced the brunt of sedition cases in Pakistan since 2018. The case of the PTM is another key example of the criminalization of dissent and activism over the past few years.

Minority resistance: the Pashtun Tahaffuz Movement

During colonial rule, Pashtuns were perceived as being 'warrior-like', 'savages' and 'lawless'; their postcolonial representations in Pakistan have persistently suffered from such stereotyping and marginalization of their communities, wherein they continue to be seen as 'violent', 'suspect' or 'dangerous communities' (Yousuf, 2020). Such representations have accompanied state narratives and perceptions of Pashtuns in contemporary Pakistan, particularly in the aftermath of the war on terror. The legal and criminological gaze through which the PTM has been viewed needs to take this historical context into account.

The PTM is a nonviolent national movement that came into being in the aftermath of Pakistan's domestic military operations against alleged terrorist groups (such as the Tehreek-e-Taliban Pakistan), primarily in the northern and western regions of the country. These military operations came alongside devastating terrorist attacks on civilians and military and law enforcement officers. Collectively, these state-driven operations and terrorist attacks had long impacted the wellbeing and human security of Pashtun communities residing in Pakistan's tribal areas. PTM's momentum escalated in 2018 in the aftermath of the extrajudicial police killing of a young Pashtun man in the city of Karachi. PTM emerges from the geographies most affected by the war on terror (Khyber Pakhtunkhwa and the Federally Administered Tribal Areas) where the Pashtun minority has long been subjected to discrimination, state violence, extrajudicial killings, disappearances and religious militancy. The PTM thus responds to the sociopolitical injustices against and marginalization of the Pashtuns over the past several decades.

Since the emergence of the PTM, some suggest, the criminalization of dissent in Pakistan has exacerbated. As our interlocutors explained, the state does not have a uniformed way to deal with this resistance movement. As such, in addition to detentions, excessive surveillance and press bans, anti-terror legislation and the law of sedition is part of broader state efforts to weaken, dismantle and delegitimize the movement. With this agenda, PTM activists have been routinely criminalized and overpoliced; arrests, illegal detentions and, in some cases, long-term detentions (as in the case of Ali Wazir) under laws such as the Anti-Terrorism Act and the Maintenance of Public Order Act, where applicable, show how the insecure regime has relied upon a range of legal and extra-legal tools, including legal colonial artifacts, to suppress Pashtun dissent and their calls for the protections of their human rights.

The law of sedition, specifically, has been weaponized to police and suppress the movement; the application of this is symptomatic of the insecurity on the part of the postcolonial state in the face of a grassroots movement that challenges its authority. In December 2020, one of PTM's primary leaders and a member of the National Assembly, Ali Wazir, along with several other leaders, were arrested by the police in the city of Peshawar, based on sedition cases registered against them in Karachi, where these activists had demonstrated earlier that month. The charge claimed that Wazir and others had used 'derogatory language' against state institutions (in other words, shown disaffection and disloyalty against the state and its institutions), including the police and military, in their speeches, and tried to 'create hatred' and 'deteriorate the law-and-order situation'. Such criminalization of their speech and opposition led to the prolonged detention of Ali Wazir.

At the time of writing, Wazir had been in custody on sedition charges for almost two years. This was not the first time Ali had found himself imprisoned; in 2005, Ali was imprisoned for violating the Frontier Crimes Ordinance (another colonial-era legislation), during which his father, brother and several other family members were killed in multiple incidents of criminal violence, including terrorism (Shah, 2022). In 2018, and in subsequent years, Ali narrowly escaped violent attacks on his rallies, in which other attendees were killed. In early 2022, while incarcerated, Ali was charged with yet another case of sedition, for another public rally in which he delivered speeches that were allegedly 'anti-state'. In total, at the time of writing, Ali was facing at least three separate sedition charges, and while some other PTM members were released, Ali's bail hearings at the anti-terrorism court were stalled and a prolonged sit-in demonstration had begun in Karachi to challenge his arrest and incarceration (Veengas, 2022). Sedition charges continued to be applied on other leaders of the PTM, including its chief Manzoor Pashteen, for criticizing Pakistan's security establishment (News Desk, 2022).

The detention and trial of Ali Wazir on grounds of sedition, for his prominent role in the PTM that calls for an end to state violence against Pashtuns in Pakistan, shows how racialized minorities suffer not just at the hands of criminals (in this case, religious militants affiliated with terrorist outfits) but also through state-mandated criminalization processes that violate their basic human and constitutional rights. It also shows how colonial laws have been usurped by postcolonial states to protect state-sanctioned violations of these rights from being construed as extra-legal, illegal or in contravention of constitutional provisions, and instead necessitated by 'extreme circumstances' that call for 'extreme measures.' In this way, the law of sedition and the laws applied in conjunction with sedition (under PPC, ATA, MPO, or other such draconian frameworks) reveal broader trends and challenges, both for activists and practitioners on the ground, as well as scholars of critical, Southern and postcolonial perspectives within criminology, criminal law and criminal justice.

Discussion

Based on our preliminary findings and the cases briefly discussed in this chapter, we note several observable trends that may be explored in future research. First, we noted that in some instances, sedition charges are usually not registered by the police unless consent is sought from the chain of command. As per one police officer, when a PTM leader was accused of seditious speech in Karachi, and the complaints were brought to a police station, the officer had to inform the senior-most officer of the police, who sought permission from the government, prior to the registration of the complaint (or what is known as the First Information Report).[4] Another police officer recounted that such political crimes unofficially fall outside the official mandate of the civilian police, even though they are registered and investigated by the police, indicating that decisions pertaining to political crimes are matters of 'high policing' and higher political or state authorities. The lawyers and police officers with whom we spoke also indicated that matters pertaining to sedition can fall under the domain of Pakistan's military and intelligence agencies, whose accountability to the public remains limited, unlike that of the police. The police are therefore *relatively* more likely to 'act formally and register cases' when sedition is suspected, to protect themselves. Curtice and Behlendorf (2021), writing about police repression in Uganda, mention how the police are the primary instrument for suppressing dissent. In Pakistan's case, the police may be the primary instrument, but often work in tandem with other institutions, and are more cautious of losing legitimacy than others.

Relatedly, the ad-hoc detentions carried out by other agencies in a pluralized policing landscape (such as paramilitary forces and intelligence agencies), signals to the police that these agencies are not held equally accountable for such extra-legal practices. This, as the police officers are all too aware, may not be the treatment that the police receive – a civilian institution that is more public-facing and reliant upon relations with local communities, but in the hierarchy of security institutions in Pakistan is placed in a junior role compared to its military and paramilitary counterparts. According to one lawyer, "the message that goes to the police is to be close to the powerful institution",[5] such as the military, or in other words, to work alongside the military and intelligence institutions, especially in cases of political crimes, such as sedition, treason, terrorism and maintenance of public order. In this way, even under democratic regimes, the military remains intimately connected to policing everyday dissent and resistance to state policies. This is exacerbated by the fact that frequently civilian police officers prefer not to get involved in political cases, as mentioned, fearing both state and civilian backlash, creating space for the military to exert its influence.

These trends show a complicated civil–military relationship in postcolonial states such as Pakistan that have long contributed to regime insecurity and state instability. They pluralize the landscape of policing (Waseem, 2021), in which matters pertaining to state and national security are, at times, beyond the purview of the regular police, but for which the formal functions of the police are still employed. A qualitative, grounded study of political crimes, such as sedition, can thus contribute tremendously to future research on the overlaps between civilian and military institutions tasked with policing and law enforcement.

Second, ethnic minorities, such as Pashtuns and Baloch, are more likely to be targeted by the postcolonial state through both legal and extra-legal means. The law of sedition becomes one component of the state's 'lawfare' against Pashtuns (the ethnic group considered here). As one lawyer commented, "the state has certain preconceived notions about Pashtuns. For them, it's not so easy to get bail".[6] The case of Alamgir, discussed earlier, demonstrates this. Alamgir, the nephew of Ali Wazir, was arrested for participating in the 2019 SSM. While others in the same case were released shortly after being detained, Alamgir's bail was rejected, and he spent four months in jail without trial and conviction. It should also be noted here that Alamgir was arbitrarily detained for almost a day by state authorities before he was formally charged. It may also be mentioned that at the time the first author was being detained, the authorities had asked him if he was Pashtun; when he confirmed he was in fact Punjabi (the majority ethnic group in Pakistan), the law enforcement officials were taken aback, indicating a continued perception that state dissent is coming from *selected* ethnic groups that deserve to be *selectively* overpoliced through racialized security and policing practices.[7]

Third, while most sedition charges are eventually dropped, the law of sedition delegitimizes those who are charged, hurting their professional and personal wellbeing. The primary author, for instance, was unable to obtain teaching jobs due to the general insecurity created in the aftermath of his detention. He was removed from his position as a university lecturer on grounds of 'national security'. As one interlocutor tells us, "Those accused of sedition are viewed as anti-national, which squeezes space for dissent and activism."[8] In this way, individuals and movements (such as PTM) are gradually disempowered, and dissenters disciplined. The fear of crime, and the associated fear of the *criminal* (the 'anti-state', 'anti-nationalist', *ghaddaar* or traitor), further creates social anxieties and apprehensions, risks creating divisions within a dissenter's social networks, as well as fragmentations within the social movement. This was confirmed by lawyers with whom we spoke who said that the registration of sedition charges through First Information Reports, although later dropped, is a process used to create fear and insecurity, and to deter critics from opining against government policies and practices.[9] Thus, while convictions and indictments remain few, the labelling and the associated trauma must be understood and evidenced further to fully capture the lawfare against political dissent and state criticism. This form of 'soft repression' (Balcells et al, 2020) is as crucial for state repression of social movements, dissent and resistance, and the discipline and isolation of activists and dissenters, as are the more substantial forms of repression (for example, killings and disappearances).

The case of Kanhaiya Kumar, who was charged with sedition, during student activism at JNU, is comparable. Singh and Dasgupta have discussed the 'hostile representations' of students at JNU, like Kanhaiya, who, as one judge argued, were suffering from an 'infection', that 'required "surgical intervention" even "amputation" before such infections could become an "epidemic"' (Singh and Dasgupta, 2019: 67). The students were represented on social media and elsewhere as being 'threats to the nation' (Singh and Dasgupta, 2019: 67). Across the border, as the case of Alamgir Wazir[10] demonstrates, student activists are similarly represented as problematic for the image of the state. During a hearing in which Alamgir's appeal was dismissed, the prosecutor noted that 'Using objectionable language against state institutions is equivalent to disrespecting the country' (Waqar, 2020). It must also be mentioned here that such representation and framing is not limited to students engaged in activism; teaching and research staff are similarly subjected to such policing processes (Cheema, 2020).

And lastly, sedition remains criminalized irrespective of the regime changes that have taken place in postcolonial Pakistan. As a senior politician explained:

'Political dissent has been controlled through the use of these [legal] provisions to further a political agenda on the part of the ruling regime. In military courts, it can amount to conviction. In civilian courts, the case will linger. It's a tool that the state uses to curb dissent, in particular progressive and left-oriented dissent.'[11]

This consistency in the criminalization of dissent and sedition resonates across the border, in India, where (as discussed), the law remains applicable despite the country's democratic political trajectory.

Conclusion

In South Asia, the law of sedition was borne out of resistance to colonial rule and authority. In postcolonial South Asia, the law continues to police sentiments critical of state policy and practice, deepening the mutual distrust between state and society. As the case of Pakistan demonstrates, postcolonial contexts continue to criminalize political dissent, incriminating activists, journalists and members of the civil society, who are framed as 'security risks', indicating a persisting level of insecurity on the part of the postcolonial state that manifests itself through processes of criminalization and securitization, operationalized through the criminal justice system.

The democratic right to dissent, criticize or resist, through protest or the written word, is gravely undermined in the global South. In Pakistan, the law of sedition is one such legal framework among many others that the undemocratic state has at its disposal to carry out lawfare against dissenting and free-thinking citizens. At the time of writing, Pakistani dissidents were at risk of having their most basic rights undermined not just through the laws discussed here, but also through a draconian Pakistan Electronic Crimes Act that sought to penalize criticism against the country's military, judiciary and other public institutions.

The law of sedition is still selectively applied in Pakistan, less liberally than perhaps other problematic legislations, such as anti-terrorism laws, and less likely to lead to many convictions. Nevertheless, its growing application undermines and threatens legitimate rights movements, opening new empirical and theoretical avenues for critical investigations. As Bakhle (2010) writes, the law of sedition was not drafted to counter terrorism in colonial India but to address growing resentment against the colonial regime; similarly, sedition's conflation with national security means sedition is criminalized in the same way as 'terrorism', and 'sedition' remains, in fact, a weapon against any expression of disaffection with punitive and discriminatory postcolonial regimes.

Therefore, decolonizing and critical agendas within criminology must shine a spotlight on the enduring, persisting and evolving legacies of contemporary application and abuse of centuries-old draconian frameworks designed to force affection and loyalty towards undemocratic regimes through authoritarian policing practices, penal procedures and criminal codes. But critical research on the policing of dissent, activism, the surveillance of activists and grassroots organizations, within the discipline of criminology remains severely limited. A critical agenda must thus be developed to focus on such modes of state repression, censorship and lawfare, especially in the context of political and state crime.

Notes

[1] Owen (2016), for instance, has written about how regime insecurity (especially in postcolonial states with a history of civil–military turmoil) is central to understanding postcolonial policing. Elsewhere, I have developed the idea of the 'postcolonial condition of policing' in which I similarly demonstrate on state insecurity results in institutional insecurity on the part of the police, creating dependency on militarized and informal policing practices (Waseem, 2022).

[2] A type of a political regime that has witnessed an incomplete transition from authoritarian governance to democratic governance.

[3] Hashmi was released a few years later.

[4] Interview 04, police officer, Karachi, 19 December 2021.

[5] Interview 01, lawyer, Lahore, 22 December 2021.

[6] Interview 04, lawyer, Lahore, 23 December 2021.

[7] Alamgir was released on bail after spending four months in custody without trial or conviction; at the time of writing, the charges against him were yet to be dropped.

[8] Interview 01, lawyer, Lahore, 22 December 2021.

[9] Interview 02, lawyer, Lahore, 21 December 2021.

[10] Alamgir Wazir was one of the activists charged with sedition during the 2019 SSM.
[11] Interview 03, politician, Karachi, 12 February 2020.

References

Agamben, G. (2005) *State of Exception*. Chicago: Chicago University Press.

Agozino, B. (2003) *Counter-Colonial Criminology: A Critique of Imperialist Reason*. London: Pluto Press.

Aliverti, A., Carvalho, H. and Chamberlen, A. (2021) Decolonising the criminal question. *Punishment and Society*, 23(3): 297–316.

Bakhle, J. (2010) Sedition and surveillance: The rule of law in a colonial situation. *Social History*, 35(1): 51–75.

Balcells, L., Dorsey, S. and Tellez, J.F. (2020) Repression and dissent in contemporary Catalonia. *British Journal of Political Science*, 51(4): 1742–1750.

Carrington, K., Hogg, R. and Sozzo, M. (2016) Southern criminology. *British Journal of Criminology*, 56(1): 1–20.

Carrington, K., Hogg, R., Scott, J. and Sozzo, M. (2018) *The Palgrave Handbook of Criminology and the Global South*. Cham: Palgrave.

Cheema, U. (2020) Shrinking space for academics who teach critical thinking. *The News*. Available from: https://www.thenews.com.pk/print/677469-shrinking-space-for-academics-who-teach-critical-thinking [Accessed 25 February 2022].

Comaroff, J.L. (2001) Colonialism, culture, and the law: A forward. *Law and Social Inquiry*, 26(2): 305–314.

Cunneen, C. (2011) Postcolonial perspectives for criminology, in M. Bosworth and C. Hoyle (eds) *What is Criminology?* Oxford: Oxford University Press, pp 249–266.

Curtice, T.B. and Behlendorf, B. (2021) Street-level repression: Protest, policing, and dissent in Uganda. *Journal of Conflict Resolution*, 65(1): 166–194.

Daly, S.F.C. (2019) From crime to coercion: Policing dissent in Abeokuta, Nigeria, 1900–1940. *Journal of Imperial and Commonwealth History*, 47(3): 474–489.

Davis, M.C. (2022) Hong Kong: How Beijing perfected repression. *Journal of Democracy*, 33(1): 100–115.

Fernandez-Bessa, C. (2019) A theoretical typology of border activism: From the streets to the council. *Theoretical Criminology*, 23(2): 156–174.

Gabol, I. (2019) Sedition cases registered against organisers and participants of student march. *Dawn*. Available from: https://www.dawn.com/news/1519976 [Accessed 12 March 2022].

Hashim, A. (2022) HRW slams Pakistan over dissent crackdown, alleged human rights abuses. *Al Jazeera*. Available from: https://www.aljazeera.com/news/2022/1/14/hrw-report-pakistan-dissent-crackdown-alleged-rights-abuses [Accessed 13 February 2022].

Heath, D. (2021) *Colonial Terror: Torture and State Violence in Colonial India*. New York: Oxford University Press.

Hussain, S. (2018) War on terror to war on dissent: Enforced disappearances in Pakistan. *Economic and Political Weekly*, 53(17): 19–22.

Jackson, J., Asif, M., Bradford, B. and Zakar, M.Z. (2014) Corruption and police legitimacy in Lahore, Pakistan. *British Journal of Criminology*, 54(6): 1067–1088.

Jaishanker, K. (2020) *Routledge Handbook of South Asian Criminology*. Abingdon: Routledge.

Jan, A.A. (2020) 'We the (seditious) people': Repression and revolution in South Asia. *Jamhoor*. Available from: https://www.jamhoor.org/read/2020/1/19/we-the-seditious-people-repression-and-revolution-in-south-asia [Accessed 17 November 2022].

Jan, A.A. (2021) *Rule by Fear: Eight Theses on Authoritarianism in Pakistan*. Lahore: Folio Books.

Jauregui, B. (2016) *Provisional Authority: Police, Order, and Security in India*. Chicago: Chicago University Press.

Kalhan, A., Conroy, G.P., Kaushal, M., Miller, S.S. and Rakoff, J.S. (2006) Colonial continuities: Human rights, terrorism, and security laws in India. *Colombia Journal of Asian Law*, 20(1): 93–234.

Kanna, M. (2020) Furthering decolonisation: Judicial review of colonial criminal laws. *Duke Law Journal*, 70(2/3): 411–449.

Lokaneeta, J. (2021) *Truth Machines: Policing, Violence, and Scientific Interrogations in India*. Michigan: University of Michigan Press.

Malik, H. (2020) Sedition law party of colonial legacy: Legal experts. *The Express Tribune*. Available from: https://tribune.com.pk/story/2267316/sedition-law-part-of-colonial-legacy-legal-experts-1 [Accessed 11 February 2022].

Manning, R.B. (1980) The origins of the doctrine of sedition. *Albion*, 12(2): 99–121.

Manuel, M. (2014) The criminalisation of environmental activism in Europe. *Studia UBB Sociologica*, 59(2): 87–103.

Mishra, M. (2020) Criminalising dissent: Sedition laws in India. *Rule of Law Journal*, 1: 14–24.

Morton, S. (2012) Fictions of sedition and the framing of Indian revolutionaries in colonial India. *Journal of Commonwealth Literature*, 47(2): 175–189.

Mullick, H.A.H. (2008) Towards a civic culture: Student activism and political dissent in Pakistan. *Georgetown Journal of International Affairs*, 9(2): 5–12.

Narrain, S. (2011) 'Disaffection' and the law: The chilling effect of sedition laws in India. *Economic and Political Weekly*, 46(8): 19–25.

News Desk (2022) PTM chief Manzoor Pashteen, four others declared proclaimed offenders in sedition case. *The Friday Times*. Available from: https://www.thefridaytimes.com/ptm-chief-manzoor-pashteen-four-others-declared-proclaimed-offenders-in-sedition-case/ [Accessed 17 March 2022].

Okonkwor, R.C. (1983) Nigeria's sedition laws: Their effect on free speech. *Journalism Quarterly*, 60(1): 54–60.

Owen, O. (2016) Policing after colonialism, in B. Bradford, B. Jauregui and I. Loader (eds) *The SAGE Handbook of Global Policing*. London: SAGE, pp 303–319.

Parmar, A. (2017) Intersectionality, British criminology and race: Are we there yet? *Theoretical Criminology*, 2(1): 35–45.

Phillips, C., Earle, R., Parmar, A. and Smith, D. (2020) Dear British criminology, where has all the race and racism gone? *Theoretical Criminology*, 24(3): 427–446.

Shah, H.A. (2022) Criminalizing the non-violent Pashtun Tahaffuz Movement: A profile of Ali Wazir. *Polis Project*. Available from: https://www.thepolisproject.com/read/criminalizing-the-non-violent-pashtun-movement-a-profile-of-ali-wazir/ [Accessed 15 March 2022].

Singh, A. (2018) *Sedition in Liberal Democracies*. New Delhi: Oxford University Press.

Singh, M. and Dasgupta, R. (2019) Exceptionalising democratic dissent: A study of the JNU event and its representations. *Postcolonial Studies*, 22(1): 59–78.

Sinha, C. (2019) *The Great Repression: The Story of Sedition in India*. India: Penguin Viking.

Veengas (2022) Pakistani state favours killers and punishes the innocent, alleges PTM founder. *The Wire*. Available from: https://thewire.in/south-asia/pakistan-pashtun-movement-military-power [Accessed 15 March 2022].

Waqar, A. (2020) Alamgir Wazir's bail petition dismissed by Lahore High Court. *Dawn*. Available from: https://www.dawn.com/news/1532820 [Accessed 20 February 2022].

Waseem, Z. (2021) 'Brothers in arms'? A police-paramilitary partnership in Karachi. *Policing and Society*, 31(2): 131–147.

Waseem, Z. (2022) *Insecure Guardians: Enforcement, Encounters, and Everyday Policing*. London: Hurst and Co.

Weis, V.V. (2022) *Criminalization of Activism: Historical, Present, and Future Perspectives*. London: Routledge.

Yonucu, D. (2018) Urban vigilantism: A study of anti-terror law, politics, and policing in Istanbul. *International Journal of Urban and Regional Research*, 42(3): 408–422.

Yousuf, F. (2020) Pakistan's 'tribal' Pashtuns, their 'violent' representation, and the Pashtun Tahafuz Movement. *SAGE Open*, January–March: 1–10.

PART II

Southern Institutions and Criminal Justice Politics

6

Reform, Restructure and Rebrand: Cursory Solutions to Historically Entrenched Policing Problems

Danielle Watson, Nathan W. Pino and Casandra Harry

Introduction

The acknowledgement of state police as important sociopolitical actors is not new (Tankebe, 2008). For many former colonies with complex diasporic histories, state police have always played a critical role in the establishment and maintenance of law and order, and often served as the most visible representation of the character of governance (Bayley, 2005). The contemporary shift in focus to a less confrontational image of police premised on the maintenance of democratic rule is largely viewed as an attempt to learn from past experiences (both local and foreign) and to disassociate from a British colonial policing model grounded in turbulent decolonization processes (Sinclair, 2017). For many countries in the global South, particularly small-island developing states (SIDS), attempts at rebranding police have neither significantly impacted police legitimacy nor positively impacted on community perceptions of police or policing (Trnka, 2011; Watson, 2016; Stamatakis, 2019; Adams, 2020). In such contexts, police legitimacy and accountability are constantly questioned.

The authenticity of the police 'service' agenda tends to be underscored by allegations of undemocratic and unlawful policing practices, along with large-scale public distrust and strongly expressed dissatisfaction with police and policing (Jauregui, 2013; Watson, 2016). Though different histories of colonial subjugation have shaped discourses on police and policing practices, several themes centred on questions of police legitimacy, fairness, susceptibility to political influence, lawfulness and monopoly of power remain concurrent throughout existing literature. Attempts at image management, posturing to gain public popularity and rebranding for improved relations with the public suggest either an awareness of a problem with the way police are perceived by the public or an identified need to revise policing strategies for improved service delivery (or both). What is evident is that the model of policing in former colonies remains a work in progress.

This chapter echoes sentiments about the importance of acknowledging colonial undercurrents that continue to inform governance processes which pervade concepts of law-and-order maintenance and enforcement. It draws on examples from Trinidad and Tobago (T&T) to support arguments about the proliferation of problematic policing models, demonstrative of the disconnect between the state and the larger populace. We draw on academic scholarship to show how the nature of policing in a former colony conflicts with contemporary policing concepts of service provision for members of marginalized groups. We further argue that attempts at police reform, restructuring or rebranding are unlikely to address issues of problematic police–community relations unless we acknowledge unrealistic claims about societal inclusivity and challenge exclusive and classist localized imperialist regimes that determine policing agendas.

This chapter has three sections. In the first, we provide an overview of the history of policing in T&T. We draw attention to the policing legacy of consent, cohesion and control that was established to protect a privileged few. In the second section, we discuss the maintenance of top-down colonial legacies and unpack the complications associated with such approaches in contemporary contexts. The third section explores postcolonial practices of importation and the impact of unstable governance arrangements on policing. We conclude the chapter by presenting modest recommendations for further consideration.

Policing former colonies: a legacy of consent, cohesion and control

In many former colonies, the establishment and presence of the state police emerged out of imperial objectives including political domination (Tankebe, 2008; Omeje and Githigaro, 2012). This arrangement has seen both local and foreign personnel charged with the responsibility and authority by the state to enforce and maintain law and order, and in many contexts this arrangement differed vastly from those that existed pre-colonization. While many police organizations have undergone significant changes and transformation, they still reflect imperial underpinnings which affect organizational function and legitimacy.

In T&T, policing in a formal sense began during the Spanish occupation starting in 1592. Six officers served under the management of the mayor in the capital, Port of Spain, while a ward watch system was implemented in country districts on other parts of the island (Ottley, 1964; De Verteuil, 1986). This arrangement lasted for two centuries until the British took control in 1797. The British expanded their sugar, coffee and cocoa plantations; and the island's population increased (Ottley, 1964). The British imperialists wanted to create a regulatory system to manage the masses by imposing new laws onto the Indigenous population (Jefferies, 1952). In his 1952 book *The Colonial Police*, Jefferies, who was the Deputy Under-Secretary of State for the Colonies, elucidated that the police's role in the colonies was based on the Royal Irish Constabulary rather than the Anglo-Saxon tradition. The colonial policing approach, emphasizing arbitrary and excessive force against the subjugated population, was thought by the colonialists to be more effective in preserving social order after the abolition of slavery in 1834 than the 'Peelian' model:

> [I]t is clear enough that from the point of view of the Colonies there was much attraction in an arrangement which provided what we should now call a paramilitary organisation or gendarmerie, armed, and trained to operate as an agent of the central government in a country where the population was predominantly rural, communications were poor, social conditions were largely primitive and the recourse to violence by members of the public who were against the government was not infrequent. It was natural that such a force, rather than one organized on the lines of the purely civilian and localized forces of Great Britain should have been taken as a suitable model for adaptation to Colonial conditions. (Jefferies, 1952: 31)

At that point, Governor Picton mandated compulsory enlistment of 'coloured men' to serve in the police force, leading many to assume that serving was a form of punishment (Ottley, 1964; De Verteuil, 1986: 29). Men from Ireland had to be brought in to fill the ranks because few local individuals wanted to join the police. A comprehensive set of rules to govern the police was then issued in 1835 (De Verteuil, 1986). English law was fully established by 1844, including trial by jury, because things were considered to be out of control (Ottley, 1964). By 1850, the Trinidadian police consisted of an inspector commandant, two sub-inspectors (one each in Port of Spain and San Fernando), ten sergeants and 100 constables consisting largely of lower-class Whites from Barbados (Ottley, 1964; De Verteuil, 1986). In 1862 a plainclothes inspector branch was instituted, and in 1874 five members of the Royal Ulster Constabulary (RUC) were appointed to reorganize and strengthen the branch. Ten years later in 1844, police pay increased and the

Police Force in Trinidad numbered 435, consisting primarily of Irish men (Ottley, 1964; De Verteuil, 1986). A little later, in the 1890s, the local senior inspector, a former RUC officer, modelled the local Police Force after the RUC, laying out San Fernando and Port of Spain into beats for purposes of crime prevention and detection (Ottley, 1964; De Verteuil, 1986).

In the late 1800s civil unrest against colonial rule became a concern. The police were tasked with quelling riots in the late 1800s, such as the Canboulay riots of 1881 and the Hosay Riots of 1884. The police were provided with firearms after a riotous crowd assaulted policemen in Arouca in 1891 (Ottley, 1964; De Verteuil, 1986). The water riots of 1903 led to protests against police brutality, but only one officer was put on trial and he was acquitted (Ottley, 1964).

Changes in 1905 to the Police Force provided the basis for how the police would function until the end of the colonial period. The Constabulary Ordinance of 1905 changed the police into an armed constabulary charged with paramilitary duties, detecting crime, repressing internal disturbances and defending the colony 'against external aggression' (Ottley, 1964: 115). By 1932, there were around 900 officers in the Police Force, almost all of them from Trinidad or Tobago, housed in 58 stations, four of which were in Tobago (Ottley, 1964). Fifteen men were formed into a local commando unit. Police continued to suppress riots and feuds between religious groups, in addition to controlling steel band activity (Ottley, 1964). By the 1950s, there were approximately 2,000 officers in the Police Force in T&T. At this time, the police started the 999-emergency call system, a police association was authorized, female officers were hired and new systems for recording crime were instituted (Ottley, 1964).

After T&T gained independence in 1962, the colonial model of policing continued in numerous ways well into the 2000s. In the 1980s and 1990s, various investigative reports found that the police were under-resourced, that morale was low, and that police deviance was rampant and found among all ranks. For example, the Committee on the Restructuring of the Police Service (CRPS) (1984) and another report by O'Dowd (1991) a few years later reported that ineffective police leadership led to a lack of interdepartmental communications, internal conflicts, managerial inefficiencies, uneven and unclear officer workloads, and ineffective disciplinary procedures. Citizens were harassed and repressed with impunity as the police engaged in arbitrary searches and arrests, destroyed the homes of squatters, and ignored urgent calls for service. In addition, internal investigations of police misconduct were never conducted (CRPS, 1984; O'Dowd, 1991). In between these two reports, Gavin Scott (1987) released what is known as the Scott Drug Report, revealing that members of the Trinidad and Tobago Police Service (TTPS) were heavily involved in the illegal drug trade. Officers were close associates of drug dealers and traffickers, and seized drugs were being recycled back into the illicit market. Seaby (1993) later discovered that police corruption had become even worse, with officers becoming wealthy from the drug trade, and officers at different ranks committing crimes including murder, rape, drug trafficking and evidence tampering. Promotions were based on whether an officer was a criminal associate alongside his superiors; officers developed a fatalistic attitude and engaged in various work-avoidance behaviours (Seaby, 1993).

Maintenance of top-down colonial legacies

The continuous international development of policing roles and responsibilities – largely due to globalization and the expanding criminal landscape – challenge police organizations to adapt (Den Heyer, 2013). Criminologists have described this internationalization of the policing agenda as fundamental to discourses about preventing and responding to cross-jurisdictional, multifaceted and multi-scaled criminal activities (Roelofse and Potgieter, 2018). They further recognize and highlight the importance of partnerships and collaboration for international, regional and national policing arrangements (Gerspacher, 2008; Lemieux, 2013). Knowledge sharing and collaboration in this sense provides necessary organizational support, while in some contexts also makes resources available to support operations.

While we recognize the importance of modernity arguments in criminological discourses and see value in knowledge mobility and drawing on lessons from other contexts, here we draw attention to operational legacies that neither align with 'best practices' in policing nor signal a shift towards the establishment of new or better practices. Scholars have attributed the continued compromise of arms of the governance machinery (such as the police) in SIDS to the endurance of problematic historically constructed institutions (Beland, 2009; Phillip-Durham, 2020). We show how the maintenance of colonial legacies impacts continuity at the organizational level and generally tends towards the continuation of previous approaches to problem solving as opposed to exploring strategies informed by empirical research on identified organizational shortcomings.

Political disruption

The existing parliamentary systems in T&T are highly representative of historical and continued implicit subscription to colonial legacies. T&T is categorized as a democratic state with executive and legislative branches of governance modelled after the British parliamentary system (the Westminster system). Despite constitutional reforms in T&T, scholars have drawn attention to the maintenance of the fundamentals of the Westminster system and governance arrangements, which distance Westernized local elites (who arguably embody characteristics of former colonial rulers) from the larger populace (Phillip-Durham, 2020). The arguable inauthenticity of the democratic system, high levels of political instability, bureaucratic bloating and interference with policing organizations do not augur well for organizational stability, strategic planning and agenda setting or general operations. The major political parties are still largely divided along ethnic lines (a legacy of divisions stoked by the British colonialists), and as soon as one party is out of power the new party jettisons previous initiatives. This political landscape, heavily underscored by colonial currents and strong sociopolitical heritage, continues to influence and impact on state organizations, particularly the police.

T&T's history of changes to the representative government along with relatively high levels of sporadic parliamentary reshuffles contribute to organizational uncertainty for police. Policing continues to be highly regime-oriented and subject to political interference. A former Commissioner of Police, Gary Griffith, publicly alleged political interference in the operations of the TTPS, a reality which he maintained resulted in him being pressured by politicians to influence appointments and termination of contracts for persons he employed during his tenure (Dowlat-Rostant, 2021). A lack of separation between the police and the ruling government, in a context where changes to the ruling political party occur regularly, means policing is highly subjected to shifting political whims (Pino, 2009; Watson and Kerrigan, 2018). Such circumstances present difficulties for stability, continuity and strategic planning. Reorganizations to suit governance changes occur, such as changes in leadership, where the 'top cop' position remains subject to political appointment; modifications to organizational and operational mandates; and discontinuation of policies implemented by previous governments.

Acceptable collateral damage: the backlash of adopting foreign policing models

Policing as a foreign concept

In addition to the imported model of policing in T&T, foreign policing policies and practices continue to be adopted without adequate adaptation to local contexts. Since the early 1990s, foreign policing policies and practices have been adopted in T&T. As we detail in this section, T&T and its police service sought and accepted numerous Western reforms that were not appropriate to the local conditions. These reforms were then adapted by local officials and police leaders in ways that suited their own interests. None of the reforms significantly changed police behaviour and were ultimately abandoned and replaced by another set of inappropriate imported reform efforts.

One significant example was the effort by the Association of Caribbean Commissioners of the Police to establish community policing in 1993 (Deosaran, 2002). Police leaders travelled abroad to the United Kingdom and United States to receive training and education on community policing. While T&T appeared to be the most committed in the region to community policing, there were concerns surrounding police capacity and conduct as well as citizen support (Deosaran, 2002). Support for community policing dwindled by 2002 in part because inadequate recruitment policies led to officers not suited for community policing getting hired, followed by inadequate supervision and oversight (Pino, 2009).

Academic research conducted after the failed community policing experiment found that ineffective, colonial-era policing still remained in the country. Police proactivity was limited and their responsiveness to calls for assistance was poor, citizens frequently had to travel to the police station to request police services and assistance, resources and equipment were often inadequate, supervision was poor, and legitimacy was low (Deosaran, 2002; Bennett and Morabito, 2006; Mastrofski and Lum, 2008). In addition, Amnesty International (2006) reported deaths in police custody, and claimed that the police officers had engaged in summary executions, kidnappings and various forms of harassment. Furthermore, authorities did not properly carry out investigations or sanction officers' misconduct.

Despite these early failures, community policing has been repackaged and exported to T&T over the years, including very recently (Mastrofski and Lum, 2008; Maguire et al, 2019). For example, Maguire et al (2010) report on a recently implemented pilot community policing programme in Gonzales, Trinidad, that aimed, in part, to reduce fear of crime among residents in the area. Prior to that, however, in 2006, a group of academics primarily from George Mason University (Virginia, USA) were brought in to implement major reforms based on the Northern Ireland reforms and Mastrofski's (1999) 'Policing for People', a model with elements of customer service principles and community policing (see Mastrofski and Lum, 2008). In addition to providing more vertical civilian control over the TTPS and giving more authority for hiring and firing to the police commissioner, the police were expected to become more service-oriented (developing more foot patrols, improving their interactions with community residents, and establishing victim assistance units). To facilitate this a number of 'model police stations' were established – in West End, San Fernando, Arouca, Chaguanas and Morvant – incorporating structural improvements and improved resources and equipment to help the police work more proactively (Mastrofski and Lum, 2008; Wallace, 2011).

Nevertheless, these reforms have still failed to significantly transform T&T policing, in part because the reforms were not suited to the postcolonial T&T context where the police had been accustomed to the colonial model and tended to resist community policing initiatives. There were various problems with management and training, including some officers using the training to get the opportunity to transfer elsewhere, high manager turnover and inadequate manager commitment (Wallace, 2011). Local non-governmental organizations (NGOs) also disapproved of these reforms, as these civil society groups were not sufficiently involved in the reform process, and thought that police deviance was still rampant, with officers remaining incompetent, corrupt, in collusion with criminals and continuing to engage in extrajudicial violence (Pino, 2009; Pino and Johnson, 2011; Wallace, 2011). In addition, police still saw largely citizens as a menace, viewing them as fractured, criminal and against the police (Wallace, 2012).

Pino (2009) interviewed local NGO leaders, and none of the interviewed leaders except one played any kind of role in the reforms; one NGO assisted with the creation of a model station for victims of domestic violence. Some had been involved in the first attempt at community policing years before, but most were unaware of the 2006 reforms or their outcomes (Pino, 2009). Those that were aware contended that the 2006 reforms had few positive outcomes, and that while the foreign consultants did try to do some good things (model stations, increases in officer pay and education, some of the TTPS restructuring) more systemic reforms and police officer buy-in were needed. In the end, many thought that paying foreign consultants was a waste of money and that the foreign consultants should not have been leading reform efforts (Pino, 2009).

The T&T government tried yet again to reform the police by appointing Canadian police leaders to top positions: Dwayne Gibbs was appointed as the Commissioner of the TTPS from 2010 to 2012, and along with Jack Ewatski and Steve Watt, he implemented what he called a '21st century policing' model (Wallace, 2011). A new police academy was established to implement a modern training program lasting 24 weeks, followed by eight weeks of field training (Dowlat, 2010). Police were expected to undertake foot and mobile patrols, as under previous attempts at reform. Again, the proposed reforms were met with resistance by the police, and only one-third of potential recruits passed the new entry-level requirements examinations (see Pino, 2021). After one year, an evaluation found that the new initiative was plagued by infrastructural and equipment challenges, a lack of enthusiasm for embracing technology, poor management by officers at all levels, and laziness on the part of some junior officers (Kowlessar, 2012). The Deputy Commissioner at the time, Stephen Williams, a native of T&T who later became the Acting Commissioner, thought that the police were becoming more proactive than in the recent past, but that the police did not show consistent quality, that police–community relations were still poor, and that criminals acted with relative impunity, causing community members to lose hope (Wallace, 2014).

The '21st century policing' model was scrapped soon afterwards and the Canadian leaders were replaced, in part because they were viewed unfavourably by the Minister of National Security at the time, Jack Warner. That being said, some elements of the initiative were retained, such as the internal unit investigating serious police misconduct allegations and the police education and training programmes (Pino, 2021). After this, Stephen Williams became Acting Commissioner and implemented new 'evidence-based policing' and hot-spot policing models. Three hundred additional officers were hired, half of whom were women (Pino, 2021). T&T still sought foreign assistance, however. Former New York Mayor Rudy Giuliani and New York City Police Commissioner William Bratton, both known for implementing 'zero-tolerance policing' in New York City, then arrived in January of 2015 to conduct an audit of the TTPS geared towards improving investigation methods, forensic testing and the crime detection rate (Clark, 2014). The audit was designed to highlight the needs of the TTPS, including improvements in intelligence gathering, covert operations, and creating new units such as a special victims unit, child protection task force, and other units to increase the crime detection rate (Ministry of National Security, 2014). The team (Giuliani Solution Point Global Services LLC) was also offering to assist with more proactive policing methods including foot patrols, customer service improvements, improving police–community relations, enhanced computerized statistics for increasing effectiveness and efficiency, anti-corruption initiatives, building cases against gang leaders and the 'proper application of the broken window theory in Trinidad and Tobago' (Ministry of National Security, 2014). No information, however, could be found by the authors of this chapter regarding the outcome of this audit, so it is assumed that the audit remained within the TTPS and was not released to the press or the public.

In sum, since the 1990s the TTPS has undergone numerous reform initiatives borrowed from the global North, often adopted in a piecemeal fashion and without any long-term strategic approach. The police in T&T continues to be perceived as incompetent, overly-militarized, violent, repressive and abusive. Police cynicism and fatalism remain common among police leaders who lack faith in officers under their command. Police typically view citizens with hostility and feel powerless to stop powerful criminals who are connected with the government and appear to act with impunity (Watson et al, 2018; Pino, 2021). What we have seen is that newly elected and appointed government officials terminate the reform initiatives of their predecessors while spearheading new initiatives of their own that are not all that different from the previous ones, while making the same false promises. Most of these initiatives have been variations of what has been promoted as community or democratic policing, promoted as a one-size-fits-all panacea from the North that can be unproblematically exported to Southern countries without having to consider the recipient country's history or context (Brogden, 2002; Pino and Wiatrowski, 2006; Ellison and Pino, 2012). Community policing has often been unable to transform policing in the global North, and yet it is marketed as a universally applicable best practice for Southern countries, a product of social progress able to overcome inequalities and political or ethnic conflict (Brogden, 2002; Blair et al, 2021). This export of contemporary policing models follows the same well-trodden paths experienced under colonialism:

> Like colonial policing, [community-oriented policing] is a particular historically and contextually bound creation. Unlike colonial policing, it does not have the same force majeure in its mission. However, like its colonial predecessor, its proponents and supporters ignore history and context in the process of transmission and installation. When it is finally rebuffed by the locals, its proponents similarly – as in the colonial period – are bemused by the ungrateful locals who fail to appreciate the inevitability of the convergence of social development through the logic of industrialism. Diversity is ignored and a unitary path presumed. (Brogden, 2002: 179)

Conclusion

Given the resilience of colonial legacies, political fragmentation, and failed and inappropriate top-down police reform efforts met with resistance by police and local NGOs, where do we go from here? While reforming, restructuring and rebranding are promoted as positive steps that can transform policing, it is important that such initiatives reflect authenticity, local ownership and locally appropriate, locally supported systemic changes that can withstand variations in political and police leadership. Reforming, restructuring and rebranding using the usual Western best practices as a political stunt, or without a clear plan of continuity, or unaccompanied by sound strategic planning, are often an inappropriate and costly use of human, financial, institutional and social resources, that can end up by further eroding police legitimacy and impacting public trust in the police and government.

Locally derived initiatives are paramount, for it is debatable as to how far policing, in both the United States and other Northern developed jurisdictions, has been significantly reformed in any meaningful way in practice (Vitale, 2017). Why export a paradigm of policing rooted in imperialism, colonial conquest and slave patrols, and aligned with the interests of the powerful and able to perpetuate human rights abuses with impunity? In professional policing, the police are typically reactive, increasingly paramilitarized and often lack effectiveness, resulting in various abuses of marginalized citizens. But even in community policing, where the police are supposed to be proactive, organizational structures and cultures have not been transformed and traditional (un)professional practices are retained (see Pino and Wiatrowski, 2006). These forms of policing are then exported, often with the interests of donors outweighing those of the recipient country, from the top down and frequently without meaningful civil society participation.

Not only do we need to see locally derived initiatives, but 'the local' must also include those that local elites and foreign donors may not wish to be considered as part of the legitimate local stakeholders: women and traditionally marginalized groups, including local NGOs and social movements that have an – often overlooked – capacity and local knowledge. As Pino (2021) contends, restructuring policing should be seen as but one part of a larger holistic approach to transformative justice geared towards human rights, civil liberties, gender equity, legal reform and citizen empowerment. Local NGOs and social movements can play a variety of roles to provide oversight, build social capital, and promote legitimacy and sustainability. This cannot be achieved without a long-term, holistic approach that eschews the status quo.

References

Adams, E.B. (2020) Police legitimacy in Trinidad and Tobago: Resident perceptions in a high-crime community. *Journal of Crime and Justice*, 43(1): 78–92. https://doi.org/10.1080/0735648X.2019.1582350

Amnesty International (2006) *Annual Report: The State of the World's Human Rights*. London: Amnesty International.

Bayley, D.H. (2005) *Changing the Guard: Developing Democratic Police Abroad*. Oxford: Oxford University Press.

Beland, D. (2009) Ideas, institutions, and policy change. *Journal of European Public Policy*, 16(5): 701–718.

Bennett, R. and Morabito, M. (2006) Determinants of constables' perceptions of community support in three developing nations. *Police Quarterly*, 9(2): 234–265.

Blair, G., Weinstein, J.M., Christia, F., Arias, E., Badran, E., Blair, R.A., et al (2021) Community policing does not build citizen trust in police or reduce crime in the Global South. *Science*, 374(6571): 1–14. https://www.science.org/doi/10.1126/science.abd3446

Brogden, M. (2002) Implementing community policing in South Africa: A failure of history, of context, and of theory. *Liverpool Law Review*, 24: 157–179.

Clark, C. (2014) Giuliani, Bratton back next month: Griffith. *Trinidad and Tobago Guardian*, 13 December.

Committee on the Restructuring of the Police Service (1984) *Report of the Committee on the Restructuring of the Police Service*. Port of Spain: Republic of Trinidad and Tobago.

De Verteuil, A. (1986) *Sylvester Devenish and the Irish in Nineteenth Century Trinidad*. Port-of-Spain, Trinidad and Tobago: Paria.

Den Heyer, G. (2013) Shape or adapt: The future of policing. *Salus Journal*, 1(1): 41–54.

Deosaran, R. (2002) Community policing in the Caribbean: Context, community, and police capability. *Policing: An International Journal of Police Strategies and Management*, 25(1): 125–146.

Dowlat, R. (2010) New positions at police academy. *Trinidad and Tobago Newsday*, 12 April. Available from: https://archives.newsday.co.tt/2010/04/12/new-positions-at-police-academy/ [Accessed 15 February 2020].

Dowlat-Rostant, R. (2021) 40 people hired by Griffity, fired on the spot from TTPS. *Trinidad and Tobago Guardian Newspaper*, 25 October. Available from: https://www.guardian.co.tt/news/40-people-hired-by-griffith-fired-on-the-spot-from-ttps-6.2.1404956.cdce8b3cb4 [Accessed 15 November 2022].

Ellison, G. and Pino, N. (2012) *Globalization, Police Reform and Development: Doing it the Western Way?* Cham: Springer.

Gerspacher, N. (2008) The history of international police cooperation: A 150-year evolution in trends and approaches. *Global Crime*, 9(1–2): 169–184.

Jauregui, B. (2013) Cultures of legitimacy and postcolonial policing: Guest editor introduction. *Law & Social Inquiry*, 38(3): 547–552.

Jefferies, C. (1952) *The Colonial Police*. London: Max Parish.

Kowlessar, G. (2012) Report on 21st century policing project: Poor management, lazy cops. *The Trinidad and Tobago Guardian*, 6 May. Available from: https://www.guardian.co.tt/article-6.2.421791.3ddacc6ca1 [Accessed 15 November 2022].

Lemieux, F. (ed) (2013) *International Police Cooperation: Emerging Issues, Theory and Practice*. New York: Routledge.

Maguire, E.R., King, W.R., Johnson, D. and Katz, C.M. (2010) Why homicide clearance rates decrease: Evidence from the Caribbean. *Policing & Society*, 20(4): 373–400.

Maguire, E.R., Johnson, D., Kuhns, J. and Apostolos, R. (2019) The effects of community policing on fear of crime and perceived safety: Findings from a pilot project in Trinidad and Tobago. *Policing and Society*, 29(5): 491–510.

Mastrofski, S. (1999) *Policing for People*. Washington, DC: Police Foundation.

Mastrofski, S. and Lum, C. (2008) Meeting the challenges of police governance in Trinidad and Tobago. *Policing*, 2(4): 481–496.

Ministry of National Security (Trinidad and Tobago) (2014) *Trinidad and Tobago Police Service to Serve You Better – Complete Audit Coming Soon*. Government of the Republic of Trinidad and Tobago. Available from: http://www.news.gov.tt/content/trinidad-and-tobago-police-service-serve-you-better-complete-audit-coming-soon#.YfK5FvXMJAd [Accessed 15 November 2022].

O'Dowd, D.J. (1991) *Review of the Trinidad and Tobago Police Service*. Port of Spain: Republic of Trinidad and Tobago.

Omeje, K.C. and Githigaro, J.M. (2012) The challenges of state policing in Kenya. *Peace & Conflict Studies*, 7(1): 1–32.

Ottley, C.R. (1964) *A Historical Account of the Trinidad and Tobago Police Force from the Earliest Times*. Glasgow: Robert MacLehose and Company Ltd.

Phillip-Durham, G. (2020) Ideas and impact: Continuity, change and constraints in the institutional landscape of Curaçao, Sint Maarten, and Trinidad and Tobago. *Island Studies Journal*, 15(1): 113–130.

Pino, N.W. (2009) Developing democratic policing in the Caribbean: The case of Trinidad and Tobago. *Caribbean Journal of Criminology and Public Safety*, 14(1&2): 214–258.

Pino, N.W. (2021) Transformative police reform in Trinidad and Tobago: Prospects and challenges. *Policing: A Journal of Policy and Practice*, 15(1): 373–386.

Pino, N.W. and Johnson, L.M. (2011) Police deviance and community relations in Trinidad and Tobago. *Policing: An International Journal of Police Strategies & Management*, 34(3): 454–478. https://doi.org/10.1108/13639511111157519

Pino, N.W. and Wiatrowski, M.D. (2006) *Democratic Policing in Transitional and Developing Countries*. Aldershot: Ashgate.

Roelofse, C. and Potgieter, P. (2018) Cybercrime, politics and their significance in the internationalisation of policing: Perspectives of academics and practitioners. *Acta Criminologica: African Journal of Criminology & Victimology*, 31(3): 161–175.

Scott, G. (1987) *Report of the Commission of Enquiry Into the Extent of the Problem of Drug Abuse in Trinidad and Tobago*. Trinidad and Tobago: Government Printery.

Seaby, G. (1993) *Final Report for the Government of Trinidad and Tobago on Investigations Carried out by Officers From New Scotland Yard in Respect of Allegations Made by Rodwell Murray and Others About Corruption in the Trinidad and Tobago Police Service*. London: Metropolitan Police Office.

Sinclair, G. (2017) *At the End of the Line: Colonial Policing and the Imperial Endgame 1945–80*. Manchester: Manchester University Press.

Stamatakis, N. (2019) Perceptions of incarcerated youth about police violence and legitimacy in Trinidad and Tobago. *Journal of Police and Criminal Psychology*, 34(3): 314–329.

Tankebe, J. (2008) Colonialism, legitimation, and policing in Ghana. *International Journal of Law, Crime and Justice*, 36(1): 67–84. https://doi.org/https://doi.org/10.1016/j.ijlcj.2007.12.003

Trnka, S. (2011) Re-mythologizing the state: Public security, 'the Jesus strategy' and the Fiji police. *Oceania*, 81(1): 72–87.

Vitale, A. (2017) *The End of Policing*. London: Verso.

Wallace, W.C. (2011) Introduction of a community involvement component in policing in Trinidad and Tobago: Reality or rhetoric? International Police Executive Symposium, Geneva Centre for the Control of Armed Forces and Cognita – For Police Reforms and Community Safety. Working Paper No 37, pp 1–45.

Wallace, W.C. (2012) Findings from a concurrent study on the level of community involvement in the policing process in Trinidad and Tobago. *The Police Journal*, 85: 61–83.

Wallace, W.C. (2014) Stephen Williams, Deputy Commissioner of Police, Trinidad and Tobago Police Service, in B.F. Baker and D.K. Das (eds) *Trends in Policing: Interviews with Police Leaders Across the Globe*. Boca Raton: CRC Press, pp 73–90.

Watson, D. (2016) 'Hotspot policing': A comparative analysis of sanctioned acts of policing versus media representations of policing in a stigmatized community in Trinidad. *Police Practice and Research*, 17(6): 520–530.

Watson, D. and Kerrigan, D. (2018) Crime, criminality, and north-to-south criminological complexities: Theoretical implications for policing 'hotspot' communities in 'underdeveloped' countries, in K. Carrington, R. Hogg, J. Scott and M. Sozzo (eds) *The Palgrave Handbook of Criminology and the Global South*. Cham: Springer International Publishing, pp 611–632. https://doi.org/10.1007/978-3-319-65021-0_30

Watson, D., Boateng, D., Pino, N.W. and Morgan, P. (2018) The interface between exercise of state power and personal powerlessness: A study of police perceptions of factors impacting professional practices. *Police Practice and Research*, 19(5): 458–471.

7

Democratic Policing in Authoritarian Structures: Policing Models and the Exercise of Authority in São Paulo, Brazil

Viviane de Oliveira Cubas, Frederico Castelo Branco and André Rodrigues Oliveira

Introduction

The police are one of the main actors in a democracy because policing is among the public services that most affects people's lives. Public policing shapes social and economic opportunities and, consequently, limits the freedom of individuals to live out their own lives. Thus, one of the tasks of police forces should be to ensure the fulfilment of democratic values for all members of society. Values such as equality, equity, participation in decisions and responsiveness are manifested when police services meet the needs of the public: if coercion is used only exceptionally and in proportion to the seriousness of the transgression; when they are receptive to public opinion about public safety policy; and when they act transparently and remove incompetent or malicious employees from their roles (Jones et al, 1996).

In terms of promoting democratic values, the influence of the police goes further. Police have the power to generate a sense of belonging to a political community, which leads to the public's commitment to democratic institutions (Loader, 2006). This sense of belonging comes from experience and the expectation that institutions, including the police, recognize the legitimate rights of all members of society. The police also function as a mediator of collective identity, a social institution that acts to recognize or deny, sometimes coercively, which voices will be heard or silenced, what claims will be considered legitimate, and how individuals and groups are integrated into the social fabric. The police do not merely guard the community, they also produce meanings about the kind of place that community is or should be (Loader, 2006). Therefore, the quality of policing has a direct impact on the quality of life in a democracy (Goldstein, 1977). The police are therefore an important indicator of the quality of a community's government and its democracy (Jones et al, 1996).

The way the police exercise their authority reflects the relationship between the state and its citizens. As the main state instrument to claim the monopoly of the legitimate use of violence in society, the police can be both a guarantor of, and a threat to, the security of citizens, and must resolve this equation in a way that meets the security demands of all social groups. This equation becomes rather more complicated when dealing with police forces originating in colonial powers, where the police's function first emerged as a highly militarized agency imposing an alien and external authority on an Indigenous population that did not have citizen status. This suggests that the way a society is policed depends substantially upon who is being policed, by whom and in whose interests. If it involves citizens, with civil and political rights, policing is undertaken carefully; but if the subjects are not citizens, the police may be free to exercise force without restraint (Anderson and Killingray, 1991, and see Squires, Chapter 2, this volume). The police's exercise of state authority is constrained somewhat by the extent to which the population is recognized as citizens and where the rule of law prevails (Waddington, 1999).

In the Latin American context, with states inheriting long colonial traditions, and where the armed forces and the police played important roles in supporting authoritarian regimes, the recognition of citizenship is still a crucial problem to be resolved in the process of consolidating democracy. Such recognition relies on social and cultural changes (Caldeira and Holston, 1999). The transitions to democracy in Brazil were relatively shallow, changing formal political institutions but leaving out deeper transformations at the level of citizenship and citizen–state relations, making the regimes vulnerable to illiberal regression (Pereira, 2021: 369).

Looking at Brazil specifically, two elements influence the structure and functioning of the police: militarization and extrajudicial activities. These elements were not new in police practices but were more firmly entrenched during the military dictatorship (1964–1985). With the transition to democracy, there were some advances in the professionalization and modernization of police forces. However, abusive practices have persisted, affecting mainly the poorest and most marginalized communities (Pinheiro, 1991).

Brazilian police officers are frequently involved in extrajudicial police killings, but also are killed in large numbers. In the state of São Paulo alone, with a population of 44 million inhabitants and the largest police force in the country (approximately 82,000 military police and 19,000 civil police), 814 people were killed by the police in 2020 (São Paulo State Public Security Secretary, 2021). During this same year, 51 police officers died, most of them while off duty, when they were engaged in other employment activities, usually as private security guards (São Paulo State Public Security Secretary, 2021). Another characteristic of police forces in São Paulo is that the quality of their work is assessed using 'efficiency' indicators. The quest for outcomes – measured exclusively by the numbers of police calls responded to, stops carried out, weapons and drugs seized, arrests made, and so on – is the primary means by which the police try to legitimize their authority.

This scenario is in stark contrast to the measures that have been adopted by the police in liberal democracies of the global North. They have focused their attention on the procedures used by their agents when interacting with the public. Especially among police forces in the Anglo-American traditions, procedural justice theory (PJT) has provided support for efforts to improve police work. PJT is based on Tom Tyler's model of social regulation, that is, a figure of authority, in order to be recognized among its subordinates as having the right to make decisions and give orders, must exercise their power impartially as well as fairly and respectfully (Tyler, 2006).

As McLaughlin (2007) has argued, police historians in the Anglo-Saxon world have tended to celebrate a tradition of authority rooted in the idea of consent, although this is now much more contested (Elliott-Cooper, 2021). Although abstract and contested, the idea has provided a moral and philosophical basis for police reform (Jacobs, 2016). Since the police in the global South are not as open to accountability in the form of studies, there is a tendency to adopt ideas and theories from the global North as if they could be applied in other contexts (Loader et al, 2016). In light of Brazil's historical particularities, its current political system and the organization of public security institutions, we present in this chapter a critical analysis of PJT. This is a way to understand the perception of democratic policing among police officers in the city of São Paulo in the context of an authoritarian legacy, tremendous social inequality and a logic of police forces tasked with social control.

Policing in Brazil

The police in Brazil were organized at the state level rather than as a national or local force, with each Brazilian state having two separate police forces responsible for public security activities: a civil police (PC) and a military police (PM). They are independent police institutions that share policing duties. The PM, made up of uniformed police officers, is responsible for overt and preventive policing. The PC is responsible for registering and investigating crimes, and these activities are carried out by plainclothes police officers. Despite being based on Brazil's democratic 1988 constitution, this model is essentially the same as the one implemented by the authoritarian military regime (1964–1985). However, this model was not created by the military government. The roots of the institutional architecture of the current public security system go back to the country's first police forces.

The transfer of the Portuguese royal family to Rio de Janeiro in 1808, at a moment when the crown intended to develop its project to civilize the colony, is the watershed event in the formation of the first police apparatus. It was during this period that the government created the General Police Intendancy (1808), the embryo of the Civil Police, and the Royal Police Guard (1809), the embryo of the PM – both inspired by the Lisbon model with its close military connections (O'Reilly, 2018), which in turn had its origins in the 'French model' of policing (Bretas and Rosemberg, 2013).

The General Police Intendancy centralized the roles of the political police, public security force and the promoter of general wellbeing. The intendant had power to decide on what behaviours were considered criminal, to establish appropriate punishments, and to arrest, judge, convict and supervise the execution of sentences (Batitucci, 2010). Meanwhile, the Royal Guard constituted the force tasked with ensuring the imperial social order – in a colonial context characterized by enslavement, which resulted in an eminently repressive and discriminatory police apparatus. It is in this context that a policing system was implanted in this Portuguese colony in the Americas, based on the maintenance of order and operationalized through military corps (Cotta, 2012).

This division of responsibilities served as a model for the provinces. During the period of the Brazilian Empire (1822–1889), the police focused on repressing slave revolts and abolitionist and republican movements. In the republican period (from 1889 onward), it started to take part in the repression of workers' strikes as well, at a time of urbanization, industrialization and the formation of a working class (Fernandes, 1974). It was during this republican period that the process of professionalizing São Paulo's police forces began.

The PC, created in 1905, laid out the duties of the chiefs of the civil police, who were asked to manage a newly formed cadre of paid professionals who would carry out the civil, judicial and investigative police functions. The military characteristics of a section of the police – which would later become the PM – were the result in the state of São Paulo of the French mission (1906–1914). French Army officers were hired to help organize the police, instituting an organizational framework that followed the criteria of military hierarchy and training (Dallari, 1977). The PM, as it exists today, is the result of a lengthy process of greater or lesser militarization of these organizations.

The 1964 military coup led to the greatest divide in the history of the PM, promoting the federalization of public security and leading to a reorganization of police forces across the country (1967). Policing the streets was entrusted exclusively to uniformed police, organized under a military hierarchy and under the control of the Armed Forces, reducing the prestige of other corporations (Guerra, 2016: 19).

During the transition to democracy (1983), the police was distanced from the army. Command of the PM returned to the hands of state governors, and the general command of the institution was now exercised by officers of the PM itself instead of by army officers. During the preparation of the democratic constitution (1988), proposals such as the demilitarization of police patrols or the unification of the two police forces were not discussed in depth, with debates around military and corporate interests prevailing. The military contours were allegedly softened by ending subordination to the army, preserving 'only' the hierarchy, discipline and military structure, aspects presented as fundamental for controlling police abuses and corruption within such a large force.

Both the PM and the PC are hierarchically and administratively subordinate to each state's secretaries of public security, with the state governors being their direct commanders, although each police force answers to a commander from their own institution. Neither police force has a unified career track. The PM is separated into officers and enlisted personnel, the former occupying the highest levels of management and command, with greater professional prestige and higher salaries; the enlisted personnel oversee operational activities. The two groups constitute distinct career tracks, each with its own admission, selection and training process. The PCs are divided into police chiefs, who also have greater professional prestige and higher salaries in their institution, and who, in addition to police attributions, are responsible for managing the police station.

Meanwhile, the subordinate careers – police investigator and police clerk – function as a distinct career path. In both police forces, entry into high-level careers requires greater availability of time and resources for training, making it difficult for those already active in the profession to enter those higher ranks, essentially preventing street-level police officers and their accumulated professional knowledge from having an influence on management positions. In this structure, lower-ranking PM or PC members frequently must submit to the command of officers and chiefs who have spent less time doing police work than they have.

As a result, Brazil is one of the few countries in the world that maintains a fragmented police system (Sapori, 2018). This model, which leads to bureaucracies with completely different forms of organization – one civil and the other military – is considered one of the main sources of inefficiency in police work in Brazil. It leads to antagonism and tension due to corporatist interests and prerogatives in police activities, in addition to the practice of one force blaming the inefficiencies of police work on the other.

Police–citizen contacts in the hands of military police officers

Another important aspect of the Brazilian model is that police officers who are socialized and inserted in a military mindset are responsible for policing civilians. Soldiers, corporals and sergeants of the PM are responsible for answering calls from the population and patrolling the streets. The disadvantages of a militarized organizational model when exercising public security tasks are well-known, such as the concentration of decision-making at the highest ranks, limiting and undermining the discretion of front-line officers in their interactions with the public; the tendency towards police performance evaluations that focus on 'quantification' (arrests, convictions) rather than the quality of street-level policing and safety (Skolnick and Fyfe, 1993). Throughout the 20th century, in order to adapt to the requirements of their roles, many police forces around the world with their origins in military systems became increasingly differentiated from the armies, incorporating aspects of a more recognizable police identity (Reames, 2008; Sozzo, 2016; Costa, 2021). In other parts of the world, however, concern has been expressed about policing systems becoming increasingly militarized (Jefferson, 1990; Kraska and Kappeler, 1997; Wright, 1998; Balko, 2014), suggesting processes of convergence rather than militarization/demilitarization (Andreas and Nadelmann, 2006).

Brazil's PM reproduces the army's functional structure, whose pillars are hierarchy and discipline. The army's values and moral principles imprint a strong military identity on the PM that goes beyond the use of military ranks and symbols, manifesting also as a military ethos (Castro, 2004). The construction of this identity begins with the professional socialization of PM officers carried out at the police academy, when the transition process from civilian life to military life takes place. It involves a process of dissolving one's civilian identity and civilian sensibilities, breaking with old values and acquiring a new military identity whose interactions strongly centred on the new group, generating what Castro (2004) defines as 'the military spirit'. Military personnel, in general, perceive themselves not only as different from civilians, but also superior to them because they have distinctive qualities, both physical (including posture, intonation of one's voice and notions of personal hygiene) and moral (sense of honesty and righteousness of character, concern with 'noble and high' causes such as the homeland, spirit of renunciation, and a respect for order, discipline and hierarchy) (Castro, 2004).

The organization of members into different ranks and careers leads to their own rules of social interaction that distinguish and differentiate each person's sense of place. Hierarchy in the PM not only serves to attribute responsibilities and competences to each member but, more than that, it is a way of demarcating the 'distinctive differences' among its members, where individuals overlap each other according to the power inherent to each stratum of the hierarchy. Thus, we have an identity that is strongly forged in social norms that distinguish and hierarchize authority in two ways: the distinction in relation to the civilian world, and the distinction among its own members (Galvão, 2016).

The demonstration of respect is an obligation required by military codes, and the officer who does not express deference to those who occupy higher ranks in the hierarchy is subject to sanctions. The control structure is strongly reactive and individualized, with a disciplinary regiment that severely limits the basic rights of police officers and often punishes behaviour that, in the civilian world, is tolerated and commonplace (Cano and Duarte, 2012). Instead of imbuing discipline with a positive characteristic, promoting self-regulation and encouraging police officers to uphold the reputation of their profession, it focuses on the threat of punishment for any mistakes. Discipline is thus considered a threat and not a source of pride (Bayley, 2001).

The military model adopted by Brazil's PM highlights even more negative characteristics common to police intuitions, such as social isolation and distrust of the outside world (Reiner, 2004), or the antagonism between those police officers who patrol the street ('street cops') and their police managers ('management cops') (Reuss-Ianni, 1983). It also makes explicit the contradiction of having police officers governed by military codes and justice but inserted into and responsible for dealing with problems in the civilian community, governed by civil legislation that is enforced by a civil and democratic judicial branch.

Military hierarchy and discipline, so important to the institution, seem to contribute little to and in fact harm the quality of police work, as they produce a model of authority that does not need to present justifications. In this model, authority is perceived almost exclusively as an axiomatic authority. An order must be obeyed without question, and the uncritical submission to norms is understood as an expression of righteousness. This type of power relationship dilutes the idea that securing the position of authority carries with it burdens, obligations and the presentation of justifications.

This entire universe of values and its inherent worldview are not limited to relationships within the institution, but spill over to relationships with the civilian world, which, governed by democratic norms, often leads to a mismatch of expectations. Is it possible, in this context, to reconcile the military model of supervision and control – with its rigid hierarchy, lack of room for dialogue, a system of differentiation and distancing that privileges vigilance within a coercive model of obedience – with the capacity and willingness of police officers to act in accordance with democratic principles?

Democratic police and procedural justice

Jones et al (1996) indicate seven 'democratic criteria' that could be applied to thinking how such adaptation of police activity to democratic principles would occur:

1. *Equity* in treatment means processing a real-life situation based on the notion of equality and justice, keeping in mind that every citizen and group has the same rights and legal protections.
2. *Participation* expresses the possibility of being part of and influencing authorities' decisions that directly affect citizens' lives.
3. *Information* refers to the transparency of police activities – that is, decisions need to be justified and well-informed, providing clarity about the criteria and procedures that guide police action.
4. *Responsiveness* indicates that the actions of the police (and government) should reflect the expectations, interests, needs and demands of citizens.
5. *Delivery of service* indicates the need to seek to act efficiently and effectively, since this implies the degree of satisfaction with the service offered and the image of the police.
6. *Redress* means that complaints about deviations will be forwarded and investigated, and that unfair and adverse measures must be reversed, with some kind of reparation when necessary.
7. *Distribution of power* highlights the importance that no one group within a police power structure always prevails over the others – which is especially important in institutions that are a fundamental part of the repressive framework of the state.

If we consider that in democracies the authority's right to govern is recognized and consented to by the governed, it is essential to observe the way in which power is exercised. During the past two decades, several studies share the idea that some criteria – such as equity, participation and information, among others – are a central part of authorities' decision-making processes and are strongly associated with the public's attitudes and perceptions about the legitimacy of these authorities (Donner et al, 2015; Nagin and Telep, 2017). These studies – in what is named by PJT – propose that authority based on the recognition of legitimacy derives from citizens' subjective perceptions that said authority is used in a fair and procedural way. This means that the justice/fairness of the adopted procedures promote and sustain the belief that the police have legitimate authority and deserve to be obeyed (Tyler, 1990; Sunshine and Tyler, 2003; Hinds and Murphy, 2007; Tyler and Fagan, 2008; Hough et al, 2010).

Procedural justice consists of a minimum core of four features: *participation, neutrality, honesty* and *respect* (Tyler, 1990). *Participation* (or *voice*) refers to the possibility of presenting one's arguments and the expectation that one's version will be considered by an authority during the decision-making process. *Neutrality* (or *equity*) indicates that all individuals, regardless of their particular characteristics (gender, age, ethnicity, social class, place of residence, work, and so on), will be treated impartially and objectively. This creates the expectation that decision-making is based on objectivity and consistent facts, which then entails an evaluation of the *honesty* (*trustworthiness/fairness*) of those in power. Finally, the perception of politeness and courtesy derived from a dignified and *respectful* treatment denotes the morality and civility of authority (Tyler, 2006; Reisig et al, 2007).

Criminal justice studies of police and procedural justice are located mainly in what is called the global North (especially the United States, United Kingdom and Australia) and have developed in two directions. One of them, in which most of the work is concentrated, deals with the perceptions of citizens about compliance with procedural justice by police officers as an explanatory variable of perceptions about satisfaction with police services, willingness to cooperate, trust and, above all, the legitimacy of police forces. The other strand addresses police officers' perceptions of procedural justice within their own organizations and its association with perceptions of police work, organization and self-confidence in the exercise of authority that is conferred to police officers (self-legitimacy) (Tankebe, 2011; Donner et al, 2015).

Overall, these studies affirm the importance of fair procedures both for public perceptions of police authority and for the organizational environment of the police. Procedural justice is positively associated with perceptions of legitimacy and trust in the police, making feasible a policing model that is desirable not only in ethical terms – because it strives for respect, information and honesty – but also because it generates greater willingness to cooperate and comply among the public (Tyler, 2006; Jackson et al, 2012; Mazerolle et al, 2013). Procedural justice carried out internally in police organizations is positively associated with greater confidence among police officers in their own authority, thus exercising it in a way that is more aligned with organizational goals and democratic values (Bradford and Quinton, 2014; Nix and Wolfe, 2015).

If the kind of policing expected in a democracy is something that promotes the perception of procedural justice in citizens, the capacity and willingness to act in this way requires the perception that internal relations within police organizations are just. According to Van Craen (2016), the conduct of supervisors can serve as a model of behaviour that is followed by subordinate police officers. Thus, the way police officers treat citizens, and their ability to respond to the various social dilemmas they face in their daily activities on the streets, may be related to how much the behaviour of superiors is guided by principles such as neutrality, respect, voice and accountability.

In this sense, there is a direct link between the way police officers exercise power on the streets and internal dynamics between police officers and their superiors and their status.

In addition to the interpersonal relationships between police officers and superiors, it is plausible that general perceptions about internal decision-making processes, transparency regarding the guidelines and results (organizational justice), and even about the way resources, work, goods and rewards are distributed within the organization (distributive justice), may also have consequences for officers' identification with and commitment to the police organization (Bradford and Quinton, 2014; Nix and Wolfe, 2015), and as a consequence, affecting their relationship with the public. In general terms, police officers' perceptions about the organization and quality of internal relations are important in promoting or inhibiting certain modes of policing, although the maintenance of internal order in police organizations is not disconnected from the maintenance and reproduction of the broader social order in which the police play a leading role (Loader, 2006). In this sense, democratic policing is the bearer and promoter of values and constitutive norms of democratic societies, which imply respecting and promoting fundamental rights, being clear about the limits of and proportionality in the use of force, and being accessible, informative, cooperative and accountable to the community and the general public (Bradford and Quinton, 2014).

Support for democratic policing in São Paulo

Considering how the principles of procedural justice theory can bring us closer to a policing strategy that is better aligned with the kind of relationships expected in substantively democratic regimes between citizens and authority, can this be extended to the case of São Paulo? Based on data from a survey conducted in 2016 by the Center for the Study of Violence of the University of São Paulo involving military and civil police officers who work in the city, we sought to think about how internal (officer) perceptions about justice in the procedures of São Paulo police may (or may not) be related to support for democratic forms of policing (Cubas and Castelo Branco, 2019).

Our general hypothesis is that internal relations, both with superiors and with co-workers, are related to the opinion police officers have of the way citizens should be treated and their perception of limits to the use of force in the exercise of their authority. The association between internal 'relations' (with superiors and peers) and the inclination towards defending a democratic form of policing would thus be mediated by how agents feel about their institution, both in terms of organizational commitment (organizational justice) and in relation to the distribution of burdens and benefits (distributive justice). In this case, both dimensions concern the group members' view of being equally (and impartially) valued, recognized and respected in the police agency to which they belong (Bradford et al, 2013; Bradford and Quinton, 2014; Nix and Wolfe, 2015).

We propose a framework of specific relationships that will allow us to observe whether the theoretical construction can be validated through empirical data modelling (Figure 7.1). This analytical strategy based on structural equation models is suitable for two main reasons: first, it allows a simultaneous analysis of the measurement of latent variables and estimation of the theoretical model, as well as their respective adjustment; and, second, it allows an estimation of direct and indirect effects of explanatory variables on response variables.

We tested eight hypotheses that support a positive relationship between the explanatory and response indicators. Objectively, the relationship between police officers and their superiors is positively related to the perception of organizational justice (H1), distributive justice (H2) and democratic policing (H5). The relationship between police officers and their peers is positively related to the perception of organizational justice (H3), distributive justice (H4) and democratic policing (H6). Finally, both the perception of organizational justice (H7) and that of distributive justice (H8) are positively related to attitudes about democratic policing. It is also important to understand which agency the police are part of, whether that is the military or civil police. All of these variables are important when observing police organizational environments; however, the differences between the two forces are central when observing relationships. Nevertheless, given the weight of hierarchy and discipline in a militarized environment, it is plausible to expect relationships with superiors to be evaluated differently by military and civilian police (H9).

The model has two covariates. The first is the amount of time that police officers have worked at their respective agencies. The expectation is that the amount of time working as a police officer affects how they perceive relational and organizational issues in their respective institutions. Finally, we controlled for police officers' adherence to the idea of democracy in a diffuse sense, based on their degree of agreement (on a five-point scale) with the following statement: 'I prefer democracy to any other form of government.' Adherence to democratic policing would not only be related to internal issues within organizations, but would also be reflected in a normative alignment with democracy as a form of government.

The operationalization of a democratic policing indicator included questions that sought to assess police officers' stance regarding respect and impartiality/neutrality in contact with citizens, along with their stance regarding limits on the use of force and possible punishment for abuses. This strategy, although different, is similar to the ideas of Bradford and Quinton (2014) concerning the way in which officers position

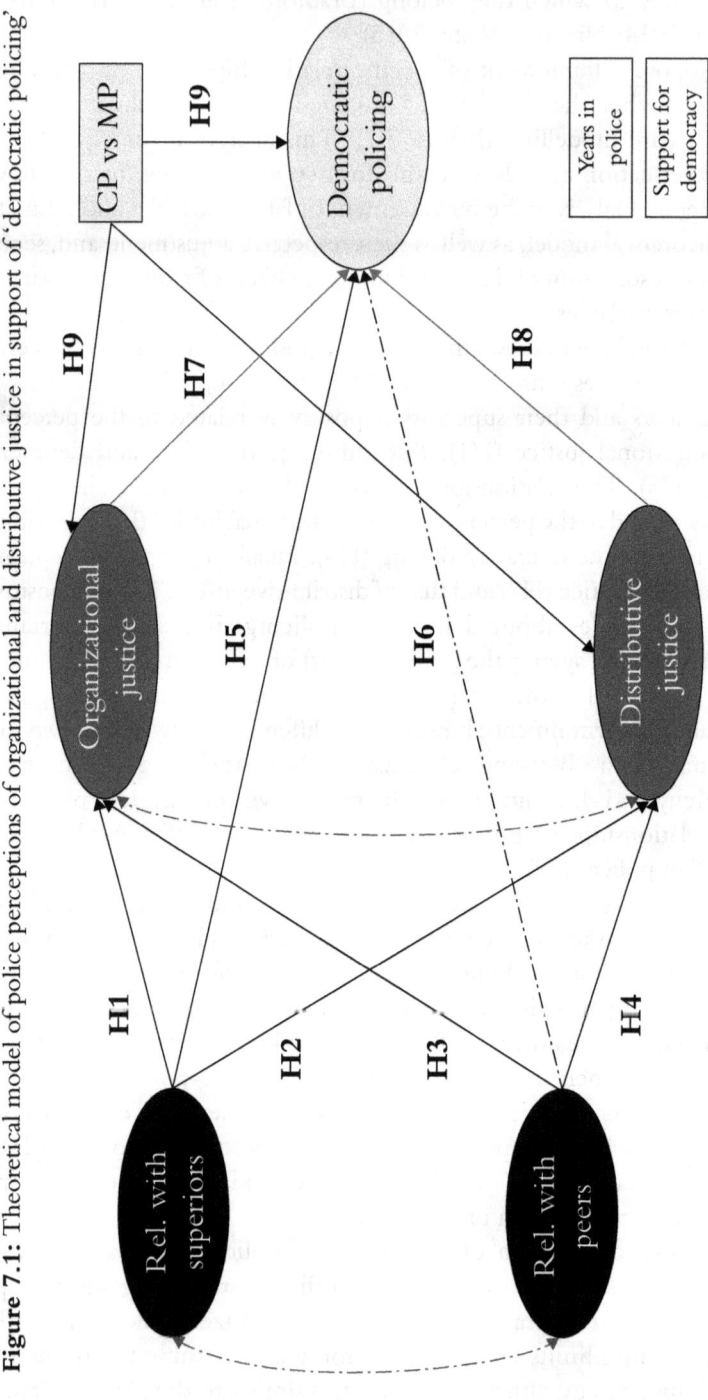

Figure 7.1: Theoretical model of police perceptions of organizational and distributive justice in support of 'democratic policing'

themselves regarding the treatment given to citizens and the use of force are essential in the prospective approach to police activity in democratic spaces and times.

It is important to make clear that our aim is not to identify whether the police are democratic or authoritarian. In this study, support for democratic policing is a continuous variable. This implies that we test the effects of independent variables on the variation in the level of support for democratic policing (as we have previously defined it).

The sample analysed in Table 7.1 consists mainly of men (83.5 per cent) who self-identified as White (65.9 per cent) and without a college education (55.8 per cent). It is possible to note some differences between respondents in the PC and PM: approximately 76 per cent of PC officers said they had a college education, much higher than the 29 per cent for PM; respondents in the PC are also, on average, ten years older than in the PM and have worked an average of five years longer as police officers than the PM group that makes up the sample. It is essential to clarify that the sample is mostly made up of police officers who interact with the public.

Table 7.1: Sample descriptive statistics

	% / Mean	SD	Min	Max	Obs
Race (Non-White=1)	34.1		0	1	149 (437)
MP	39.9		0	1	119 (298)
CP	21.6		0	1	30 (139)
Gender (Man=1)	83.5		0	1	365 (437)
MP	83.9		0	1	250 (298)
CP	82.7		0	1	115 (139)
Education (Higher=1)	44.2		0	1	193 (437)
MP	29.2		0	1	87 (298)
CP	76.3		0	1	106 (139)
Adm. Process (No=1)	46.8		0	1	202 (430)
MP	41.8		0	1	123 (294)
CP	58.1		0	1	79 (136)
Age	36.7	9.34	20	66	437
MP	33.7	8.01	20	66	298
CP	43.1	8.77	26	66	139
Years in police	11.0	9.24	0	49	437
MP	9.62	8.50	1	49	298
CP	14.05	10.1	0	45	139

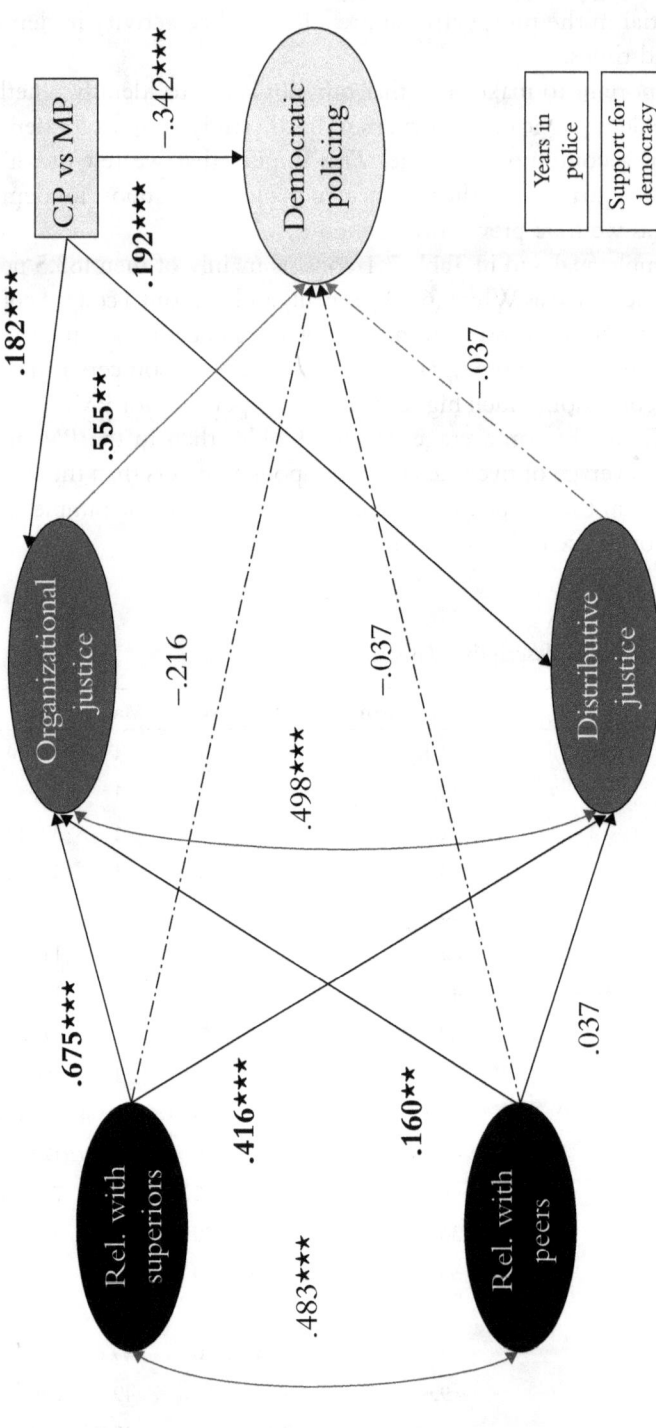

Figure 7.2: Police perceptions: research results

Regarding the results, we can first see that internal 'relations' are positively related to a perception of justice in the organization. In the case of one's relationship with superiors, the results indicate that the better this perception, the greater the assessment of organizational justice ($\beta=0.675/P=0.000$) and distributive justice ($\beta=0.416/P=0.000$). Regarding one's relationship with peers, the association is only observable for organizational justice ($\beta=0.160/P=0.003$). It is important to highlight that being a PM is related to better assessments in regard to both organizational justice ($\beta=0.182/P=0.000$) and distributive justice ($\beta=0.192/P=0.000$). Finally, the amount of time on the force has a negative relationship to organizational justice ($\beta=-0.139/P=0.002$), indicating that police officers with more experience in the institution tend to perceive justice in the organization in a more negative way, which means: the longer the agent's time in the police activity, the worse the perception of organizational justice, what indicates, for example, a more critical view regarding the prospect of being recognized and remunerated for good performance.

Regarding democratic policing, only the organizational justice variable ($\beta=0.555/P=0.003$) is related to support for this view. This means that the greater the perception that police officers are valued and respected in their respective institutions, the greater the defence of procedural justice practices and limits to the abusive use of force in police activity. As for the relationship with superiors, the results allow us to state that this variable is indirectly associated with democratic policing, being mediated by the perception of organizational justice ($\beta=0.314/P=0.008$). In this sense, we can verify the existence of a thread that links neutrality, respect, voice and accountability to the way in which officers perceive the treatment they receive from their superiors and to the way in which police officers view their behaviour when in contact with civilians on the streets (Van Craen, 2016).

A result that was expected and confirmed is the overlap between police officers who think democracy is the best form of government and those who favour democratic forms of exercising power ($\beta=0.212/P=0.000$). Finally, one result that stands out refers to the difference between the PC and PM. Being a PM officer diminishes support for democratic policing ($\beta=-0.342/P=0.000$), which implies less support for procedurally just policing and a less emphatic stance regarding limits on the use of force.

Conclusion

Two results should be noted. First, we have shown that the police institution has tremendous influence on the way its officers act on the streets. In their contacts with the public, police officers not only carry out the law but also interpret it at their discretion, deciding when and how to enforce it. This interpretation is not neutral, but rather is influenced by their perceptions of social class, ethnicity, religion, gender, age and their values (Goldstein, 1977). The police organization serves as a filter through which senior management's objectives are translated into expectations about how police officers should interact with the public. It guides officers not only through the techniques and rules that it requires them to follow in the execution of their duties (legality of action), but also in terms of the values that are shared within the institution. In this sense, if the institution's objective is to have police officers who exemplify democratic ideals on the streets, the experience of democracy within the department is an important incentive for the acquisition of these values (Trinkner et al, 2016). From this starting point, then, police agencies might seek to train newly recruited officers and encourage their acceptance of new ways of thinking, seeing and acting in order to take the demands of different audiences into consideration and thereby seek to promote the ideals of a democratic police force in an increasingly diverse society. In other parts of the world, for instance, police training has sought to incorporate new ideals of race, sex and gender awareness, although, it has to be said, not always successfully, as police culture has often tended to 'push back' (Chan, 1997; McLaughlin, 2007: 143–171; Loftus, 2009).

Second, we showed that among the PM there is less support for democratic policing practices. Previous studies have noted the limitations of a military organizational model on the execution of police work (Goldstein, 1977; Reiner, 2004) and the existence of problems in the quality of relationships between members of the organization that result from strict military discipline and hierarchy (Cubas, 2012; Cubas et al, 2020, 2021). The results presented here go further, revealing that the less democratic stance of these police officers is related to the dynamics, processes and practices adopted by the militarized police institution. The judgements that police officers make regarding their organization's behaviour towards its members – including the quality of officers' relationships with their superiors – helps define whether or not these officers support democratic attitudes in policing. Most likely, this result can be explained both by the institution's austere hierarchy and its authoritarian actions, which reproduce and deepen the inequalities found outside the police force, reaffirming a hierarchical notion of society split between those who command and those who must obey, and a discipline that is enforced through the regular and routine use of force.

The principles that constitute the foundation of a military organization produce an authoritarian environment that undermines the fundamental democratic values that should guide policing – an essentially civilian service, conducted in a civilian environment. How can the institution create 'good police officers' who, among other qualities, need to develop, in Muir's terms (1977), the pleasure of conversation, with the understanding that eloquence enriches their repertoire of potential responses to violence, allowing officers to 'touch the souls of citizens' – their hopes, their fears, their needs, their consciences – and to discuss with their peers the intellectual and moral issues inherent in coercive power? How can the institution overcome those disciplinary restrictions that end up limiting police skills, generating a 'poor' way of preparing the police to fulfil their responsibilities (Goldstein, 1977: 261)? This helps explain the perception, said to be held by many police officers, that people nowadays no longer respect the police as they used to and that the justifications that the public demands for police behaviour pose an affront to their authority.

Obviously, other aspects also influence this less democratic stance of the PM. However, it is no longer possible to ignore the institution's role in this worldview, which engenders a rationale about the exercise of power that is immune to slight modifications in recruitment, procedures or training lacking a critical analysis of management practices.

Tradition weighs heavily on the police. Even when oppressive regimes are superseded, their structures tend to remain (Waddington, 1999: 27). In Brazil, policing by consent never existed, as it was never necessary to obtain the population's voluntary acceptance and agreement for the police to exercise their authority. The maintenance of order by force is, in effect, supported by a socially implanted authoritarianism (Pinheiro, 1991) – deeply rooted authoritarian practices that permeate both politics and society – that manifests itself in the form of racism, sexism, elitism and other socially entrenched hierarchies. We have a spiral of authoritarianism: massive insecurity increases demand for even tougher measures, even if this means giving up rights and putting democratic principles at risk (Loader, 2006).

The transition to democracy in Brazil did not break the authoritarian structures that hindered advances in the democratic ways of exercising police authority. More recently, after Brazilian 2018 presidential election, it is evident that a *'mano dura'* public security agenda has gained prominence again. This movement reveals the resurgence of latent forces that have never ceased to exist, especially within institutions whose role should be to guarantee the democratic state of law.

The military framework has been shown to be one of those structures that do not provide the environment for the development of a democratic approach to policing. The PJT, with its focus on rights, participation, accountability and transparency, exemplifies democratic ideals, helping us to identify more clearly the negative impact that militarized organizations have on policing and on the authority relations to which police officers themselves are subjected (Cubas et al, 2021). This does not mean that a police department should be run like a democracy. What is needed is not a radical replacement by some new management style, but rather a movement away from the radically authoritarian climate that is sweeping across police agencies, and towards a more democratic form of organization (Goldstein, 1977: 264).

The implications of a militarized agency to the exercise of authority by police in a democratic society needs to be better understood. The literature has not yet given due attention to this topic. The militarized policing model, so rooted in the Brazilian context, can help to understand problems that may arise for the democracies in the Global North, currently experiencing their own police militarization pressures (Kraska, 2007; Balko, 2014; Turner and Fox, 2018; Moule et al, 2019). The main one is that it poses significant challenges to the very legitimacy of the police.

Acknowledgements

The study received financial support grant# 2013-07923-7, São Paulo Research Foundation (FAPESP), as part of the project 'Building democracy daily: human rights, violence, and institutional trust', developed by the Center for the Study of Violence of the University of São Paulo (NEV/USP).

Appendix

Table A.1: Constructs and measures

	Estimation	SE	z	p-value	95%	CI
Relationship with superiors						
Senior managers in this force value and listen to the views of their staff	0.845	0.016	51.08	0.000	0.813	0.878
My superiors make decisions that are based on objective criteria, not personal judgements	0.801	0.019	40.55	0.000	0.762	0.840
Decisions are made fairly by senior managers in this company	0.871	0.019	60.07	0.000	0.843	0.900
My superiors treat me with respect	0.749	0.023	32.01	0.000	0.703	0.795
Superiors give us explanations for decisions they make that affect us	0.744	0.023	31.41	0.000	0.698	0.790
I am treated fairly by the senior officers in this company	0.839	0.017	48.88	0.000	0.805	0.872
Relationship with peers						
I feel respected by colleagues in this police station	0.715	0.032	22.29	0.000	0.652	0.778
I feel respect for my colleagues in this police station	0.718	0.031	22.56	0.000	0.656	0.781

Table A.1: Constructs and measures (continued)

	Estimation	SE	z	p-value	95%	CI
I trust my colleagues in this police station	0.737	0.029	25.23	0.000	0.680	0.795
My colleagues in this police station trust me	0.613	0.037	16.17	0.000	0.539	0.687
I feel supported in my work by my fellow officers	0.756	0.028	26.62	0.000	0.700	0.811
Distributive justice						
I am rewarded fairly for the work I do	0.505	0.044	11.24	0.000	0.417	0.593
The amount of work I am expected to do is fair	0.696	0.035	19.42	0.000	0.626	0.767
My work schedule is fair	0.766	0.033	23.03	0.000	0.701	0.832
Transfers in military police are made in a way that is fair to all police officers	0.510	0.045	11.13	0.000	0.420	0.600
Organizational justice						
Good performance is recognized and rewarded	0.689	0.033	20.69	0.000	0.624	0.755
The military police is fair when it comes to promotions and career advancement	0.665	0.035	18.84	0.000	0.596	0.734
The objectives of the military police are clear to me	0.651	0.035	18.45	0.000	0.581	0.720
Commanders are aware of what happens to police officers on the streets	0.525	0.041	12.65	0.000	0.444	0.606
Democratic policing						
People must be treated with respect, regardless of how they treat the police	0.394	0.052	7.51	0.000	0.291	0.497
People who break the law do not deserve to be treated with respect by the police	0.631	0.047	13.38	0.000	0.538	0.723
For police officers, it makes little sense to try to be impartial because that is impossible in police work	0.417	0.052	7.92	0.000	0.313	0.520

(continued)

Table A.1: Constructs and measures (continued)

	Estimation	SE	z	p-value	95% CI	
It is sometimes acceptable for police officers to take matters into their own hands	−0.497	0.048	−10.20	0.000	−0.592	−0.401
It is sometimes acceptable to use force, beyond what is allowed, to make an arrest	0.495	0.049	9.93	0.000	0.397	0.593
Police officers who abuse physical force in police activities must be investigated and punished	−0.533	0.049	−10.74	0.000	−0.630	−0.435

Table A.2: Structural model

	Estimation	SE	z	p-value	95% CI	
Organizational justice						
Pol. agency	0.182	0.045	4.04	0.000	0.094	0.271
Years in police	−0.139	0.043	−3.17	0.002	−0.225	−0.053
Support for democracy	0.038	0.043	0.87	0.385	−0.047	0.124
Rel. superiors	0.675	0.045	14.7	0.000	0.584	0.765
Rel. peers	0.160	0.054	2.94	0.003	0.053	0.268
Distributive Justice						
Pol. agency	0.192	0.052	3.65	0.000	0.088	0.295
Years in police	0.041	0.052	0.80	0.425	−0.061	0.144
Support for democracy	0.059	0.053	1.12	0.262	−0.044	0.163
Rel. superiors	0.416	0.060	6.88	0.000	0.298	0.535
Rel. peers	0.037	0.066	0.57	0.572	−0.093	0.169
Democratic policing						
Org. justice	0.555	0.184	3.00	0.003	0.192	0.917
Dist. justice	−0.145	0.105	−1.38	0.166	−0.351	0.060
Pol. agency	−0.342	0.063	−5.36	0.000	−0.468	−0.217
Years in police	0.007	0.066	0.12	0.905	−0.122	0.137
Support for democracy	0.212	0.060	3.53	0.000	0.094	0.330
Rel. superiors	−0.216	0.128	−1.69	0.091	−0.467	0.034
Rel. peers	−0.037	0.079	−0.47	0.639	−0.192	0.118
Cov. org. justice/dist. justice	0.498	0.076	6.53	0.000	0.349	0.648
Cov. rel. sup./rel. peers	0.483	0.043	11.04	0.000	0.397	0.568

Table A.3: Indirect effects

Indirect effects	Estimation	SE	z	p-value
Democratic policing				
Pol. agency	0.073	0.043	1.98	0.048
Years in police	−0.083	0.002	−2.11	0.035
Support for democracy	0.012	0.010	0.53	0.599
Rel. superiors	0.314	0.058	2.66	0.008
Rel. peers	0.083	0.037	1.98	0.48

References

Anderson, D.M. and Killingray, D. (1991) Consent, coercion and colonial control: Policing the Empire 1830–1940, in D.M. Anderson and D. Killingray (eds) *Policing the Empire: Government, Authority and Control, 1830–1940*. Manchester: Manchester University Press, pp 1–16.

Andreas, P. and Nadelmann, E. (2006) *Policing the Globe: Criminalization and Crime Control in International Relations*. Oxford: Oxford University Press.

Balko, R. (2014) *The Rise of the Warrior Cop: The Militarization of America's Police Forces*. New York: Public Affairs Books.

Batitucci, E.C. (2010) A evolução institucional da Polícia no século XIX: Inglaterra, Estados Unidos e Brasil em perspectiva comparada. *Revista Brasileira de Segurança Pública*, 4(7): 30–47.

Bayley, D. (2001) *Padrões de Policiamento*. São Paulo: Edusp.

Bradford, B. and Quinton, P. (2014) Self-legitimacy, police culture and support for democratic policing in an English constabulary. *British Journal of Criminology*, 54(6): 1023–1046.

Bradford, B., Quinton, P., Myhill, A. and Porter, G. (2013) Why do 'the law' comply? Procedural justice, group identification and officer motivation in police organizations. *European Journal of Criminology*, 11(1): 110–131.

Bretas, M.L. and Rosemberg, A. (2013) A história da polícia no Brasil: balanço e perspectivas. *Revista Topoi*, 14(26): 162–173. doi:10.1590/2237-101X014026011

Caldeira T.P.R. and Holston, J. (1999) Democracy and violence in Brazil. *Comparative Studies in Society and History*, 41(4): 691–729.

Cano, I. and Duarte, T.L. (2012) *Análise Comparativa das Legislações Disciplinares das Corporações de Segurança Pública: uma proposta de Matriz de Lei Disciplinar para o Brasil*. Brasília: Senasp

Castro, C. (2004) *O espírito militar: um antropólogo na caserna* (2nd edition). Rio de Janeiro: Zahar Ed.

Chan, J.B. (1997) *Changing Police Culture: Policing in a Multicultural Society*. Cambridge: Cambridge University Press.

Costa, A.T.M. (2021) A Polícia Militar e seus dilemas identitário. *Contemporânea*, 11(1): 287–312.

Cotta, F.A. (2012) *Matrizes do Sistema Policial Brasileiro*. Belo Horizonte: Crisalida.

Cubas, V.O. (2012) A Ouvidoria e o controle da atividade policial na percepção dos policiais militares. Tese de Doutorado, FFLCH, Universidade de São Paulo, São Paulo. doi:10.11606/T.8.2013.tde-30102013-112807

Cubas, V.O. and Castelo Branco, F. (2019) Desafios y obstáculos em las encuestas de opinión con la polícia. *Revista Latinoamericana de Opinión Pública*, 8(2): 219–235.

Cubas, V.O., Alves, R.A. and Oliveira, A. (2020) Tão diferentes e tão iguais: As percepções de policiais civis e militares de São Paulo sobre suas instituições. *Dilemas – Revista de Estudos de Conflito e Controle Social*, 13(3): 801–825. doi:https://doi.org/10.17648/dilemas.v13n3.26235

Cubas, V.O., Castelo Branco, F., de Oliveira, A.R. and Cruz, F.N. (2021) Predictors of self-legitimacy among military police officers in São Paulo, Brazil. *Policing: An International Journal*, 44(6).

Dallari, D. de A. (1977) *O Pequeno Exército Paulista*. São Paulo: Editora Perspectiva.

Donner, C., Maskaly, J., Fridell, L. and Jennings, W.G. (2015) Policing and procedural justice: A state-of-the-art review. *Policing: An International Journal of Police Strategies and Management*, 38(1): 153–172.

Elliott-Cooper, A. (2021) *Black Resistance to British Policing*. Manchester: Manchester University Press.

Fernandes, H.R. (1974) *Política e segurança*. São Paulo: Ed. Alfa-Ômega.

Galvão, M. (2016) *Sim, senhor! Não, senhor! Discutindo o relacionamento social militar*. Curitiba: Appris.

Goldstein, H. (1977) *Policing a Free Society*. Cambridge, MA: Ballinger.

Guerra, M.P. (2016) *Polícia e ditadura: a arquitetura institucional da segurança pública de 1946 a 1988*. Brasília: Ministério da Justiça e Cidadania.

Hinds, L. and Murphy, K. (2007) Public satisfaction with police: Using procedural justice to improve police legitimacy. *Australian and New Zealand Journal of Criminology*, 40(1): 27–42.

Hough, M., Jackson, J., Bradford, B., Myhill, A. and Quinton, P. (2010) Procedural justice, trust, and institutional legitimacy. *Policing: A Journal of Policy and Practice*, 4(3): 203–210.

Jackson, J., Bradford, B., Hough, M., Myhill, A., Quinton, P. and Tyler, T.R. (2012) Why do people comply with the law? Legitimacy and the influence of legal institutions. *British Journal of Criminology*, 52(6): 1051–1071.

Jacobs, J. (2016) Policing, the rule of law and civil society: A philosophical perspective, in B. Bradford, B. Jauregui, I. Loader and J. Steinberg (eds) *Global Policing Studies: A Prospective Field*. London: SAGE, pp 82–103.

Jefferson, T. (1990) *The Case against Paramilitary Policing*. Milton Keynes: Open University Press.

Jones, T., Newburn, T. and Smith, D.J. (1996) Policing and the idea of democracy. *British Journal of Criminology*, 36(2): 182–198.

Kraska, P.B. (2007) Militarization and policing: Its relevance to 21st century police. *Policing*, 1(4): 501–513. doi:10.1093/police/pam065

Kraska, P. and Kappeler, V.E. (1997) Militarizing American police: The rise and normalization of paramilitary units. *Social Problems*, 44(1): 1–18.

Loader, I. (2006) Policing, recognition, and belonging. *The Annals of the American Academy of Political and Social Science*, 605: 202–221.

Loader, I., Bradford, B., Jauregui, B. and Steinberg, J. (2016) Global policing studies: a prospective field, in B. Bradford, B. Jauregui, I. Loader and J. Steinberg (eds) *Global Policing Studies: A Prospective Field*. London: SAGE, pp 1–10.

Loftus, B. (2009) *Police Culture in a Changing World*. London: Oxford University Press.

Mazerolle, L., Antrobus, E., Bennett, S. and Tyler, T.R. (2013) Shaping citizen perceptions of police legitimacy: A randomized field trial of procedural justice. *Criminology*, 51(1): 33–63.

McLaughlin, E. (2007) *The New Policing*. London: SAGE.

Moule Jr, R.K., Burruss, G.W., Parry, M.M. and Fox, B. (2019) Assessing the direct and indirect effects of legitimacy on public empowerment of police: A study of public support for police militarization in America. *Law & Society Review*, 53(1): 77–107.

Muir, W.K. (1977) *Police Streetcorner Politicians*. Chicago: University of Chicago Press.

Nagin, D.S. and Telep, C.W. (2017) Procedural justice and legal compliance. *Annual Review of Law and Social Science*, 13: 5–28.

Nix, J. and Wolfe, S.E. (2015) The impact of negative publicity on police self-legitimacy. *Justice Quarterly*, 8825(December): 1–25.

O'Reilly, C. (2018) Introduction: Policing and the Lusaphone community across time and space, in C. O'Reilly (ed) *Colonial Policing and the Transnational Legacy*. New York: Routledge, pp 1–13.

Pereira, A.W. (2021) Samuel P. Huntington, Brazilian 'decompression' and democracy. *Journal of Latin American Studies*, 53: 349–371. doi:10.1017/S0022216X21000250

Pinheiro, P.S. (1991) Autoritarismo e Transição. *Revista USP*, 9: 45–56. https://doi.org/10.11606/issn.2316-9036.v0i9p45-56

Reames, B.N. (2008) Neofeudal aspects of Brazil's public security, in M.R. Haberfield and I. Cerrah (eds) *Comparative Policing: The Struggle for Democratization*. London: SAGE, pp 61–87.

Reiner, R. (2004) *A Política da Polícia*. Série Polícia e Sociedade. São Paulo: Edusp.

Reisig, M.D., Bratton, J. and Gertz, M.G. (2007) The construct validity and refinement of process-based policing measures. *Criminal Justice and Behaviour*, 34(8): 1005–1028.

Reuss-Ianni, E. (1983) *Two Cultures of Policing: Street Cops and Management Cops* (1st edition). New York: Routledge.

São Paulo State Public Security Secretary (2021) Secretaria de Segurança do estado de São Paulo. Estatísticas Trimestrais. Available from: http://www.ssp.sp.gov.br/Estatistica/Trimestrais.aspx [Accessed 11 October 2021].

Sapori, L.F. (2018) The dual civil and military models for policing in Brazil, in V. Riccio and W.G. Skogan (eds) *Police and Society in Brazil*. New York: Routledge, pp 29–42.

Skolnick, J.H. and Fyfe, J.J. (1993) *Above the Law: Police and the Excessive Use of Force*. New York: The Free Press.

Sozzo, M. (2016) Policing after dictatorship in South America, in B. Bradford, B. Jauregui, I. Loader and J. Steinberg (eds) *Global Policing Studies: A Prospective Field*. London: SAGE, pp 337–355.

Sunshine, J. and Tyler, T.R. (2003) The role of procedural justice and legitimacy in shaping public support for policing. *Law and Society Review*, 37(3): 513–548.

Tankebe, J. (2011) Explaining police support for the use of force and vigilante violence in Ghana. *Policing and Society*, 21(2): 129–149.

Trinkner, R., Tyler, T.R. and Goff, P. (2016) Justice from within: The relations between a procedurally just organizational climate and police organizational efficiency, endorsement of democratic policing, and officer well-being. *Psychology, Public Policy, and Law*, 22(2): 158–172.

Turner, F.W. and Fox, B. (2018) *Police Militarization: Policy Changes and Stakeholders' Opinions in the United States*. Cham: Springer International Publishing.

Tyler, T.R. (1990) *Why Do People Obey the Law?* New Haven: Yale University Press.

Tyler, T.R. (2003) Procedural justice, legitimacy, and the effective rule of law. *Crime and Justice: A Review of Research*, 30: 283–357.

Tyler, T.R. (2006) Psychological perspectives on legitimacy and legitimation. *Annual Review of Psychology*, 57: 375–400.

Tyler, T.R. and Fagan, J. (2008) Legitimacy and cooperation: Why do people help the police fight crime in their communities? *Ohio State Journal of Criminal Law*, 6: 231–276.

Van Craen, M. (2016) Understanding police officers trust and trustworthy behaviour: A work relations framework. *European Journal of Criminology*, 13(2): 274–294.

Waddington, P.A. (1999) *Policing Citizens*. London: UCL Press.

Wright, A. (1998) Slippery slopes? The paramilitary imperative in European policing. *International Journal of Police Research and Management*, 2(2): 31–41.

8

Rioting Struggles in Brazil: Prison Gangs, Staff and Criminal Justice Hegemony

Vitor Dieter

Prison riots, criminological theories and hegemony in the Brazilian context

The orderliness of prison regimes is a central theme of criminological literature and continues to have great historical importance in the field. Yet, despite riots generating academic interest into prison (Sparks et al, 1996), riots as a phenomenon themselves have generally attracted rather less theoretical attention (Adams, 1992). This is partly reflected by the view that riots are perceived as a pathology within the system, an outcome of disorder, either caused by prisoners (Fleisher and Decker, 2001) or the authorities (Boin and Rattray, 2004). However, as I will argue, that might not necessarily be the case. Instead of the order/disorder dyad that has predominated since the era of the Chicago School (Whyte, 1943), in this chapter I argue that riots can be understood as part of the hegemony of the prison apparatus – that is, an aspect that reveals its central functioning mechanisms, rather than representing an exception to it. The argument here draws upon results from three case studies in Brazil that discuss the dynamics of prison riots, their potential causes and perceived outcomes.

The work of Useem and Kimball (1991, 1987) and Salla (2006; Adorno and Salla, 2007) are key references to understand prison riots and their specificity in Brazil – one emanating from a North American right-realist perspective and the others from the Brazilian context. In their analysis of a series of riots occurring in the United States, Useem and Kimball (1991) found that a common cause of prison riots was a systemic type of crisis that stemmed from lack of adequate administrative control. In their view, riots were neither 'purposeless emotional outpourings', nor instruments of prisoners to express 'grievances' and 'persuade elites' (Useem and Kimball, 1991: 202). Social dynamics are insufficient causal explanations to these events – although they did identify increasing ideological militancy among prisoners, for example, the Black Panther Party, Black Muslims, Latin Kings, and so on. Instead, Useem and Kimball (1991) argue that the effective causal mechanisms that maintain order are twofold: the establishment of a presumption of legitimacy among inmates; and a capacity of the state to contain and disrupt disturbances. Thus, they dislocate their interest away from the organization of inmates (their grievances and riot as protests) to the administration of prison by the state. According to this perspective, causes of riots are not to be found in the cultural motivations or in the protests of prisoners, but ultimately are tied to administrative vulnerabilities and the inadequate safe operation of prisons, or as Boin and Rattray (2004: 60) further develop their argument: 'prisoners do not riot in furtherance of a "cause" in a political sense – riots are an effect of the interaction between structural and cultural pathogens'. In sum, riots are seen as a pathology caused by the lack of legitimacy from the 'disorganisation of the state' (Useem and Kimball, 1991: 218–219), rather than the social dynamics between prisoners and their organizations.

In Brazil, Salla (2006) develops a different argument in which riots are the product of organized crime. In his view, the poor conditions in Brazilian prisons – understaffing, overcrowding and the lack of adequate prison welfare – contribute to riot-prone environments, but ultimately, he argues, prison gangs play the major role in these events. In his view, from the late 1990s to 2006, precarious prison conditions have contributed to a crisis of authority that ended by conceding power to criminal organizations. Organized crime, on their part, sought to further expand their power by eliminating opposing gang members – a response that fostered further riots and disorder. The consequence is that riots are being caused by 'movements that re-organize power amongst the criminal groups present among the prison population and over which the prison administration has very limited control' (Salla, 2006: 287). Authorities became passive observers that created these conditions by neglect, but gangs are the ultimate engines of violence. However, this gang violence, the vying for power, is not without self-interest. According to Adorno and Salla (2007: 15), 'these leaders, to a large degree, became stronger because they understood how to manipulate and monopolise the resources available in prison to accumulate wealth'. In other words, prison gangs use riots as means to control a group of inmates and expand their violent enterprises (see also Skarbek, 2014) and gain the monopoly of violence (Dias, 2011).[1] Therefore, for Salla (2006) and Adorno and Salla (2007) the core explanation of contemporary Brazilian prison riots can be found in the combination of poor governance with the vying for power between gangs for a greater share in the governance of illicit markets. This has become a mainstream view especially in the Brazilian states where the Primeiro Comando da Capital (PCC) – the largest and most widespread *facção* (faction/prison gang) of prisoners in Brazil – is deeply rooted (Adorno and Salla, 2007).[2]

There are important differences in both perspectives. While a right-realist approach gives emphasis to the lack of proper state management of prisons, the organized-crime perspective stresses the role of prisoners and criminal markets. Nevertheless, what both dominant perspectives have in common is that they draw from a liberal viewpoint in which riots are a disturbance, a pathology with individual, organizational or structural causes that represent the opposite of a legitimate prison order (Carrabine, 2005). As such, these theories are limited in their scope because riots become events detached from the underlying relations of order and domination in prison (Matthews, 1999). The interest in *legitimacy* measures prison order according to a preconceived standard – often drawn from affluent Western prison systems (Armstrong and Jefferson, 2017) – that risks concealing the centrality of riots in the power relations that shape prison life in Latin America.

In a more critical vein, prison order has been theorized in the global South as comprising a necessary shared governance between state authorities and groups of prisoners (Macaulay, 2013; Antillano, 2017; Narag and Jones, 2017), which, despite the precarious conditions of prisons, fosters the production of order rather than its disruption (Darke, 2018). To a certain extent this both draws upon and develops Sykes's (2007) original perspective in which prison order is a fundamental compromise, a negotiation between captives and custodians. From this perspective, Weegels (2020: 16) has argued that riots in Nicaragua can be understood as a rupture in the co-governance equilibrium, as a means to call wider social attention to the 'the system's structurally poor conditions' and 'the authorities' willingness to use violence' – aspects of imprisonment that the Nicaraguan state is deeply interested in keeping out of the wider political debate (maintaining a state of *public secrecy*). Riots then enter the cycle of co-governance as instances of *scripted performance* (*a creative violence*) by which prisoners seek to rearticulate, negotiate and develop prior arrangements of power (Weegels, 2020). This last critical perspective turns its attention back onto the cultural and political dynamics in which prisoners and the governance of prison participate, positing a distinctive understanding of riots from the perspective of order.

Contributing to this critical perspective, this chapter foregrounds the notion of struggles, rather than governance, to explore prison riots beyond the dominant right-realist approach and, instead, views the Brazilian riot as an event caused by the interests of organized crime. In that vein, I will argue that prisons are sites of struggles in which order represents the *stabilization* of struggles through covert means rather than a component that is disturbed in somewhat atypical circumstances. More than a crisis of legitimacy or the dispute for criminal markets between gangs, prison riots are an expression of tensions, contradictions and limitations deeply embedded by mechanisms of power that are already in place in prison before and during the event. Order shares a common gene with disorder, therefore, riots should be understood as the expression of an order – not its opposition.

In that sense, a dialogue with the Gramscian theory of hegemony can further clarify the mechanisms by which the stabilization of struggles (and their disruption) occurs. According to this perspective, the concept of hegemony posits that arrangements of power in modern society are a project of domination that seeks the consent of subaltern groups, but those social arrangements remain always unstable because within them lie social conflict (Coutinho, 2010) – even if those struggles are not fully manifested (Lukes, 2005) or appear only in covert forms (Scott, 1990). Gramsci 'sees hegemony as one aspect of social control arising out of social conflict' (Strinati, 2004: 154). It is in this sense that Gramsci suggests we can identify two important forms of struggle occurring within the modern state apparatus: the 'war of manoeuvre' (a frontal attack against hegemony) and the 'war of position' (when groups organize and struggle within dominant hegemony to improve their stances) (Egan, 2016). In light of this, we can establish a dialogue with this theory, but going beyond it, to formulate my main problem in the following way: can prison riots be understood from the vantage point of strategies of struggle around hegemony? This question draws insight from critical theories of power in Gramsci, but approaches hegemony as the outcome of a variety of mechanisms in a particular apparatus (the prison). In this sense the analysis moves beyond traditional Gramscian perspectives in criminology (Hall et al, 1978; Hall and Jefferson, 2006; Stephenson, 2015).

My research is based on seven months of ethnographic observations in four prisons between 2016 and 2017, complemented by 52 interviews and four focus groups. The data was collected in the state of Paraná. The state is in the southern region in Brazil and incarcerates approximately 40,000 prisoners. This research is part of a larger research project that sought to discuss the maintenance of order in prison with both prison staff and prisoners. In addition, the contributions of other authorities, such as human rights organizations, judges, government authorities and anti-riot special forces of the police, were also key to the research. The PCC was very active and influential in three of the four prisons where the ethnographic research took place and the remaining facility was a prison that contained an opposition faction to the PCC as well as a number of sexual offenders who had to be protected from the general prison population. In addition to the field research, data on the number of riots was collected from media sources in physical and digital archives. Gatekeepers with official access to documents also shared affidavits and appeals from cases that triangulated crucial evidence arising during the interviews.

Results are presented in three case studies. The first one situated near the capital of the Paraná is often considered the main prison of the region, the PCE (Penitenciaria Central do Estado or Central Penitentiary of the State), which holds between 1,000 and 2,000 prisoners. The second case study focuses on a 'model' prison which had never seen a riot before 2014. Finally, the third case study focuses on the surge of riots during 2013 and mid-2015 across the state. Each case study comprises a brief analysis but common aspects are drawn together in the final section.

Case 1: The 2010 PCE riot – prison officers and prison *factions* struggling for influence

The PCE is the oldest penitentiary still functioning in Paraná and the second largest prison in the south of Brazil. According to Bodezan (2011), it was constructed in the 1950s as a model rehabilitation unit that sought to comply with the deliberations of the United Nations (UN) on the Minimum Rules for the Treatment of Prisoners. Initially planned for 522 inmates, by the standards of the time, it was publicized as the largest and most modern penitentiary in Latin America (Bodezan, 2011: 74). Nevertheless, from the start the PCE developed an overcrowding problem that led to several reforms, which, throughout the decades, expanded its inmate capacity and reorganized many of its rehabilitative structures for new purposes (Bodezan, 2011: 76). As the state and the prison population grew, despite enlarging its official crowding capacity to approximately 900 prisoners, the penitentiary averages around 1,400 prisoners (Reis, 2014: 193) and, thus, has long lost its status as a model – while also suffering from budget constraints (Moraes, 2005: 187) and becoming foremost a space of confinement rather than of rehabilitation (Bodezan, 2011).

The PCE is not unfamiliar with riots, in effect, among the senior staff interviewees many were direct witnesses of a riot in the unit. From 1955 to 1989 despite the PCE being only one in a system of another seven large prisons, the unit was the primordial stage for major disturbances, escapes, assassinations and riots (Reis, 2018). Nevertheless, the penitentiary system of Paraná stood out in the national arena. For instance, in 1988 a visiting report concluded that the overall prison system in Paraná proved that 'there is the possibility of the existence of an excellent penitentiary system in the country' (Moraes, 2005: 198) and throughout the 1990s penitentiaries in the state saw no major public scandal arise – despite the growing national public perception of chaos and institutional violence in the Brazilian prison system (Human Rights Watch, 1998; Varella, 1999; Dias and Silvestre, 2009). That perception was to change when conditions at the PCE came to significantly worsen after its facilities were significantly damaged in the early 2000s during a six-day riot, in which, according to the memoirs of a staff hostage (Bitencourt, 2012: 256–257, 265), prisoners were for the first time collectively organized around the PCC. Other inmates found inspiration in this, subsequently creating a local faction (the Paranaense group), which would later develop in opposition to the PCC.

The immediate outcomes of the riot were the following: three staff were held hostage; and six prisoners died, directly as a result of the riot, some of them burned and three decapitated. The event was eventually followed by a criminal prosecution that convicted the security chief of the unit. Some of the prison wings were damaged to such an extent that prison cells had their doors destroyed, including the walls around them. Having nowhere to provisionally house over 1,400 inmates from the PCE, state authorities decided to bring in armed police officers (*polícia militar*) to maintain control of the prison unit. The effect was an 'intense militarization ... accompanied by the hardening of the internal regime ... with increasing number of complaints ... of violence committed by police officers' (Moraes, 2005: 189–190). While the state government greatly increased the number of new prisons, the problems of the PCE were not to be solved, conditions took a long time to improve, and overcrowding remained a constant variable through the 2000s. From 2001 until 2010 the presence of heavily armed police officers maintained a regime of subordination while the state government kept a small number of prison staff (*agentes penitenciários*) responsible for the remaining concerns of prisoners and the prison unit.

The particular background to the riot involved discontented security officials who, since 2002, had been pressuring the government into withdrawing the armed police support and returning the control and security to the penitentiary department. In the view of high-ranking officers of the police forces, their actions had been necessary as a temporary measure, but it was not their role to replace prison guards on a permanent basis, draining resources that could be used for street patrols (Kikuchi, 2003: 34). After nine years of this informal arrangement, the night after the government conceded to these pressures and withdrew 20 of the 48 officers attending the unit, a riot broke out: 'As soon as police officers withdrew from the unit, prisoners rebelled, destroying part of the facilities and demanding transfers to another establishment' (Bodezan, 2011: 77).

The riot started in the wings of PCC prisoners, who took three staff hostage, and then spread to the rest of the prison, as described by a local newspaper the day after the event:

> With their bare hands, prisoners managed to break the cell doors and took three staff hostages. They ripped the bricks off the walls. At dawn, prisoners destroyed the unit, such as the prison's infirmary, and

set fire to the wards and mattresses. In the morning, inmates began to burn the water tanks. One of the strongest scenes recorded was the head of a detainee displayed by prisoners on a tray. (Monteiro, 2010)

The riot represented a total loss of control over prison. Inmates took over the entire unit and held it for around 18 hours until surrendering it back to the authorities in an orderly manner. Six prisoners died directly as a result of the riot – some of them burned and three decapitated.

The prison staff union initially blamed the precarious working conditions and the withdrawal of the police (Ribeiro, 2010), while the command of the police attributed it to turf wars between rival prison gangs (Agência Brasil, 2010; Gruner, 2011). However, prisoners had a different version, accusing prison staff of intentionally designing a criminal confrontation between opposing groups to use the turmoil as a way to pressure the government into reversing the withdrawal of the police (Gruner, 2011: 8). Whereas this last version did not make it into the headlines, in the aftermath, due to captured conversations of prisoners on mobiles by the intelligence agencies and the reports given by the crisis negotiator teams, the government opened an investigation and eventually a criminal prosecution against the PCE chief of security.

The riot was mentioned in many conversations during my ethnographic work, but the legal process itself provided a firmer background of testimonies from prisoners and staff that helped in triangulating and developing an understanding of the riot events as they unfolded.

According to the criminal investigation the main cause for the riot was a malicious attempt by the chief of security to eliminate the influence of the PCC (increasingly becoming popular among prisoners) within the prison. What was particularly interesting regarding this case was that although the PCC outnumbered other prisoner groups; there was also another prison faction, the Paranaense group, operating in the prison. According to my interviews, this group originally emerged around a common platform together with the PCC in 2002 but clashed with them in the following years by combining some of the leaderships of street gangs in prison. Since then, despite the Paranaense group being more locally based and better connected at street level, the PCC had expanded considerably among prisoners themselves, and this established the State Central Penitentiary – the largest prison unit in the state – as the cornerstone of their disputes.

In contrast, the prison staff argued that the core issue revolved around the withdrawal of the police forces from the surveillance and control of the prison. In the view of prison officers, withdrawing the police would put them in danger, chiefly because of their inability to contain and control the threat of prison gangs.

Within the prison each group was housed in a different wing. According to police investigations and the prosecution, Tácio (pseudonym), the chief of security, engineered a confrontation between the two groups – attempting to potentially reduce the influence of the PCC within the prison and demonstrating the need for continued police support in managing the prison regime. As the police officer, Alpha, who negotiated with prisoners, recalled the event:

> 'I participated directly in the 2010 riot, I recall that three people were killed, several hostages. … There were three officers held hostage, also three guys were beheaded, it was very violent. … In this particular riot there were a lot of complaints [from prisoners], a prison officer was punished because they [prison officers] wanted to end the PCC inside prison, and so they set up the [opposing group] inside the jail to kill the PCC guys. But the PCC guys rioted before. They did it to be transferred, right? Because if they stayed they would be killed, so they took the officers hostage, so they could be transferred, and I think they were almost all transferred at the time.' (Alpha, interview, December 2016)

Official documents with the testimonies of prison staff and prisoners confirmed those suspicions. Especially revealing were the depositions of some of the direct witnesses to the events, among them the prisoner Romeu (pseudonym) who declared that he knew about the riot before it happened because:

> 'The chief of security Tácio did a deal with prisoner Germano to weaken the PCC; Germano gave to the chief of security Tácio at his request, a list with 45 names of members of the PCC with the intention that these were to be transferred. Germano knew who were the "heads" of the PCC because he sold seized cell phones to them. This happened one month before the riot. The effective transfer of PCC prisoners occurred the day the Military Police left the prison a few days before the riot; and according to Germano the intention of Tácio was to weaken the PCC and put the opposition in an advantageous situation over the members of the PCC with the intention that they would riot after the police left. Originally, the intention was just to intimidate the members of the PCC, but if they resisted there was supposed to be violence … initially the people from the PCC killed Nuno and Heron; They also killed Jael, taking Martim and Benicio hostage. Caio and Germano later escaped through the football field … a member of the prison staff gave a bag with knives and shivs to the prisoners of the opposition when they were accommodated in the 8th and 10th wing. … The riot began in the 10th wing eventually taking over all the prison.' (Romeu, legal deposition, January 2010; all names are all pseudonyms)

In other words, according to the accusation, the manoeuvre of moving members of the Paranaense group in the wings of the PCC was planned by the chief of security to promote a clash between opposing factions (*facções*), but with the acquiescence of the less influential group who saw in this plan an opportunity to push back against the PCC and grow their influence among inmates. As a deposition from a member of the Paranaense group stated: "he agreed with the ideas [the leaders of the Paranaense] and believed the others who were moved to that wing also agreed; the intention was to convince the general prison population without the use of violence". However, despite being prepared for confrontation with weapons, thanks to the support of prison officers, the PCC in desperation acted sooner and derailed the plan of the Paranaense group and the chief of security.

This case study illustrates a three-way struggle between the staff and groups of prisoners. Two things appear to be at stake here that we will return to later. In the first place, a strategy of confrontation by the staff in collusion with gang members to undermine the PCC, which was at the time the strongest group in the prison among inmates. And secondly a war of position, because as the affidavits point out, the balance of influence among other inmates was very much an issue considered at stake by rival groups. The chief of security sought to seize the opportunity for the opposing faction to grow stronger with the intention of leveraging the field against the PCC and drawing more inmates onto their side, while fragmenting the culture of inmates in two opposing sides.

Case 2: The Guarapuava penitentiary riot and the revolt against the judicial system

The Industrial Penitentiary of Guarapuava is a model rehabilitative prison in the west of Paraná, which was, at the time of the riot, housing around 250 prisoners. Prison officers often referred to the Guarapuava penitentiary as a model prison in the state. In effect, according to a visit of the national prison monitoring body (DMF-CNJ, 2010), the prison was in an exceptionally good state. In terms of staffing, it was above the regional level: the prison had 105 prison officers per a total prison population of 239 and it also had the support of other staff and private contractors. In addition, according to ethnographic research (Faria, 2008: 133), it deemed itself as a model in low recidivism rates and quality services of rehabilitation. Starting off with the accommodation, the 120 cells provided adequate bedding and sanitation to prisoners, while offering work to 82 per cent of inmates, comprising laundry, gardening, barber shop and cleaning, besides two companies within the prison that hired most of the prison population (around 170 inmates) to produce footwear (shoes) and industrial protective gear (boots, gloves and garments). All types of work gave inmates better sentencing conditions (favouring them for probation, parole and quicker progression to more lenient prison regimes) while also providing them with regular wages (Faria, 2008: 135; DMF-CNJ, 2010: 111).

Education was also adequately provided. Prisoners had access to a library available to all prisoners on Fridays and Saturdays – being allowed to borrow books for the remainder of the week; four classrooms were operating with primary and secondary school (DMF-CNJ, 2010). Some prisoners could attend professional courses through distance learning (DMF-CNJ, 2010). Occasional partnerships with civil society offered digital training and other qualifications to inmates. The ample provision of education (179 inmates studying) allowed many prisoners to have simultaneous access to education and work (Faria, 2008). The infirmary included medical, pharmaceutical and dental care from Monday to Friday. The unit also had adequate space for legal, psychological and social assistance, offering free legal counselling and both a psychiatrist and a psychologist available at the institution (Faria, 2008) – although the latter was on sick leave during the inspection (DMF-CNJ, 2010: 112) – besides the provision of permanent Alcoholics Anonymous meetings. In sum, along with very few other prisons in the region, the industrial penitentiary of Guarapuava was founded with an effective rehabilitative project that state authorities wished to reproduced in other prisons (Faria, 2008: 139).

As such, since its foundation the Industrial Penitentiary of Guarapuava was designated as a low-security prison in which the authorities select disciplined and compliant prisoners that would fit their rehabilitative ideals (Faria, 2008). According to my interviews, part of that selection excludes inmates classified as problematic, those with disciplinary problems and especially those associated with the PCC or any other problematic groups. Yet, despite the selection process and the apparently ideal rehabilitative setting, in 2014 the Guarapuava penitentiary was the place of one of the biggest riots in the region, in which prisoners held hostages, destroyed significant parts of the prison, and only released it to the authorities 48 hours after the initial take-over. The destruction was such that it took more than four years to reconstruct and reopen the industrial training departments, and even then this only resulted in a partial return of prisoners to the shopfloor (Secom, 2019).

This was also the first considerable disturbance identified in the prison unit since it was first established 15 years earlier. The causes of the riot had less to do with the type of prisoners incarcerated or the apparent order and quality of the penitentiary itself. Instead, the riot stemmed from a juridical debate, a theoretical issue, regarding the calculation of the length of prison sentences, which once adopted by the local judge affected the whole prison population.

The Brazilian penal system is divided in three prison regimes: closed, semi-open and open. Convictions distribute prisoners to one of those regimes according to the nature of the crime committed and the length of their sentence. In normal circumstances, after a given proportion of the sentence has passed, a prisoner has the right to progress to a more lenient regime (for instance from a closed prison, which was the case of the Guarapuava Industrial Penitentiary, to a semi-open regime), provided they have not been subjected to any disciplinary measures and not sentenced for other crimes. However, juridically speaking, there had been a long-running legal debate (Roig, 2016: 198; Prado et al, 2017: 172; Giamberardino, 2021: 210) occurring at the national level concerning the question of progression between prison regimes. The issue was similar to the question about how time 'on remand' should be treated, whether as part of an overall sentence or not, and this involved the case of prisoners serving time for one offence, but still awaiting sentencing for other offences. Different interpretations of the sentencing law and guidance could significantly impact the length of overall sentences and therefore the speed that prisoners might pass through the different stages of their sentences and, consequently, the speed at which they might transition to a more lenient regime.[3]

This can clearly be a significant issue for prisoners in general as it sometimes occurs that offenders will not have been sentenced for all their offences. In such cases the tougher interpretation of the calculation of an overall sentence might double, triple or even further expand the time they are due to spend in the harsher prison regimes. Unfortunately, at this time the Supreme Court (Superior Tribunal de Justiça, STJ) was developing a juridical consensus around a harsher stance; a position referred as the *res judicata* (*trânsito em julgado*) (Fonseca, 2015). In this context, the problem that suddenly arose in Guarapuava was that the local sentencing judge decided to follow the growing jurisprudence at the higher courts and issued an ordinance that overnight changed all the sentences of prisoners in her jurisdiction.

Often prisoners remained oblivious as to how they might be impacted by changing sentencing policies or the reasons they were not progressing to more lenient prison regimes. Yet, at the Guarapuava penitentiary inmates had sufficient legal counselling to collectively understand the dramatic changes that many prisoners had suffered overnight to their expected rights of regime progression. This led to major dissatisfaction among the prison population. According to a public defendant interviewed, as soon as prisoners understood the judge had adopted the more punishing interpretation, greatly increasing their time of conviction in a worse prison regime, prisoners in Guarapuava were outraged. As one judge, Sol (pseudonym), remarked in interview, this change had a domino effect on rioting at the Guarapuava penitentiary and beyond: "Then, this was the great trigger for the major riots from Guarapuava, Londrina and to a certain extent Cascavel."

The riot at the Guarapuava penitentiary, however, surprised my participants because of its massive scale and its reputation as a model prison, with disciplined prisoners – perceived as uninvolved with the PCC or other factions. Nevertheless, the riot quickly escalated to a full-blown take-over and a major conflict in which inmates took staff hostages and destroyed substantial parts of the prison – including those spaces of work and leisure that benefited them. As Deno (pseudonym), a police officer who responded to the riot, explained:

> 'In Guarapuava, prisoners were questioning the juridical deadlines for progression. ... The prisoners wanted to know what position the judge adopted, how she was counting the prison term for prisoners in that region. And she explained ... so we exposed this person, put them in contact with the prisoners there, so that she could clarify their doubts, briefly, and then we removed her from there. This contact brought something in return, release of a hostage, a return to physical integrity and the end of the crisis.' (Deno, interview, December 2016)

The riot that erupted as a direct result of the new sentencing policy led directly to the serious violence and vandalism. In effect, for a model prison the riot caused great and unexpected concern. News outlets described the ending of the riot only after 48 hours, with prisoners on the roof holding banners citing their grievances, destroying and burning the prison, and, according to the account of interviewees, writing on the walls of the prison 'down with the *res judicata*' ('*abaixo o trânsito em julgado*'). In that process, 13 staff were taken as hostages; prisoners severely damaged the prison administrative offices, the industrial sector, the health sector, and the roofs of the unit. 'Rioters had a list of demands to the negotiators, such as improvements in conditions at the penitentiary, a change of prison governor and the progression of prisoners to the semi-open regime' (Cordeiro, 2014). Clearly, inmates were severely affected by their own riot and state authorities quickly sought a negotiated solution to their grievances. Some prisoners were transferred out of that jurisdiction, while others counted upon the support of the secretary of justice to discuss the '*res judicata*' matter with the local prosecutor and judge. Even if the STJ still took a couple of years to alter its course in favour of more lenient interpretation (Cruz, 2018), in Guarapuava the ordinance was eventually returned to a favourable stance regarding prisoner regime progression.

Here, the core protagonists of the riot were not prison officers and inmates, but rather juridical authorities and prisoners. Inasmuch as the Guarapuava prison was a model unit with adequate conditions, sufficient staffing, rehabilitative opportunities and disciplined prisoners, prison staff participants were shocked to see it descend into rioting. In effect, the riot was a form of overt conflict, in which prisoners revolted against the juridical and prosecutorial authorities, not merely the conditions of prison itself. Therefore, this case study indicates that dynamics of riots extrapolate conflicts between gangs or precarious conditions in prisons. Albeit many prisoners decided not to participate in the riot, many of them actively revolted as a group with a shared interest. The prison apparatus is a terrain in which imprisonment also means attaining some degree of consent from prisoners regarding their own conditions of incarceration. More than the staff–prisoner relation or the possibilities of a humane system, this entails their sentencing conditions (among this the expected progression between prison regimes). When a juridical decision affects the shared interests of inmates, the riot takes the form of an overt collective form of struggle against the authorities themselves (in the Guarapuava case, the juridical and prosecution authorities).

Understanding prison as a hegemonic project means that it can be seen from the light of an apparatus that must successfully subordinate individuals to its form of domination, not just by using coercion but producing consent. Hegemony in Gramsci means seeking to attain consent from subaltern groups, but in this framework, consent is also attained through struggles. This case study reflects power dynamics in a wider hegemonic project, within which lies a covert or hidden tension, a struggle, between the legitimacy sought by the authorities and the interests of prisoners. When the opportunity arises for the prisoners to see themselves as a subaltern collective with a common interest and a capacity for revolt, that struggle can take the form of a *war of manoeuvre* in which state authorities (here, judges, courts and prosecutors) appear directly as the representatives of the structures of domination. It is significant here that state authorities did not opt to subdue rioters with direct police coercion, they acted to re-establish consent by compromising and progressively re-adopting the original juridical interpretation. This act of compromise is less an act of common sense or grace towards prisoners and more of a need to de-escalate the crisis and dismantle inmate solidarity spurred by their (suddenly overt) common interest. Although the riot can be seen as a victory for the inmates, the authorities gained a greater victory in the long run: the concealment of their domination behind the formal legitimacy of the legal system.

Case 3: Facilitating riots – struggles between authorities and the staff union

In both of the previous two case studies prisoners themselves were a catalyst mechanism of the riots – together with the chief of security and judges and prosecutors, respectively. Now, this third case, by contrast, illustrates the importance of the prison staff and their relationship with prison authorities. The weight of this relationship can be identified in a quantifiable historical process (see Figure 8.1). However, in tandem with the quantification of riots, interviews and participant observation allowed us to identify potential causal mechanisms at play. Ethnographic interviews with prison staff and police officers attached to the 'crisis management' special units (responsible for negotiating, disrupting riots and taking back prisons) indicated that a trend comprising three stages can be identified in the dynamics of riots. These trends are:

1. From 1999 most riots arose from a failed escape attempt, in which prisoners took over to demand better conditions and reduce the severity of prison punishments.
2. From 2003 onwards some riots were part of a decision from the PCC to protest prison conditions. Most noticeably, in 2006, prisoners rioted in jails across the state of Paraná making more than localized demands, such as demanding the abolition of solitary confinement, of violent and abusive punishment practices and overall better conditions in other prisons (across the state). Smuggled mobile phones connect PCC members helping them coordinate their actions throughout the system. This form of coordination has a long history. The police captain interviewed, Bigode, found that the influence of the PCC in this form of riots has been apparent since 2003.

'[It started] right there from 2003, in which I participated, we had already realized, they had a very close connection with the "party" [*partido*, PCC] leadership in Brazil ... so it was quite difficult, because you are not negotiating with the people in that local prison, you're negotiating with the "party" ... that's the problem, it depends on them [local prisoners] the resolution. And suddenly they were saying "The boss ordered the jail to be delivered only tomorrow".' (Barol, interview, December 2016)

The PCC has used rioting as a strategy of resistance for years, yet there seems to have been a quantitative expansion and an intensification of coordination efforts after 2010, which made them a key mediator in organizing riots throughout the region.

3. From 2013 onwards, many riots were caused by hostage situations, mostly small and quick acts in which prisoners asked to be transferred to another facility (referred to in the field as *pegar o bonde* [taking the bus]). This last type consisted mostly of a couple of prisoners taking one or two prison officers hostage for a brief period of time before negotiating the *bonde*.

In the perspective of prison officers, there are two types of prison riots: the *guentos* and *rebelião*. The *guentos* generally involve only a small part of prison, often limited to the boundaries of a prison wing and with little involvement from the rest of prison, they are often associated with hostage-taking and a relatively speedy resolution. The *rebelião* is a more significant take-over often

Figure 8.1: Paraná riots in prisons and jails (1998–2017) and total state prison population (2003–2014)

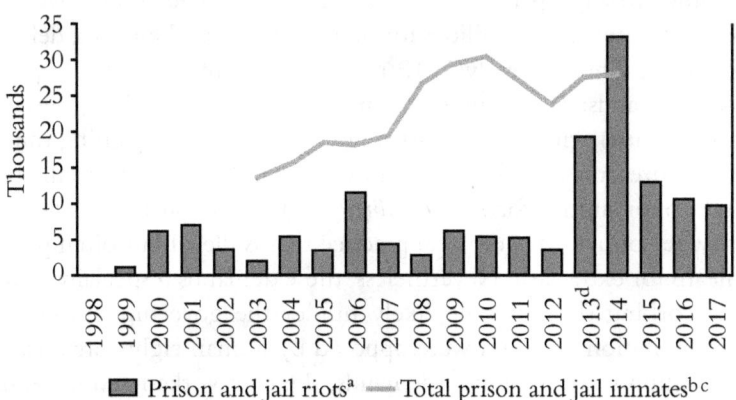

Notes: [a] Parana newspaper archive of news on riots in prisons and jails; [b] Penitentiary Department December of each year (Ministry of Justice, 2017); [c] Includes convicted and provisional – from prisons, jails and asylums; does not include convicted, but not incarcerated, prisoners under surveillance, such as the open regime (*regime aberto*) or electronic monitoring (*monitoramento eletrônico*); [d] Estimative considering July of the past and subsequent year.

with more significant consequences and a more complex resolution – such as in Case Studies 1 and 2. Prison staff interpret most of the recent episodes simply as *guentos* for *bondes* (demands of transfers from prisoners to county 'jails' where they are closer to their families). Riots in Figure 8.1 entail both *guentos* and *rebelião*. The smaller size of *guentos* (also called *motim* or *small riots* by participants in the field) could pass unnoticed if research on prison only considered major disturbances, but measured quantitatively throughout time, they also reflect the development of a longer underlying trend. Indeed, the growing usage of riots as a means to request a transfer (*pegar o bonde*) was a prevalent issue among prison staff.

Yet, the standard explanation given by prison staff for the causes of riots from 2013 to early 2015 seems only a rather partial perspective. Prisoners, prison authorities and police officers also added a different explanation for the considerable growth in the number of riots. According to them, the major cause of riots was an emerging conflict between the prison staff union and state authorities.

In 2013 a neoliberal candidate – in place of a left-wing administration – succeeded in gaining election to the position of state governor, introducing both a strategy of fiscal discipline and a strengthened stance on human rights. The governor appointed a human rights advocate within the Justice Secretariat, whose prime responsibility in the prison department was to move prisoners from overcrowded jails to less crowded penitentiaries and to increase education, visiting and other prison rights. This policy of tackling crowding by transferring inmates to different prisons, coupled with the pressure of delivering improved conditions, triggered a conflict between state authorities and prison staff, because it demanded substantially more work and greater responsibilities for staff, without, in their eyes, delivering any benefits. Thus, in early 2013 the union started to increase pressure on two demands: (1) changing their working shifts to long periods of work (24 hours) with longer breaks (48 hours); and (2) gaining the right to possess firearms outside prison. Both demands sought to facilitate and expand opportunities for *moonlighting* (*bicos*) by prison officers as private security personnel – an informal practice that is illegal but often practised as a means for extra cash. Nevertheless, these demands (especially a change in the working shifts) would likely hinder the government's crowding and rehabilitation plan and were opposed by human rights organizations. Thus, in support of the union demands, the overworked and increasingly discontented rank-and-file staff started to take industrial action, further straining the prison population.

From July 2013 the frequency of riots started to increase significantly, only waning from early 2015. In 2012, overall, four riots were recorded by media outlets, whereas 2013 saw 22; 2014, 38, and 2015, 15. A penal judge, Sol, pointed out how this development came about:

> 'Because see, she [the secretary of justice] arrives and she says that she wants 100 per cent [of the prison population] working, 100 per cent studying. Who is affected first? The correctional officer. They have to be there dealing with the prisoner. ... So, they were pulling in more prisoners, until it reached its 100 per cent [crowding capacity], right. Then, a little more ... it incited riots. ... It's not really riots, right? Most were small.' (Sol, interview, April 2017)

Adding to those elements, a number of these riots arose from unusual places, such as the security wings – usually associated with vulnerable prisoners, such as those convicted for sexual offences, or those accused of informing on other inmates – contexts where prisoners are more subordinate to staff and officers generally have greater control.

Some participants referred to this escalation as staff-*facilitated* riots. For instance, according to Deno, a police officer directly engaged with the management of crisis in riot situations, it was possible to observe an odd combination of behaviours arising in the immediate prison conflict settings. As he argued:

> 'The prison guards' union was left-wing, they were against the state government, so they were acting strongly ... as soon as a riot broke out [the union] was already in front of the penitentiary with union banners

... whenever someone left the "crisis" [the riot], either a prisoner or hostage, we would talk to them, and noticed in some, not all cases, that the staff were very calm. ... I'm not saying it's always like this, but there was a clear facilitation [from the part of prison officers], because if the riot is seen it affects the state [government].' (Deno, interview, December 2016)

In a similar vein, the secretary of justice argued:

'In fact, they [some prison officers] created an environment to have prisoners riot, to make some noise. Because there was no death ... there was nothing! It was just noise! ... They didn't want to move the prisoners around. They wanted to maintain the same status of "I just look at them at a distance, the guy is trapped inside the cell and I'm not going to worry about his rehabilitation" ... in these riots, the deal was: no one will hurt the prison officer. The officer stays inside. So much so that, during the entire term, no staff were injured.' (SJ, interview, December 2016)

For most prisoners the escalation of riots during these years resulted in a further deterioration of conditions – every time a riot occurred prisoners had to go on lockdown and endure stricter security. Nevertheless, common prisoners did not blame the new administration, but the prison staff, for causing these disturbances. These riots also divided officers. It appears that the climate in prison became one of division among those who were either for or against the 'human rights' secretary of justice. In effect, even two years after the upsurge in the number of riots it was possible to observe a marked difference between two groups of staff, those working closer to inmates who were mostly still opposing the policies of the secretary of justice, and some others, more in charge of administrative matters, who continued to support the new approach.

Nevertheless, in the longer term the riots were significant in that, during early 2015, the secretary of justice stepped down, a significant victory for the prison staff union that nevertheless continued to press for higher wages, pension benefits and access to firearms while continuing to protest and organize industrial action.

In sum, certainly the role of prisoners is of central relevance in any episode of prison riot, nevertheless as this case study shows, dynamics of power are much more complicated than a mere relation between prisoners/gangs, prisoners/staff or prisoners/authorities. In particular, the great increase in the number of riots since 2013 cannot be understood simply as an output of increasing crowding, worsening conditions, loss of situational control or gang violence. On the contrary, far more than just inmate disorder, the rising frequency of riots was more directly associated with the struggles between the prison officers' rank-and-file and the policies of the state authorities.

Prison hegemony as struggles: riots from the vantage point of wars of manoeuvre

These three case studies suggest a different perspective from the dominant literature on riots. First, while Useem and Kimball (1991) gave greater emphasis to the role of immediate prison authorities (state disorganization in terms of legitimacy and control), in these case studies rioting emerged as part of the interplay of different group-interests (prisoners, prisoners' groups, prison officers and prison authorities). Second, less relevant than gang violence promoted by the poor quality of prison conditions in Brazil (Salla, 2006; Adorno and Salla, 2007) and in Northern accounts of the penal crisis (Adams, 1992; Cavadino and Dignan, 2007), these case studies show a bigger picture in terms of the relations of struggles in prison.

There are large differences surrounding the causes and motivations behind each case. Some issues did not appear as direct causes in the three case studies, such as overcrowding, understaffing or poor living conditions; there were also few major political and ideological narratives voiced by inmates (such as 'Black liberation' or prisoners struggles for recognition) and nor were there significant issues relating to the contraband-market-oriented governance by prison gangs.

Instead as we have seen, there appeared a variety of causes for these three diverse riots: (1) major penal policy initiatives were a key feature (pressuring for greater surveillance; sentencing time; fostering rehabilitation); (2) the struggle for power among prison staff was also a major aspect of the PCE riot of 2010 and in the upsurge in disturbances and lockdowns in 2013 and 2015; and (3) the struggle of prisoners, not for their criminal governance (in terms of a competition for economic interests), but concerning the culture of inmates and their perceptions regarding the legitimacy and fairness of incarceration itself. In this sense, the dominant theoretical approaches and explanations for prison disorder are insufficient as analytical frameworks to make sense of the causes influencing the riots discussed in the three Brazilian case studies discussed here.

An analysis of the causes of the riots foregrounds the relations of struggle between the competing interests in prison: between prison politics, the daily governance of prison and the cultural agency of prisoners. The covert and overt relations of struggle between these interests tend to be overlooked by right-realist perspectives that limit their analysis to the loss of prison control, the market interests of gangs and the disorderly precariousness of prisons.

The analysis presented here suggests that the policy level and the group-interests are still of major relevance to understand prison order dynamics – especially evident in the disruption of that order. As we have seen in the first and third case studies, the PCC, for example, used the riot as a strategy of struggle to influence the arrangement of power within prison. The PCC directed a frontal attack against opposing groups at the State Central Penitentiary riot, to oppose a prison governance seeking to annihilate their influence, but also remained somewhat passive during the 2013–2015 surge of riots when these appeared against their interests. In the second case study, the overt mobilization of prisoners against the judicial authority demanded the re-establishment of the juridical status quo ante – a condition to their consent to the prison regime. In the third case, prison staff found that facilitating riots by manipulating conditions and vulnerable inmates could be an effective leverage in their favour.

Looking beyond violence and disorder, the cultural agency of prisoners is of considerable relevance to understand riots. Contrary to Adorno and Salla (2007: 12) who argued that '[a]ppealing to unchecked violence, without sparing deaths, and capable of terrorizing society, [the actions of the PCC] place them in direct conflict with police and judicial authorities', these case studies do not suggest rioting of the PCC as terrorism. Quite the contrary, it appears as a strategy around hegemony, but one that is exceptional and undesirable. Since riots can lead to unforeseen consequences and disturbances can worsen their conditions in the long term, rioting, unchecked violence or gang terrorism is not a convenient means of struggle within prison.

Instead, factions (*facções*) and other prisoners find more incentives to engage in securing petty concessions within an established order (Weegels, 2020) or indefinitely withhold from expressing their interests (Carrabine, 2005) because of the potential likelihood of a negative outcome from rioting. Thus, the vying for power of the PCC has limited explanatory power. The same applies to non-faction prisoners, as the second case study indicates major changes to their legal situation (a shared condition of subalternity to the penal system) may lead prisoners into sacrificing gains to their immediate prison conditions with the attempt of collectively pressuring authorities. While an unexpected issue might well be the immediate catalyst – the spark – for a revolt, riots only gain traction among prisoners when they are transformed into a strategy of struggle, in which prisoners can find some common cause. In a war of manoeuvre, the outcomes are always uncertain, but sporadically may appear worth the risk, especially when there is strength in numbers.

The prison staff are important actors in hegemonic struggles, not just in the establishment of a presumption of legitimacy. Whenever, as a group, they perceive that they may be losing ground within the prison system, they assess if a frontal confrontation – against inmates or the political authorities – can benefit or worsen their conditions. The prison authorities cannot maintain a penal hegemonic project without the assistance of prison officers, while inmates depend on staff to have their minimal survival conditions met. They are therefore at a deeper level of the production of consent (the level of staff–inmate interactions) within the apparatus but with consequences significantly beyond that level. This position gives them a good leverage opportunity to achieve their interests. Nevertheless, like prisoners, a direct confrontation with the authorities is problematic, leading them, instead, to engage in a *petty politics* of the war of position (negotiating perks), before taking more significant measures (formal protests and industrial action). The same applies to their relations with prisoners, as long as they share a group identity, prison officers can together manipulate their working environment in their favour (neglecting prisoners deemed bothersome, restricting rights, boycotting goods, imposing disciplinary sanctions, and so on), but to some extent they must also adapt their behaviour to a point in which prisoners recognize their authority as legitimate and follow their instructions. Thus, episodes in which prison officers engage in direct confrontation (a *war of manoeuvre*) with the authorities – like the third case study, where prison officers were seen to be facilitating riots – or with prisoners – like the first case, in which prison officers criminally planned the direct victimization of prisoners – are likely to be rare. Nevertheless, the occurrence of such events does indicate that riots cannot be understood as a phenomenon relating exclusively to the crisis of legitimacy and the violent vying for power among prison gangs. Instead, a dialogue with the Gramscian theory of hegemony allows us to understand prison staff playing a major role in maintaining the hegemonic penal project for the authorities (imprisonment and its conditions) while being an interest group that often conflicts with and struggles against the hegemonic project authorities planned for them.

Finally, the hegemony of the authorities and their penal policies are also a major aspect in the dynamics of riots. To maintain a large prison population as passively subordinate they can and do rely on *wars of manoeuvre*. The response to riots is a good illustration of these direct confrontational strategies, as authorities can lengthen the sentence of prisoners (by criminalizing their conduct), worsen conditions by imposing lockdowns and use police forces to neutralize riots. Regarding prison staff, state authorities can increase their workload (as in the third case), transfer prison officers to undesirable positions, put limitations upon the progress of their careers, dismiss them or even criminalize their attitudes (as in the first case study). Yet, as before, strategies of direct confrontation can risk losing their hegemony over the governance of the prison apparatus (the prison staff), in which a crisis may challenge their competence and legitimacy as regards society as a whole; or it can result in them losing the consent of prisoners and risking a general organized opposition that exposes the prison hegemony as crude domination (such as in the second case study). In either case, authorities are better positioned than both of these groups.

In most crises, authorities have greater ideological and material resources to attain consent through wars of position, that is, negotiating and producing an image of fairness. Prison authorities aspire and often achieve the spontaneous consent of subaltern groups, as Gramsci had put it (1992: 12) 'to the general direction imposed on social life' – a reason why most prisoners remain fatalistic on their chances to change their environment (Carrabine, 2005). As the second and third case studies reveal, official governance may appear in the hands of prisoners, factions or prison officers, but beneath it lies a direct relation in which the authorities play a leading role. Nevertheless, political authorities are significantly shielded from engaging in overt hegemonic struggles around imprisonment, however their general invisibility in the immediate rioting event should not conceal their role in struggles around strategies of consent, nor their agency in the strategies of domination. Riots give exceptional insight into the mechanisms by which authorities govern prisons and their forms of maintaining hegemony.

In sum, while the dominant perspective understands riots as pathologies of disorder within the prison setting, especially caused by a loss of administrative control, poor institutional conditions and the violence of gangs, this chapter has drawn from the results of three case studies of riots in a southern Brazilian state to argue that, more than a consequence of lack of legitimacy and governance, riots are an integral part of the prison apparatus. As an event, it is more than a disturbance, it sheds light onto hidden forms of governance (Sykes, 2007; Weegels, 2020), yet, in my view, riots reveal an important aspect of prison power: the pervasive struggles for hegemony through different means. These struggles comprise more than simply violent exchanges between gangs and other prisoners. Because prisons are spaces of hegemony, interest groups in prison – especially state authorities, prison officers and prisoners – are struggling to maintain their respective positions, if possible, without resort to overt coercive measures. Therefore, a dialogue with the Gramscian theory of hegemony (1992), but beyond this, to consider it in the relations of prison, provides a vantage point beyond the predominant dyad of order/disorder (where riots may be reduced to a disturbance to legitimate order) and repositions them in the critical framework of power, not in opposition to it, but as a moment within it.

Although Gramsci never theorized the mechanics of prison power, his reflections on the key strategies being used to gain and maintain hegemony in modern societies differentiated between the wars of manoeuvre (Gramsci, 1992: 120) and the war of position (Gramsci, 1992: 238). The prison as a modern apparatus needs a good degree of consent to function in democratic societies, which offers a battleground for both strategies. Strategies of struggles can be explicit (in the case of riots as wars of manoeuvre) or they may arise as a part of a tug-of-war between authorities, staff and inmates (in the petty politics that revolve around the prison). Thus, riots can be understood as an intrinsic part of the struggles for hegemony, when groups use strategies of frontal confrontation (wars of manoeuvre) seeking to dramatically change a certain arrangement of power or counteract such a change.

In any case, while strategies may vary, their common ground is the political content of the cultural responses of inmates to prison order and control, that is, maintain their subordination with as much consent as possible. This must be intermediated by prison officers and staff, the effective on-the-ground foremen, with their interests and hierarchies. Nevertheless, they are not in ultimate subaltern position, but negotiating their interests with the plans established by the authorities. In this regard, authorities in general are ahead of prisoners. They are dominant not simply because they control the means of coercion within prison; they are also in the privileged position of being able to shape the consent of subaltern groups within penal apparatuses. Thus, it is not surprising that, as Carrabine (2005) has argued, most prisons are orderly. Yet, while inmates may often simply adapt to prison domination (Carrabine, 2005; Sykes, 2007), seeing the penal system from a Gramscian perspective, the prevailing social conformity of inmates does not eradicate the inevitable underlying tension between the interests of prison as an apparatus and that of inmates as its subaltern group (Lukes, 2005). On the contrary, thinking with Gramsci but beyond him has allowed us to critically conceive how power is shaped in prison through its contradictions, limits and struggles, see domination beyond overt coercion to its more nuanced mechanisms of consent, and pay attention to the often-neglected group interests that may appear as storming heaven – but is a spectre long haunting the system itself.

Notes

[1] Dias (2011) has used the concept of hegemony in her work associated to the idea of a monopoly of violence by gangs that may take away state sovereignty. Her approach draws the concept of hegemony from Norbert Elias' framework, which in its turn is used within the context of wars between states – therefore connected to violence, coercion and sovereignty. In this chapter, I will use hegemony from a different framework (Gramsci, 1992), which conceives it not as a conflict of sovereignty, but as one where dominant social groups assume a leadership to produce consent.

[2] Brazil has a complex cultural formation comprising larger prison gangs (mainly for our purpose of interest here, the Primeiro Comando da Capital [PCC] are known as a *facção* [literally translated as faction]). The PCC is considered the strongest and most widely dispersed network among a small number of nationally widespread factions. They emerged in Sao Paulo between the late 1980s and early 1990s inside prisons (Dias, 2009). According to the most popular version of the origins of the PCC (Jozino, 2005), a couple of prisoners came up with the idea of forming a sort of 'union' (*sindicato*) of prisoners. These prisoners, mostly serving very long sentences, sought to organize against the institutional violence of prison staff and create some pressure to change a law that had exacerbated prison conditions (Jozino, 2005: 26–29). Although there are various versions of the origin of the PCC (Biondi, 2010), relevant to our purposes is that from

1998 leaders of the PCC were transferred to the state of Paraná (Silva and Soares, 2001) to help contain their expansion within the São Paulo prison system. However, after a number of failed escape attempts from part of the PCC leadership that escalated into major riots (Bitencourt, 2012), the PCC slowly started to grow within Paraná itself (Bodezan, 2011; Reis, 2018) and can now be found in the vast majority of prison units (jails and penitentiaries) across the state (Dieter and Freitas, 2020). In the course of its growth the PCC has organized riots, promoted violent attacks against the authorities and became part of the national debate on 'organized crime' and drug trafficking in Brazil.

[3] The debate occurring at a national level that had a sudden impact in Guarapuava dealt with whether the time spent for a certain conviction should be considered if the prisoner is convicted of another crime (a conviction for a crime that might have happened before or after the first sentence, for which the inmate had been serving time in prison). If the time spent in prison due to the first conviction is not taken into consideration in the new conviction, then the length spent in a harsher regime of the sentence can be considerably longer. As an abstract example concerning only the time of conviction awarded in a sentence, for instance, someone is charged with (non-armed) robbery and drug trafficking. If they are convicted for five years for drug trafficking, after two years they are expecting to progress to a more lenient regime, but if before progressing they are convicted for the robbery (supposing) for eight years then there is a complication regarding when they will move to the more lenient regime. In abstract terms, the robbery imposes more or less two extra years to the closed regime, however the legislation is not clear how that time affects the time already spent overall in prison for the first conviction (in this example, for the drug trafficking). In practical terms, in a more lenient interpretation they would progress to the semi-open regime adding only two more years to the time already done in prison; however, in a more punitive interpretation the time spent for the drug trafficking would have to restart (two years, again, regardless of the time already spent), plus the time of the non-armed robbery (two years). Again, using this example, in the punitive interpretation if any other conviction (a third, non-related conviction) occurs while the prisoner is doing their time for the drug trafficking and the robbery, the time would restart again in the worse prison regime for both crimes, plus the time of the new conviction and so forth.

References

Adams, R. (1992) *Prison Riots in Britain and the USA*. London: Palgrave Macmillan.

Adorno, S. and Salla, F. (2007) Organized criminality in prisons and the attacks of the PCC. *Estudos Avançados*, 21(61): 7–29.

Agência Brasil (2010) Rebelião Em Penitenciária Do Paraná Deixa Cinco Mortos, Diz PM. *Último Segundo*, 15 January. Available from: https://ultimosegundo.ig.com.br/brasil/rebeliao-em-penitenciaria-do-Parana-deixa-cinco-mortos-diz-pm/n1237610062998.html [Accessed 7 April 2022].

Antillano, A. (2017) When prisoners make the prison: Self-rule in Venezuelan prisons. *Prison Service Journal*, 229: 26–30.

Armstrong, S. and Jefferson, A.M. (2017) Disavowing 'the' prison, in D. Moran and A.K. Schliehe (eds) *Carceral Spatiality: Dialogues between Geography and Criminology*. London: Palgrave Macmillan, pp 237–267.

Biondi, K. (2010) *Junto e Misturado: Uma Etnografia Do PCC*. São Paulo: Terceiro Nome.

Bitencourt, C.R. (2012) *Penitenciária: Estágio Para o Inferno*. Curitiba: Maximus.

Bodezan, S.J. (2011) *Penitenciárias No Paraná: Contribuição Aos Estudos Sobre Sociologia Da Punição e Políticas de Segurança*. Master's Thesis, Universidade Estadual de Maringá.

Boin, A. and Rattray, W.A.R. (2004) Understanding prison riots: Towards a threshold theory. *Punishment & Society*, 6(1): 47–65.

Carrabine, E. (2005) Prison riots, social order and the problem of legitimacy. *British Journal of Criminology*, 45(6): 896–913.

Cavadino, M. and Dignan, J. (2007) *The Penal System: An Introduction*. London: SAGE.

Cordeiro, S. (2014) Presos Libertam Reféns e Terminam Rebelião Em Guarapuava Após 48h. *G1 Paraná*. Available from: https://g1.globo.com/pr/campos-gerais-sul/noticia/2014/10/presos-libertam-refens-e-terminam-rebeliao-em-Guarapuava-apos-48h.html [Accessed 11 November 2018]

Coutinho, C.N. (2010) *O Estruturalismo e a Miséria Da Razão* (2nd edition). São Paulo: Expressão Popular.

Cruz, M.R.S. (2018) STJ - Recurso Especial 1557461 / SC.

Darke, S. (2018) *Conviviality and Survival: Co-Producing Brazilian Prison Order*. London: Palgrave Macmillan.

Dias, C.N. (2009) Da Guerra à Gestão: A Trajetória Do Primeiro Comando Da Capital (PCC) Nas Prisões de São Paulo. *Revista Percurso: Sociedade, Natureza e Cultura*, 2(10): 79–96.

Dias, C.N. (2011) *Da Pulverização Ao Monopólio Da Violência: Expansão e Consolidação Do Primeiro Comando Da Capital (PCC) No Sistema Carcerário Paulista*. Doctoral Thesis, Universidade de São Paulo.

Dias, C.N. and Silvestre, G. (2009) Situação Carcerária No Estado de São Paulo, in L. Souza (ed) *Políticas de Segurança Pública No Estado de São Paulo: Situações e Perspectivas a Partir Das Pesquisas Do Observatório de Segurança Pública Da UNESP*. São Paulo: UNESP, pp 91–105.

Dieter, V.S. and Freitas, R.A. (2020) The 'prison-presence': Prison culture beyond its walls. *Antigone*, 15(2): 62–83.

DMF-CNJ (2010) Mutirão Carcerário Realizado No Estado Do Paraná: Relatório Geral. Brasilia. Available from: https://www.justica.pr.gov.br/sites/default/arquivos_restritos/files/migrados/File/sigepsemiaberto/CNJ_relatorio_Parana.pdf [Accessed January 2020]

Egan, D. (2016) Gramsci's war of position as siege warfare: Some lessons from history. *Critique*, 44(4): 435–450.

Faria, E.C. (2008) *Trabalho e Pena: O Desvelamento Do Discurso Crítico Pela Penitenciária Industrial de Guarapuava*. Curitiba: UFPR.

Fleisher, M.S. and Decker, S.H. (2001) An overview of the challenge of prison gangs. *Corrections Management Quarterly*, 5(1): 1–9.

Fonseca, M.R.S. (2015) STJ - Agravo Regimental no Agravo em Recurso Especial 598723 / MG.

Giamberardino, A.R. (2021) *Comentários a Lei de Execução Penal*, edited by C. Paiva (3rd edition). Belo Horizonte: CEI.

Gramsci, A. (1992) *Selections from the Prison Notebooks*, edited by Q. Hoare and G. Nowell Smith. New York: International Publishers.

Gruner, C. (2011) 'Virando a Unidade': Análise Comparada de Duas Rebeliões Nas Prisões Paranaenses, in *Anais Do XXVI Simpósio Nacional de História – ANPUH*. São Paulo: ANPUH, pp 1–16.

Hall, S. and Jefferson, T. (2006) *Resistance Through Rituals: Youth Subcultures in Post-War Britain*. London: Routledge.

Hall, S., Critcher, C., Jefferson, T., Clarke, J. and Roberts, B. (1978) *Policing the Crisis: Mugging, the State and Law and Order*. London: Macmillan.

Human Rights Watch (1998) *Behind Bars in Brazil*. New York: Human Rights Watch.

Jozino, J. (2005) *Cobras e Lagartos: A Vida Intima e Perversa Nas Prisoes Brasileiras. Quem Manda e Quem Obedece No Partido Do Crime*. Rio de Janeiro: Objetiva.

Kikuchi, J.C.H. (2003) *Gerência de Segurança No Sistema Penitenciário*. Master's Thesis, UFPR.

Lukes, S. (2005) *Power: A Radical View* (2nd edition). London: Palgrave Macmillan.

Macaulay, F. (2013) Modes of prison administration, control and governmentality in Latin America: Adoption, adaptation and hybridity. *Conflict, Security & Development*, 13(4): 361–392.

Matthews, R. (1999) *Doing Time: An Introduction to the Sociology of Imprisonment*. New York: St. Martin's Press.

Ministry of Justice (2017) *Levantamento Nacional De Informações Penitenciárias – INFOPEN*. Brasilia: DEPEN.

Monteiro, J. (2010) Encerrada Rebelião Mais Cruel Do Paraná. *Tribuna do Paraná*, 16 January. Available from: https://tribunapr.uol.com.br/painel-do-crime/encerrada-rebeliao-mais-cruel-do-Parana/ [Accessed 15 November 2020]

Moraes, P.R.B. (2005) *Punição, Encarceramento e Construção de Identidade Profissional Entre Agentes Penitenciários*. São Paulo: IBCCRIM.

Narag, R.E. and Jones, C.R. (2017) Understanding prison management in the Philippines: A case for shared governance. *Prison Journal*, 97(1): 3–26.

Paciornik, M.J.I. (2017) STJ - Habeas Corpus 355522 / RS.

Prado, L.R., Hammerschmidt, D. Maranhão, D.B. and Coimbra, M. (2017) *Direito de Execução Penal*, edited by L.R. Prado (4th edition). São Paulo: Revista dos Tribunais.

Reis, W.P.S. (2014) *A Fundamentação Ideológica Do Poder Punitivo e o Cárcere Como Meio de Controle Social- a Punição Para Além Do Cumprimento Da Pena*. Master's Thesis, UFPR.

Reis, W.P.S. (2018) *As Raízes Dos Discursos Midiáticos Sobre a Questão Penitenciária No Paraná: Os Primeiros Conflitos Carcerários Que Antecederam a História Das Rebeliões a Partir de 1982*, edited by K. Silene Cáceres Arguello and P. Placha Sá. Curitiba: EVG.

Ribeiro, A. (2010) Cinco Presos Morreram Em Rebelião Na PCE; 90% Das Celas Foram Destruídas Motim. *Gazeta Do Povo*, 15 January. Available from: https://www.gazetadopovo.com.br/vida-e-cidadania/cinco-presos-morreram- em-rebeliao-na-pce-90-das-celas-foram-destruidas-9pnfp1byy1dcadozooqyvqr7y/ [Accessed 11 April 2022].

Roig, R.D.E. (2016) *Execução Penal: Teoria Crítica* (2nd edition). São Paulo: Saraiva.

Salla, F. (2006) As Rebeliões Nas Prisões: Novos Significados a Partir da Experiência Brasileira. *Sociologias*, 8(16): 274–307.

Scott, J.C. (1990) *Domination and the Arts of Resistance: Hidden Transcripts*. London: Yale University Press.

Secom (2019) Presos Precisam de Oportunidades de Ressocialização, Defende Moro. *Jornal Extra Guarapuava*, 3 April.

Silva, A. and Soares, R. (2001) Transferência Deu Origem a Facção No Paraná. *Folha de São Paulo*, 25 February.

Skarbek, D. (2014) *The Social Order of the Underworld: How Prison Gangs Govern the American Penal System*. Oxford: Oxford University Press.

Sparks, R.J., Bottoms, A.E. and Hay, W. (1996) *Prisons and the Problem of Order*. Oxford: Clarendon Press.

Stephenson, S. (2015) *Gangs of Russia: From the Streets to the Corridors of Power*. London: Cornell University Press.

Strinati, D. (2004) *An Introduction to Theories of Popular Culture* (2nd edition). London and New York: Routledge.

Sykes, G.M. (2007) *The Society of Captives: A Study of a Maximum Security Prison* (2nd edition). Princeton: Princeton University Press.

Useem, B. and Kimball, P.A. (1987) A theory of prison riots. *Theory and Society*, 16(1): 87–122.

Useem, B. and Kimball, P. (1991) *States of Siege: U.S. Prison Riots 1971–1986*. New York: Oxford University Press.

Varella, D. (1999) *Estação Carandiru* (1st edition). São Paulo: Companhia das Letras.

Weegels, J. (2020) Prison riots in Nicaragua: Negotiating co-governance amid creative violence and public secrecy. *International Criminal Justice Review*, 30(1): 61–82.

Whyte, W.F. (1943) Social organization in the slums. *American Sociological Review*, 8(1): 34–39.

9

The Political Economy of Punishment in the Global Periphery: Incarceration and Discipline in Brazilian Prisons

Luiz Dal Santo

Introduction

The Political Economy of Punishment (PEofP) is a traditional theoretical framework present in criminological debates. Since Rusche and Kirchheimer (henceforth R&K, 2003 [1939]), then Melossi and Pavarini (1977) and Hall et al (1978), and several other scholars more recently (De Giorgi, 2002; Sutton, 2004; Lacey, 2008; Cheolitis and Xenakis, 2010; Martins, 2016; Melossi et al, 2018; Dal Santo, 2021, forthcoming c; Cheliotis, 2022), the PEofP brings a materialist approach to the analysis of trends and patterns of punishment. As De Giorgi (2018: 1) puts, the PEofP 'hypothesizes the existence of a structural relationship between transformations of the economy and changes in the penal field'.

After experiencing a 'culturalist turn' in the 1990s, the sociology of punishment saw a 'renaissance of the political economy of punishment' in the early 2000s (Sozzo, 2018). This theoretical framework has undergone some changes, among which we could highlight: (1) the overcoming of unemployment rates as the only indicator of the lowest labour class standards of life (Sutton, 2004); (2) the consideration of symbolic dimensions of punishment, as well as the influence of cultural, political and institutional elements on its trends (De Giorgi, 2002, 2013, 2018); and (3) the growth of a comparative approach between different countries (Sutton, 2004; Cavadino and Dignan, 2006, 2011; Lacey, 2008). Nonetheless, the PEofP still faces some problems.

Despite expanding its comparative approach, the PEofP remains oriented by, and limited to, the experiences of core countries. When peripheral countries are considered, it seems that some of the main premises of the PEofP may not be empirically observed. For instance, Latin American countries have experienced increasing incarceration rates even during times of social inclusion (Fonseca, 2015; Azevedo and Cifali, 2016; Hernandez and Grajales, 2016; Paladines, 2016; Sozzo, 2017; Iturralde, 2019; Dal Santo, 2020, forthcoming a). In addition, Brazilian prisons have been marked by low numbers of prisoners involved in working/teaching activities (Dal Santo, 2019, forthcoming b). This chapter is then aimed at answering whether the PEofP is a theoretical framework *from* and *for* core countries only, or if this may also be helpful to make sense of punishment in peripheral regions.

For this purpose, this work engages with three main claims from R&K's *Punishment and Social Structure* (2003 [1939]): first, what is known in the literature as the 'R&K's Hypothesis', which means there is a 'direct positive relationship between changing imprisonment rates and changing unemployment rates' (Melossi, 2003: xxiii); then, the productive dimension of punishment, better represented by the famous statement that 'every system of production tends to discover punishment which correspond to its productive relationships' (R&K, 2003 [1939]: 5); and, finally, the principle of less eligibility, which orients 'the necessity of keeping prisoners' living standard below the living standard of the lowest classes of the free population' (R&K, 2003 [1939]: 108). The chapter is then divided in three main parts, following these three PEofP main premises.

Quantitative dimensions of punishment: how many to be punished?

From a historical-materialist perspective, Rusche and Kirchheimer observed that variations in punishment trends are not driven by changes in crime rates, but by variations in the surplus labour force. In about the 1980s, the 'R&K Hypothesis' was explored in a series of quantitative analyses that tried to find a correlation between imprisonment and unemployment rates (for example, Greenberg, 1977; Jankovic, 1977; Laffargue and Godefroy, 1989; Chiricos and Bales, 1991; Chiricos and DeLone, 1992). Trying to make sense of contemporary penality, in particular mass incarceration, authors such as Giorgi and Wacquant have made efforts to refine what some considered a 'materialist reductionism' (Garland, 1990: 108). The authors, respectively, found in post-Fordism and neoliberalism the causal explanations for mass incarceration. Put simply, both accounts see the historical targets of incarceration being expanded – post-Fordism in promoting structural unemployment (De Giorgi, 2002) and neoliberalism in increasing poverty and social insecurity (Wacquant, 2009).

Mass incarceration has also been a phenomenon observed in Brazil. Between 1990 and 2016 the imprisonment rates (prisoners for every 100,000 inhabitants) increased by nearly six times, from 61 to 352 (MJSP, 2017). For many scholars, Wacquant's 'neoliberal penality thesis' fits well enough with the Brazilian context (for example, Wacquant, 2003; Arguello, 2007; Batista and Abramovay 2010; Batista, 2012; Toscani, 2018). This thesis found a favourable context as it was recognized that political choices determined the rise of neoliberalism in the country in the 1990s (Antunes, 2004; Martins, 2011), the precise moment when Brazilian imprisonment rates started to escalate. However, this approach ends up ignoring the subsequent period of economic growth and social inclusion that Brazil underwent from 2002 to the mid-2000s (Azevedo and Cifali, 2016; Dal Santo, 2020). Not only had Brazil had a dramatic decrease in its unemployment rates (from 13 per cent in June 2003 to almost 4 per cent in December 2014 [IPEA, 2017]), the country also experienced a significant decline of its inequality levels (GINI index from 58.1 to 51.9 between 2002 and 2015).

At first glance, the reproduction of mass incarceration in times of economic growth and inclusion in Brazil might represent a contrast to the PEofP perspective. Importantly, Brazil does not represent a mere exception in this context: nearly all Latin American countries have experienced similar trends (see Sozzo, 2016; Iturralde, 2019). Elsewhere I have analysed the conditions of possibility for mass incarceration in that specific context, arguing three key points that Brazilian criminologists have been asking the wrong questions about. Rather than asking why we have high imprisonment rates now, we should first understand why we had imprisonment rates comparable to Scandinavian countries up to the 1990s. Next, we should stop uncritically reproducing Northern theories and understand the *local* conditions of possibility for mass incarceration in times of social inclusion (going beyond the presumed equation of more poverty, more punishment; more social investment, less punishment). Finally, rather than focusing upon politicians (and political changes), we ought to better understand internal struggles in the criminal justice system and, in particular, the pivotal role played by judges in the reproduction of mass incarceration in Brazil (Dal Santo, forthcoming a). Here I will only retrace the key points of that argument.

In the preface to Rusche and Kirchheimer's *Punishment and Social Structure*, Melossi (2003: xxxvii) claimed that 'Rusche's hypothesis has to be negotiated with many other aspects of social reality and especially with the historical specificity of each country's history'. Similarly, I argued that before understanding why Brazil has such high rates of imprisonment now, one should comprehend why the country had such low imprisonment rates until 1990. In that year, the Brazilian imprisonment rate was 60 per 100,000 inhabitants, comparable to the historically low Scandinavian rates of incarceration. To do so, one needs to consider at least two major elements: the prevalence of a more 'domestic' form of punishment until the late-20th century and the peculiar institutional practices of the military dictatorship, that lasted over 20 years in the country (from 1964 to 1985). I consider the former but not the latter issue in the following section.

Similarly, and before *Punishment and Social Structure*, Rusche himself had highlighted the complex interplay between economic and punitive systems. He acknowledged 'the dependency of crime and crime control on economic and historical conditions does not, however, provide a total explanation. These forces do not alone determine the object of our investigation and by themselves are limited and incomplete in several ways' (Rusche, 1978: 3). The Rusche and Kirchheimer hypothesis therefore should not read as a mechanical, determinist statement, but rather as a trend. As in anything pertaining to social reality, human action cannot be neglected (Archer, 1998; Bhaskar, 1998). This is not, though, to deny the importance of structure and to return to a microanalysis of punishment. Nevertheless, the role played by human agency in the reproduction of mass incarceration in times of social inclusion must be considered. In some contexts, politicians might have had a more pivotal role (Paladines, 2016; Sozzo, 2017). In the Brazilian case, judges have been the key actors. A fuller analysis of this will exceed the scope of this chapter (for a more detailed analysis, see Dal Santo, forthcoming a).

Finally, the last element to be considered here is that the so-called period of economic growth and social inclusion in Brazil (and in Latin America) could be seen through different lenses. This period could be seen as a later part of a wider historical moment in the region, representing a period of *mass incorporation*. This comprises, for example, the late processes of industrialization, the transition from a rural to urban society, and the modernization and enlargement of the state. Regarding the late process of industrialization, although its development started in about the 1930s in Brazil (Marini, 2000 [1973]: 75; Fernandes, 2008 [1964]; Antunes, 2016: 84), it is only from the second half of the 20th century that this trend started to grow faster until the 1970s (Pochmann, 2012: 16) – when neoliberalism had already ascended in other countries (Anderson, 1995; Harvey, 2005; Wacquant, 2009). Linked to this, it was only in the early 1970s that the urban population became larger than the rural one in Brazil (IBGE, 2006). Following these demographic and socioeconomic changes, Brazil underwent a process of modernization and enlargement of its state apparatuses, bringing larger sections of society into its sphere of influence. The modernization (Fonseca, 2018) and expansion (Dal Santo, forthcoming a) of the state penal apparatus are part of a wider state-building process that directly increased the state institutional and formal capacity to punish. These are therefore relevant changes that also pertain to the structural domain, despite being overlooked by Northern literature, which at times has been overly concerned with quantitative indicators such as rates of inequality, poverty and unemployment (Sutton, 2004; Downes and Hansen, 2006).

A direct, positive relationship between imprisonment and unemployment rates is not observed in 21st-century Latin America (Sozzo, 2021). This, however, does not determine the failure of the PEofP. The consideration of other elements from a political-economic viewpoint is needed and, when thoroughly addressed, will shed light on considerable changes in the penal domain.

Qualitative dimensions of punishment: productive relations

After discussing some quantitative elements of punishment from a PEofP perspective, this section starts engaging with some of its qualitative dimensions. In particular, it takes a historical approach to analyse transitions in patterns of punishment in Brazil. In so doing, it verifies how applicable the paradigmatic claim that 'every system of production tends to discover punishments which correspond to its productive relationships' is in a peripheral setting.

Three historical facts are crucial for setting the scene. To begin with, the first Latin American 'modern prison' – Rio de Janeiro's House of Correction – began construction in 1834 and was completed only in 1850 (Aguirre, 2009). Secondly, slavery lasted four centuries in Brazil, being abolished only in 1888, making Brazil the last country in the so-called West to officially abolish slavery. Thirdly, and as already noted, after slavery was abolished, Brazil remained as a predominantly rural country until early 1970s.

These facts can help us understand the close relations between punishment and social structure. Aguirre (2009: 215) argues that the time it took for the Rio de Janeiro House of Correction to be completed suggests a number of economic and political difficulties to be overcome when designing prison regimes according to 'liberal principles'. Several other projects for 'modern prisons' were developed but not put into practice (Koerner, 2001). Were modern prisons meeting local elites' interests, these reforms would not have faced so many economic barriers and political contestation. The very social structure was a limitation for that new system of punishment to thrive. At that historical moment, slavery was still in force. It follows that punitive practices were chiefly enforced in a private context, within the plantations, and at the behest of the plantation owners (Zaffaroni et al, 2015: 414). As Koerner (2001) asserts, the enforcement of the punishment of slaves by their masters meant there were no standardized rules for crime and punishment; each master would define their own set of crimes, adopt their own criminal 'procedure', and enforce their own punishment as they pleased.

The way the new Penal Code of 1930 dealt with punishment of slaves also illustrates this dilemma well. While the 1830 Penal Code recognized slaves not as 'things', as they were defined in contemporary civil law, but as responsible subjects, even so the code preserved the 'slave owners' autonomy to punish their slaves. Bodily injury to a slave for disciplinary purposes was not considered unlawful (Dieter, 2012: 621). In practice, there was only one main exception to that masters' autonomy, that is, some criminal offences would also demand a civil reparation. This Code established that if a convicted person were unable to economically repair the damage caused, they would serve a prison sentence to dispose of their work for the time necessary to pay off the debt. This provision was directed to slaves (Dieter, 2012). Before this Code, the civil reparation was a responsibility of the slave owner, who, in turn, would make them free, avoiding the debt assumption. However, the purchase of slaves was legally forbidden at that time. In the end, the slave owner would free their slave; the offended would not have any compensation for the damage suffered; and the slave would become free, but indebted and dispossessed, with no means to meet the debt. The Code then 'fixed' that situation as per local elites' interests. In addition to slaves caught while trying to escape from bondage (Koerner, 2001), this was the main reason enslaved people were taken to prison.

Even after slavery was abolished, domestic patterns of punishment remained predominant. It is true that several political, economic, and social changes took place in the country between the 18th and 19th centuries (see Fernandes, 2008 [1964]; Leal, 2012 [1976]; Ribeiro, 2015 [1995]). Migration from rural to newly urban cities started to increase. Take the city of São Paulo: its population soared from 35,000 to 600,000 inhabitants between 1880 and 1924 (Fausto, 1984: 10). The role of the state in practices of punishment and social control was considerably larger in urban than in rural areas. In the latter, rural areas, as I argued elsewhere (Dal Santo, forthcoming a), large landowners played a significant role in dispensing criminal justice. Even official documents show cases of delegation of punitive power to large landowners, who kept ordinary people in custody in their own properties (Franco, 1997 [1969]: 153–162). In the urban areas, police had a larger role in controlling Black people – seen as responsible for a 'white fear' (Azevedo, 1987; Flauzina, 2006) – and, during a specific historical moment and place, also controlling White immigrants (Fausto, 1984). However, a major part of Brazilian society lived in rural areas until the early 1970s, making domestic practices of punishment predominant from the 16th to the 19th, but also until mid-20th century.

Considering the preceding points, the PEofP allows us to understand why domestic/privatized practices of punishment were predominant in Brazil throughout that period, whereas prisons were becoming the main form of punishment in core countries. While Brazil had a slave labour force until the late 19th century, the Industrial Revolution had already taken place almost a century earlier in the United Kingdom (Hobsbawm, 1996 [1962]), having deeply reshaped the modes of production and, consequently, the social relations in that region. The newly industrializing social order demanded specific forms of discipline and control, which were reproduced within prisons (Melossi and Pavarini, 1977). In a slaveholding, rural Brazil, as well as in other Latin American and peripheral countries, domestic punishments were a more effective mechanism of social control and order production. Corporal, domestic punitive practices enforced a pattern of discipline and subordination based on a close, physical relation between dominant and dominated, guaranteeing the material conditions and social relations for the reproduction of that given social structure. That punishment reproduced relations of personal dominance and a duality of 'social distance and physical closeness' (Koerner, 2001). Core and peripheral countries had significantly different modes of production and social structures, as well as different predominant punitive practices. This then corroborates the idea that every system of production tends to discover punishments which correspond to its own productive relationships.

Qualitative dimensions of punishment: less eligibility and discipline

In addition to transitions in predominant forms of punishment, the PEofP framework is also useful to make sense of historical traits and peculiar elements of prison life. In this section, I explore historical roles played by violence within Brazilian prisons. I first analyse how this relates to the principle of less eligibility (the idea that prison conditions should be worse than those attainable by the lowest class of free labourers), and then explore how violence also plays a pivotal role in reproducing discipline. These are two dimensions of punishment in peripheral settings that corroborate two main assumptions from the PEofP viewpoint.

As per the principle of less eligibility, living conditions in prisons are dependent upon the living conditions of the 'lowest socially significant proletarian class' (Rusche, 2014 [1933]: 255–256). In peripheral contexts, often characterized by fundamentally higher levels of poverty, inequality, hunger and homelessness, for prisons to be 'less eligible' must entail additionally punitive hardships and deprivations. In the first section of this chapter, I mentioned that Brazil recently experienced a period of economic growth and social inclusion. Yet the country has remained much poorer and more unequal than any core country. The lowest recorded GINI index in Brazil was of 51.9, in 2015, as indicated earlier. The highest recorded GINI indexes in the United Kingdom, United States and Australia were 38.4 (2000), 41.5 (2014) and 35.4 (2008), respectively. The lower the GINI index, the less unequal a country is. This means that even in the best Brazilian context, the country remained far more unequal than core countries. Other data can better represent what poverty means in the local context. Brazil remained in the United Nations World Food Programme's Hunger Map until early 2010s, having had over 22 million inhabitants living below internationally established nutritional standards in the 1990s (UN, 2015). Nearly 40 million people lived in extreme poverty up to the early 2000s. Housing issues are also relevant here. Although there is no official data on the number of homeless people (see Natalino, 2016), other information illustrates well the country's reality. As per official demographic data released by the Brazil Institute of Geography and Statistics (IBGE) in 2017, approximately 11.4 million people were living in *favelas* in 2010. In 2015, nearly 30 per cent of urban households lacked at least one of the three basic sanitation services – access to sewerage, running water and garbage collection (as per the data released by the IBGE in 2017). Despite a considerable improvement in Brazil's socioeconomic reality, the living standards of the lowest classes of its free population remain fundamentally worse than those achieved in core countries.

In this wider context of inhumane living conditions, violent relations have always played a crucial role in social relationships within Brazilian prisons. Violence, in all its different dimensions, has been an intrinsic feature of life in prisons since the 19th century. This comprises more structural and indirect elements, such as overcrowding (Dal Santo, 2019, forthcoming b), spoiled food, precarious and unhealthy facilities, and lack of medical care (MJSP, 2017), as well as more direct violent relations, both in inmate–inmate and staff–inmate relationships, resulting in torture, massacres and a high death toll.

In terms of staff–inmate relations, violence has always been a key instrument of prison governance. Since its very earliest 'modern' form and until at least the early 1990s, prison guards used to torture prisoners on a regular basis (Adorno, 1991; Koerner, 2001; Salla, 2007; Dias, 2011). Prisons were even known to have special rooms, often informally and ironically called *human rights cells*, where torture would take place (Adorno, 1991: 73; Dias, 2011). Extremely violent action was also the standardized intervention to contain prison riots. Several prison riots in the 1980s and 1990s ended up each with a dozen or more prisoners killed by the police (Salla, 2007: 75). The most well-known case is the Carandiru massacre, in 1992, when military police killed at least 111 prisoners. Several factors were involved, including the organization of prisoners as a collective of equals (Feltran, 2008; Dias, 2011; Biondi, 2016; see also Dal Santo, forthcoming b) and torture (although beatings did not take place as often and as openly as in the recent past) (Varella, 2012). Nonetheless, these abuses still happen systematically (Brazil, 2009; Pastoral Carcerária, 2010; HRW, 2015; UN, 2016). For instance, in the last three years, the number of complaints concerning torture has increased (Minuano, 2021), clearly suggesting that this is not a vanishing feature of Brazilian prisons.

Within prisons, violence is endemic and not limited to the relations between prison guards and prisoners. As Coelho (2005 [1985]: 84) puts it, the latter is not only physically beaten by the former but are also subjected to the brutality of other inmates. Adorno (1991: 72) argues that violence constituted a normative code of behaviours, and being violent represented an 'act of bravery and heroism that gives [inmates] prestige, as a form of personal respectability'. Until the 1990s, rape was a central element in prison sociability. It used to be the most common form of violence and subjugation between inmates (Coelho, 2005 [1985]: 84–96; Ramalho, 2008 [1979]: 41–43). Dias (2011: 203) suggests that until the 1990s, 'the ability to impose physical force was the basis for sustaining a personal and individualized form of power, and sexual subjugation through violence was an important element in asserting that power'. She also argues that this individualized capacity to use physical force used to be the central element to establish social hierarchies within prisons.

Often, prison management had little interest in regulating or prohibiting interpersonal violent relations. Prison staff used to see sexual violence as something 'normal within prisons' (Coelho, 2005 [1985]: 95–96). Similarly, describing living conditions in prisons where rival gangs are in custody together, Godoi (2017) reports that inmates from a specific gang are responsible for cooking for all inmates. As a consequence, inmates from the rival gang often receive food with glass powder, animal faeces, insects and even rat poison. By allowing food to be prepared by direct enemies, Godoi argues that state agencies ensure that the prison experience is the worst possible (Godoi, 2017: 170). This represents a passive, institutional approach that allows violence to be reproduced.

As mentioned before, though, there have been important changes in prison relationships. For instance, Primeiro Comando da Capital (PCC), a major Brazilian gang, has prohibited rapes – both in prisons and in local communities (Feltran, 2008; Dias, 2011). However, it does not follow that physical violence is over, but that it is not the primary basis of relations of domination anymore. Prison violence may no longer be a power possessed and exercised from an individualized perspective (Dias, 2011: 204). Homicides within prisons illustrate this well. Dias (2011) argues there were significant quantitative and qualitative changes in prison homicides before 1993, and between 1994 and 2001. In the previous period, homicides were usually a consequence of petty, personal quarrels between one inmate and another. The period between 1994 and 2001, which represents the rise of the PCC, was marked by increasing rates of homicide, but this was driven mostly by cases with more than one death caused in the same context, all of which suggests the patterns of collective and gang conflict. In this context, 'beheading becomes a hallmark of murders committed in the name of gangs' (Dias, 2011: 161). More recently, a number of inmate-on-inmate massacres took place in northeast Brazil, resulting in over a hundred deaths (Darke, 2018: 101–138). Although social relations in prisons may have changed, elevated levels of (deadly) violence still represent a key aspect of prison life.

The role played by physical violence in Brazilian prisons is not limited to the principle of less eligibility. Violence also works as a means of discipline. In fact, Brazilian prisons have always had low levels of inmates involved in educational and/or working activities – generally less than a quarter of the total prison population (Dal Santo, forthcoming b). This has given space for claims that Brazilian prisons operate merely as workhouses (Arantes, 2012; see also Godoi, 2017; Dal Santo, 2019). This wider context of idleness – or lack of prison labour – in tandem with the widespread violence may lead people to believe Brazilian prions have operated more as a destructive influence upon Brazilian society. Here lies an important differentiation between notions of discipline imposed within prisons and the 'rehabilitative ideal' sought through prison labour. As Melossi (2018: 30) argues, 'the point of discipline is not really to teach actually useful skills to potential workers … as a certain rhetoric of "resocialization" or "rehabilitation" would suggest. The point of discipline, rather, is to teach (at least programmatically) the lesson of what we could call "subordinate inclusion", obedience'. In a given context, even deaths can work towards discipline if one considers their effects beyond the dead body (Dal Santo, 2022). Earlier, I discussed how violent corporal relations mirror and reproduce social relationships in the Brazilian society in three different domains.

A form of 'violent sociability' has historically been a common trait of Brazilian society. Franco (1997 [1969]) describes violence as an institutionalized element in old, rural Brazil. She argues this was a common behavioural pattern in a social order in which individual courage was well regarded. Violence permeated the entire social order, Franco argues, and the use of force was widespread, including as means to solve minor and trivial conflicts (Franco, 1997 [1969]: 27–51). Yet in a more modern and urban Brazil, violence still remains central. Misse (2019) has pointed out that what he coined as a 'social accumulation of violence', a process originating in the 1950s, is still at work. He believes that the rise of 'death squads', mainly composed of off-duty police officers, in that decade represents the beginning of a new kind of urban violence in the country. The frequency of lynching (Martins, 2015), the elevated rates of homicide (Dal Santo, 2022) and gender-based violence (Gomes et al, 2018), as well as the extremely powerful and organized gangs (see, for example, Feltran, 2008; Willis, 2015; Biondi, 2016) also illustrate the violent sociability in contemporary, urban Brazil.

Violence has also been used by the Brazilian state, particularly as a means of governance and control. Repression has been a key instrument in producing and preserving social order throughout Brazilian history even beyond prisons. Between the 1920s and the 1940s, Brazil relied on its police apparatus to contain workers and union leaders, chasing and persecuting communists, socialists and anarchists (Zaffaroni et al, 2015: 455). In 1964, a coup d'état established a military dictatorship that lasted until 1985. That period was characterized by, for example, the suppression of political mandates and rights, persecution of workers' and peasants' leaders, closure of unions, censorship, torture and unlawful arrests (Teles and Safatle, 2010). The end of the military dictatorship and the following transition to democracy, however, did not end the state's widespread use of violence. Brazil is the only Latin American country where police lethality has increased *after* military dictatorship (Sikking and Walling, 2007). Broader public security policies have then been marked by 'extreme levels of everyday violence' (Cavalcanti and Garmany, 2020) and, since 2017, police have been responsible for killing over 5,000 civilians annually (Dal Santo, 2022). Therefore, violence is a feature both of sociability and governance in Brazil.

Conditions of labour are the last element to be considered in order to understand the relevance of violent, physical relations within Brazilian prisons. High levels of exploitation and submission, as well as its predominantly physical character, are historical features of labour in Brazil. While it is true that the country has a colonial past and that slavery lasted four centuries there, explaining the present purely through this would overlook those facts, relations and conditions that have allowed those old practices to be reproduced and/or reshaped. The Marxist critique of dependency (Bambirra, 2013 [1970]; Marini, 2000 [1973]; Santos, 1970) can help us to better understand contemporary conditions of labour and relations of production. After reaching its formal independence from Portugal and overcoming its colonial condition, Brazil stepped into a new condition of dependency. According to Santos (1970: 231), dependency is a 'situation in which the economy of certain countries is conditioned by the development and expansion of another economy to which the former is subjected'. However, different from colonialism, these new relations of subordination are necessarily between two formally independent nations (Marini, 2000 [1973]: 109). The consolidation of industry and the consequent establishment of a new international division of labour in the 19th century is the moment when the relations of dependency were set. From that moment, Brazil (and the whole of Latin America) has had a clear role in supplying raw materials and agricultural commodities to most developed countries. In the second half of the 20th century, Brazil also occupied a position in the lower stages of industrial production, such as the extraction of raw materials and primary manufacture, which enabled core countries to concentrate both on the more advanced stages of industrial production employing a monopoly of more developed technologies (Marini, 2000 [1973]: 145). More recently,

Brazilian foreign trade has returned to its former role as supplier of primary goods to the capitalist market (Martins, 2011). This situation has led to an uneven international trade and the most common way disadvantaged and dependent nations found to compensate the loss of income produced by this unbalanced international trade is through a greater exploitation of workers (Marini, 2000 [1973]: 122). Because Latin American production works to meet core countries' demands and interests based on a global market, the region's internal consumption capacity is limited. With the circulation and production of goods primarily for the foreign market, the conditions for workers to reproduce their labour force are not always met – and are not always an actual goal. This is particularly the case given the wide possibility of labour replacement through the incorporation of unemployed workers. This enables a qualitatively higher degree of exploitation called 'super-exploitation'. For our purposes, two main points are taken from this: the international division of labour determines the predominance of more physical, and less technological, forms of work, while the conditions of production and patterns of wealth accumulation impose greater levels of exploitation of workers.

What do these labour conditions have to do with prison conditions? Violent, corporal relations within prisons then have a productive rationale and should not be seen as if they operate according to a merely destructive logic. On the one hand, this is a form of imposing brutality on inmates, mirroring, to some extent, the predominant physical labour in the country, which, in turn, demands more corporal control and interventions. On the other hand, this context also reproduces relations of more extreme submission, oppression and dominance in a society marked by greater degrees of exploitation and subjugation. In that context, violent corporal relations work to instill subordinate inclusion.

Conclusion

In this chapter, I have shown how useful the PEofP is to make sense of penal changes in Brazil. In fact, there are several contested theoretical understandings involving the PEofP even within Northern penal regimes. It is not so surprising that these issues resurface in core–periphery dialogues. Despite sometimes looking contrary to some of the main claims of PEofP, the Brazilian case instead corroborates them. Neither the reproduction of mass incarceration in times of economic growth and inclusion, nor the historical lack of prison labour in Brazil, refute the PEofP. To make sense of penal changes, though, one must always consider local and historical particularities, as well as structural differences and elements. Some of these elements may be simply taken for granted in Northern analyses, such as in state-building processes and in the transition from rural to predominantly urban societies.

Other elements may be peculiar to regions beyond the core, such as relations of dependency and the super-exploitation of the labour force.

After engaging with some key premises and claims from Rusche and Kirchheimer's *Punishment and Social Structure*, it is clear that the PEofP is not a theoretical framework for core countries only. A historical analysis of punishment in colonial, slave and rural Brazil indicates that systems of production indeed tend to find patterns of punishment that correspond to their productive relations. This explains both the predominance of domestic punitive practices and the intense brutality of prison life. The centrality of violent corporal relations within Brazilian prisons is more thoroughly appreciated from the PEofP perspective. On the one hand, the active and passive stances of prison staff towards violence work to reduce living conditions in prison below the living standards of the free population in a context of extreme poverty and inequality. This reiterates the principle of less eligibility. On the other hand, Brazilian historical sociability and governance, as well as Brazil's position in the international division of labour and conditions of production, also explains the roles violent physical relations have played in Brazilian prisons: they have worked as means to achieve a subordinate inclusion. Finally, social structure also helps us understand quantitative changes in punishment, not by offering accurate predictions in terms of specific numbers, but merely indicating trends. In the end, this chapter has shown that the PEofP is crucial for understanding both qualitative changes in punishment and is helpful to grasp quantitative changes. This theoretical approach, however, should not be employed to make rigid, mechanical predictions.

Acknowledgements

I am thankful to Hallam Tuck for his helpful feedback on a previous version of this work.

References

Adorno, S. (1991) Sistema prisional no Brasil: problemas e desafios. *Revista USP*, 9: 65–78.

Aguirre, C. (2009) Cárcel y sociedad en América Latina (1800–1940), in E.K. Garcés (ed) *Historia social urbana: espacios y flujos*. Quito: FLACSO, pp 209–252.

Anderson, P. (1995) Balanço do neoliberalismo, in E. Sader and P. Gentili (eds) *Pós-neoliberalismo: as políticas sociais e o Estado democrático*. Rio de Janeiro: Paz & Terra, pp 9–23.

Antunes, R. (2004) *A desertificação neoliberal no Brasil (Collor, FHC e Lula)*. Campinas: Autores Associados.

Antunes, R. (2016) De Vargas a Lula: caminhos e descaminhos da legislação trabalhista no Brasil. *Pegada*, 7(2): 83–88.

Arantes, P.E. (2012) Zonas de espera. Uma digressão sobre o tempo morto da onda punitiva contemporânea, in V.M. Batista (ed) *Loïc Wacquant e a questão penal no capitalismo neoliberal*. Rio de Janeiro: Revan, pp 229–280.

Archer, M. (1998) Introduction: Realism in the social sciences, in M. Archer (ed) *Critical Realism: Essential Readings*. London: Routledge, pp 189–205.

Arguello, K. (2007) Do Estado social ao Estado penal: invertendo o discurso da ordem, in W. Bitar (ed) *A criminologia no século XXI*. Rio de Janeiro: Lumen Juris/IBCCRIM, pp 119–144.

Azevedo, C.M. (1987) *Onda negra, medo branco: o negro no imaginário das elites – século XIX*. Rio de Janeiro: Paz & Terra.

Azevedo, R.G. and Cifali, A.C. (2016) Seguridad pública, política criminal y penalidad en Brasil durante los gobiernos Lula y Dilma (2003–2014): cambios y continuidades, in M. Sozzo (ed) *Postneoliberalismo y penalidad en América del Sur*. Buenos Aires: CLACSO, pp 29–94.

Bambirra, V. (2013 [1970]) *O capitalismo dependente latino-americano*. Florianópolis: Insular.

Batista, V.M. (2012) *Introdução crítica à criminologia brasileira*. Rio de Janeiro: Revan.

Batista, V.M. and Abramovay, P. (eds) (2010) *Depois do grande encarceramento*. Rio de Janeiro: Revan.

Bhaskar, R. (1998) Societies, in M. Archer (ed) *Critical Realism: Essential Readings*. London: Routledge, pp 206–257.

Biondi, K. (2016) *Sharing This Walk: An Ethnography of Prison Life in Brazil*. Chapel Hill: University of North Carolina Press.

Brazil (2009) *CPI Sistema Carcerário*. Brasília. Available from: https://www.inflation.eu/en/inflation-rates/brazil/historic-inflation/cpi-inflation-brazil-2009.aspx [Accessed 17 November 2022].

Cavadino, M. and Dignan, J. (2006) Penal policy and political economy. *Criminology & Criminal Justice*, 6(4): 435–456.

Cavadino, M. and Dignan, J. (2011) Penal comparisons: puzzling relations, in A. Crawfor (ed) *International and Comparative Criminal Justice and Urban Governance*. Cambridge: Cambridge University Press, pp 193–213.

Cavalcanti, R. and Garmany, J. (2020) The politics of crime and militarised policing in Brazil. *International Journal for Crime, Justice and Social Democracy*, 9(2): 102–118.

Cheliotis, L. (2022) Depression and repression: Global capitalism, economic crisis and penal politics in interwar Greece. *European Journal of Criminology*, 19(3): 419–441.

Cheliotis, L. and Xenakis, S. (2010) What's neoliberalism got to do with it? Towards a political economy of punishment in Greece. *Criminology & Criminal Justice*, 10(4): 353–373.

Chiricos, T.G. and Bales, W.D. (1991) Unemployment and punishment: An empirical assessment. *Criminology*, 29(4): 701–724.

Chiricos, T.G. and DeLone, M.A. (1992) Labor surplus and punishment: A review and assessment of theory and evidence. *Social Problems*, 39(4): 421–446.

Coelho, E.C. (2005 [1985]) *A oficina do diabo e outros estudos sobre criminalidade*. Rio de Janeiro: Record.

Dal Santo, L.P. (2019) Cumprindo pena no Brasil: encarceramento em massa, prisão-depósito e os limites das teorias sobre giro punitivo na realidade periférica. *RBCCRIM*, 151(27): 291–315.

Dal Santo, L.P. (2020) Reconsiderando a tese da penalidade neoliberal: inclusão social e encarceramento em massa no Brasil. *Revista da Faculdade de Direito da UFG*, 44 (1).

Dal Santo, L.P. (2021) Economía Política del Castigo en la periferia global: ¿Desde el silencio del norte a las importaciones acríticas? *Delito y Sociedad*, 53. https://doi.org/10.14409/dys.2022.53.e0053

Dal Santo, L.P. (2022) Killing and letting die: Depicting the Brazilian conundrum between police killings and private lethal practices, in W. Wallace (ed) *Guns, Gun Violence and Gun Homicides: Perspectives from the Caribbean, Global South and Beyond*. London: Palgrave Macmillan, pp 327–346.

Dal Santo, L.P. (forthcoming a) Mass incarceration in times of economic growth and inclusion? Three steps to understand contemporary imprisonment in Brazil. *Theoretical Criminology*.

Dal Santo, L.P. (forthcoming b) Brazilian prisons in times of mass incarceration: Ambivalent transformations. *The Howard Journal for Crime and Justice*.

Dal Santo, L.P. (forthcoming c) *A punição no Brasil: crítica do giro punitivo*. D'Plácido: Belo Horizonte.

Darke, S. (2018) *Conviviality and Survival: Co-producing Brazilian Prison Order*. Cham: Springer.

De Giorgi, A. (2002) *Il governo dell'eccedenza: postfordismo e controllo della moltitudine*. Verona: Ombre Corte.

De Giorgi, A. (2013) Punishment and political economy, in J. Simon and R. Sparks (eds) *The SAGE Handbook of Punishment and Society*. London: SAGE, pp 40–59.

De Giorgi, A. (2018) Punishment, Marxism, and political economy, in *The Oxford Research Encyclopedia of Criminology*. Available from: https://oxfordre.com/criminology/view/10.1093/acrefore/9780190264079.001.0001/acrefore-9780190264079-e-358 [Accessed 17 November 2022].

Dias, C.N. (2011) *Da pulverização ao monopólio da violência: expansão e consolidação do Primeiro Comando da Capital (PCC) no sistema carcerário paulista*. São Paulo: USP.

Dieter, M. (2012) Sistema econômico e tutela penal do escravo no Brasil Imperial. *Discursos Sediciosos: crime, direito e sociedade*, 17(19–20): 613–647.

Downes, D. and Hansen, K. (2006) Welfare and punishment in comparative perspective, in S. Armstrong and L. McAra (eds) *Perspectives on Punishment: The Contours of Control*. Oxford: Oxford University Press, pp 133–154.

Fausto, B. (1984) *Crime e cotidiano: a criminalidade em São Paulo (1880–1924)*. São Paulo: Brasiliense.

Feltran, G. (2008) *Fronteiras de tensão: um estudo sobre política e violência nas periferias de São Paulo*. São Paulo: Universidade Estadual de Campinas.

Fernandes, F. (2008 [1964]) *A integração do negro na sociedade de classes: o legado da 'raça branca'* (5th edition). São Paulo: Globo.

Flauzina, A.L. (2006) *Corpo negro caído no chão: o sistema penal e o projeto genocida do Estado brasileiro*. Brasilia: Universidade de Brasília.

Fonseca, D.S. (2015) Punishment and democracy in Brazil: Mass incarceration in times of social inclusion. *Crime, Justice and Social Democracy: Proceedings of the 3rd International Conference*, pp 37–45.

Fonseca, D.S. (2018) Expansion, standardization, and densification of the criminal justice apparatus: Recent developments in Brazil. *Punishment & Society*, 20(3): 329–350.

Franco, M.S. (1997 [1969]) *Homens livres na ordem escravocrata*. São Paulo: Fundacao Editora da UNESP.

Garland, D. (1990) *Punishment and Modern Society: A Study in Social Theory*. Oxford: Oxford University Press.

Godoi, R. (2017) *Fluxos em cadeia: as prisões em São Paulo na virada dos tempos*. São Paulo: Boitempo.

Gomes, M., Falavigno, C. and Da Mata, J. (eds) (2018) *Questões de gênero: uma abordagem sob a ótica das ciências criminais*. Belo Horizonte: D'Plácido.

Greenberg, D.F. (1977) The dynamics of oscillatory punishment processes. *The Journal of Criminal Law and Criminology (1973-)*, 68(4): 643–651.

Hall, S., Critcher, C., Jefferson, T., Clarke, J. and Roberts, B. (1978) *Policing the Crisis: Mugging, the State and Law and Order*. London: Macmillan.

Harvey, D. (2005) *A Brief History of Neoliberalism*. Oxford: Oxford University Press.

Hernandez, L. and Grajales, M. (2016) Chavismo y política penal (1999–2014), in M. Sozzo (ed) *Postneoliberalismo y penalidad en América del Sur*. Buenos Aires: CLACSO, pp 99–162.

Hobsbawm, E.J. (1996 [1962]) *The Age of Revolution 1789–1848*. London: Weidenfeld & Nicolson.

HRW (Human Rights Watch) (2015) *The State Let Evil Take Over: The Prison Crisis in the Brazilian State of Pernambuco*. Available from: https://www.hrw.org/report/2015/10/19/state-let-evil-take-over/prison-crisis-brazilian-state-pernambuco [Accessed 17 November 2022].

IBGE (Instituto Brasileiro de Geografia e Estatística) (2006) *Estatísticas do século XX*. Rio de Janeiro: IBGE.

IPEA (Institute for Applied Economic Research) (2017) *Brazilian Economic Outlook*. Available from: https://www.ipea.gov.br/cartadeconjuntura/wp-content/uploads/2017/12/171113_brazilian_economic_outlook_4rdq_2017.pdf [Accessed 17 November 2022].

Iturralde, M. (2019) Neoliberalism and its impact on Latin American crime control fields. *Theoretical Criminology*, 23(4): 471–490.

Jankovic, I. (1977) Labor market and imprisonment. *Crime and Social Justice*, 8: 17–31.

Koerner, A. (2001) O impossível 'panóptico tropical-escravista': práticas prisionais, política e sociedade no Brasil do século XIX. *Revista Brasileira de Ciências Criminais*, 35: 211–224.

Lacey, N. (2008) *The Prisoners' Dilemma: Political Economy and Punishment in Contemporary Democracies*. Cambridge: Cambridge University Press.

Laffargue, B. and Godefroy, T. (1989) Economic cycles and punishment: Unemployment and imprisonment. *Contemporary Crises*, 13(4): 371–404.

Leal, V.N. (2012 [1976]) *Coronelismo, enxada e voto. O município e o regime representativo no Brasil*. São Paulo: Alfa-Omega.

Marini, R.M. (2000 [1973]) *Dialética da dependência: uma antologia da obra de Ruy Mauro Marini*. Petrópolis: Vozes.

Martins, C.B. (2016) *Distribuir e punir?: capitalismo dependente brasileiro, racismo estrutural e encarceramento em massa nos governos do Partido dos Trabalhadores (2003–2016)*. PhD Thesis, UFG.

Martins, C.E. (2011) *Globalização, dependência e neoliberalismo na América Latina*. São Paulo: Boitempo.

Martins, J.D.S. (2015) *Linchamentos: a justiça popular no Brasil*. São Paulo: Ed. Contexto.

Melossi, D. (2003) Introduction to the transaction edition: The simple 'heuristic maxim' of an 'unusual human being', in G. Rusche and O. Kichheimer (eds) *Punishment and Social Structure*. London: Routledge, pp ix–xlv.

Melossi, D. (2018) Between struggles and discipline: Marx and Foucault on penality and the critique of political economy, in D. Melossi, M. Sozzo and J. Brandariz García (eds) *The Political Economy of Punishment Today*. London: Routledge, pp 23–36.

Melossi, D. and Pavarini, M. (1977) *Carcere e fabbrica: alle origini del sistema penitenziario*. Bologna: Il Mulino.

Melossi, D., Sozzo, M. and Brandariz-García, J.A. (eds) (2018) *The Political Economy of Punishment Today: Visions, Debates and Challenges*. London: Routledge.

MJSP (Ministério da Justiça e Segurança Pública) (2017) *Levantamento Nacional de Informações Penitenciárias: atualização – Junho de 2016*. Brasília: DEPEN.

Minuano, C. (2021) Denúncias de tortura em presídios sobem 70% durante pandemia. *Ponte Jornalismo*, 23 January.

Misse, M. (2019) The puzzle of social accumulation of violence in Brazil: Some remarks. *Journal of Illicit Economies and Development*, 1(2): 177–182.

Natalino, M.A. (2016) *Estimativa da população em situação de rua no Brasil*. Brasília: IPEA.

Paladines, J. (2016) La 'mano dura' de la Revolución Ciudadana (2007–2014), in M. Sozzo (ed) *Postneoliberalismo y penalidad en América del Sur*. Buenos Aires: CLACSO, pp 163–206.

Pastoral Carcerária (2010) *Relatório sobre tortura: uma experiência de monitoramento dos locais de detenção para prevenção da tortura*. São Paulo: CNBB.

Pochmann, M. (2012) *Nova Classe média? O trabalho na base da pirâmide social brasileira*. São Paulo: Boitempo.

Ramalho, J.R. (2008 [1979]) *Mundo do crime: a ordem pelo avesso*. Rio de Janeiro: Centro Edelstein de Pesquisas Sociais.

Ribeiro, D. (2015 [1995]) *O povo brasileiro: a formação e o sentido do Brasil* (3rd edition). São Paulo: Global.

Rusche, G. (1978) Labor market and penal sanction: Thoughts on the sociology of punishment. *Crime and Social Justice*, 10: 2–8.

Rusche, G. (2014 [1933]) Labour market and penal sanction: Thoughts on the sociology of punishment. *Social Justice*, 40(1–2): 252–264.

Rusche, G. and Kirchheimer, O. (2003 [1939]) *Punishment and Social Structure*. London: Routledge.

Salla, F. (2007) De Montoro a Lembo: as políticas penitenciárias de São Paulo. *Revista Brasileira de Segurança Pública*, 1: 72–90.

Santos, T.D. (1970) The structure of dependence. *The American Economic Review*, 60(2): 231–236.

Sikking, K. and Walling, C.B. (2007) The impact of human rights trials in Latin America. *Journal of Peace Research*, 44(4): 427–445.

Sozzo, M. (ed) (2016) *Postneoliberalismo y penalidad en América del Sur*. Buenos Aires: CLACSO.

Sozzo, M. (2017) ¿Más allá de la 'tesis de la penalidad neoliberal'? Giro punitivo y cambio político en América del Sur. *Revista Brasileira de Ciências Criminais*, 25(129): 321–348.

Sozzo, M. (2018) The renaissance of the political economy of punishment from a comparative perspective, in D. Melossi, M. Sozzo and J. Brandariz García (eds) *The Political Economy of Punishment Today*. London: Routledge, pp 37–64.

Sozzo, M. (2021) Inequality, welfare and punishment: Comparative notes between the Global North and South. *European Journal of Criminology*. doi: 10.1177/14773708211060164

Sutton, J. (2004) The political economy of imprisonment in affluent western democracies, 1960–1990. *American Sociological Review* 69(2): 170–189.

Teles, E. and Safatle, V. (eds) (2010) *O que resta da ditadura*. São Paulo: Boitempo Ed.

Toscani, E. (2018) *As disputas dóxicas no campo da revista Discursos Sediciosos (1996–2016): metacriminologia, engajamento político, e os debates sobre raça e gênero.* Brasília: Universidade de Brasília.

UN (United Nations) (2015) *The State of Food Insecurity in the World: Meeting the 2015 International Hunger Targets: Taking Stock of Uneven Progress.* Available from: https://www.fao.org/publications/sofi/2015/en/#:~:text=About%20793%20million%20people%20are,regions%2C%20despite%20significant%20population%20growth [Accessed 17 November 2022].

UN (United Nations) (2016) *Report of the Special Rapporteur on Torture and Other Cruel, Inhuman or Degrading Treatment or Punishment on His Mission to Brazil.* Available from: https://digitallibrary.un.org/record/831519?ln=en [Accessed 17 November 2022].

Varella, D. (2012) *Carcereiros.* São Paulo: Companhia das Letras.

Wacquant, L. (2003) Toward a dictatorship over the poor? Notes on the penalization of poverty in Brazil. *Punishment & Society*, 5(2): 197–205.

Wacquant, L. (2009) *Punishing the Poor: The Neoliberal Government of Social Insecurity.* Durham, NC: Duke University Press.

Willis, G.D. (2015) *The Killing Consensus.* Berkeley: University of California Press.

Zaffaroni, E.R., Batista, N., Alagia, A. and Slokar, A. (2015) *Direito Penal Brasileiro: primeiro volume: Teoria Geral do Direito Penal.* Rio de Janeiro: Revan.

PART III

Southern Narratives and Experiences: Culture, Resistance and Justice

PART II

10

Colonial Violence, Contemporary Conflict and Socio-Ecological Renewal: Analysis from Bougainville

Blaise Iruinu and Kristian Lasslett

Introduction

Colonization as practised by the European imperial powers represented at its heart a prolonged period of state-organized violence, sociocultural destruction and ethnic cleansing, enacted on an immense scale. Initial acts of colonial incursion and annexation presaged elongated periods marked by the political, economic, cultural and social usurpation of Indigenous social systems. For the proud custodians of these systems, this entailed a profound social dislocation from a way of life in which their identity and subjectivity was indelibly rooted, and their gradual incorporation into an introduced system, at a position of extreme disadvantage. The complex legacies of these processes are alive today, in the economic, political and social antagonisms that continue to prime insecurity, conflict and crisis in the global South, albeit sometimes with a subtlety that obscures their origins.

In order to excavate the multidimensional magnitude of colonial violence, and its enduring legacies, a process of epistemological upheaval is required. The methodologies, analytical tools and theoretical concepts we use must be part of a democratizing process of epistemic and analytical diversity, which is receiving renewed emphasis inside and outside academia through social movements demanding a decolonization of knowledge (Agozino, 2003; Connell, 2007) and, as Satia would have it, 're-telling' the stories of the past, and 'reinterpreting what it is to be human' (Satia, 2020). This especially concerns the topic at hand, embracing the different ways of knowing and analysis which have emerged from within the geopolitical 'ground zeroes' of colonial violence, knowledge that is delivered on occasions through conventions and frames that may not sit easily with the traditions designed and established in and through institutions of the metropoles.

The following chapter presents one such analysis. The lead author, Blaise Iruinu, a village elder and traditional leader from Bougainville in the South Pacific, delivered a series of oral presentations and reflections for a community-based oral history project organized by film-makers and scholars from Bougainville, France, and Australia between 2014 and 2015. These presentations have been transcribed and edited for this chapter. Extended film highlights from Iruinu's contribution to the project are available online on the project website (see Lasslett and Saovanna, 2020). We also draw upon other presentations from the oral history project, that add texture to Iruinu's thesis and analysis.

In the presentations and associated conversations, Iruinu presents a novel analysis of the Bougainville conflict (1988–2001). The war erupted in the easternmost province of Papua New Guinea (PNG) during late 1988, after customary landowners employed industrial sabotage to close a large-scale copper and gold mine (Panguna mine) operated by the Anglo-Australian mining corporation, Rio Tinto (see Lasslett, 2014). A heavy-handed response from the PNG military, aided both by the former colonial power, Australia, and Rio Tinto (through its subsidiary Bougainville Copper Limited), ignited an armed conflict that took up to 20,000 lives. During its most intensive period, the Australian and PNG militaries jointly organized a blockade around the island of Bougainville, denying civilians access to humanitarian aid. This was followed by an expansive counterinsurgency campaign, featuring systematic, egregious human rights abuses documented by a number of monitors (Amnesty International, 1990, 1993, 1997; Havini, 1995, 1996; see also series 5 in Lasslett and Saovanna, 2020).

The landowning leaders who initially led sit-in protests, road blockades and carried out industrial sabotage against the mine countered the campaign of state-corporate violence employing guerrilla warfare tactics, forming the Bougainville Revolutionary Army (BRA). The hostilities soon encompassed the entire island of Bougainville, and Buka, as the BRA forces took root well beyond the mine-impacted areas.

The BRA sought independence for Bougainville and a cessation to large-scale mining. Hampered by internal tensions within its leadership, the co-optation of the BRA brand by criminal gangs, and a diminishing support in certain regions following violent BRA reprisals over perceived collaboration with the Papua New Guinea Defence Force (PNGDF), the BRA nonetheless defeated the PNG and Australian forces. A political settlement was negotiated that included a referendum over independence. When the referendum was held in 2019, Bougainville voted emphatically for independence (almost 98 per cent were in favour: Lyons, 2019), which is now being negotiated by Bougainville's president, Ishmael Toroama, a former BRA commander.

The scholarship and formal commentary on the conflict, written primarily outside Bougainville, has largely framed it as a war initially sparked by landowner grievances over the Panguna mine, which then transformed into an ethnonationalist struggle, in part due to Bougainville's distinctive ethnic identity and sense of geopolitical distance from PNG. Less sympathetic accounts in this vein portray the inception of revolution on Bougainville as a knee-jerk reaction against modernity by hardliner political extremists (Regan, 1996; Dorney, 1998), or a cynical ploy by reactionary members of the landowning community to grab greater power and wealth from the mine, which then unintentionally ignited Bougainvillean nationalism (Callick, 1990). More sympathetic accounts recognize the serious forms of inequality, environmental degradation, and social dislocation engendered by the mine, which fuelled a wider sense of alienation from the PNG state and the socioeconomic model emerging around it (Spriggs, 1990; Wesley-Smith and Ogan, 1992; Böge, 1995).

Blaise Iruinu's analysis offers a strikingly different framing of the conflict, both in terms of its historical perspective and the meaning attributed to different events. Iruinu argues that the Bougainville crisis – the name often given to the decade-long war – in fact began in 1886, the year when Bougainville was first annexed by the German state. The armed conflict that erupted over a century later in 1988 was, in Iruinu's conception, a visceral manifestation of this longer crisis. And while he recognizes the dreadful human toll brought about by the war, Iruinu argues that out of this deprivation, brought about by the conflict, came a process of cultural renewal where people found strength in their Indigenous roots. In his view, an opening was created by the Bougainville crisis to start again on a new footing liberated from its colonial foundations.

While Iruinu's theoretical treatise pertains specifically to Bougainville, it is also about much more than one region alone. It is an attempt to conceptually grapple with a generalized process of cultural disruption brought about by colonization, of violence not only against the body, but against the inherited forms of social tradition in which the mind and body are acutely invested. It is also about how this particular nexus of structural and interpersonal violence presaged by colonialism is experienced by its subjects, creating social and personal contradictions that can erupt well after the colonial flag has lowered. Finally, Iruinu's analysis examines questions of transition, or what we might call transformative justice (Evans, 2016), in the wake of colonial and neocolonial violence. Iruinu considers how communities can begin to remove the shards of colonialism embedded deep within the social body, creating the conditions under which a process of cultural renewal can begin. Not, though, in order to return to a mythologized past, or to reject the possibility of social exchange with other cultures and civilizations, but rather to build a future grounded in the best of Indigenous cultures, customs and values, utilized as forces for progressive change.

While Iruinu's theoretical argument has been composed independently from key anti-colonial theorists of the global South, what is remarkable about his thought is how it sings in tune with the theoretical treatise of thinkers and revolutionaries such as Franz Fanon (1952, 1964), Walter Rodney (1972), Amilcar Cabral (2004, 2016) and Thomas Sankara (1999, 2006). Like Fanon, Iruinu theoretically unpacks the deep psychological incision made into Bougainville, when a people adjusted intellectually, spiritually and physically to a way of life forged over many thousands of years are cast into a system for which they lack capital, in all senses, economic, political, cultural and symbolic. Like Walter Rodney, Iruinu sees in Bougainville's past a rich history of progress and discovery that was disrupted in fundamental ways by the heavy hand of the colonial powers. In syncopation with Cabral, Iruinu argues that local culture has kept alive many of the social resources bequeathed from the past, which must be drawn upon now as a resource to build anew. And Iruinu does not argue for a rose-tinted view of the past or a definitive rejection of all 'Western' influence, but a nuanced conversation undertaken on firm Indigenous-led footing. Finally, echoing Sankara, Iruinu believes in building a progressive political project, grounded in pride and the independence of 'upright men', but which is also internationalist in orientation.

In the first section of this chapter, Iruinu explores Bougainville's pre-colonial past. It is not an attempt to conduct an exact history. Rather, it aims to underline the social achievements of Bougainville that existed prior to colonization, which were subsequently discounted by the colonizer. Iruinu then examines how a process of personal dislocation and political-economic dependency engineered through colonization created a set of powerful antagonisms that were heightened by the impacts of industrial mining in central Bougainville. This, he argues, found articulation in a revolutionary movement, which faced violent reprisals from the state, leading to the fault-lines for armed conflict. To conclude, despite its traumatic human toll, the conflict nonetheless provided an opportunity to reflect on and break with key colonial legacies, and to rebuild an independent Bougainville that is both grounded in its Indigenous cultural traditions, but which is also internationalist in its political programme to disrupt the damaging impacts of globalized capitalism on its environment and future social development.

Independence on Bougainville prior to colonization

[Historically] the land of Bougainville was isolated and separated from PNG, Australia and other islands by sea. It was complete, with mountains of her own, valleys, rivers and plains. It was complete with ecosystems, fish and other aquatic wildlife, forestry, and vegetation. It was blessed with minerals and other resources. It was blessed with birds and other animals. It was blessed with fertile land. Untouched virgin land, that is Bougainville. That is how God created Bougainville and blessed the land.

God created the island of Bougainville and he gave his breath for it to breathe and to keep life, the vegetation, the environment, the forest, the rivers and so forth. And on top of the land, God created human beings to manage the land of Bougainville as a custodian, to be the owner of the land, to cultivate it, to sustain their livelihood, and their ancestors, and to ensure the livelihood of future generations. The land of Bougainville, because it is a sacred land, there is no need to exploit it. The purpose of man is to cultivate the land and look after it as a custodian. He is not to exploit the land and the environment.

God also gave Bougainville Man his capacity to think, to manage, to cultivate and to look after. With this mental capacity he came to know about science. With science he knew about things such as astronomy – the sun, the moon and the stars, what are their purpose. And he knew about biology. Examples include breeding animals. Using his mental faculties and capacity for knowledge, Bougainville Man knew about physics. For example, he knew about friction, and could create fire. Bougainville Man knew about chemistry. For example, medicines extracted from the local environment. If he did not feel well, Bougainville Man used herbal medicines. Bougainville Man used the environment for his survival, for his health. He knew what was bad for him.

Bougainville Man also knew about mathematics. He had counting systems in his language. He also, relatedly, had a calendar system. He knew weeks, months and years. Another example is the division of time. For example, he divided the day into three parts. Because he is a knowledgeable man, Bougainville man had language and linguistic skill. He can communicate with other people within the dialect of each particular community, or each region of Bougainville. He had poems, he knew about poems. He had other aspects of culture too, like art and craft. He could do carvings that depict stories, historical stories of his clan's movement. Even though he was a naked man, even though somebody might see him as a primitive he had all these aspects of civilization.

Above all, he had the foundation of knowledge which is wisdom. And he had other forms of knowledge too. Spiritually, Bougainville Man has been inspired from time immemorial. He believed in God, the creator of heaven and earth. He believed in life after death. He knew before anyone else arrived here that there was a being above him, whom he knew as a creator of heaven and earth. How did he know? He saw the environment and he said, yes, there is somebody above me. He knew that when his ancestors died they communicated with that creator. He knew about sacred places. Rivers, mountains and stones where he would worship for whatever needs and wants, through his ancestors to God.

Bougainville Man had government structures and systems. And he had a system of administration. Special people in high positions like high priests, who served as priests to sustain spiritual living. And he had chiefs, in the families, in the community, for administration of community affairs. For that, I can say Bougainville Man had his government structure and his system of administration long before any 'civilization', any colonizer, any missionaries, came here.

Another aspect of his civilization was the material side, to provide for his physical needs and to sustain his living. For food he ate what he grew. He did not wait for miracles. He did not wait for any 'cargo' that the ship or aeroplane will bring. He was a farmer in his own right, because he had land to provide for his wants and needs. It was rich, fertile land. Whatever he grew he had abundance of. There was no poverty. There were no poor people. There were no street people. Hunger and poverty, he did not know about those. In the past, with knowledge of astronomy, with his calendar system, Bougainville Man knew when to rest the land and look for food elsewhere.

With regards to the shelter he built, Bougainville Man used a style of architecture most appropriate for his environment in order to protect himself from the weather, and to provide security. Technical knowledge of architecture, he had all these things. He developed from the cave to the bush-material shelter like banana leaves, and eventually he started developing and building houses from sago palm leaves. And he built his houses on posts. Bougainville Man's architecture was still developing.

Bougainville Man also had trade. For trade he exchanged for items that he cannot produce in his environment, because there were other neighbouring societies he was in contact with, producing under different environmental conditions. In the monetary system he used shell money instead of coins and notes which we are using today. He had shell money to buy whatever goods he needed, that he did not have in his environment.

Bougainville Man knew about the banking system. One of the commercial banking systems in our local Kieta language, it is called *kerekasi*. And he also had a reserve banking system, which in Kieta language we called *dakotare*. That reserve bank in our custom contains such things as pigs. That is one example of what our ancestors used as a store of wealth. They looked after pigs for big ceremonies, which they then used along with the shell money.

All the aspects of Bougainville's civilization noted here are examples of an integrated form of human development which formed the foundation of our society from time immemorial. Bougainville Man was complete as a human being. Whatever he did was for his own survival. For that matter I can say Bougainville Man from creation, from time immemorial, he was a complete man. He was a full man, and he was an independent man.

For that reason, nobody 'gives' independence to Bougainville Man. He was a complete man and independent man from time immemorial, from the era of creation. With the different aspects that I have outlined, mental, spiritual, physical, political, he was a complete man. As a result there is no need for anybody to talk about independence for the Bougainville Man, he in fact had it to begin with.

But then somebody, from somewhere, came to Bougainville and disrupted that reality. This someone thought that the Bougainville Man was a primitive. He needed education, he needed religion, and much more.

Disrupting independence: colonization, social dislocation and dependency

Bougainville fell into the path of the power struggles between superpowers in Europe. The colonizer, poisoned and blinded by pride, jealousy, greed, hatred, ignorance, leave their own land and culture in search of the new world to satisfy their own ego. The colonizer was a man with many problems. The problems that were created in his own land, when he came to Bougainville, his problems then became the problems of Bougainville Men [see also series 1 in Lasslett and Saovanna, 2020, for local reflections on the colonial period in Bougainville].

A virgin island full of resources catches the eye of the colonizer at the very first glimpse. Mistaken for the biblical Solomon's riches, the colonizer undergoes a heart-breaking experience when he discovered that this paradise, this garden of Eden, is guarded by – in his eyes – a naked Man armed with a bow and arrow with nothing but a confused look on his face.

The colonizer's reaction is a mixture of feelings. He sees the Bougainville Man as an inferior, dirty, primitive being just above an animal. That is how the colonizer described the Bougainville Man. But even though he was 'naked', and even if he 'looked' primitive, he had all the aspects to be a full and independent man. That is when the Bougainville Crisis or the Conflict began, when the colonizer came to Bougainville and landed in Bougainville.

Germany was the first country to set itself up in New Guinea. They then named it German New Guinea, which included the island of Bougainville. Germans built colonial mission stations on Bougainville, and established plantations and mines. They bribed the local people with the axes, knives, salt and tobacco, and the Indigenous people let the Europeans operate alluvial gold mine operations in Kupe, on the far northern side of Panguna. That was the start of gold mine operations. Then during 1914, the First World War, the allied forces defeated Germany, and Australia then took over Bougainville's administration from Germany.

This colonial period was marked by indoctrination, destruction and confusion. The colonizer started his work on the Bougainville Man by disturbing different aspects of his civilization.

First, there is the material effect. The colonizer gave Bougainville Man axes, knives, which were superior, because at that time our ancestors were only using stone axes. When the colonizers brought knives, axes and other items, that disturbed the physical side. There was clothing also, which was manufactured in the colonizer's homeland. He brought them with him and clothed the 'naked' Bougainvillean.

The colonizer brought tools and utensils like cooking pots. In pre-colonial times the Bougainville Man used bamboo for fire, for his cooking. But when the colonizer gave him cooking pots and better tools life seemed easier. That is how the material side of life started to be influenced and disturbed.

Then there was the political display of superiority in weapons. Impressed by this technology, the Bougainville people accepted the newcomers as masters and perceived themselves as an inferior. This permitted the enforcement of the foreign laws, which the colonizer brought. Political oppression on Bougainville really began as a reality when the colonizer came and imposed his rules. Before that the Bougainville Man was independent, he was free, he had everything he needed for his survival. This was disrupted.

The colonizer also disturbed the spiritual side of life on Bougainville. So impressed beyond all limits the Bougainville Man saw the colonizer as a god or a being next to god, who brought with him new biblical doctrines … the colonizer brought in materials which influenced and manipulated the Bougainville Man. All sorts of conflicting biblical doctrines emerged, and as a result confusion set in.

The colonizer, by contrast, saw Bougainville Man as a pagan, a worshipper of darkness. When the colonizer told the people of Bougainville each of their fathers' spirits was in fact a devil, the Bougainvillean Man bowed down, and began to worship a European spirit. He forgot about his ancestors' spirits. The colonizer had arrived with another God. This confused the Bougainville Man spiritually. The colonizer's influence also disturbed the Bougainville Man's marriage initiations, and sacred initiations. Whatever rituals he practised, such as feasts, the colonizer disturbed.

There were other changes brought by the colonizer – mentally the colonizer never taught the Bougainville Man how, and where, the Europeans got their knowledge from. The colonizer never disclosed how to make or manufacture the things which the colonizer brought with him and then gave to the Bougainville Man. The colonizer changed the Bougainville Man physically, spiritually, politically, socially and economically, 'raising' his needs to the level of the colonizer, but did not provide him with the means to meet these needs. We can see this dependency in changing practices of consumption. Housing built from imported materials. Clothing, fashion imported from overseas. Cars, ships, airplanes, helicopters and so on, all imported. Hungry for goods that we cannot produce, we became consumers, we became dependent. Now we are just waiting to 'eat' what is coming out from somewhere else.

The education that the colonizer did design for the Bougainville Man was education to live in towns, education for adoration of the colonizer's ways. Education to suppress the Bougainvillean Man's mind at dependency level, thus preventing him from reaching his full potential in mental advancement. Education to be a consumer.

But today, with this so-called education system a lot of our children roam the streets, even with their master's degrees, doctorates, PhDs. Grade 11 students, grade 12 students, they have no jobs. Once they come out of whatever institutions, the University of PNG, Unitech Lae and all the other universities, they are roaming the streets because they have no jobs with the education that they are getting.

Then there is the example of PNG's political situation. PNG obtained independence in 1975. But this is the common practice of every colonizer. After making the Bougainville Man obedient, after making the Black man's mentality dependent on satisfying the artificial physical, spiritual, economic and political needs incorporated into him by the colonizer, the colonizer kicks him out of 'empire' by granting the colonized political independence, which is not really independence.

Let me explain. First there is the political side, the introduction of Westminster government, which is a huge administrative system. It is an expensive system designed for the management and distribution of imported goods and services. The colonizer set up laws and rules for its own interest. Now PNG then had to borrow from somewhere to sustain her huge government.

PNG's first prime minister, Chief Michael Somare, told the Australian government at the time of 'independence': "I have no money to run the government and the services for the people." Australia advised Somare to borrow from the World Bank and begin mining. "Open mines in your country, that will sustain your economy for the running of your government" [see, for example, Barnes, 1969]. That is why PNG now has no way to go. Instead of surviving, she is dying. Borrow money [capital], borrow for services, PNG became a slave to the master.

PNG was in this sense designed for doom. A dumping ground of White man's junk and nothing but a marketplace for the extraction of its resources. That is how I see PNG, and Bougainville was forced into this setup in 1975, when they proclaimed Bougainville as part of PNG.

Therefore, the solution to the Bougainville crisis does not exist in the constitution of PNG. The only logical solution is to break away from PNG. PNG is living beyond her means. PNG's trend of development has been backwards since 1975. Instead of progressing it has been sinking. That is why we had the Bougainville revolution.

A new independence: crisis, revolution and renewal

A complex dialectic exists between colonialism, capitalism and local resistance on Bougainville. The industrial mine in Panguna accelerated the tensions contained within these intertwined dynamics and thus its history is an important thread in Iruinu's thesis.

This history of the mine dates back to the 1960s, as the first proto-independence organizations emerged on Bougainville. During this period the Anglo-Australian mining multinational Conzinc Rio Tinto of Australia (CRA) was invited to conduct exploration activity in the Panguna region of the Crown Prince Range, where there were large low-grade deposits of copper and gold (see Lasslett, 2014). CRA elected to proceed with the mine following exploration, with significant support from the Australian administration. The Australian government believed that the mine would generate a significant stream of income for sustaining PNG's approaching independence.

The mine opened in 1972, three years prior to independence. It generated a significant environmental impact, both due to the mine construction process, the associated forms of residential, industrial and commercial development, and the waste disposal method used in the mining region, which caused significant harm to the Jaba river (see Böge, 1995). Local communities participated in the mine operations largely through lower paid employment at Bougainville Copper Limited (BCL), CRA's PNG subsidiary. A small business and executive class emerged from within the mining impacted communities. They set up the Panguna Landowners' Association (PLA) to secure for Bougainville, and local landowners, greater levels of compensation and royalties from the mining operation, which during the 1970s had realized super profits for CRA (Okole, 1990). In 1987, a younger generation of activists emerged from the mine area. They successfully challenged the initial PLA executive, and obtained election to the association's board, placing the PLA on a radical new footing.

The new PLA, as it became known, organized protests and civil disobedience during 1988, and famously called for the mine to be closed, and for CRA to pay K10 billion (approximately US$12 billion) in reparations (Lasslett, 2014). A lack of progress with BCL management led the PLA to undertake a campaign of industrial sabotage. This triggered a militarized response from the government of PNG, which was materially supported by the Australian state and BCL. In reaction to government security force incursions, the BRA emerged, seeking independence.

Following a brutal decade of conflict, a referendum over independence was incorporated into the Bougainville Peace Agreement signed in 2001. Bougainville was also granted greater autonomy, with the devolution of key national powers to the Autonomous Bougainville Government (ABG). As noted in the introduction Bougainville voted 98 per cent in favour of independence during 2019. However, there is still no clear timeline or operational process in place for ratifying and implementing this referendum decision.

Nevertheless, for Iruinu this result represents an opportunity for substantive decolonization and Indigenous renewal for a form of meaningful independence.

> What is revolution? It is the total change in one's mental, spiritual, social, economic and political direction towards a new directive vision. That is why we had the crisis in Bougainville. It is a new way forward.
>
> We have violated and exploited the natural creations which we are custodians of. We have destroyed the natural habitats, with her natural laws. That is why the crisis occurred. It was a process through which to progress self-discovery and rediscovery of the Bougainville Man. We have to go back, to start a new journey [see also Bryar and Lasslett, 2021]. We have to rehabilitate the mindset and the hearts of the people, mentally, spiritually and physically, to prepare them for political and economic independence. That is why the crisis occurred.
>
> The Bougainville revolution is not an accident, nor a mistake. Before the conflict, even during the administration of Australia, there were attempts to resist. First, there was the first arrow shot at the 'discoverer'

or the intruder during first contact with the colonizer. There were other early confrontations with the colonizer. Organizations like the Hahalis Welfare Society were part of the resistance, there was the Rorovana case, and the emergence of other organizations such as the Napidakoe Navitu group. Those are all signs that we did not agree with what was coming, that is why the tensions finally escalated into a crisis.

Then came the 1988 revolution. CRA and its mine in Panguna, operated by BCL, was a catalyst. Because with mining, it was the time of cultural invasion. What I mean by cultural invasion is that during the mine exploration period, and during the mining operations, local landowners, and Bougainville as a whole, were not looked upon as sovereign peoples by the colonizer. They did not respect our culture and traditions, or ability to choose [see series 2, chapters 2 and 3, in Lasslett and Saovanna, 2020].

Our society is a matrilineal society, which means the women are the leaders of this land and this traditional system (see Saovanna, 2007). Under the matrilineal society women are the mothers of this land. So, in our custom, women are at the forefront of protecting the land. Women did not want the land to be mined. But when the men came from the Australian government, with its company BCL, they did not recognize the women or their wishes. The Australian colonial administration in fact suppressed the customary landowners' laws. That is where these two cultures clashed, and with that we lost our sovereignty, our identity, our dignity and integrity.

And that loss in part is linked also to the damage that has been done to our environment, which women were attempting to prevent [see series 3, chapters 1 and 2, in Lasslett and Saovanna, 2020]. During the mine operations, and at the beginning during the construction phase, BCL employed chemicals to spray the jungle, for the trees to be cleared out in the mining area. And what happened was that the trees, the forest, all the vegetation, and even the animals, like the possums, flying foxes, birds, all died. During the mining operations the rivers became the primary waste dump area. And so now the river system has been intoxicated by chemicals from the mining operation [see Human Rights Law Centre, 2020].

You cannot separate the land, the environment, from the people. They are integrated. Well, that is how the Bougainvillean Man lives. That is our culture, our tradition and our custom. That is why a young leader from the mine area named Francis Ona agitated. To begin with, Francis Ona had been working within the mining company, initially as a surveyor. He saw the effects of the mine operations first-hand and became deeply frustrated with the Panguna mine operations. And so he started to mobilize some of the younger people.

Out of this mobilization a new revolution was born. First came the formation of a new landowners' association to represent the communities surrounding the mine [see also Okole, 1990]. It stood on the side of the people, the women, the chiefs, the children and the community, under the leadership of Francis Ona and his two cousin sisters. One cousin sister, Perpetua Serero, was the Chairlady of the new association, while Francis Ona was the secretary.

The new landowners' association countered BCL's management and the old landowners' association. The old landowners' association was in effect working on behalf of BCL, and BCL management. There were only a few 'educated' people from the mine region who worked for BCL at a more senior level, and they formed the basis for the old landowner association [see also series 5, chapter 4 in Lasslett and Saovanna, 2020]. Instead of telling BCL management that they were exploiting people, these so-called 'educated' people of Bougainville sided with BCL management.

That is why we simple people, with only limited educational qualifications like myself and Francis Ona, rose up. Various demonstrations took place, as the new landowner association negotiated with BCL's management calling for an end to all mining activities and the payment of significant compensation. But in negotiation with BCL's management, our negotiations fell on deaf ears.

So the young men, mobilized by Francis Ona, then seized control of the mine operations. They started blowing up, dynamiting the pylons that powered the mine. When the PNG government saw that the mining operations were shut down, they responded by sending police riot squads and the PNGDF. The government security forces started burning houses. They started taking prisoners. They started beating everybody up. And they even shot the militant landowners, as they called them. They called us militants! A lot of our people died during this initial operation that functioned under a 'shoot to kill' order, which PNG's Prime Minister Sir Rabbie Namaliu authorized [Umau, 2019].

Out of frustration came the birth of the BRA, emerging as an organized military force in 1989. The BRA, led again by Francis Ona, fought for three basic principles [see series 4, chapters 1, 2 and 3 in Lasslett and Saovanna, 2020]. The number one basic principle, which the BRA fought to defend, was to protect our land and environment. The second principle was to protect local culture and traditional customs. And the third principle was to protect the future generations of Bougainville.

The BRA, however, did not fight like a regular army. They undertook guerrilla-style actions. That is why even the well-trained PNGDF, and the riot squads, could not contain the BRA force. The

BRA formed into small groups of around five members and initiated hit and run attacks. In response to the rise of the BRA, a state of emergency was issued by the prime minister of PNG. Then there was a declaration of all-out war by Prime Minister Namaliu. To stop the war on Bougainville major funding and military support came from the Australian government and the Australian Defence Force. Following this state of emergency declared by PNG, with Australia's assistance, they introduced a military blockade around Bougainville. Nothing was permitted in, not even medicines. They even blockaded assistance from humanitarian organizations [see Evans, 1992]. The purpose of the blockade was political, to suppress and oppress the people of Bougainville and make them surrender. Military planners thought that the Bougainville people would surrender to the multinational corporations and government.

During the initial phases of the conflict, a lot of the people and families lost their belongings and were displaced. The military planners hoped the blockade would make the people turn against their defenders, their sons in fact, the BRA. They knew if they blockaded essential services, it is the people who will suffer, and while they are suffering, they will turn against the BRA. The real purpose was to create division among Bougainvilleans.

Then there were the care centres, where civilians were placed by the government security forces. For example, when the PNGDF killed a BRA soldier, they would cut up this BRA soldier into small pieces, take them to the concentration camp and throw them to the people and say to them "These are your pieces of pig. You cook them and eat them." Women were raped in those 'care centres' in front of their brothers, sisters, fathers and mothers. Chiefs were treated with no respect. There were also revenge killings. To avenge dead comrades, the PNGDF soldiers would take civilians from the care centre and kill them in retaliation [see series 5, Lasslett and Saovanna, 2020].

Despite the tragedy and suffering, the conflict in the end was a new way forward for Bougainville developing itself towards true independence. It was also a period of growth that had been stunted and limited by colonization. And ultimately, because of this, the PNG security forces could not contain the BRA movement, and the awakening that the conflict provoked. That was when the PNGDF and the Australian Defence Force saw that they could not win the war on Bougainville. Accordingly, they came up with a ceasefire in 1997 and a peace agreement 2001.

So after the war came a ceasefire. Then the withdrawal of PNG rule under a neutral observer which was the United Nations Observer Mission. Then there were the negotiations following the ceasefire. After that came the 2001 Peace Agreement. There were many problems with how the Peace Agreement was produced and its final format, which I will not go into now.

Suffice to say though, the answer to resolving the Bougainville crisis is independence. But independence equals fullness to determine one's own future on one's own footing. To do that we have to go back to our origins. The origin does not mean that we will walk naked. But rather that we will base our progress on customary means, we start from there, and we move forward. The origin does not mean we go back to the stage where our ancestors were, it means to revive our novel customary norms and practices. To revive our traditions to find an independent way forward, to progress into the future [see series 6, in Lasslett and Saovanna, 2020].

So let us now outline the general guidelines for independence. Start with what you know and what resources you have and only absorb from the outside what is useful. Shed the bad history hoisted on us by the colonizer. To taste something new, first empty your cup.

To be truly sovereign we must again live as an independent nation free from the relations of dependency created by the colonizer. We must have our own government, we must have our own service departments, and most of all we must have our own people united, we must have our own development model, and we can on that footing build diplomacy with other countries. And we will need support from people who have the same problems or grievances as us, who have stood up against the capitalist liberal order. If we cannot mobilize and organize and speak with one voice internationally against these multinational corporations with their capitalist mindset, we will not last long.

So, for independence to flourish there must be the right environment. First there must be secure land and resources, blockaded from outside interference. And to do that we must overthrow both PNG's and the colonizer's rules. Second, there must be the regrowth of Bougainville Man towards maturity, so we see life with a new vision. Research and discovery must be the foundation of this process. Know how to produce for your basic needs, stand on Indigenous wisdom and learn from outside only to enrich them. Think simple and bring your vision to the present. Reason as a Bougainvillean.

What can we do to support the material side of independence? First, sacrifice our physical desires for foreign food. Focus on improvement of our Indigenous cuisine. The development of Me'ekamui cooking for example. And the same goes for housing, develop Me'ekamui architecture, building from our resources, from what material we have. We must live within our means, establishing industries to satisfy our essential needs. For example: rice industries, clothing, making clothes from our own materials. Soap, we have raw materials like coconuts for making soap. Salt, we have sea down there which we can make salt out of, and other industries, which would sustain our standard of living.

Third, there is the need to rebuild social relations. Re-establish, revive, noble customary values to revitalize marriage, social initiations, community feasts, respect for one another, movement between societies and communities, kinship and entertainment.

Fourth, there is a need to establish a political programme. Government must be a facilitator, building one political vision for independence. Independence is not an event, but a process of growth. Bougainville was independent from time immemorial. Now we have reclaimed that independence. What we have been struggling for is formal recognition.

There are some tensions between the government created out of the colonial and postcolonial experience, and Indigenous systems of government that re-emerged during the conflict. For some people, they see Me'ekamui and the Autonomous Bougainville Government (ABG) as two different bodies, but from the perspective of Me'ekamui, ABG and Me'ekamui they are not different. Me'ekamui is the traditional system of governance, which operates on three Indigenous principles:

Sipungeta, which means regulating life through our traditional customs, norms and values.

Osikaiang, which means you are a Bougainvillean by tradition. That is, by being part of its customary norms and values, you are from Bougainville.

Me'ekamui, which means holy and sacred land. Me'ekamui in other words is perfectness, the land of Ophir. Ophir means land of riches, full of resources, which we must preserve as custodians. The Me'ekamui Man, or the Bougainville Man, has to be holy, he has to align himself with the environment.

What we are currently lacking between Me'ekamui and the ABG is alignment. If the ABG can allow and let Me'ekamui concentrate on the traditional governance system, and the ABG concentrates on public administration, there is no problematic difference or tension. Once we come together in unity, that will be the day to proclaim the real Bougainville government for the people of Bougainville. At this current point of time, ABG is just a system, it is just a structure which came out of the Peace Agreement, it is not yet fully Bougainvillean.

That moment of unity is some time in the future. At the moment, financially, Bougainville is not yet capable of bringing these systems of government together as one. Even Me'ekamui is also in the same situation. She has no financial capacity to run her own government. Economically, Me'ekamui and ABG, they are relying on funding from the PNG government. That's why, for our own government to survive, we need to have an economy of our own.

But now the ABG is talking about the reopening of the Panguna mine. But for us, for the Me'ekamui side, I think there are other sources to find funding that should be explored, to recover our economy on an independent footing. We have rich and fertile land, if we go into agriculture, with the right support and sources of capital, we can generate sustainable revenue through agriculture. We can build our own spin-off industries through agriculture. Like, for example, we can look after cattle. We can even plant rice, we can produce our own rice. But more importantly I think we can rehabilitate the cocoa plantations, and even coconuts, to produce copra. I think those are essential cash crops which we can revive our economy with.

With the current mining projects in PNG, and even back during the BCL operations on Bougainville, instead of us getting fat, somebody outside was getting fat, with our resources. And here you can see, us feeding the foreigner. It is our job to create our own standard of living on our own footing, not to be dependent on somebody else, not to be dependent on money from the mine.

After all that blood that has been spilled on the land of Bougainville, and given all the people who lost their lives and properties, we cannot return to past extractive practices. The people are still mourning, they are still mourning about the bloodshed, the lives lost and the property they lost. Bougainvilleans will fight to the last man to stop mining. We will fight to the end, through whatever means, through politics and through justice.

Ultimately you cannot live on money. It is the land which is the source of material wealth needed for life. All the resources, all the material that you use to create whatever power you have as a human being, and whatever social system we operate, it ultimately depends on and comes out of the land. If you destroy the land, then there is nothing. You cannot breathe air out of space. It is the land that provides, which gives life to the environment. And out of the land oxygen is created. It provides oxygen, which you breathe. And once you destroy the land, and everything on it, especially Bougainville island, everything on earth will be extinct.

You must understand, despite the gains we on Bougainville are still in the colonial era, because all these superpowers, along with organizations such as the World Bank and International Monetary Fund, they have already dominated the minds and hearts of the people of Bougainville. There is a great struggle ahead if we are to fully realize the independence disrupted by colonization.

I do not know the future, maybe next year I will be gone. But that is why I am presenting this to you, it is for the children, it is for the future generations. If all this land is dug up, through mining, and the environment is destroyed, I do not know how our children, our grandchildren, will survive.

Those are just some ideas I wished to share for our way forward. We will need support, immediate support, because it is not only the Bougainville people that are suffering. Out there across the world right now, there are a lot of people who are suffering, because a small minority are living in luxury, the capitalist. The only way to conquer or minimize that is to organize within our own regions and mobilize. Because only by mobilizing ourselves can we force the capitalist system to think twice.

That is it from me. If you think I am crazy, saying this and warning you, I do not know what to say, but from my end something inspired me to reveal this to you. I think it is not too late for me to tell you. Even if you think I am crazy, I am telling you, you have to think about your future generation.

References

Agozino, B. (2003) *Counter-Colonial Criminology: A Critique of Imperialist Reason*. London: Pluto Press.

Amnesty International (1990) *Papua New Guinea: Human Rights Violations on Bougainville 1989–1990*. London: Amnesty International Secretariat.

Amnesty International (1993) *'Under the Barrel of a Gun': Bougainville 1991–1993*. Available from: https://www.amnesty.org/en/documents/asa34/005/1993/en/ [Accessed 16 November 2022].

Amnesty International (1997) *Bougainville: The Forgotten Human Rights Tragedy*. Available from: https://www.amnesty.org/en/documents/asa34/001/1997/en/ [Accessed 16 November 2022].

Barnes, C.E. (1969) Business and investment opportunities in New Guinea *Current Notes on International Affairs*, 40(6): 333–334.

Böge, V. (1995) Mining and conflict on Bougainville, in *Development as a Cause of Conflict: The Bougainville Issue in Papua New Guinea*. Proceedings of a Conference held in the Evangelische Akademie Bad Boll/Germany from 10 to 12 March 1995 (= Protokolldienst 22/95), Bad Boll.

Bryar, T. and Lasslett, K. (2021) 'To taste something new, first empty your cup': Bartleby politics, anti-colonial resistance and state violence. *State Crime*, 10(2): 217–237.

Cabral, A. (2004) *Unity and Struggle: Speeches and Writings*, edited by M. Adams and C. Cocks. Pretoria: Unisa Press.

Cabral, A. (2016) *Resistance and Decolonisation: Reinventing Critical Theory*. London: Rowman & Littlefield.

Callick, R. (1990) Stench of war likely to linger on Bougainville for years to come. *Australian Financial Review*, 1 February, p 16.

Connell, R. (2007) *Southern Theory: The Global Dynamics of Knowledge in Social Science*. Cambridge: Polity.

Dorney, S. (1998) *The Sandline Affair*. Sydney: ABC Books.

Evans, L. (1992) The health and social situation on Bougainville, in D. Denoon and M. Spriggs (eds) *The Bougainville Crisis: 1991 Update*. Bathurst: Crawford House Press, np.

Evans, M. (2016) Structural violence, socioeconomic rights, and transformative justice. *Journal of Human Rights*, 15(1): 1–20.

Fanon, F. (1952) *Black Skin, White Masks*. London: Pluto Press [1986].

Fanon, F. (1964) *The Wretched of the Earth*. Harmondsworth: Penguin.

Havini, M.T. (1995) *A Compilation of Human Rights Abuses Against the People of Bougainville: 1989– 1995*, Vol 1. Sydney: Bougainville Freedom Movement.

Havini, M.T. (1996) *A Compilation of Human Rights Abuses Against the People of Bougainville: 1989– 1995*, Vol 2. Sydney: Bougainville Freedom Movement.

Human Rights Law Centre (2020) *After the Mine: Living with Rio Tinto's Deadly Legacy*. Available from: static1.squarespace.com/static/ 580025f66b8f5b2dabbe4291/t/5e7d7cce47c7f816da86005f/158528 2297310/AfterTheMineRioTintoDeadlyLegacy.pdf [Accessed 16 November 2022].

Lasslett, K. (2014) *State Crime on the Margins of Empire*. London: Pluto Books.

Lasslett, K. and Saovanna, R. (2020) *The Colonial Syndrome*. Available from: www.colonialsyndrome.org [Accessed 16 November 2022].

Lyons, K. (2019) Bougainville referendum: Region votes overwhelmingly for independence from Papua New Guinea. *The Guardian*, 11 December.

Okole, H. (1990) The politics of the Panguna Landowners' Association, in R.J. May and M. Spriggs (eds) *The Bougainville Crisis*. Bathurst: Crawford House Press, pp 16–24.

Regan, A.J. (1996) *The Bougainville Conflict: Origins and Development, Main 'Actors', and Strategies for its Resolution*. Port Moresby: University of Papua New Guinea Faculty of Law.

Rodney, W. (1972) *How Europe Underdeveloped Africa*. London: Verso [2018].

Sankara, T. (1999) *Women's Liberation and the African Freedom Struggle*. London: Pathfinder Books.

Sankara, T. (2006) *Thomas Sankara Speaks: The Burkina Faso Revolution: 1983–87*. London: Pathfinder Press.

Saovanna, R. (2007) *Gender and Peace: Bougainvillean Women, Matriliny, and the Peace Process*. PhD, Australian National University.

Satia, P. (2020) *Time's Monster: History, Conscience and Britain's Empire*. London: Penguin, Random House.

Spriggs, M. (1990) Bougainville December 1989 – January 1990: A personal history, in R.J. May and M. Spriggs (eds) *The Bougainville Crisis*. Bathurst: Crawford House Press, pp 25–30.

Umau, P. (2019) Sir Rabbie apologises for B'ville crisis. *Papua New Guinea Post-Courier*, 8 November.

Wesley-Smith, T. and Ogan, E. (1992) Copper, class, and crisis: Changing relations of production in Bougainville. *The Contemporary Pacific*, 4(2): 245–267.

11

Exploring the Moving Lines of the 'Global South': Citizenship and Political Participation in a Rio de Janeiro *Favela*

Elizabete Ribeiro Albernaz

Introduction

"I don't defend classes, I want to unite what the city has separated, because this city *made* this *favela*." This is how Robson, a *community leader* from a *favela* called 'Morro do Palácio', likes to define his work. Since 2016, I have been following his trajectory as a 'community leader' and wannabe 'politician' from Niterói, a municipality located in the Metropolitan Area of Rio de Janeiro, in the southeast of Brazil.[1] Repeated to exhaustion during his campaign to become a councillor in 2020, Robson's catchphrase translates to perfection his deep sense of the forces in place when it comes to producing the *favela* as a 'margin' (Das and Poole, 2004)[2] in the city of Niterói.

In the current chapter, I describe the efforts of Robson to become a legitimate representative of Palácio, a position that is defined by the authority to 'speak on behalf of the community', intermediating the relationship of the *favela*, an 'illegal settlement', with public and private agencies to improve the lives of the inhabitants.[3] I show how Robson's efforts to become a *favela politician*, moving from being a community leader, can dramatize the complex social processes implicated in the construction of Palácio as a 'place' (Bourdieu, 1997). I argue that the constitutive tension between his capacity to mobilize resources located 'outside' the *favela*, and the symbolic and material manipulation of insignias of 'belonging' that connects him to a place tainted by the stigma of violence, illegality and social disorganization are key to the understanding of his 'political tactics'.

I'm calling *political tactics* the manoeuvres applied by the community leaders to 'bring improvements' to the *favela* (such as street paving, electricity or a creche for the kids), 'pressuring the authorities' for adequate service delivery, using the personalistic power of political mediators[4] (as the 'politicians') to reclaim some participation in what Chatterjee (2004) called the 'practical helms of citizenship'.[5] By doing so, I explore the relationship between violence, mobility and inequality, developed in previous works (Albernaz, 2018; Albernaz and Pires, 2021), as an insight into the concept of 'global South' as a moving border, where the ambivalent coexistence between connection and separation produces zones of intense exchange and conflict promoting the 'subaltern integration' of Palácio in the cultural, political and economic life of the city of Niterói.

As movements through space are also indices of social status (Virilio, 1986; Pires, 2011, among others), I argue that they can be good analytical keys to try to grasp the everyday, mundane expressions of long-term structures of social inequalities and their effects on people's lives. Therefore, moving away from the prevailing macroeconomic framework of international studies addressing social inequality – centred on income, wealth and consumption standards (Piketty, 2014)[6] – I'm interested in the workings of localized grounded social mechanics, operating at the intersection of values (symbolic and economic) and power relations. As an anthropologist, the relevant question, however, is how to build intelligible connections between the workings of those powerful forces, and the everyday lives of real people in real-life settings, how those forces are felt by the common people and what vernacular is used to symbolize these relations.

Setting the grounds: a place called Palácio

I was living in Niterói for my doctoral fieldwork, a bubbly beach city just outside Rio de Janeiro, known to have one of the best municipal HDI scores (Human Development Index) in Brazil, and for being the hometown of the Universidade Federal Fluminense (UFF), where I received my doctorate in anthropology. Two of those lovely years were spent in a place called Morro do Palácio ('Palace Hill'). The name, however, can be misleading. Instead of being a royal residence, Palácio is a medium-size *favela* (1,851 inhabitants), home to a mostly non-White (Figure 11.1), lower-class, migrant population, carved in the heart of a well-established mostly White upper-middle-class area of Niterói (Figure 11.2), at the intersection of three of its wealthiest suburbs, Icaraí, Ingá and Boa Viagem.[7]

The name of the *favela*, though, comes from a real palace. Oral history holds that the first generation of Palácio inhabitants were domestic workers of the old palace that used to be the headquarters of the provincial government of Rio de Janeiro, back when Niterói was its capital city.[8] Coming mostly from

Figure 11.1: Morro do Palácio and the ethnic distribution in the surrounding neighbourhoods

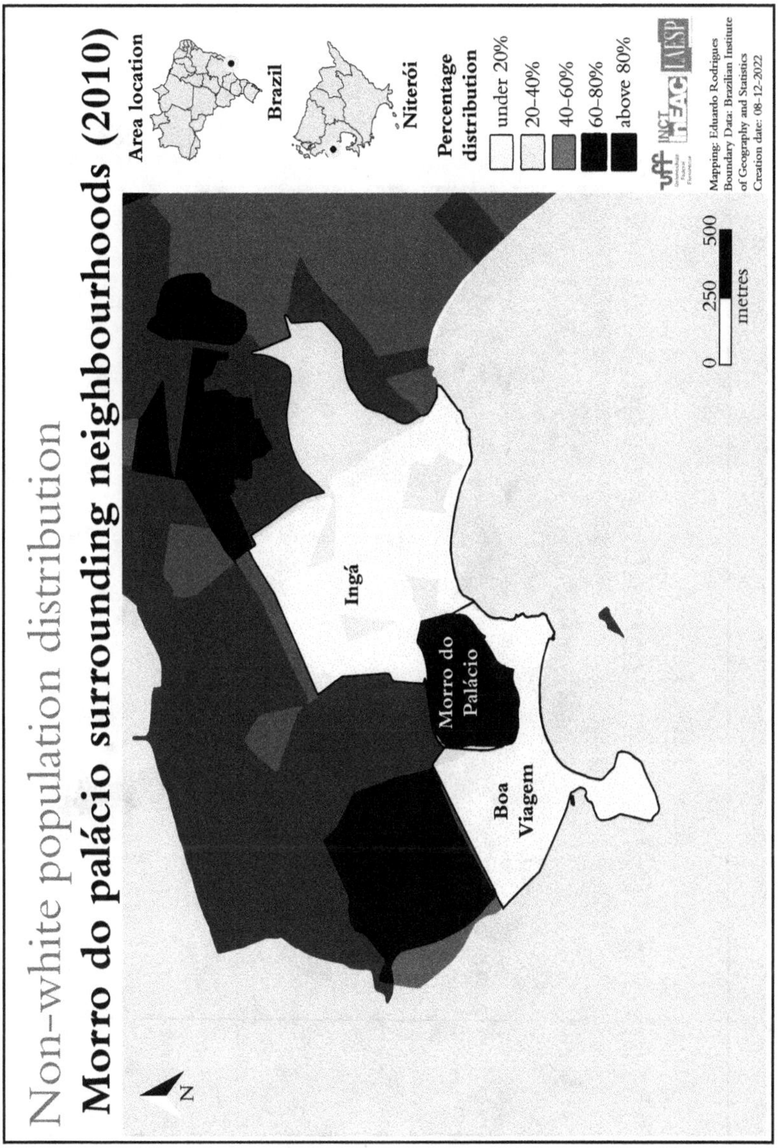

Figure 11.2: Morro do Palácio and the income distribution in the surrounding neighbourhoods

High income distribution
Morro do Palácio surrounding neighbourhoods (2010)

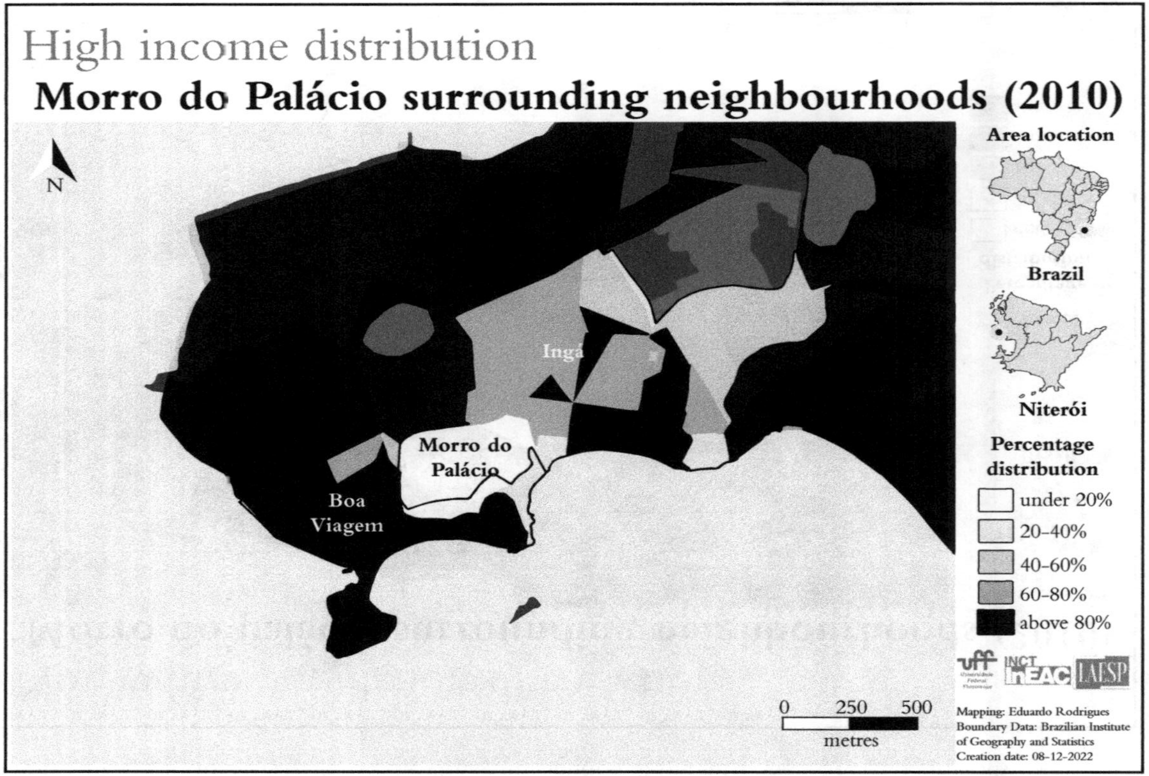

Source: http://nephu.sites.uff.br/programa/mapeando-conflitos/mapeando-comunidades/comunidades-de-niteroi/morro-do-palacio/

neighbouring cities and unable to sustain the financial and logistic burdens of daily commuting, this first generation witnessed two great periods of expansion of the *favela*: the first, in the turn of the 19th and 20th centuries, when Niterói went through major urban reform, dislodging the urban poor from its city centre; the second, in the 1960s and 1970s, when the 'illegal occupation' of the hill was intensified by migration flows coming from the north and northeast of Brazil.[9] The migrant population living in Palácio told me that they moved to the *favela* to enjoy the benefits of living in a central area, such as having close proximity to job opportunities, major transport hubs, public education, health and so on.

The proximity to Niterói city centre, however, never meant a sustainable form of inclusion for Palácio dwellers. The *favela*, as an urban formation, can be seen as a sort of gateway to better life conditions, a promise of escape, in spite of the striking levels of poverty and violent crime, police violence, poor service delivery and infrastructure affecting their everyday lives. *Favelas* like Palácio can be also seen as places of social struggle and symbolic dispute, challenging hegemonic ideals of 'city' (Burgos, 2012) for the right to actively build the 'urban' as a space of diversity, of creative expression of collective forms of life (Lefebvre, 1991 [1968]). But here is another curious thing about the name of the *favela*. As one of the oldest living residents of Palácio, Dona Luiza,[10] once told me, the name of that area used to be 'Travessa do Ingá'.

> 'The name "Palácio" wasn't our idea, it didn't come from the community; it was given by the police! The police would call us that and the newspapers would repeat it. Palácio! Palácio! They would repeat it so often that no one remembers our real name anymore, even some residents that don't know the history of our *favela*.' (Dona Luíza, interview, October 2016)

That said, the *favela* can be many things. Like other peripheries, *favelas* are vividly cultural and creative environments, places of resistance and affirmation of counter-hegemonic forms of life, of living together and making a living (De Certeau, 2012). This multilayered approach to the *favelas* goes against the dominant view of those places as a 'problem' (Preteceille and Valladares, 2000; Alvito and Zaluar, 2003; Mello et al, 2012). Under that light, we cannot avoid still pointing out the critical role in defining these places by their specific relationship with the state.[11] *Favelas* like Palácio have figured as a *problem* (of housing, health, security) to what I've called 'forces of public interest'[12] for at least a century. This long-term deep-rooted process of stigmatization had worked in tandem with the *subaltern integration* of the *favelas* and its residents to the city's economy and in the universe of rights that constitutes the foundation of formal democracies. Wherever that *subaltern integration* cannot be achieved, we observe the systematic elimination of those populations already subjected to the consequences of precarious citizenship status, their legal, symbolic and oftentimes material annihilation (Medeiros, 2017, 2018; Silva, 2019; Albernaz, 2020, among others).

Prior to my fieldwork, I was constantly bombarded with derogatory remarks about *favelas* and their inhabitants. Not surprisingly, I had limited experience with other *favelas* before starting my fieldwork in Palácio, but not because they were a distant experience for me. I grew up surrounded by them, seeing them covering the hills around me, stamping newspaper covers and on the daily crime news shows on TV. Despite their relative proximity, however, I had a very vague idea of how ordinary life occurred in those interdicted places, which is not an uncommon experience for people living outside *favelas*. This interplay of 'visibility' and 'invisibilization' is key to understanding how politics are articulated in Rio de Janeiro *favelas*, producing a subaltern form of political action based on two main characters, the 'community leader' and the 'politician'.

The community leader is necessarily a resident, whether or not he or she has been born in the *favela* that they presume to 'represent'. Ideally, a community leader would be recognized as duly representative based on considerations of origins and belonging, family ties and trajectory as a respectable member of the community. The most important feature of the community leader, however, is his or her capacity to build 'networks' that extrapolate the boundaries of the *favela*. As Robson once explained to me:

> '"Network" is when you connect people. It's to know to whom you're going to appeal when you need help; and this guy that I take my problem to, has a problem himself. You don't waste human material! You might not know how you can help me now but this favour will come back one day, and vice-versa. Life is an exchange. … So there are two types of community leaders, the ones that establish their leadership based on money, and the ones that do that based on connections, networking; the first, only can give you money, the second will use his connections to bring improvements. It's the government's obligation to provide water, sanitation, electricity but if you don't have mediation [referring to the relationship of the community leader and the politician] things will never happen in the favela.' (Robson, interview, October 2016)

One key connection that should figure in any respected community leader network is the politician. The politician is an elected representative of the people or someone holding an executive position in the municipal government, where the issues more directly affecting the *favelas* tend to be decided. The politician needs the community leader to gain access to the *favela* to campaign during the elections, or for the development of localized projects. These two activities are deeply interconnected, projects will be capitalized on by the community leader to give rise to the electoral success of the politician in the *favela*. In Palácio, this is called 'carrying the flag of the politician'. The existence of politicians and community leaders are relevant to each other once the *favelas* are considered 'places that you shouldn't go to' (Albernaz and Pires, 2021), where social and spatial mobility are highly restrained due to urban violence, and where social rights are transacted as concessions, benefits granted by the politician of the time. Although conservative in nature, those transactions are paramount to the viability of life in those places.

In the case of Palácio, what I've called a 'radical neighbourhood situation' (Albernaz, 2018, 2020), referring to the abrupt discontinuity, in terms of life conditions, between the *favela* and its 'surroundings',[13] represents a tactical opportunity of political action for local community leaders like Robson. "Palácio is a highly political *favela*," he told me at the beginning of my fieldwork. "Everything that happens here resonates in the media because Palácio's neighbours are people with influence, and I believe in those *influences* [emphasis]; other *favelas* in Niterói, don't have the same visibility." Robson was a pragmatic and witty political actor; and was able to turn the disadvantages of Palácio's subaltern position into tactical advantages for his own political ambitions. He wanted to, one day, become a politician himself, and he knew how to use Palácio's location among the well-to-do of Niterói as part of his political tactics. To be able 'to speak on behalf of the community', however, Robson had to walk a thin and turbulent line between the recognition of his peers, other residents like himself, the sabotage of his 'adversaries', and the favours of local politicians.

Speaking on behalf of the community

Robson was 46 years old when I first met him in 2016. He had moved to Palácio some 25 years earlier, and was at the time one of its more prominent community leaders. His wife had family in the *favela*. During a short visit to her relatives, they decided to buy a little shack for no more than 5,000 reais[14] and try to make a living in Niterói. Robson had moved around a lot throughout his life, mostly in search of job opportunities. His family could not provide for him, as he told me, and the small town where he was born was also limited in terms of opportunities for low-skilled workers like himself. On his pilgrimage through several provinces in Brazil, during his young age, he learned how to use the relationships with 'important people' to explore the opportunities available for people like himself. In his view, this was the most important thing he had learned from his nomadic years. That, and his ten professions. As he told me:

> 'I can say I have ten professions! That may not sound so good for you but for people like me it is crucial. So, when I got to Niterói, I started to offer myself to the people in the surroundings, to offer my services, because in the *favela* people didn't need what I had to offer. Working for the construction company was definitely crucial [to his career as a community leader]. They worked for the municipal government, so I met people with political relations. And you know me, Bete, I'm a very outgoing person, so I always stood out in what I was set out to do, and I always ended up in the favour of the bosses, the supervisors. I think I was always a leader, since I was a kid. People called me "baba" in the construction company because I was like a boss [laughs]! But I was smart. I was working beside people whom I could influence and whose influence I could use. And I also knew how to make myself useful to people, to become intimate, and I knew how they could be useful for me too. But you cannot know people working the whole day, you have to circulate.' (Robson, interview, July 2016)

Robson thought that his mobility was so important to his successful career as a community leader that in 2020, during the local elections, when he launched his first-ever candidacy as a municipal councillor, he defended the same 'right' for the youngsters in Palácio, restrained in their mobility by financial limitations but also by the violent rule of the drug dealers:

> 'My first bill will be to allow the use of riocard [a social grant card used in public transportation] over the weekends. This prohibition is discriminatory! They want to keep the kids restrained to the *favela*. Our youngsters want to go to the beach, they have to live together, to circulate, otherwise you will breed animals up here!'[15]

Despite his view about the importance of mobility, his campaign slogan, 'I'm here!', would be crafted to project a message of stability. When I asked about its meaning, he promptly responded that he picked the slogan because he wanted to differentiate himself from other politicians that campaign in the *favela*, and then "are never seen again until the next elections".[16] Later on in the conversation, he brought up his own conflicts about the matter. Robson was not born or raised in Palácio, and after more than 20 years living in the *favela*, the fact that he was considered an outsider still raised suspicion about his intentions and methods. Rumours about his past were constantly recycled by his political opponents to undermine his claims to represent the community. The political slogan was also a message to his *adversaries*. His ballot name was 'Robson from Palácio', making clear his link to the *favela*.

Once Robson decided not to be a wanderer anymore, he lived the dilemmas of a 'stranger', as defined by Georg Simmel (1950). Being someone that embodies distance and closeness at the same time, the *stranger* possesses a more critical and objective view of society, and therein lies its importance to the community of people it decided to join. Over the *stranger's* head will always hover the shadow of its potential departure, as well as speculations about its past. However, Robson wanted to acquire social and material status by becoming a *favela* politician, a career that would unfold from its trajectory as a community leader. In that matter, his political tactics, but also his daily struggles to make his life viable in the *favela*, would constitute singular opportunities to explore the complex interconnections between violence, mobility and inequality (Albernaz and Pires, 2021). By drawing attention to this, I intend to highlight the processes of border formation embedded in the everyday life of segregated areas like Palácio in their relationship with the state.

In response to his critics, Robson argued that, although he was an outsider, his son and granddaughter were both '*crias*' from Palácio. *Cria* is a slang word widely used in Rio de Janeiro *favelas* to refer to the *born and raised*. The term literally means 'the offspring of an animal' and implies a deeply rooted origin in the *favela* where one presently lives. Although irrelevant to the world outside, the status of *cria* is critical for everyday life in the *favelas*. Working as a sort of marginal citizenship status, the *cria* is the personification of an informal (and, therefore, often disputed) code of conduct drawing the lines between acceptable and unacceptable behaviours in areas like Palácio.[17] "People know your family, know that you worked hard to raise your kids, your grandkids, that you're a decent person, and this says something about your behaviour in other matters too," explained one of my interlocutors (Wellerson, interview, July 2016).

However, it's in the association of the *cria* to a demarcated territory that resides the most critical implications of the use of the category. As the *favelas* are violently disputed by different illegal armed groups, being a *cria* from a certain area, you can only circulate in *favelas* dominated by the same group or faction. Disobeying this basic rule will most certainly bring about deadly consequences for the transgressor. In your own area, however, being a *cria* can protect you, producing some predictability in the relationship with those same untamed forces based on a set of unwritten precarious rights. For people like Robson, occupying the position of community leader, not being able to claim the marginal citizenship status of the *cria* can expose him to violence. This thin and oftentimes indiscernible line that Robson walks daily to bring improvements to the community he lives in can be exemplified by the following episode.

A few years after he moved with his family to Palácio, the municipality of Niterói started negotiations with a previous generation of community leaders to provide piped water for the houses. For decades prior, Palácio's residents had to tackle the hilly terrain, carrying buckets to get access to potable water from public taps, located in the lower sections of the *favela*, closer to its urbanized surroundings. Back in those days, Robson already had plans to become part of the select group of community leaders, people with powerful connections with the world outside the *favela*. His ambitions to join the 'favela bourgeoisie' (Da Silva, 2011), however, were frustrated by the widespread distrust of his *outsider* status. But that was about to change. Having "more than ten professions", most of them derived from his engagement in lower-skilled construction jobs, Robson was unemployed and decided to closely follow the installation of Palácio's water piping system. That decision was key, according to him, to grant access to the powerful networks associated with the role of a community leader:

'I think making friends and using our friendship to progress both of us is one of my most outstanding features. So, as I was unemployed, and being an interested person, I had plenty of time to stay the whole day with the city hall engineers and workers following the installation of the piped water system. At the end of the process, almost two years, not only did I know everything about the operation of the system but I also managed to secure a job as its operator in Palácio. Every *favela* has one operator, and I made myself that person for Palácio! So that's how it all started for me as a community leader. My network started to expand, I got a second job fixing public schools for the municipality, and I met more people, including the politician for whom I "carry the flag" today here in Palácio. He works with Education. But it all started with the water, by acquiring a knowledge that no one had about the operation of the water in the *favela*. No one has that knowledge still. That's actually a problem. I have to start thinking about making a successor. This situation you heard about the drug dealer threatening to kill me, pointing a gun to my face in front of everyone, is proof of that. In the beginning, it was useful for me; the community needed me and for that I was embraced as part of this community. But now it's time. I need to be able to rest, I need to be able to leave the *favela* on vacation and not to come back to the mess you saw last month.'
(Robson, interview, April 2017)

The situation with the drug dealer, mentioned by Robson, happened during my fieldwork. It was high summer in Rio de Janeiro, a time of the year when not having access to piped water can become a critical issue. Robson had left on vacation, leaving another resident as the person responsible for receiving the technician from the water company that would operate the system during his absence. Being a *favela*, Palácio is classified by the water company as a 'risk area'. In practical terms, this means that the technician cannot be in any way compelled by the water company to enter the *favela* if he or she feels unsafe, and without the support of a local person. The person designated by Robson also did not fully master the intricacies of the process, and was unable to perform the *water manoeuvre*, a journey of opening and closing junctions to allow the water to reach all sections of the *favela*, without the support of the technician. One night, after an especially violent week in the *favela*, the technician could not find the local person and decided to leave, not returning to Palácio even in the subsequent week.

Soon people started to struggle to access water, especially those in the houses located at the top of the *favela*, distant from the urban infrastructure of the surrounding areas. Subsequently, someone decided to take the matter to the drug dealers, "poisoning them with lies", like Robson would tell me later, not just about his alleged "disappearance" during the then water crisis, but about his overall conduct as the one responsible for *manoeuvring the water* in Palácio. He was accused of privileging his relatives and coreligionists, people that "would vote with him", supporting his candidates in the local elections, in the distribution of water in the *favela*. When Robson came back from his vacation "the circus was set", he said; everybody was looking for him, including the drug dealers. One afternoon, he was walking around the *favela* assessing the damages – both to his reputation and to the water supply – when he bumped into one of the drug dealers. The man threatened to kill him, accusing him of "the most vicious improprieties".

I interviewed him twice after the episode. The first time, after the encounter with the drug dealer; the second, a couple of months later. During the first interview, Robson appeared angry, and repeatedly mentioned how insulting it was to have a gun pointed to his face in front of everyone:

> 'He pointed a gun to my face! To my face! A guy that just got out of jail! I always thought I could talk my way out of anything but this time I wasn't allowed to talk! This guy doesn't know what is going on here, and he was poisoned with lies about me, about my work, by envious people! People that question my role as a community leader, that dispute my position to speak on behalf of this *favela*. And he simply believed them! He should have asked around before confronting me like that, in front of everyone. … You know, politics has two sides, and there's always someone looking after your mistakes, there are always political adversaries.' (Robson, interview, March 2017)

In the second interview, I found Robson deeply resentful and exhausted by the extensive negotiations he had had to go through, talking to other residents, providing his version of what happened and gathering support. People who were supportive of Robson's plea would say that the drug dealer acted disrespectfully, exceeding his due right to exert violence to keep behaviours in check in the *favela*. His detractors, however, questioned his present conduct as a 'community leader', questions also fuelled by rumours about his past. "Why did he end up living in Palácio after moving so much? Was he running from something? We don't know. But people say that he must have done something wrong," I heard from a female Palácio resident. Robson, on his part, felt vulnerable. The gossip about his past was on the verge of becoming a matter of life and death after the episode with the drug dealer. The untamed violence that had created the necessity of mediators, frontier explorers like himself, had turned against him. In the next section, I present one of the political manoeuvres used by Robson when negotiating Palácio's unique neighbourhood situation when seeking to channel those same marginal forces to secure improvements and access to basic rights for its residents while progressing his own personal project to become a politician himself.

Political tactics

Robson is a pragmatic and shrewd political actor, although with a fairly ruthless view of society, and a very sharp sense of place. In his life, he learned that he could not allow himself the luxury of wasting any opportunities to establish informal networks that he saw as critical to his own material survival. At a certain point, he also realized that electoral politics worked in a very similar way, and his eyes were open to seeing the opportunities to live from his politics, the politics of everyday life (Albernaz, 2018). He was one of the few who knew exactly how to use the terrain and apply the meagre resources available to advance his political tactics. In this section, I explore these tactics a little further. Despite dealing with sometimes contradictory expectations about his role as a community leader, his social ascension ambitions as a wannabe politician, and his material needs as a member of the popular classes himself, Robson still managed to secure improvements to Palácio and its residents, without losing sight, however, of the conservative nature of his own achievements:

> 'As a community leader, you're compelled to do something for your community but you also become a hostage of the person that did you a favour. So you're never free to do what you want. People calling themselves community leaders have to know how to negotiate, and make deals with politicians. You have to have the councillor's cell number but also that of the technician of the electricity company to call him in the middle of the night, unofficially, to come to Palácio to restore the power so people can wake up the next day to go to work,

and have power to make coffee and toast bread. There is the politics of electricity, the politics of the nursery, of the soccer field, of asphalt. Politics is not just electoral politics. But when you're involved with politics you lose your pressure capacity in a way. In my case, I carry the flag of a politician here in Palácio. I also have a job that is derived from this political affiliation. I do my best not to displease people, but to be an appointed public servant and a community leader can be contradictory sometimes. But we all have to make a living. The bread must be shared, or we'll take it! … People say that in Palácio we don't pay taxes. That's right, and we don't have to pay them! Why can some people have everything while we have nothing? But they need the *favela*. They made this *favela*, and people outside use the *favela* as a bargaining chip. They use you, and you use them. You have to know how to follow the law of the situation, of the moment, the law of necessity. That's why it's always the same people and the same ideas. People repeat themselves.' (Robson, interview, October 2016)

When Robson talks about the *favela* as a 'bargaining chip' he is referring to its political use to propel power projects extracting value from the radical discontinuity, in terms of human occupation, between Palácio and its urbanized *surroundings*. This undesirable proximity with poverty was profusely represented by stigmatizing markers of social distance as places existing on the outskirts of legality, social order and civilization (Valladares, 2005; Da Silva, 2008; Amoroso, 2012). In this sense, the symbolic work of defining the *favela* as a 'public problem' is a key dimension of the complex ways in which politics can emerge from the daily struggles for ensuring basic survival for people living in the margins of the state order (Das and Poole, 2004; Das and Randeria, 2015). Robson also knew very well how to navigate these two distinct worlds, exploring the frictions produced by the close contact between them to create opportunities to improve life conditions while becoming a relevant political actor in the city of Niterói. The effectiveness of his political tactics, as we're going to see, implied walking a thin line between embracing and fighting, at the same time, the consequences of social stigmatization.

Many attempts were made to remove Palácio from its 'privileged' location throughout the years. These measure were strongly resisted by most residents. Besides depriving them from many of the benefits of centrality, increasing costs of daily commuting, the removal of the *favela* would also destabilize well-established solidarity and mutual-help networks, critical to making viable the conditions for basic survival. The relentless work of Palácio's community leaders, past and present, was key in dodging those removal attempts. Many were the reasons given by the local government to justify the measure. In the 1960s and 1970s, Palácio was depicted in public policy and by the local media as a 'health hazard', and its 'promiscuous livelihood conditions' accused of promoting the spread of diseases. It was constantly accused of being an 'aesthetic aberration', obscuring the splendour of its surrounding areas. But if in the past the *favelas* were publicly handled mostly as a 'housing problem', the last 40 years witnessed the consolidation of the *favelas* as a 'police problem', and a legitimate object of violent forms of state repression (Burgos, 2005, 2012).

Palácio was known as a 'violent place', and that stigma tended to be reinforced by public policies informed by restricted forms of public participation. As part of my research, I attended the monthly meetings of the local Community Safety Council, a public participation instance created by the government, and run by representatives of civil society, to discuss issues of public safety affecting the communities. During those meetings, the members of the 'community', mostly small business owners and residents from the urbanized areas of the city, would voice their preoccupations regarding the state of public safety in Niterói. More or less consciously, the *favelas* were always a key element for the ways they would represent the problems affecting the city and its inhabitants. Community leaders from the *favelas* in Niterói rarely attended those meetings. A common complaint would be about alleged Palácio residents who were "coming down from the *favela* to rob people in its surroundings". In this case, as mentioned, Palácio's proximity to more well-to-do neighbourhoods could be a source of great distress and discontent.

Highly visible and politically sensitive, "everything that happens in Palácio attracts police attention", whose presence is tempered between brazen corruption, the search for 'police productivity' and extreme levels of violence (Albernaz, 2018, 2020).[18] However, as I show, the effects of Palácio's public visibility are not unidimensional. The stigmatizing attributes discussed here, imposed from the 'outside', were vivid in the hearts and minds of the good citizens of Niterói, people who 'pay their taxes' and who expect to see a solution for the 'problem' represented by the *favelas* in return. In the realms of public opinion, the authorities' ability to handle the issue, keeping the *favela* 'under control', played a critical role in the local elections, often determining the political futures of established groups, accused of being 'inept' or even 'compliant with the criminality'. In this case, the political role of the community leader is paramount.

The political tactics applied by Robson were pragmatic, based in an acute sense of place, both of the *favela* in the social landscape of the city of Niterói and of himself as a community leader, as mentioned. One of these tactics – observed in Palácio, but widely spread in other *favelas* – is known as '*fazer a favela descer*' or 'to take the *favela* down', meaning to incite its residents to manifest their discontent in the 'asphalt', a metonymic way of referring to the *favela*'s surrounding urbanized areas.[19]

In Palácio, this happened a handful of times in the past ten years; usually because of a serious discontinuation in service delivery, or when a *trabalhador* (worker), a resident not involved with the drug-dealing cartels or factions, was killed by the police. In both cases, the *favela* is usually taken by a deep sense of outrage, that an unacceptable injustice occurred, an insult even for those already used to a life under duress (Cardoso de Oliveira, 2008). The political powers unleashed in those episodes, if handled carefully by community leaders, can be highly effective in achieving immediate results, like in the restoration of electricity and water supplies, or the appointment of a medical doctor for the local health care centre. However effective, those movements rarely manage to promote enduring social justice or to achieve substantive structural changes. For the community leader, they can also be an opportunity to display political strength to adversaries and politicians, showing the amount of local support and control exerted over the always disruptive and unpredictable nature of those gatherings.

The inherent danger of this tactic, however, is that it can be seen by politicians and especially the municipal government as a threat to their electoral projects. According to Robson:

> 'When the *favela comes down* it generates a huge political problem for the municipality, and we need the politicians to bring improvements for the *favela*. So we cannot push too hard, but it's also hard to keep people under control once you instigate their revolt. There are also occasions when you don't want to do it, you don't want to *bring down* the *favela* but you have to do it anyway or people will lose their trust in your capacity to represent them as a community leader. ... There are community leaders that use that power to incite people's outrage to undermine the electoral ambitions of the municipality, to project opposition candidacies etc. It's a risky move, though. We have to always be on good terms with the politicians and the government.' (Robson, interview, October 2016)

When the '*favela* comes down' what usually happens is that the residents block the roads located in its immediate vicinity using their own bodies or whatever materials are available, like garbage, rocks, burning tires, and so on. People shout and sing, asking for the presence of the municipal authorities, naming the victims of gun violence, and demanding justice. Soon the press shows up, interviewing people, asking questions. What is being said, however, has very little face value for the politicians. People vote in the *favelas*, of course, but what is decisive in gaining their votes is the everyday work of the community leader, bargaining for improvements and distributing social grants on behalf of a specific politician. During those protests, what really brings about the recognition of the demands of Palácio residents is the outrage of the good (or 'respectable') citizens of Niterói. Frightened by the sight of the poverty next door, and willing to disseminate the message that the politicians cannot 'handle' the favela, those 'orderly taxpayers' expect to see the mostly non-White and migrant population of the *favela* 'under control', confined to the spaces and opportunities reserved to them.

Conclusion

'Global South' is a politico-theoretical category that seeks to distance itself from old teleological and stigmatizing terminologies such as 'third world' or 'developing countries', adding another geopolitical division between countries that were victimized and the ones that have benefited from the colonial expansion of the capitalist system and its planet-wide social division of labour. It also implies a shared political, theoretical and academic framework of concerns derived from peripheral or counter-hegemonic positions in the circulation of values, people and knowledge in the 'global economy' (Santos, 2002a, 2002b; Dias et al, 2008; Dias and Trajano Filho, 2015; Hollington et al, 2015; Ribeiro and Dwyer, 2015), a position that some authors have also described as 'subaltern' (Spivak and Guha, 1988; Appadurai, 2001; Spivak, 2010).

An important criticism of the concept, however, is that by thinking about the global South in opposition to the North one does not consider the continuous influence of *Northern* ideological and material lineages in the so-called 'post-colonial world', embodied in the actions of its economic elites (Eriksen, 2014). By breaking this hemispheric opposition, the political, economic and cultural asymmetries created by the colonial enterprise, characteristic of this *Southern* position, unfold into countless forms of oppression endorsing long-term structures of social inequalities internal to the countries, on both sides of the globe. In the current chapter, I have explored the possibility of thinking of the *global South* as a fluid and moving border, showing how social and spatial mobility can disrupt the *North/South* oppositions in the everyday relations of ordinary people in real-life settings.

In Palácio itself, I have explored the political relevance of the everyday struggles of community leaders to ensure conditions for life and its reproduction to reveal the very mundane social processes producing the radical borders between the *favela* and its *surroundings* as an example of the moving nature of the *global South*. I've shown how the physical and symbolic borders defining the *favela* could emerge from marginal, semi-official forms of governing producing the *subaltern integration* of Palácio as a 'no-go' area in the city of Niterói. The deeply perverse nature of the social processes highlighted here challenges the very possibility of real democracy in countries overwhelmed by high levels of social and legal inequalities. Ultimately, the case of Palácio illustrates how state and governmental forms can actively operate to prevent (instead of promote) the establishment of a universal, egalitarian ideal of citizenship.

Notes

1. I performed two sets of interviews with Robson. In July 2016, I did one interview about his trajectory and, in the following October, another about his routine and 'tactics' as a community leader in Palácio. In March 2017, I decided to interview Robson again, right after the episode with the drug dealer and a second time in April of the same year, trying to capture more settled perceptions about what had happened to him.
2. For Veena Das and Debora Poole, the 'margins of State' are privileged places to observe the practical limits of democratic ideals. For the authors, the discursive production of the *margins* as the outskirts of the political order is actually a strong conveyer of political powers.
3. According to Bourdieu (1992), struggles of 'representation' are also struggles over ethnic or regional identity, to impose the legitimate definition of the divisions of the social world, of frontiers and territory, a power whose authority is under permanent contestation
4. The importance of political mediators for the negotiation of precarious citizenship status in the many peripheries of capitalist societies is widely documented (Chatterjee, 2004; Da Silva, 2011; Das and Randeria, 2015, among others).
5. According to Chatterjee (2004), the 'democratic State' should not be approached by social researchers as a given reality. What the author calls the 'practical helms of citizenship', therefore, would emerge from the observation of localized governance techniques, developed in direct contact with people living on the fringes of enclaves of law and order in Indian society (the 'governed').
6. See the World Inequality Database (https://wid.world/), the World Income Inequality Database (https://www.wider.unu.edu/project/wiid-%E2%80%93-world-income-ine quality-database) and the Inequality and Shared Prosperity reports and data (https://www.worldbank.org/en/topic/isp) (accessed 11 August 2021).
7. Palácio is located within a 20-minute walk from my old home in Niterói. In this short time, it was possible to experience the transition from an HDI of 0.962 and an average monthly income of 5,146.21 reais, characteristic of the living conditions in Icaraí Beach, to an HDI of 0.661 and an average income of only 427.35 reais per month, a reality lived by the residents of Palácio. In its classic formulation, the HDI is composed of three indicators, representing the opportunity to have long and healthy lives, to have access to knowledge and to have command over resources in order to guarantee a decent standard of living (UNDP/IPEA, 2014).
8. Niterói was the capital city of the province of Rio de Janeiro between 1834 and 1894, and again from 1903 to 1975.
9. This was largely due to broader economic and social transformations happening in Brazil in the 1960s and 1970s, with the intensification of internal migrations and the accelerated urbanization of cities like São Paulo and Rio de Janeiro, but also of a series of regional urban reforms aiming to relocate poverty and fix the working classes at a safe commutable distance from the city centres. But if São Paulo was relatively successful in producing its peripheries, largely due to the conjugation of strict land use controls and an efficient public transportation system, in Rio de Janeiro, the close coexistence of extreme levels of inequalities became the city's most striking feature (Silva, 2012).
10. Dona Luiza became known to me through the recounting of a famous story in Palácio in which she lay down in front of the municipal tractors that were in the *favela* to execute one of the many judicial orders to demolish some of the residents' houses in the early 1980s.
11. The spatialized analysis of the everyday process of state formation reveals that state powers have no institutional stability on either theoretical or historical grounds. In this

sense, in the present chapter, the state is depicted as a porous entity, the by-product of everyday, very mundane relations with society, recognized by its effects more than by any other discernible *a priori* feature, never obtained solely through national institutions or in governmental sites (Abrams, 1988; Mitchell, 1999; Trouillot, 2001; Ferguson and Gupta, 2002; Ferguson, 2006).

12 Combined with the logic of reproduction of political and economic oligarchies, what I've called in my thesis 'forces of public interest' is a collusion of institutional actors symbolically and politically consecrated by the illocutionary power of the state field to say the 'public interest'. By promoting a project of 'city', on behalf of which they would exercise their power, representing neoliberal forms of spatialization operating in a blurred area between the interests of the state, powerful market forces, and a mostly complicit segment of civil society in the city of Niterói.

13 In Portuguese '*entorno*', a euphemistic but clear-cut term used to demarcate the frontier with the supposedly law-abiding community of 'taxpayers' that is located in the immediate vicinity of the *favelas*.

14 Which would be equivalent to 800 US dollars based on the current exchange rate.

15 Excerpt from campaign video posted on Robson's Facebook profile on 7 October 2020 (accessed 29 November 2021).

16 In one of his social media posts, he uploaded a video in October 2020, right before the municipal elections, saying "A lot of people are coming up here in the community now telling their stories [claiming responsibility for betterments and campaigning] but when something goes wrong I'm the one that is here. I'm here!"

17 One can say, for example, "This is not the type of behaviour expected from a *cria*!" judging someone's conduct in a specific situation. On the same spectrum, being a *born and raised* also works for the granting of 'credit' in pecuniary and reputational terms. During my fieldwork I was always actively pursuing to pay credit ('*fiado*', in Portuguese) in small shops and bars in Palácio. However, I was only allowed to do that because one of my main interlocutors was a *cria* and was the guarantor of my good conduct in the *favela*. I'll never forget the first time someone gave me credit in Palácio. The woman running the shop told me, "There's no problem, if you don't pay your debt I'm going after him [referring to my friend]. You might leave, but he'll be always here." So if I hadn't paid my debt, disappearing from the *favela*, she could take my friend's name to the drug dealers. As he was a *cria*, the due process to charge him would start with a warning. If he was an 'outsider', however, it wouldn't be seen as inappropriate if they had recurred straightaway to violent methods of collection.

18 In the last two months of my fieldwork, I was following the developments of a series of four police killings that took place in Palácio. The four young men, aged between 18 and 23 years old, were killed in 'self-defence', according to the police, and accused of being drug dealers. However, instead of being held accountable by civil society for their lethal actions, the local police commanders would be enthusiastically congratulated for their great work 'fighting criminality' during the Community Safety Forum meetings (see Albernaz, 2020).

19 As an example of a protest resulting from a serious discontinuation in service delivery, in 2013, see https://www.youtube.com/watch?v=K13kEfqJmJM&t=7s; in 2021, again the *favela came down* to protest after a resident was killed by the police, see https://www.youtube.com/watch?v=wYsleeN2G9Q [Accessed 16 November 2022].

References

Abrams, P. (1988) Notes on the difficulty of studying the state. *Journal of Historical Sociology*, 1(1): 58–89.

Albernaz, E. (2018) *Palácios sem reis, democracias sem cidadãos: política, cotidiano e a formação de mercados da exclusão em dois contextos do 'sul-global'*. Tese de Doutorado defendida no Programa de Pós-Graduação em Antropologia da Universidade Federal Fluminense (PPGA/UFF), Niterói.

Albernaz, E. (2020) Economias-Políticas Marginais: Produtividade Policial, Vizinhanças Radicais e a (Re) Produção Cotidiana das Desigualdades em uma Favela de Niterói-RJ. *Antropolítica-Revista Contemporânea de Antropologia* 50: 107–127.

Albernaz, E.R. and Pires, L. (2021) 'Places you shouldn't go to': (Im)mobility, violence and democracy in Brazil and South Africa. *Oñati Socio-Legal Series* 11(6): 1365–1391.

Alvito, M. and Zaluar, A. (eds) (2003) *Um Século de Favela* (3rd edition). Rio de Janeiro: FGV.

Amoroso, M. (2012) Duas faces da mesma fotografia: atraso versos progresso na cobertura fotojornalística de favelas do Correio da Manhã, in M.A. Mello, L. Freire and S.S. Simões (eds) *Favelas cariocas: ontem e hoje*. Rio de Janeiro: Garamond, pp 191–212.

Appadurai, A. (2001) *La modernidad desbordada*. Buenos Aires: Trilce/Fondo de Cultura Económica.

Bourdieu, P. (1992) *Language and Symbolic Power*. Cambridge: Polity.

Bourdieu, P. (1997) Efeitos do Lugar, in P. Bourdieu (ed) *A miséria do mundo*. Petrópolis: Vozes, pp 159–175.

Burgos, M.B. (2005) Cidade, territórios e cidadania. *Dados*, 48(1): 189–222.

Burgos, M.B. (2012) Favela: uma forma de luta pelo direito à cidade, in M.A. Mello, L. Freire and S.S. Simões (eds) *Favelas cariocas: ontem e hoje*. Rio de Janeiro: Garamond, pp 373–391.

Cardoso de Oliveira, L.R. (2008) Existe violência sem agressão moral? *Revista Brasileira de Ciências Sociais*, 23: 135–146.

Chatterjee, P. (2004) *The Politics of the Governed: Reflections on Popular Politics in Most of the World*. New York: Columbia University Press.

Da Silva, L.A.M. (2008) *Vida sob cerco: violência e rotina nas favelas do Rio de Janeiro*. Rio de Janeiro: Editora Nova Fronteira.

Da Silva, L.A.M. (2011) A política na favela. *Dilemas-Revista de Estudos de Conflito e Controle Social*, 4(4): 699–716.

Das, V. and Poole, D. (2004) Anthropology in the margins of the state. *PoLAR: Political and Legal Anthropology Review*, 30(1): 140–144.

Das, V. and Randeria, S. (2015) Politics of the urban poor: Aesthetics, ethics, volatility, precarity: An introduction to supplement 11. *Current Anthropology*, 56(S11): S3–S14.

De Certeau, M. (2012) *A invenção do cotidiano: artes de fazer*. Petrópolis: Editora Vozes.

Dias, J.B. and Trajano Filho, W. (2015) O colonialismo em África e seus legados: classificação e poder no ordenamento da vida social. *Anuário Antropológico*, 2: 9–22.

Dias, J.B., Thomaz, O.R. and Trajano Filho, W. (2008) Brazilian anthropologists in Africa: Remarks on theory, politics and fieldwork overseas. *Vibrant Virtual Brazilian Anthropology*, 5(2): 277–303.

Eriksen, T.H. (2014) *Globalization: The Key Concepts*. London: A&C Black.

Ferguson, J. (2006) *Global Shadows: Africa in the Neoliberal World Order*. Durham, NC: Duke University Press.

Ferguson, J. and Gupta, A. (2002) Spatializing states: Toward an ethnography of neoliberal governmentality. *American Ethnologist*, 29(4): 981–1002.

Hollington, A., Salverda, T., Schwarz, T. and Tappe, O. (2015) *Concepts of the Global South*. Cologne: Global South Studies Centre.

Lefebvre, H. (1991 [1968]) *O direito à cidade*. São Paulo: Moraes.

Medeiros, F. (2017) A necropolítica da 'guerra': tecnologias de governo, 'homicídios' e 'tráfico de drogas' na região metropolitana do Rio de Janeiro. *Abya-Yala: Revista sobre acesso à justiça e direitos nas Américas*, 1(3): 73–94.

Medeiros, F. (2018) O morto no lugar dos mortos: classificações, sistemas de controle e necropolítica no Rio de Janeiro. *Revista M*, 3(5): 72–91.

Mello, M.A.S., Machado da Silva, L.A., Freire, L. and Simões, S.S. (2012) *Favelas cariocas: ontem e hoje*. Rio de Janeiro: Garamond.

Mitchell, T. (1999) Society, economy, and the state effect, in G. Steinmetz (ed) *State/Culture: State-Formation after the Cultural Turn*. Ithaca, NY: Cornell University Press, pp 76–97.

Piketty, T. (2014) *Capital in the 21st Century*. Cambridge, MA: Harvard University Press.

Pires, L. (2011) *Esculhamba, mas não esculacha! Uma etnografia dos usos urbanos dos trens da Central do Brasil*. Niterói: EDUFF.

Preteceille, E. and Valladares, L. (2000) Favela, favelas: unidade ou diversidade da favela carioca, in L.C. Ribeiro (ed) *O futuro das metrópoles*. Río de Janeiro: Editora Revan, pp 375–403.

Ribeiro, G.L. and Dwyer, T. (2015) *Social, Political and Cultural Challenges of the BRICS*. Sao Paulo: Langaa RPCIG.

Santos, B.S. (2002a) Para uma sociologia das ausências e uma sociologia das emergências. *Revista crítica de ciências sociais*, 63: 237–280.

Santos, B.S. (2002b) Between Prospero and Caliban: Colonialism, postcolonialism, and inter-identity. *Luso-Brazilian Review*, 39(2): 9–43.

Silva, G. (2019) 'Quantos ainda vão morrer, eu não sei': O regime do arbítrio, da curtição, morte e a vida em um lugar chamado de favela. Tese de doutorado. Niterói: PPSD/Universidade Federal Fluminense.

Silva, M.L.P.D. (2012) Os urbanistas e seu debate: reflexões sobre 'Aspectos humanos da favela carioca', in M.A. Mello, L. Freire and S.S. Simões (eds) *Favelas cariocas: ontem e hoje*. Rio de Janeiro: Garamond, pp 101–119.

Simmel, G. (1950) The stranger, in K. Wolff (trans) *The Sociology of Georg Simmel*. New York: Free Press, pp 402–408.

Spivak, G.C. (2010) *Pode o subalterno falar?* (1st edition), translated by S.R.G. Almeida, M.P. Feitosa and A. Pereira. Belo Horizonte: Editora da UFMG.

Spivak, G.C. and Guha, R. (1988) *Selected Subaltern Studies*. New York: Oxford University Press.

Trouillot, M.R. (2001) The anthropology of the state in an age of globalization: Close encounters of a deceptive kind. *Current Anthropology*, 42(1): 125–138.

Valladares, L.P. (2005) *A invenção da favela: do mito de origem a favela.com*. Rio de Janeiro: FGV.

Virilio, P. (1986) *Speed and Politics: An Essay on Dromology*, translated by M. Polizzotti. New York: Semiotext(e). (Originally published in French in 1977.)

12

Social Mobilization and Victims of Violence: Emotional Responses to Justice in an Urban Periphery

Valéria Cristina de Oliveira and Jaqueline Garza Placencia

Introduction

1 March 2017, Wednesday, residents of Santana, a slum in the Sapopemba district in the city of São Paulo, were following their daily routine. Soccer night, Corinthians and Brusque were competing for the Brazilian Cup. A group of young people are hanging out at a well-known corner, on a street that marks the border between the '*asfalto*' and the '*favela*'.[1] Everything was quite normal until the sound of gunshots made that night atypical. These happenings would change some residents' lives forever and would become a milestone in the recent history of social movements in that neighbourhood.

The very negative outcome was one young man murdered (Rogério[2]), another seriously injured, and the suspicion that it had been an execution carried out by police officers who were not wearing uniforms and were driving regular civilian cars. The shooters didn't try to hide their faces: "The two men came openly, walking ... into the *favela* and then they [shooters] executed him [one of the young guys]," Beatriz, an important district leader, tells us. "It was like a movie," describes Fabio, a teenager who knew the victim and accompanied us during the fieldwork. Then the 'movie', registered by security cameras installed in nearby properties, goes on showing neighbours running to see what had happened, the mother's desperation and the arrival of other men who identified themselves as members of the Forensic Services, collecting the bullet cases that were scattered on the street after the shooting.

Our research in the east side of São Paulo began a few days after this fact and, given our research subject, that is, collective responses to violence and local social action, the case of Rogério's death was always brought up in conversation and interviews with residents. Some mentioned a big mobilization that had stopped an important avenue in the district the day after the homicide. Others added that it was an injustice that the young man had been killed this way, even though he was not 'involved' in crime anymore. Others were concerned about the physical integrity of the survivor. However, in general everyone had an opinion on what happened that March night and to how it unfolded an important social mobilization in the neighbourhood.

★★★

Numbers of homicides in Brazil leave no doubt that, like Rogério, the biggest victims of this violence are young, Black, poor and, consequently, often residents of urban peripheries. There are so many victims with this profile that the gap between their percentage and the one of young and Whites surprises even the reader less inclined to quantitative data: according to the Brazilian Public Security Yearbook, in 2020, of all people killed as a result of police intervention, 78.9 per cent were Black (Fórum Brasileiro de Segurança Pública, 2021).

If the homicide victim is young, 'involved in crime', 'takes drugs' or 'messes with the wrong things', Brazilian society seems to be allowed to justify and to minimize the seriousness of the crime. Police, media and sometimes the victims' own neighbours describes the violent deaths of these youths as inevitable considering their criminal backgrounds. As a consequence, some lives seem to be worth less than others and therefore when they are taken, those deaths receive more impersonal and general meanings that signify the fact (the death or the number of deaths) and not people (the victims) (Pita, 2018).

For those deaths in Brazil, there are lower chances of a fair judicial process in criminal proceedings (Lima and Ratton, 2011; Ribeiro et al, 2014). The reason is a huge socioeconomic inequality that differentiates access to justice and strengthens the collective feeling that nothing should be said or done about the homicides in peripheral areas.

The situation changes when the victim is brought to light with a name, face and, most important, a history. He or she is no longer a record on a public safety department database. Family and friends are there to give him or her a voice that it is even more listened to when that crime produces a sense of injustice in society. This collective feeling of grievance can have a cathartic effect that motivates social acts such as mobilizations that request punishment for the murderers or the making of T-shirts and painting the victim's image on walls (Fireman and Gamson, 1979). Emotions and affection seem to be capable of returning centrality to people, usually hidden amidst the police narrative of violent deaths in peripheral areas (Vianna and Farias, 2011; Gayol and Kessler, 2018).

We argue that such mechanisms motivated the intense mobilization of residents and local human rights institutions around Rogério's execution in 2017. The publication of an open letter and a march that closed the main avenue of the region with intense media coverage were just some of the responses to this case that still had a survivor who lacked protection and medical attention.

This contrasted with an apparent social apathy about other youth homicides in the neighbourhood. The area is known for high levels of violence, perpetrated by police officers against young people (Feltran and Motta, 2021). Even during our fieldwork there were some violent deaths in similar conditions and they did not provoke the same popular engagement against violence practised by the state. What makes the social reactions to those violent events so different? What are the strategies to engage people to oppose the violence against youth in the neighbourhood?

The contact with community leaders and other residents have indicated the role of emotions and affection in defining the contours and adaptations of local responses to cases of violence. Considering this, and following answers to these initial concerns, this chapter analyses the role of emotions building different and coordinated responses from residents of a peripheral area in São Paulo, Brazil. Results are based on a qualitative research conducted by the authors between 2016 and 2017, during our postdoctoral internship at the Center for Metropolitan Studies (CEM) at São Paulo State University (USP).

We argue that a common element of collective manifestations in the face of youth deaths is the community's identification with the victims. It happens through a retrieving of victims' affections, the social ties established throughout their lives and referring to the values that the friends and relatives wish their dead to express. The literature that discusses the affections and emotions configuring popular manifestations in response to violence and human rights violations supports this work (Moore Jr, 1987; Pita, 2010, 2018). We mainly triggered the concept of emotional language designated by Myriam Jimeno (2010) analysing Colombian social movements in the 2000s.

The text goes through collective public gestures that illustrate residents' strategies to signify the violent youth deaths in the neighbourhood, focusing on the victims. This involves remembering their lives and disclosing the circumstances of their death, especially when the murderers are public agents such as police officers.

The repercussion of Rogério's killing is an example of collective action with an institutional contour that fits even the stricter concept of social movement in political science. However, we also will describe less structured – and maybe more silent – responses to youth violent deaths in the Brazilian periphery. They are the material support of the residents to the victims' families or the emotional local tributes usually paid to loved ones who passed away in violent circumstances. In this category, there are tributes such as the indoor soccer team that have printed their team shirts with the face of a friend executed by the police, or what we call here memory writings, which are messages stamped on the walls, remembering friends who were killed in that area.

We argue that these manifestations expose different ways of expressing the feelings of grievance and injustice brought by violence. Economic deprivation and the lack of access to formal justice forms the bases to some of these responses in disadvantaged areas in Brazil. Using emotional language seems to remove from invisibility the homicide victim in a scenario in which for most of society they are just one more case in criminal records of homicides.

Emotional language: affections and mobilization

In the last two decades, the debate about the role of affect and emotions in collective action has gained prominence in social science research agendas (Hochschild, 1975; Moore Jr, 1987; Jasper, 2012; Poma and Gravante, 2018). Emotions linked to feelings of injustice and moral grievance feed the system of relationships that produces collective action. Therefore, affective bonds are key motivations for social organizing and mobilization. Moreover, emotions can trigger political and cultural transformations in subjects affected by violence (Moore Jr, 1987; Pita, 2010).

However, emotions are not always triggered and act in the same way. Jasper (2012) proposes that several emotions are observed in the configuration of social movement. However, those that are able to activate a sense of belonging and engagement with common issues are those that arise from what he calls a moral shock. The concept describes information or events that suggest to people that the world is not as they believed it to be until that moment. A moral shock is part of the flow of action towards political activism, but it does not change people's moral principles, only activates or clarifies them, sometimes causing the visceral unease produced by shock to lead to political action in the quest for reparations (Jasper, 2012: 46–66).

Emotions function as a tool to foster or to contain the social mobilization. Groups seem to be strengthened when they share reflex emotions[3] (fear, commotion, sadness) in response to certain events. These emotions evolve to become affective loyalties and moral emotions. For Jasper (2012), affective loyalties are understood as shared and reciprocal emotions among members of a group towards a common goal, while moral emotions are feelings of approval or disapproval – about ourselves and our actions – that are based on moral institutions or principles, such as shame, guilt, pride, indignation, anger and compassion.

Sharing negative emotions (for instance, anger, fear or grief) can strengthen positive reciprocal emotions. As an example, experiences with fear can build a sense of collectivity that the author has called collective solidarity (Jasper, 2012). However, this does not guarantee that the same feeling – fear – will not paralyse or infuse panic into a group, making collective responses impossible. In other words, the author argues that same emotions can affect collective action in different ways.

Emotional language is neither spontaneous (automatic) nor rational (calculated). It is built over time to express messages comprised of reflexive, affective or moral emotions. That is the reason why the speech and the gestures are so important to produce this language that materialize itself in texts, images and graphics. This emotional language does not only serve to express people's misfortune. It also involves moral judgements and it shapes views of social reality and identifications among diverse subjects (Jimeno, 2010: 99–121). In this sense, a collective force is formed when testimonies describe events, point out the perpetrators of the crime, distinguish who the victim is, and demand rights and ways to repair the damage through emotional language.

The consequence of a reinforced use of emotional language is the creation of a social truth. It may not be a legal truth, but it suggests some understandings of the violent situations and the social drama that affects residents' daily lives (Jimeno, 2010). Moreover, emotional language is a potential tool to constitute a new relationship between the subjective experience of the victims of violence and the political making, especially by those excluded from the formal circuits of participation (Zaragoza and Moscoso, 2017).

With the analytical resource of the emotional language, political and social action give a role to the affections. If they were unnoticed and individually irrelevant in traditional social movements, in this approach they occupy a central place. They become visible as a vehicle in social organization and political action. Victims' family members, friends and neighbours give up their anonymity to turn the suffering that comes from their losses into something publicly significant to society. This takes their loss beyond their private circle. A violent death, and especially one caused by state agents, has a meaning, and that meaning is injustice (Mate, 2008).

When events such as the one we analyse in this chapter take place in Brazilian *favelas*, the stigma and criminalization of public safety agents towards family members tends to generates in residents feelings of moral aggravation, a sense of injustice, anger and indignation. However, this is not enough to engage people in public political acts. It is also necessary that they conceive of themselves as capable of achieving their intentions.

The emotional expressions forming part of this search for recognition for someone who was violently killed build a shared and broad sense of outrage and injustice. Those practices give meaning to life and death of friends and family members. In such everyday practices community members create the space to consolidate local narratives about the importance of victims.

In both cases, in organized collective action and in local and sometimes silent practices of tribute, emotions and their varied forms of languages gain prominence as an analytical category that helps to understand the relationship between peripheral social groups and death.

We argue that urban peripheries are spaces in which violence permeates social relations in many dimensions. It is present in the fear of circulating through some areas (at certain times), in reports of victimization by acquaintances and friends, in fear of police approaches, and, consequently, in the frequency of 'unnatural' deaths. Everyone knows about friends, family members or neighbours who were fatal victims of violence. It makes emotions a central issue in many of the individual and collective responses to these deaths. Therefore, this chapter describes some evidence of the role of the emotional language in the answers of a *favela* to their youth violent deaths.

Victims of violence and the search for recognition in daily activities

At the turn of the 20th century, victims of violence began to make themselves visible in the public international arena with the increase in civilian victims of wars and the subsequent appearance of associations such as the Red Cross and Doctors Without Borders. Images of injured and sometimes mutilated people aroused the ire of the world, which was informed at every moment of the human rights violations by television broadcasts. For instance, television coverage with colour images of corpses piling up in Rwanda in 1994 generated a public mobilization that forced the United Nations to appoint a tribunal to judge those responsible for the genocide (Robertson, 2008).

But violence cannot be understood only by the use of physical force or the pain it brings. Violence acts are assaults on the victims' personality, dignity, and their value to both self and society (Azaola, 2012). The arguments of high crime rates have led states to set more repressive security policies, especially in Latin America (Pinheiro, 1991). Consequently, victims of violence, and primarily victims of state violence, tend to remain anonymous. When the person is part of the numbers of 'deaths by violence', the victim loses his or her personality. They are bodies without identity or a life story (Pita, 2018).

In view of this scenario, the relatives and friends of the victims are those who have been fighting for their recognition in a great number of civil associations around the world. This is the emblematic case of the Abuelas de Plaza de Mayo (Grandmothers of the Plaza de Mayo) in Argentina. Women mobilized for the right to the identity of their children and grandchildren who were victims of disappearance or kidnapping during the last military dictatorship in that country.

The movement of families affected by police violence remains vibrant in Argentina. Even those who are not formally engaged in civil society groups are known as 'Families of *gatillo fácil*[4] Victims'. The movement fights for recognition of victims of police violence and tries to get the perpetrators convicted for the execution cases. Hence the name 'easy trigger', used to speak of the 'lightness' or 'ease' with which the police kill or injure someone in various situations, sometimes by the extreme use of police force, sometimes by false confrontations (Pita, 2010).

Also in Brazil there is an increasing leading role of family members in the social civil movements against police violence. In Rio de Janeiro, since 2004, the Rede de Comunidades e Movimentos contra Violência (Network of Communities and Movements against Violence) has been active. It is formed mostly by family members of people killed by the Military Police in *favelas*. The activists employ several strategies to create recognition places for these losses to state violence. Participating in court hearings, trials, protests in front of police units, taking part in events of the Human Rights Commissions of the Legislative Assembly of the State of Rio de Janeiro (ALERJ) and of the House of Representatives are just some activities undertaken by these activists and family members (Vianna and Farias, 2011).

In the city of São Paulo, the group known as Mães de Maio (Mothers of May) has mobilized for the unsealing and federalization of the investigations into the crimes that occurred between 12 and 20 May 2006. Over those eight days, there was a daily average of 55 homicides in the city. Police officers perpetrated most of the killings as a retaliation for a huge prison riot led by Primeiro Comando da Capital (First Command of the Capital; PCC), now the biggest crime organization in the country. In addition to the violent actions inside the prison, the riot led to attacks on police stations and some days of curfew for the population in many areas of the city (Galdeano, 2012: 230). The result was the murder and disappearance of 493 victims, of which more than 400 were young Black, Indigenous and/or poor people, when police and paramilitary groups promoted what they called a 'response wave' to the 'PCC attacks' (Fundo Brasil, 2019). In addition to the struggle for justice, the Mães de Maio gives material and psychological support to relatives and friends of victims; participates in meetings or conferences related to the institutional violence subject; and organizes social mobilizations, such as protests, marches and vigils (Fundo Brasil, 2019).

In short, the category of victim functions as a mobilization resource used by political movements to consolidate popular participation, to mobilize public opinion, and thus to expand the possibilities of reparations, one of the main issues of these movements led by families (Jimeno, 2010). The Santana residents fight daily for recognition of their victims. Their engagement takes different shapes and levels, depending on how strong the ties of affection are that bind them to the victims. Engagement also depends on their perception of the chances of contributing material proof to the case. In other words, it depends on whether the evidence of rights violations is well-documented. Therefore, if residents, local leadership and organizations have strong evidence (that is, videos and photos) about the criminal act of the state agents, there is a higher likelihood of greater social mobilization, as happened after Rogério's execution.

In next section we describe daily situations in which family members, friends and residents fight for recognition for victims of violent deaths, highlighting particularly three situations:

1. legal defence and mobilization of public opinion around cases of violence committed by the police;
2. support networks for family members; and
3. tributes and acts of remembrance for the victims.

Affections, mobilization and memory among the Santana community

In order to answer why some police killings generated public mobilization while people were indifferent to other deaths caused by the same institution we revisited field notes and interviews carried out in Parque Santana between 2016 and 2017. In this process we identify some clues that became our categories of analysis to explain this contradiction.

The first aspect is how solid is the material proof about the rights violations practised by public agents. Observing the reactions to Rogério's execution, we knew that besides the march stopped local traffic, the most important local organization offered professional legal support to the victim's family. As mentioned by Beatriz and Carlos, the lawyers and activists in charge of the case, the large amount of evidence (photos, videos, testimonies, and so on) that had been raised to support the argument of an execution was essential to the criminal prosecution.

If this human rights organization can't collect enough evidence of violations committed by the police, for instance, through videos or testimonies, the organization focuses on providing material and psychological support to relatives of the victims. They know how difficult a conviction and incarceration of the guilty parties is because official forensic investigations tend to hide the state's faults. Therefore, the community is the only source of information and when they don't have strong evidence, the organisation handles the lack of human and financial resources, choosing to pursue only the cases in which they have higher chances of winning court battles. In general, when this happens, the media's engagement typically tends to be less intense than in Rogério's case. Thus, there's a certain pragmatism justifying the willingness of individuals and groups to put effort into social actions (Gusfield, 1981). In the view of the interviewees, this situational analysis is what allows them to design strategies for the defence that reduce the means of obstruction of the investigation and the processing by the public security and justice institutions themselves.

In this way, deaths of adolescents and young people who became victims during crimes such as thefts and robberies, something so common in that region, are not the cause of large public mobilizations. Not because their lives are less worthy, but because the leadership understand that the circumstances mean that there is a higher chance of the case being dismissed, both within the criminal justice system and by public opinion. The activists anticipate the arguments that could be used in the prosecution in order to favour the state, in the figure of the agents who perpetrated the violence. The existence of important material proof, the violence and ostensible purpose of the action, and finally the victims' reputation (as *workers* or someone who didn't have a history of criminal practices) are some of the factors considered by the social movement leaders when they have to trace strategies to face police violence in peripheral areas.

Rogério's homicide was one of those in which everything favoured collective action. The crime took place in atypical circumstances even for a *favela* in São Paulo. It didn't happen late at night. The perpetrators showed their faces. The crime scene was an open area, a corner frequented by all residents. The fatal victim had no conflicts with the police. He had a "phase in which he got involved in bad things", in the words of Adriana, a resident who knew Rogério and was in the neighbourhood that night. However, at that point he was in a new stage of his life as a husband and father of a young daughter. It became easy to mobilize efforts to build evidence, to identify witnesses, and to define a proper legal representation of the victim, guaranteeing the initiation of the police investigation and the other phases of prosecuting.

Nevertheless, only rationality cannot explain social movements in response to violent deaths caused by police. After all, even with solid legal arguments, the population may not support the actions. At this point, affection seems to be one of the most important assets for engagement. The violent death of Rogério, an 'innocent person', born and raised in the area, being part of a 'respected' family, touched the population in a very intense way. The news spread in many spaces, from the privacy of Santana's houses to the most public arena in our society, the internet. Everyone could signify that event according to their own repertoire of beliefs and values.

The murder of a loved one who did not participate in the local criminal dynamics is a trigger for the outbreak of many popular demonstrations. The 'innocent', the 'worker' or 'the one who was in the wrong place at the wrong time' are categories that, for some, highlight more strongly the injustice and violence of state action in the urban peripheries. Rogério was not in the group of those whose way of life put them at permanent risk of disappearing at the hands of the police. The residents' perception of this was quite clear for us since our first visit to Santana, just a few day after the execution.

Another factor that activated emotional language was the mother's attitude from the moment after the shooting. According to our interlocutors, she cried desperately, hugging her son's dead body. The pain was public and intense, but the same woman was also one of the leaders of the public demonstration that happened after the burial. She gave interviews to the media covering the march, chanted for justice and warned the youth about how important it was to avoid their own mothers having to go through what she was going through.

Rogério's mother proved to be strong and turned pain into engagement, something that has become common in São Paulo and in other parts of Brazil through the groups of mothers of victims of violence (Vianna and Farias, 2011). This is how the Mães de Luto (Mothers in Mourning) was born in the neighbourhood, a group of mothers that provides support to other families who have lost their loved ones because of police violence, just like the Mães de Maio (Fundo Brasil, 2019).

In these groups the emotional language, expressed in the pain and outrage of the mothers, works as a political tool to make their voices heard. According to Vianna and Farias (2011: 83), the condition of being a mother carries in itself a certain moral authority in political acts. By the ties of blood and affection these women have the legitimacy to make a public denunciation of their experiences of injustice. It creates relevant transits in contemporary political and judicial scenarios: the mothers of victims of violence live 'between personal pain and collective causes; between suffering and rights; between distinct forms and dimensions of mourning … an individual and social process' (Vianna and Farias, 2011: 83).

In Santana the Centre for Defence of Human Rights (CDHS) offers support to the Mães de Luto group that meets weekly in the centre building. They meet to organize themselves to follow the legal processes of their loved one's death in court, to help each other assimilate the suffering, to cry and dry each other's tears. They were also present at the march for justice. They added their sadness and indignation to the sadness and indignation of that new mother in mourning, Rogério's mother.

Families in Santana make up a network of mutual support also handling other consequences of living in a violent place. Adriana, a 30-year-old educator who works at the centre for defence of human rights, gave us an example of how this extended family operates. The daughter of a woman who lived for some years in the streets of downtown São Paulo, Adriana has lived in Santana since she was five years old. When we interviewed her to talk about collective responses to youth deaths in the neighbourhood, she immediately described the common practice of contributing to funeral service expenses when the relatives do not have enough financial resources to do so. She told us about the funeral of Andrezinho, a young person also killed by the police in Santana:

Adriana: It was a funeral that raised so much money. You have no idea! His name was André. People called him Andrezinho. ... Then everybody mobilized themselves, "Let's help to make the coffin." ... My mother and I raised money. I got R$1,000 just from one of his friends. There were so many [funeral] crowns. So many crowns and there were some of those very expensive ones, that cost R$ 150, R$ 200.
Researcher: And who was sending these flowers?
Adriana: His partners [in crime], his friends. (Interview conducted on 9 September 2017)

Unlike Rogério, Andrezinho died while trying to commit a robbery. It was an unfair killing as there was no reaction on his part. However, there was also no great mobilization of local public opinion around his death. No march on the street. The community, which interviewees referred to as 'Santana's family', was there to support the young man's family. The perception of the vulnerability of a poor family that has just lost a son is capable of awakening a sense of collectivity that makes mutual support almost inevitable. Suddenly people who accuse each other of gossip and disunity, a recurrent complaint among residents, organize themselves to prepare the funeral of someone whose family is as vulnerable as their own.

As with Andrezinho's funeral, the social mobilization that happened after Rogério's death counted on the youth. His friends were important in organizing the march and displaying publicly their sadness, anger and revolt. They brought their youthful energy, their motorcycles, and even their willingness to argue with the drivers who complained about the road closure for the march. The bonds established by the victim, including in the 'world of crime' (Feltran, 2008), seem to have been fundamental for people to feel encouraged to participate in the tributes and demonstrations. Knowing that he was a nice, handsome, polite person with a well-regarded family were important elements for the movement for justice.

Beatriz mentions in our conversation the importance of removing anonymity from cases of violence as a way to face the depersonalization of criminal statistics. Especially if it is a case of police violence. This signification involves a process in which family and friends take death as a factor to give meaning to their longings (especially in the public arena) and to their interpersonal relationships (Pita, 2018). The dead are not just lines in a database of homicide or killings by the police. The living interpret the dead's trajectory and reconstruct it as political symbol or to emphasize desirable values and attitudes.

This struggle for recognition of the value of lives provides motivation for actions that transform recurrent events, such as the violent deaths of adolescents at the hands of public security agents, into public issues (Gusfield, 1981). This brings to light not only the relevance of lives that have already ended. Also, the importance of the lives of all who share characteristics such as age, skin colour and place of residence. It is death speaking more about the living than about the dead (Pita, 2018).

From this perspective, mobilizing public opinion in large demonstrations is not the only strategy to ensure recognition for victims of violence. Another murder in Santana illustrates another aspect of this struggle (for recognition). Moisés was also a neighbourhood resident. He was around 30 years old when, early one morning in 2015, police officers chased and killed him on his way home after a night-shift as a private security guard.

Moisés was very popular and loved by Santana's residents, especially Bel. She is one of the most popular people in the *favela*. As Adriana's mother, Bel used to live on the streets, but she moved to Santana in the 1990s when Beatriz created a social project – a shelter for girls exposed to violence on the streets. From that moment on, Bel became part of Santana's family. In that place, she gave birth to her child. She was a victim of domestic violence. The PCC helped her to leave her partner. She saw her child become addicted to drugs.

However, despite all the suffering she is a signal of the joy of living in that neighbourhood. Usually, hanging out on the streets. Sometimes arguing with some neighbours. Always ready to help and to talk about her friends. Moisés was one of them.

In Bel's words, he was spontaneous, irreverent and a good friend. He used to have close ties with the *favela*'s indoor soccer team, and, about this relationship, she says: "Moisés used to drive us by bus. Moisés and Pedrão. Moisés used to command the bus, he was used to take the lead. Then he is dead and a little bit of the team died too."

Moisés' death created a great emotional shock that generated a movement similar to that brought on by Rogério's execution: manifestations of support, investment in a well-structured legal defence strategy, gathering of material proof and the identification of witnesses. Coincidentally, among these witnesses was one of Rogério's family members, making up the network of pain and mutual support that connects family members of victims of police violence in a neighbourhood. Overcoming his fear, this witness was willing to make a statement, testifying against the police officers who shot Moisés, and thereby gaining even more support from the population when suffering knocked at his door.

Figure 12.1: Writings of memory on walls in Parque Santana

Notes: The left image reads 'We miss you a lot' and the right image reads 'Continuously in our thoughts. Eternally in our hearts'.
Source: Fieldwork records (2 September 2017)

Nevertheless, in Moisés' case, what draws more attention than the civic engagement is the expression of recognition through memory. A lively person, dedicated to the soccer team, who liked to drive his friends to parties, Moisés is always remembered through the image of the team's mascot painted on some of the neighbourhood walls. As Bel says, the mascot, a "*maconheirinho*[5] throwing a bomb", became a symbol for the soccer team, the subject of texts written on the walls where friends portrayed through street art how they both missed a friend and expressed their outrage against violence. Both on the neighbourhood walls and on the team's uniforms the dead friend was remembered (see Figure 12.1). The images are no longer on the walls, as someone erased them. According to Bel, this was because "not everyone in Santana likes these things [writings, paintings or graffiti]". However, it is the intention that deserves our register and analysis.

In our perception, the sense of injustice catalyses public demonstrations that remember or honour the dead. A loved one who dies in unnatural circumstances becomes an image that alters – even for a while – the routine in that physical and symbolic space. In scenarios of intense violence, this effect manifests itself in dialogue with symbols of strict political and well-coordinated resistance. But it is important to consider that emotional representations such as messages on walls or in the tribute paid by the soccer team are also affected by the sense of injustice.

Literally, unlike the metaphor drawn by Bel, the team did not end. They are active and participating in local championships and organizing their post-game events. They also continue honouring Moisés in the image and in the words that are printed on the team's T-shirts. They recognize him as someone who stands out from the rest through affection. He should not have died so young, he should not have been murdered, and, above all, it was not his place to die at the hands of the police.

The prosecution of Moisés' murder is a success of political action of the centre for defence of human rights. In 2017, the policemen responsible for the execution had been removed from the streets and were in jail awaiting a trial. But beyond that, the acts in memory to that important resident is a demonstration of how the victim's recognition is built by people daily in different ways.

The *writings* drawn on walls in the neighbourhood, such as those mentioned by Bel, are repeated on other walls in the streets and alleys of the *favela*. 'Saudades 1.000',[6] 'Forever remembered', 'Eternal Angel', are just some of the many messages written in honour of young people who died in that region. The interviews led us to identify the stories of some of those to whom these images refer. In most cases, they are young, and were described by their neighbours as involved in the 'world of crime', which does not prevent them from being considered (or esteemed) in the territory, mainly, by colleagues who are also connected in some way to the same *world*.

Estalinho was part of a large family, who came from the north of Brazil. He was the nephew of Clarinha, a hairdresser who had a small beauty salon located very close to the site of Rogério's murder. As we already mentioned, the area is a place of confluence and gathering of residents due to the proximity of small bars, grocery stores and, in our opinion, mainly because it marks the border between the *favela* and the *asfalto*. This implies that Estalinho's aunt, as well as himself and his family, are well known in the region. The teenager was killed in 2015 when he tried to rob the lottery house located on a busy street in the neighbourhood, in front of a large supermarket in the area. The store's security guard (a retired police officer) was carrying a gun and shot him. It was a weekday, in the afternoon, and the street was crowded, which caused people to gather to see what had happened. Nevertheless, despite being witnessed by a large number of people, there were no public demonstrations afterwards.

Paco, another teenager, was shot dead in 2016 at the large street market held in the neighbourhood every Sunday. His body was exposed for a long time until the arrangements for registration and forensics of the homicide took place. He was also killed by policemen who chased him after an attempted robbery on the same avenue where the march took place. The fair takes place in a very long street that starts at the entrance of the neighbourhood and ends at the main access to the *favela*. The teenager was caught and shot by the police when he was already at the end of the street in a space free of stalls. The body was left lying in the gutter, under the sun, and the blood dripped down the sloping street. People gathered to watch and comment on the sad scene (another 'movie') and, even now, they talk about what happened as an important episode in the recent history of the *favela*. Apparently, the shooting in public space could have been avoided as, after all, it put the lives of everyone passing by at risk. However, no one protested or even signed an open letter.

Paco and Estalinho have in common the fact that they were victims of violent deaths, caused by public agents, in circumstances associated with the practice of crime. The most violent face of the *world of crime* is the fact that these interrupted lives are the ones that most often are labelled as just one more young death due to being 'involved' in drug trafficking or because they were 'doing bad things'. We would hardly remember their names and their stories. Even in this chapter, we are hiding their true names, covering part of the writings in order to guarantee their friends' safety. If they had not become the subject of the tributes on those walls they would be even more in the shadows of anonymity.

According to Bel these are not *pichações* (graffiti tags). After all, the message is understandable and addresses any reader (this is not always the case in the *pixo*/graffiti culture). She prefers to call them 'writings' and, in our perspective, they are the silent way of personifying the one who passed away violently by practising a reprehensible act for a large part of the population. This is the citizen who society – even some of Santana's residents – allows the state to kill. But even for him there are people willing to mourn his death, to celebrate his life, and to declare how much he is missed.

Many factors play against the use of conventional means of public political demonstrations about these violent deaths. People's engagement in collective action depends on whether there is evidence of rights violation. If the victim was committing a crime just before the homicide. If the victim has a job or a family. If the victim was already in jail. Therefore, letters of support directed to the media and published on internet profiles, or public actions such as a march or an avenue closure, would hardly be planned or supported by a large number of residents if the victim is one of the *killable* young people. The memory *writings* emerge as a possible alternative to express feelings about dead friends, and this practice is not limited to Santana, or to Brazil.

The same gestures of the rescue of the memory of those killed in violent events are described in works such as those of María Victoria Pita (2018) and Eugenia Cozzi (2018), developed from long ethnography in peripheries in Buenos Aires, Argentina. Respectively, with greater and less centrality, the authors describe and analyse writings very similar to those found in Santana. The making of the drawings is also similar, that is, the colleagues themselves, sometimes partners in crimes, are responsible for choosing the sayings and painting the walls.

In her analysis of these public messages, Cozzi (2018) highlights the double meaning of the act and the phrase ('*yo no miento sólo engaño, tomo, fumo y meto caño*'[7]) to characterize the region of '*La retirada*', an area in which she conducted her research. The mural would signify the courage and loyalty of the honoree to his group, values that also the living would like to maintain. The choices of the living about how to represent and remember the dead speak, in Pita's (2018) view, about the social uses of death and how the types, circumstances and actors involved in each of them interfere with that use. We share this perspective and rely on it to understand the differences in the responses of the same population to different violent deaths in the neighbourhood, although many of them have important commonalities, such as the participation of public agents.

Memory is the result of a complex work of recovery of the past, which acts through diverse testimonies. Some of them are similar, some are contradictory (Calveiro, 2012: 21–30). In this active reconstruction of the past actors with different interests and perspectives intervene. Official accounts coexist and are questioned and reinterpreted by alternative versions of the facts. Despite the silence imposed by fear and the preponderance of official versions of events, the community's memory cannot be easily erased and changed. Victims' friends have become 'memory entrepreneurs', as with their strategies and resources they make visible the story of that person who was killed by violence (Jelin, 2012). Mainly, people united to the victims through ties of kinship and friendship use graffiti and carry the image of the victim printed on the t-shirts of the *favela*'s indoor football team.

Participation in major events involves empathy, and empathy can be lost when people do not identify themselves with the one who is dead or with their family members. Perhaps, involvement in crime puts 'these boys', as residents often refer to them, in a position of distance, despite their geographical closeness. Not to mention those who are far away from the neighbourhood. There, empathy tends to be lost for good when people do not perceive the victim as a good citizen, a student, a worker or a father.

In spite of this, the recognition brought by affection is not lost. We can see this considering expressions like that of the *writings*. Possibly, among all the characteristics of Santana (*favela* and *asfalto*), one of those that most caught our attention since the first visit to the field were these messages. Whether by the quantity (spread over many streets) or by the emotion in the words, those *writings* are public expressions of the pain caused by a death. Regardless of how that friend lived, they show that all lives matter, including those that, lost, tend to 'become statistics'. The *writings* function as an alternative for the residents to make memory of the *killable* in a different shape, but in the same register of what occurs in the demonstrations that demand justice for the non-killable.

Conclusion

In this chapter we revealed three distinct forms of routine actions that seek social recognition for victims of violent deaths in Parque Santana. Popular mobilization enhanced by the mothers' movement and the legal aid movement, the writings on the walls and the tributes by football teams, all demonstrate socially creative uses of distinct attempts organized by the community to denounce and shed light on youth whose lives were interrupted by violence. All are connected by the threads of emotion, by the bonds of affection that oppose the movement that standardizes the victim of urban violence (Machado da Silva, 2004) as a young, Black male. Rogério, André, Moisés, Paco and Estalinho are more than numbers; they are sons, fathers and friends of people who make an effort to keep their memory alive.

Public opinion is triggered in different ways in each of the situations, with the movement triggered by Rogério's murder being the broadest in this sense. However, the actions vary in levels, from the public sphere being occupied by texts written on neighbourhood walls, to the actions of the mothers' movement in the public demand for justice for their children.

Acknowledgements

Valéria Cristina de Oliveira: this research was developed during a postdoctoral internship at the Centro de Estudos da Metrópole (CEM) with a scholarship granted by the Fundação de Amparo à Pesquisa do Estado de São Paulo (FAPESP), through the Process 2016/15899-7, in the period between 1 October 2016 and 31 July 2017.

Jaqueline Garza Placencia: this research was developed during a postdoctoral internship at the Centre for Metropolis Studies (CEM), with a fellowship granted by the Consejo Nacional de Ciencia y Tecnología (CONACYT) Mexico, in the period between 1 October 2016 and 31 July 2017 in São Paulo, Brazil.

Notes

[1] In this text the terms *favela* and *asfalto* distinguish the two main forms of occupation of space in the Parque Santana neighbourhood. The first is the Santana slum, a very steep area that surrounds a stream that once used to run in the open in the lower part of the neighbourhood. Therefore, unlike the hill-shaped *favelas* commonly seen in Rio de Janeiro, Santana, for those arriving from the street, presents itself as a large descent through narrow alleyways, occupied by self-built houses that share walls, have low finishing standards, and improvised electrical, water and sewage facilities. The *asfalto* is the neighbourhood area in which the houses have better finishing standards, wider and paved streets and that, therefore, set the boundaries for the most adequate provision of public services such as garbage collection, mobile emergency health care and postal services, to name only those we witnessed to be quite deficient in the *favela*.

[2] All names in the text are fictitious in order to protect the collaborators who may be participating in some way in police and legal proceedings that are still in progress and which, therefore, require the confidentiality of information.

[3] Reflex emotions: quick and automatic responses to events and information, often taken as the paradigm for all emotions, such as fear, joy, sadness (Jasper, 2012).

[4] The Spanish language expression that could be translated as 'easy trigger' describes the violent police approach that results in crimes such as executions, disproportionate use of force and false confrontations with victims (Pita, 2010).

[5] A pothead or someone who habitually uses marijuana.

⁶ There is not a literal translation for this Portuguese expression. However, in urban and youth slang it could be a synonym of 'We miss you a lot'.
⁷ "I don't lie, I just cheat, drink, smoke, and do the pipe."

References

Azaola, E. (2012) La violencia de hoy, las violencias de siempre. *Desacatos. Entender la violencia*, 40: 13–32.

Calveiro, P. (2012) La memoria en tanto espacio ético y político, in A Huffschmid and V. Durán (eds) *Topografías conflictivas. Memorias, espacios, ciudades en disputa*. Buenos Aires: Nueva Trilce, colección memoria, pp 21–30.

Cozzi, E. (2018) *De ladrones a narcos: Violencias, delitos y búsquedas de reconocimiento en tres generaciones de jóvenes en un barrio popular de la ciudad de Rosario*. PhD dissertation, Universidad de Buenos Aires.

Feltran, G. (2008) O legítimo em disputa: as fronteiras do 'mundo do crime' nas periferias de São Paulo. *Dilemas Revista de Estudos de Conflito e Controle Social*, 1(1): 93–126.

Feltran, G. and Motta, L. (2021) Polícia e ladrão: uma abordagem etnográfica em pesquisa multimétodos. *Runa, Ciudad Autónoma de Buenos Aires*, 42(1): 43–64.

Fireman, B. and Gamson, W.A. (1979) Utilitarian logic in the resource mobilization perspective, in M. Zald and J.D. McCarthy (eds) *The Dynamics of Social Movements*. Boston: Winthrop, pp 8–44.

Fórum Brasileiro de Segurança Pública (2021) *Anuário Brasileiro de Segurança Pública*. Fórum Brasileiro de Segurança Pública.

Fundo Brasil (2019) *Mães de Maio*. Available from: https://www.fundobrasil.org.br/projeto/movimento-independente-maes-de-maio/ [Accessed 20 November 2020].

Galdeano, A.P. (2012) A gestão social da violência: de como ativistas de direitos humanos, líderes de associação de bairro e evangélicos se mobilizam, in N. Vieira da Cunha and G. Gabriel de Santis (eds) *Sobre periferias: novos conflitos no Brasil contemporâneo*. Rio de Janeiro: Editora Lamparina/FAPERJ, pp 101–117.

Gayol, S. and Kessler, G. (2018) *Muertes que importan: una mirada sociohistórica de casos que marcaron la argentina reciente*. Ciudad Autónoma de Buenos Aires: Siglo XXI Editores Argentina.

Gusfield, J.R. (1981) *The Culture of Public Problems: Drinking-Driving and the Symbolic Order*. Chicago: Chicago University Press.

Hochschild, A.R. (1975) The sociology of feeling and emotion: Selected possibilities, in M. Millman and K. Moss (eds) *Another Voice*. New York: Anchor, pp 280–307.

Jasper, J. (2012) Las emociones y los movimientos sociales: veinte años de teoría e investigación. *Revista Latinoamericana de Estudios sobre Cuerpos, Emociones y Sociedad*, 4(10): 46–66.

Jelin, E. (2012) *Los trabajos de la memoria* (2nd edition). Lima: IEP.

Jimeno, M. (2010) Emoções e política: a vítima e a construção de comunidades emocionais. *Mana*, 16(1): 99–121.

Lima, R.S. and Ratton, J.L. (2011) *As ciências sociais e os pioneiros nos estudos sobre crime, violência e direitos humanos no Brasil*. São Paulo: Associação Nacional de Pós-Graduação e Pesquisa em Ciências Sociais.

Machado da Silva, L.A. (2004) Sociabilidade violenta: por uma interpretação da criminalidade contemporânea no Brasil urbano. *Sociedade e Estado*, 19(1): 53–84.

Mate, R. (2008) *Justicia de las víctimas. Terrorismo, memoria, reconciliación*. España: Anthropos.

Moore Jr, B. (1987) *Injustiça: as bases sociais da obediencia e da revolta*. São Paulo: Brasiliense.

Pinheiro, P.S. (1991) Police and political crisis: The case of the military police, in M.K. Huggins (ed) *Vigilantism and the State in Modern Latin America*. New York: Praeger, pp 167–188.

Pita, M.V. (2010) *Formas de morir y formas de vivir 1 ed*. Buenos Aires: Editores del Puerto.

Pita, M.V. (2018) La historia de un mural o acerca de la muerte, de los muertos y de lo que se hace con ellos. Muertes violentas de jóvenes de barrios populares en la Ciudad de Buenos Aires. Revista M. *Estudos sobre a morte, os mortos e o morrer*, 3(5): 53–71.

Poma, A. and Gravante, T. (2018) Manejo emocional y acción colectiva: las emociones en la arena de la lucha política. *Estudios Sociológicos*, 108: 595–618.

Ribeiro, L., Couto, V., Vasconcellos, F., Souza, J., Ratton, J. and Franco, M. (2014) *Mensurando o tempo do processo de homicídio doloso em cinco capitais*. Brasília: Ministério da Justiça, Secretaria de Reforma do Judiciário.

Robertson, G. (2008) *Crímenes contra la humanidad. La lucha por una justicia global*. Madrid: Siglo XXI.

Vianna, A. and Farias, J. (2011) 'A guerra das mães' dor e política em situações de violência institucional. *Cadernos Pagu*, 37: 79–116.

Zaragoza, J.M. and Moscoso, J. (2017) Presentación: Comunidades emocionales y cambio social. *Revista de Estudios Sociales*, 62: 2–9. Doi.org/10.7440/res62.2017.01

13

Women, Peace, Security and Justice: A Postcolonial Feminist Critical Review

Giovana Esther Zucatto

Introduction

Throughout history, women have been systematically excluded from the battlefield, but that certainly does not mean they are absent from wars. The legions of combatants were invariably followed by women taking on all sorts of tasks: throughout history they have been healers and nurses, laundresses, cooks, prostitutes, in charge of correspondence or even of searching the battlefield at the end of the confrontation, collecting valuables from fallen bodies (Trustrum, 1984). In the Second World War, the unprecedented scale of the conflict, both in terms of geographical scope and in terms of the mobilization of human and material resources, led to the incorporation of women into the military ranks of several countries, especially in auxiliary cadres, which made it possible that a greater number of men be allocated to the *fronts* of combat (Campbell, 1993; Wheelwright, 2020). Women started to work as nurses, as in the Brazilian case, operating lines of communication and logistics and, mainly, working in factories of products destined for war. Also, in the United States and the Soviet Union, some women served as combat aircraft pilots. From the 1970s onwards, women began to be admitted to the armed forces – mostly in Western liberal democracies – in times of peace, with full military status (Carreiras and Alexandre, 2013).

However, this timeline is a partial portrait of the relationship between women and conflict. On the one hand, they were an important part of the most varied armed organizations, especially from the 20th century onwards. In several European countries, many women joined national resistance militias during the Spanish Civil War and the Second World War. During the

US Civil War and Mexican Revolution, they were present on both sides of the conflicts, occasionally reaching command positions within the differing forces. Even in Mexico, the *solderaras* tradition continued until the 1930s, when they were banned by the military on the grounds that they would be a source of immorality. These women followed the armies performing various services and even fighting in combat (Salas, 1990; Browder, 2006).

More than that, the gaze on the relationship between war and women cannot be focused solely on the battlefield. Armed conflict has important consequences for women around it, even if they are not directly engaged in combat. Sexual violence, forced migrations, poverty, prostitution, the involvement of children and husbands in conflict and the very prolonged absence of men are some of the effects of wars on the lives of women and girls during and after conflagrations. This chapter discusses the fact that it is important to study these issues with a gendered lens: the way in which armed conflict affects women and men is different in important respects, and these experiences are precisely determined by gendered factors (Benard, 1999; Skjelsbaek, 2001; Cohn, 2013).

According to Cheryl Benard (1999), two other aspects are relevant when studying the relationship between war and women. First, although they are traditionally associated with peace, the relationship between women and peace is not uniformly positive. The post-conflict period is a crucial moment to think about the relationship between gender and violence (Jacobson, 2013). It is important to understand that peace will not necessarily indicate a better scenario. Peace does not mean the same thing to men and women. When peace is defined purely in terms of the absence of war, women can still experience extremely high levels of violence. Therefore, a study of conflict that takes into account the experiences of women and girls needs to be aware of the interconnectedness between all forms of violence – domestic, societal, state-based and interstate (Weber, 2006).

Second, and in a complementary way, Benard (1999) points out that peace agreements, postwar reconstruction and humanitarian assistance programmes often exclude or discriminate against women. In this sense, the author highlights that the disadvantages that women face are of three orders: (1) as part of a deliberate mechanism imposing and maintaining the inferior social status of women; (2) an unconscious and automated part of structural violence against women; or (3) a more or less accidental part of the fact that decision-makers are not aware of and do not consider the needs and interests of women.

At the same time, war can be an opportunity for women, as a social and political group, as the prolonged absence of men can (albeit temporarily) elevate women's status (Greenwald, 1980; Summerfield, 2012). The problem is, precisely, that the period following the conflict is usually a time of cultural repression against women, so that they return to their places of origin.

Examples of this are varied, such as the Soviet fighters who took decades to receive recognition for their participation in the fight against the Nazis; or in post-Liberation France, where the punishment of women accused of collaborationism was seen as a priority over other demands, such as the demand to address the problem of hunger.

In an effort to integrate the understanding of gender dynamics with the study of war, Inger Skjelsbaek (2001) draws generalizations about the identities associated with women in three moments: among the guerrillas in El Salvador during the 1980s; in the Vietnam War; and in the conflict in Yugoslavia in the 1990s. In the first case, femininity was reinterpreted in terms of liberation, in the sense that women would be an integral part of the revolutionary struggle and women's independence was associated with the liberation ideology and emancipation more broadly. In El Salvador, women's participation was used as an equality token, but it was also possible to perceive a new sense of collective female consciousness developed through the years of conflict.

In the second, in conservative terms – the traditional meaning of 'woman' has changed little in Vietnamese society, and the broad female engagement in conflict has typically been based upon an extension of work traditionally already done by women, especially in the field of care. Finally, in Yugoslavia, femininity was largely associated with the role of victim, where war meant nothing but insecurity and grief for women, especially in a context where rape was systematically used as a weapon of war and an instrument of ethnic cleansing (Skjelsbaek, 2001). Skjelsbaek's research brings the lesson that there is no single way to understand the relationship between women and the very social construction of gender, peace, security and justice.

This chapter represents an attempt to systematize the main issues related to the articulation of women, peace, security and justice, which currently has as its maximum concrete expression the so-called UN Women, Peace and Security (WPS) Agenda, which will be presented in the next section. In addition, I will seek to synthesize some issues relevant to the topic in Latin America, as a way of illustrating the theoretical points presented here. Then, I bring some of the main criticisms of the Agenda, developed mainly from the framework of postcolonial feminism. Finally, I make some considerations in which I seek to reflect on the landmarks of coloniality on women in the global South and the importance of this for us to develop contributions that critically think about the relationship between women, peace, security and justice.

The UN Women, Peace and Security Agenda

The international framework aimed at the articulation between women, peace, security and justice is currently based mainly on a series of UN

Security Council resolutions that were passed from 2000 onwards. These resolutions, however, are anchored in one previous series of conventions, treaties and other international documents aimed at defending the rights of women, which largely left aside the issues of peace and security. It is only in the 1990s that the first international norms that really address the conditions of women directly or indirectly involved in armed conflicts begin to appear, as well as more specific concerns about the place of women in peacebuilding. These changes were driven, on the one hand, by reports of abuse and sex trafficking in the UN Peacekeeping Missions, as well as by the systematic use of sexual violence in conflicts, especially in the case of Rwanda and Bosnia, and, more specifically, by the World Conference on Women in Beijing in 1995, whose central theme was 'Action for Equality, Development and Peace'. In both, there is a fundamental role envisaged for civil society organizations, especially those concerned with the human rights of women.

The Platform for Action adopted in Beijing brought as one of its 12 thematic axes 'Women and armed conflict'. It was the first time that the theme of war appeared explicitly on the organization's gender agenda. More specifically, there is the link between peace and gender equality as inseparable and the recognition of the differentiated effects of armed conflict on women. From this derive strategic objectives outlined at the Conference, which include increasing the participation of women in decision-making for conflict resolution, protecting women in war zones and promoting the contribution of women to the development of a culture that favours peace.

In October 2000, the UN Security Council (UNSC) unanimously approved Resolution 1325 of 2000 (hereinafter Res. 1325), which demarcated the institutionalization of the idea of *gender mainstreaming* and gender equality (*gender balancing*) within the peace and security concerns of the United Nations (UN) and recognized women as agents in both war and peace. In the resolution, the parties demand that the member countries promote greater female representation in different political settings and at the most varied levels of decision-making, as well as an increase in women's participation in the prevention and management of conflicts and in the construction of peace processes. More specifically, the inclusion of a gender perspective in planning the disarmament, demobilization and reintegration of ex-combatants is outlined (Article 13) and the mandatory inclusion of women in the military and civilian components of Peace Missions proposed (Article 15).

Res. 1325 permanently included the theme 'Women, Peace, and Security' on the UN agenda. Since then, efforts carried out within the institution with regard to conflict management and peacebuilding have sought to adopt mainstreaming and gender equity strategies, in other words, placing gender perspectives and concerns as a central part of these initiatives. This was translated into strongly normative discourses that associate greater gender equality – at least in terms of representation – with the possibility of guaranteeing peace in a lasting way. This appears in the form of positive conceptions of peace that prioritize gender equality, considerations about victims of violence – that is, war in its individual aspect – and postwar social justice (Karim and Beardsley, 2016). In a way, the ideals of classical liberalism and the conception of democratic peace that have permeated the UN's ideals since its creation are updated to include a gender variable, as already discussed.

Since Res. 1325, the UNSC has already had nine new resolutions related to this theme: Res. 1820/2008; Res. 1888/2009; Res. 1889/2009; Res. 1960/2010; Res. 2106/2013; Res. 2122/2013; Res. 2242/2015; Res. 2467/2019; and Res. 2493/2019. Without going into details, these resolutions sought to deepen the discussion on gender and peace within the organization, as well as guide more specific actions to advance the Agenda. Also, from 2014 onwards, one of the main points of convergence of the processes of review of the UN peace and security architecture – the High Level Independent Panel on Peacekeeping Operations, the Advisory Group of Experts on the Review of the Consolidation Architecture of the Peace and the Global Study on the Implementation of UNSC Resolution 1325 (2000) – is the need to 'insert a gender perspective in all aspects related to the promotion and maintenance of international peace and security' (BRASIL, 2016).

It is also worth mentioning UNSC Res. 2282 of 2016 and Res. 70/262 of the same year of the UN General Assembly (UNGA), which, although not directly covered under the umbrella of the Agenda, bring an important innovation which is the concept of 'sustainable peace' (*sustaining peace*). The framework provided by the resolutions foresees, among other measures, 'the promotion of sustainable development; the eradication of poverty; national reconciliation and inclusive dialogue; access to justice; the promotion of gender equality; and the mobilization in a coordinated manner of the various organs and entities of the UN System' (BRASIL, 2016) as a way to guarantee the support of peace in the long term. These measures would not only be worked on in the post-conflict period but would also have a preventive nature. Accordingly, the idea of 'sustainable peace' reinforces the normative association between gender equality and peacebuilding characteristic of the WPS Agenda.

Some considerations on Women, Peace, Security and Justice in Latin America and the Caribbean

As stated, the WPS Agenda envisages building sustainable peace beyond simply a no-conflict scenario. It means, therefore, that it foresees a series of areas in which governments – and also civil society – must act. Overall, the UN strategy to adopt a gender approach is based on the concepts of gender balance and gender mainstreaming (Gianinni and Vermeij, 2014), which means parity between men and women in different instances and that its security efforts will be always crossed by concerns about gender issues. In general, the main mechanism that the organization has encouraged its member countries to adopt is the preparation of National Plans of Action (NAP), with plans for the Agenda to be carried out internally.

As for the issue of gender balance, efforts are aimed at a more balanced representation of women in different spheres. Although the immediate attention is for a greater number of women in peace missions and at the negotiation tables, the WPS Agenda also has fundamental concern with greater female political participation. Why is it important, in the context of implementing the WPS Agenda, for women to occupy seats in the legislature and ministerial cabinets? As mentioned earlier, one of the bases of the Agenda is the idea of a gender balance and its relationship with the construction of lasting peace. On the one hand, this is anchored in the idea – which works almost like a norm – in the framework of UN documents and missions, that peace tends to be more sustainable when built with the participation of women, as will be discussed later in the case of Colombia. Furthermore, there is a certain updating of the idea of democratic peace, and a suggestion that democracies with more women in their political ranks tend to be more peaceful – an argument that ends up sounding quite essentialist.

However, the issue to be highlighted is that the WPS Agenda brings a series of forecasts of what countries should implement internally, even those that are not in conflict situations, to build more peaceful, secure and egalitarian societies. Among them, these include policies to combat gender violence – in its different forms, the promotion of autonomy and economic independence of women and access to education, among others. A greater presence of women in these spheres would be a way of guaranteeing a state interest in promoting this type of policy. In fact, what experience has shown is that women tend to be more directly involved in developing policies that address women's and children's rights. Promoting the greater participation of women would thus be a way of inducing the creation of efficient and lasting public policies aimed at gender equality.

In reflecting upon these developments, we also need to be aware of the resurgence of conservative politics in Latin America and how this is directly related to the *implementation* of policies and initiatives aimed at women in the areas of peace, security and justice. In the case of Brazil, there is a longer movement of contesting the rights of minority political groups, which already in 2015, during the government of President Dilma Rousseff, resulted in the amalgamation of the human rights portfolios of the secretariats for the Promotion of Racial Equality and Policies for Women within a new Ministry of Women, Racial Equality and Human Rights.

Under Jair Bolsonaro's government, this ministry was renamed the Ministry of Women, Family and Human Rights, under the command, since 2019, of evangelical pastor Damares Alves, thereby subordinating women's rights, once again, to 'family politics'.

A paradigmatic case, in this sense, is the change in the position of Brazilian diplomacy regarding debates on gender and women in international bodies, mainly in the UN. While, traditionally, Brazil had adopted a very progressive posture in advancing these agendas internationally, in the new government, the Itamaraty directives require Brazilian diplomats to defend an understanding of gender as a biological sex. Furthermore, Brazil has adopted a position against mentioning themes such as sexual and reproductive health, women's autonomy of choice and sexual education. In its candidacy for re-election to the UN Human Rights Council (UNHRC), the Brazilian government presented a platform that excluded mentions of gender, poverty and torture, and instead included the defence of family structures as a central aspect of its work in the UNHRC. This has direct effects on peace and security issues, including peacekeeping missions. In 2019, the US delegation threatened to veto the Resolution on Women, Peace and Security at the Security Council if a reference to the need for UN bodies and donors to give timely 'sexual and reproductive health' assistance to survivors of sexual violence in conflict were not withdrawn from the resolution since it was perceived by the Trump administration as a code for abortion.

This conservative advance can also be discerned in Colombia, especially from 2012, and with greater force in the period of debate about the peace agreement with the Revolutionary Armed Forces of Colombia – People's Army (FARC-EP). In November 2016, the historic peace agreement between the Colombian government and the FARC-EP was formalized. The dialogue between the government of Juan Manuel Santos and the FARC-EP began in 2012 and was mediated by Cuba, Venezuela and Norway and was initially signed in September 2016. In October 2016, the agreement was submitted to a popular plebiscite, which was rejected by 50.02 per cent of voters in a complex and polarized political process. As a result, the government and the FARC returned to the dialogue table in Havana to incorporate the revised demands into the text. With the update, the text was submitted to Congress and officially approved on 24 November 2016, with implementation scheduled to start on 1 December of the same year. The main axes of peace agreements were: rural and agrarian reform; a model of political-institutional and party participation by the FARC; the end of the conflict and the demobilization of the guerrillas; agreements on victims and reparation; and mechanisms for implementation, verification and endorsement of the terms set down.

It is important to draw attention to the fact that the Colombian peace process is one of the most emblematic cases of integration of the WPS

Agenda in the peace negotiations and represents an important shift from the paradigm based on women as victims of conflict to women as participants in the process of peace.

> When negotiations started in 2012, none of the negotiating teams (guerrilla and government) had women. In 2013, the parties signed an agreement [including the commitment] that the entire content of the agreement would be implemented with 'a gender perspective and guaranteeing the participation of women' ... [and a] Gender Subcommittee. Thanks to the Gender Subcommittee, Colombian women's organizations were directly represented and actively participated both in the peace table in Havana and in the national and regional consultations held throughout the country. Although this is not the first time that a gender subcommittee has been created in a peace process. ... Women constituted up to a third of the participants at the table, approximately half of the participants in the consultations, and more than 60 percent of the victims and experts who visited the peace negotiating table. (Casanova, 2017: 15, our translation)[1]

It should be noted that, in the plebiscite on the Agreement, the right-wing and conservative forces coalesced around the 'no', mobilizing a campaign based on fear of a possible 'Venezualization' of Colombia, and upon a supposed FARC plan to impose a 'gender ideology' aimed at destroying the family and subverting traditional social values. One of the mottos used was 'Vote no to the referendum: defend the family'. To be against the peace agreement was, therefore, to be against the disintegration of the family – especially over the issue of same-sex marriage, against abortion and against the supposed 'communist atheism' of the FARC.

The Colombian Peace Agreement brings, in its text, a commitment to a 'comprehensive and gender approach, based on the principles of equity and progressive realization. The parties commit to address the historic inequality and vulnerabilities of women and girls, the lesbian, gay, bisexual, transgender and intersex (LGTBI) population and religious minorities'.[2] Another point that stands out is the fact that the Peace Agreement excludes any possibility of amnesty or forgiveness for crimes of sexual violence, an aspect that is a direct consequence of the participation of women in peace negotiations through the Gender Subcommittee (Casanova, 2017).

Critical views of the UN Women, Peace and Security Agenda

An important limitation of the Agenda seems to be in the very conception of gender that the UN and member countries have adopted. As the name already implies, gender equality is automatically associated with the inclusion of perspectives, demands and more women in the fields related to conflict and peace. This is problematic in two ways: first, it obscures an important dimension of gender-based violence that is perpetrated against men and boys, especially civilians, making them absent from UN gender policies (Drumond, 2012). The same is also true for issues concerning LGBTQ+ populations, which constitute an especially vulnerable group. Second, both the repeated emphasis on sexual violence and the direct normative association between the inclusion of women and sustaining peace often ends up reinforcing stereotypes about the identity and role of women, as always a victim of conflict or as having an inherently peaceful nature.

The theme of peace missions concentrates a significant portion of the criticisms of the WPS Agenda. The first and most poignant problem are the recurring cases of sexual abuse committed by UN 'blue helmets' in different peacekeeping missions – in the case of Bosnia, for example, the allegations have even involved networks of international trafficking in persons linked to UN forces. International pressure, especially from feminist organizations, in relation to abuses committed in UN missions in the 1990s was one of the main causes that led the UNSC to approve Res. 1325 in 2000. One of the proposals was precisely to employ more women in missions as a way to reduce cases of sexual violence, in addition to further training on gender issues for UN forces. However, in more than 20 years of Res. 1325, there have been no profound changes in this regard – as is evident in the allegations of sexual violence and the abandonment of children of UN soldiers in Haiti.[3]

An Associated Press investigation of UN missions during the past decade found nearly 2,000 allegations of sexual abuse and exploitation by peacekeepers and other personnel around the world. And since we are talking about sexual crimes, we can expect a great under-reporting. This situation involves not only profound gender inequality, and a clear problem of deep-rooted machismo, but also profound social and economic disparities that appear when a peace mission is installed in a deprived and unsettled country with a population in a situation of extreme vulnerability. The issue of accountability is already a huge challenge and there are not enough inputs on 'gender awareness', the employment of a minimum contingent of women or any other specific measures that seem likely to reverse this situation, even though all of these would be important.

This situation is aggravated by two factors. The first is that there is a legal impasse over who to blame in cases of rape and sexual violence, as well as the recognition of paternity. Would it be the UN – which has international legal personality – the state of origin of the peacekeeping personnel or the individuals themselves?[4] What would be the appropriate court of law? Faced with this legal uncertainty and the UN's inertia in advancing investigations, little or nothing has been done and victims remain helpless. The second factor is that the percentage of female presence *in loco* in peace missions is still very low – only around 5 per cent of the universal total of blue helmets, as opposed to the 20 per cent target stipulated by the UNSC resolutions on women, peace and security. Added to this is the factor noted out by Gizelis (2018) that military women serving in peace missions tend to be deployed in low-risk operations or conflict areas. However, in these areas, rates of gender-based violence tend to be significantly lower than in high-risk conflicts. *Ceteris paribus*, it could be expected that a greater number of women would mean a reduction in rates of gender violence. However, there is so far no concrete evidence that the increase in female personnel reduces the number of incidents of sexual assault and exploitation in peacekeeping missions. It is true that the difficulty of measuring the impact of women's participation in peacekeeping missions may be due to the extremely low level of female personnel, which makes it difficult to measure effects or significant changes (Gizelis, 2018: 6).

Soumita Basu (2017), based on the idea of a political economy in the WPS Agenda, presents three central issues, which are often ignored by much of the literature on the subject:

1. the scarcity of resources, which increases the power and the influence of major donors on the Agenda's content and initiatives;
2. relative silence on the issue of economic rights and the wellbeing of women, which should be related to the functions of the Economic and Social Council (ECOSOC), another important UN body;
3. the form of neoliberal peacebuilding, which ends up by conflating post-conflict social reconstruction with a largely pro-market reform agenda.

Harrington (2011) explains that, during the Cold War, debates on women's rights at the UN revolved around the criticism of capitalism, both for the diplomatic action of the Soviet Union and of the so-called Third World countries. With the US hegemony from the 1990s onwards, there has been a change in the way the issue is approached internationally. The recognition of violence against women as a matter of international security and Res. 1325 itself are associated with international responses to the so-called new wars and defined by a neoliberal logic that involves market-oriented development measures as a solution for post-reconstruction conflict. As previously demonstrated, the WPS Agenda arose during this period – therefore, the international debate was (and still is) dominated by this logic. Basu (2017) argues that the ideological domination prioritizing pro-market reforms ultimately leads to a process of feminization of poverty in these countries. It remains difficult to see how neoliberal reforms and improving women's quality of life can be achieved when the norm of employment precariousness prevails, leading women in particular towards the informal labour market.

In other words, if the WPS Agenda was intended to empower and advance the quality of life of women, its practical policies can end up having the opposite effect.

Finally, some authors have taken a more critical look at how, especially since the adoption of Res. 1325, the mobilization of the gender equality discourse within the international security sphere has served as a way to reassure the current geopolitical order within the framework of the neoliberalism; also serving as a way of legitimizing growing military interventions. Butler (2015) coins the idea of 'coercive instrumentation of freedom' when addressing how the feminist discourse is appropriate in the intention to publicly justify and legitimize the US invasion of Iraq, while not overlooking the use of similar supposedly 'progressive' precepts by countries of the European Union even as they implement xenophobic policies to curb Muslim immigration.

In the specific case of the WPS Agenda, the approval of Res. 1325 itself seems to operate by seemingly legitimizing the expansion of UN intervention mandates. This is what Dianne Otto (2016) argues, that the UNSC, Res. 1325 and its sister resolutions symbolize its commitment to include women in decision-making and address the gendered effects of armed conflict. According to the author, Res. 1325 is conceived, in this perspective, as a form of symbolic capital developed by the UNSC to maintain its legitimacy in times when the organization's structure and mandate are questioned in the post-Cold War context. The WPS Agenda is developed within a broader context of thematic resolutions, which also cover issues such as refugees and HIV, as the legitimacy of international institutions is increasingly measured by the extent to which their actions are consistent with contemporary notions of justice and human rights (Otto, 2016). The instrumentalization of gender agendas in the UNSC and in international politics in a broader way will be a recurrent theme of this research, being developed in further in the Brazilian case in subsequent research.

Conclusion

In view of the debates presented in this chapter, the question remains: how to propose alternatives to think about the relationship between women, peace, security and justice based on the specificities of the global South? The very use of a concept of the global South can provide important clues. One of the most defining markers of countries and populations in the global South is the experience of European colonization. If we take the experiences of European colonization as a fundamental landmark for historic inequalities, gender relations need to be moved to the centre of the analysis. Here, it is worth noting that it is impossible to hermetically isolate gender relations from other social relations, especially those of class and race. This is further accentuated when we take colonial enterprises as a starting point. Colonial violence must be understood as a continuum that does not privilege one form or another of oppression, but adds them together, creating new layers; the universalizing project, after all, is the project of the global North, as the so-called postcolonial feminists have argued for some time (Rajan and Park, 2000).

At first, it is necessary to critique the idea that there is a single historical or universal woman who can respond to all the aspirations for classification and also for political emancipation in the global South. Just as it is difficult to categorize what the global South is, there is a profound difficulty in defining the category of women. This ontological challenge actually seems counterproductive. Here we follow the trail left by Mohanty (1988), who argues that 'woman' is a cultural and ideological composition constructed by different discursive representations (scientific, literary, legal, and so on). Women are real and material subjects of their collective histories. What brings them together can also distance them. 'False universals like the "postcolonial woman" or the "postcolonial other" obscure [sic] relationships not only between men and women, but also between women', argues McClintock (2010), similarly 'the relations between a French tourist and the Haitian woman who washes her sheets are not the same as the relations between their husbands' (McClintock, 2010: 24).

What interests us is that colonization was built from gender relations and is maintained even today by these characteristics. In 'post-colonial' Brazilian society, Indigenous women are relegated to tiny communities, struggling to survive the colonization processes that continue today in the doubtful and compromised name of 'civilization' and 'progress'. White women, despite a relatively successful emancipation process that has developed in recent decades, continue to be judged on the basis of values that were not carved by them, but against them. Even so, they continue to represent the most privileged portion of the Brazilian female population. And there are many women who exploit the work of Black women: the Black mother remains in the figure of the Black nanny from the periphery, who lives in her employers' house and raises the children of the wealthier classes. The hypersexualization of the Brazilian woman's body, both here and abroad, and especially the Black body, remains constant in both advertising media and popular imagery. Coloniality is deeply patriarchal.

In addition to these permanencies, there are recurrences of the relationships between imperialism, coloniality and gender still today, precisely what Judith Butler (2015) calls the 'coercive instrumentation of freedom'. The war on terror is a paradigmatic example in this sense, in which the feminist discourse is appropriate in order to publicly justify and legitimize the US invasion of Iraq, or even Israel's colonialist advance on the Palestinian territories. Colonial undertakings legitimated under the pretext of 'freeing Muslim women from the yoke of Muslim men'. Likewise, we can cite the use of progressive precepts by countries of the European Union to carry out xenophobic policies that block the immigration of Muslims and imperil the travels of refugees. Finally, there are the successive cases of sexual violence committed by UN blue helmets in countries of the global South.

In other words, what is argued here is that when thinking about the articulation between women, peace, security and justice in and from the global South we must understand the ways in which violence was – and continues to be – inserted in these women's lives and bodies today. This allows us to look critically at initiatives such as the UN Peacekeeping Missions, for example, and their legacies in the countries where they are implemented. The shift towards criticism, then, becomes obvious. How should we think about building peace when one of the great marks of these missions seems to be precisely the imposition of new forms of (post)colonial violence on women's bodies?

On the other hand, a postcolonial feminist perspective needs to understand women's emancipatory potentials and go beyond the perspective of women as universal victims of violence and, more specifically, of war. In this sense, it is essential to recover history and build a collective memory about the women who joined the fronts that fought the national liberation wars in Africa and Asia and were part of guerrilla struggles against dictatorial governments in Latin America. These traditions are central challenges in thinking about a truly emancipatory project for the global South. Because one of the basic principles of feminism, whatever the precise field, is that all theorizing must be accompanied by a commitment to transforming reality.

Acknowledgements

This chapter builds on my doctoral research, which was funded by the Brazilian National Council for Scientific and Technological Development through a full doctoral fellowship.

The section on 'The UN Women, Peace and Security Agenda' is a central part of my doctoral research and was developed from other works such as Zucatto, Giovana E. and Monteiro, Giovanna L. (2020) Peace, feminine noun (?). *Horizontes ao Sul*. Available from: www.horizontesaosul.com/single-post/2020/10/01/PAZ-SUBSTANTIVO-FEMININO-; and Zucatto, Giovana E. (2020) 20 years of UN Resolution 1325: Implementation and challenges to the Women's Agenda, Peace and Security in South America. *OPSA Bulletin*, 3: 24–30.

Notes

[1] In the original: 'When negotiations started in 2012, no one from the negotiating teams (guerrilla and government) counted with women. In 2013, the parties signed an agreement with 15 points on political representation, one of which established that all content of the agreement would be implemented with 'a gender approach and ensuring the participation of women'. In fact, thanks to the Gender Subcommittee, Colombian women's organizations were directly represented and actively participated both in the peace table in Havana and in the national and regional consultations held throughout

the country. Only this is the first time that a gender subcommittee is created in a peace process, in the case of Colombia, the Gender Subcommittee is very present throughout the entire process. The women constituted up to a third of the participants at the table, approximately half of the participants at the consultations, and more than 60 because of the victims and the experts who visited the peace negotiation table.'

2   'Annual report of the United Nations High Commission for Human Rights on the situation of human rights in Colombia', presented on 16 March 2017, session of the Human Rights Council (A/HRC/34/3 /Add.3, p. 4), our translation.

3   There are thousands of allegations of sexual harassment and hundreds of lawsuits about children of MINUSTAH soldiers abandoned after the departure of UN forces from the country. About Brazilian soldiers, more specifically, see: https://brasil.elpais.com/internacional/2019-12-27/os-filhos-abandonados-da-onu-no-haiti.html [Accessed 25 February 2021].

4   Felipe Alves debates the responsibility of the Brazilian state for the children that the military generated – and abandoned – in Haiti in this text: https://www.conjur.com.br/2020-jan-13/felipe-alves-uniao-answer-military-children-haiti [Accessed 25 February 2021].

References

Basu, S. (2017) The UN Security Council and the political economy of the WPS resolutions. *Politics & Gender*, 13(4): 721–728.

Benard, C. (1999) *Assessing the Truths and Myths of Women in War and Peace*. Comunicação Oral. United States Institute of Peace. Conference Perspectives on Grassroots Peacebuilding: The Roles of Women in War and Peace.

BRASIL (2016) *Ministério das Relações Exteriores. O Brasil e a consolidação da paz*. Available from: www.itamaraty.gov.br/pt-BR/politica-externa/paz-e-seguranca-internacionais/143-o-brasil-e-a-consolidacao-da-paz [Accessed 20 August 2019].

Browder, L. (2006) *Her Best Shot: Women and Guns in America*. Chapel Hill: University of North Carolina Press.

Butler, J. (2015) *Quadros de guerra: quando a vida é passível de luto?* Rio de Janeiro: Civilização Brasileira.

Campbell, D. (1993) Women in combat: The World War II experience in the United States, Britain, Germany and the Soviet Union. *The Journal of Military History*, 7(2): 301–323.

Carreiras, H. and Alexandre, A. (2013) Research relations in military settings: How does gender matter? in H. Carreiras and C. Castro (eds) *Qualitative Methods in Military Studies*. Abingdon: Routledge, pp 97–115.

Casanova, M.R. (2017) La aplicación de la Agenda Mujeres, paz y seguridad en los procesos de paz: la participación de mujeres em la prevención y resolución de conflictos. *Revista Electrónica de Estudios Internacionales*, 34: 1–37. DOI: 10.17103/reei.34.04

Cohn, C. (2013) Women and wars: Toward a conceptual framework, in C. Cohn (ed) *Women and Wars*. Cambridge: Polity, pp 1–35.

Drumond, P. (2012) Gênero ou Feminismo? As Nações Unidas e as políticas de gênero nas operações de paz, in K.M. Kenkel and R.F. Moraes (eds) *O Brasil e as operações de paz em um mundo globalizado: entre a tradição e a inovação*. Brasília: Ipea, pp 69–92.

Giannini, R. and Vermeij, L. (2014) Women, peace and security: Gender challenges within UN peacekeeping missions. *Policy Brief*, v 5. Norwegian Institute of International Affairs, pp 1–5.

Gizelis, T.-I. (2018) Systematic study of gender, conflict, and peace. *Peace Economics, Peace Science and Public Policy*, 24(4): 1–10.

Greenwald, M.W. (1980) *Women, War and Work: The Impact of World War One on Women Workers in the United States*. Ithaca: Cornell University Press.

Harrington, C. (2011) Resolution 1325 and post-Cold War feminist politics. *International Feminist Journal of Politics*, 13(4): 557–575.

Jacobson, R. (2013) Women after wars, in C. Cohn (ed) *Women and Wars*. Cambridge: Polity, pp 215–241.

Karim, S. and Beardsley, K. (2016) Explaining sexual exploitation and abuse in peacekeeping missions: The role of female peacekeepers and gender equality in contributing countries. *Journal of Peace Research*, 53(1): 100–115.

McClintock, A. (2010) *Couro Imperial: raça, gênero e sexualidade no embate colonial*. Campinas: Editora da Unicamp.

Mohanty, C. (1988) Under western eyes: Feminist scholarship and colonial discourses. *Feminist Review*: 61–88.

Otto, D. (2016) *Women, Peace and Security: A Critical Analysis of the Security Council's Vision*. LSE Women, Peace and Security Working Paper Series.

Rajan, R.S. and Park, Y.-M. (2000) Postcolonial feminism/postcolonialism and feminism, in H. Schwartz and S. Ray (eds) *A Companion to Postcolonial Studies*. Oxford: Blackwell Publishing, pp 53–71.

Salas, E. (1990) *Soldaderas in the Mexican Military: Myth and History*. Austin: University of Texas Press.

Skjelsbaek, I. (2001) Is femininity inherently peaceful? The construction of femininity in war, in I. Skjelsbaek and D. Smith (eds) *Gender, Peace and Conflict*. London: SAGE, pp 47–67.

Summerfield, P. (2012) *Women Workers in the Second World War: Production and Patriarchy in Conflict*. London: Routledge.

Trustrum, M. (1984) *Women of the Regiment: Marriage and the Victorian Army*. Cambridge: Cambridge University Press.

Weber, A. (2006) Feminist peace and conflict theory, in *The Routledge Encyclopaedia on Peace and Conflict Theory*. Available from: https://www.uibk.ac.at/peacestudies/downloads/peacelibrary/feministpeace.pdf

Wheelwright, J. (2020) *Sisters in Arms: Female Warriors from Antiquity to the New Millennium*. Oxford: Bloomsbury Publishing.

PART IV

Conflicts, Criminalization and Protest in the New Neoliberal Internationalism

14

The Contemporary Criminalization of Activists: Insights from Latin America

Roxana Pessoa Cavalcanti, Israel Celi and Simone Gomes

Introduction

The scene quiets when President Piñera comes out to make a speech on television. 'We are at war with a powerful, relentless enemy that respects nothing and no one'. It's just violent delinquents, violent delinquents – same old, same old. (Domi, 2019: 8)

Domi is describing how political rhetoric operates in stark contrast to scenes of ecstasy, chanting and resistance in protests against high living costs and inequality in Chile in October 2019, when over a million people took to the streets. What follows are more organized and intense[1] brutal police responses, a growing number of deaths, reports of injuries, rape, torture and disappearances. Political rhetoric used to denigrate opponents, insurgents and activists is not a new phenomenon, nor is it unique to Latin American countries. It is part and parcel of a wider contested version of politics in which activists and social movements have been systematically persecuted through diverse state and corporate mechanisms. A growing body of research emerging in Latin America focuses on understanding this phenomenon as it is experienced through the criminalization of activists, social movements and protesters (Buhl and Korol, 2008; Doran, 2017; Alcazar, 2020; Celi et al, 2022). This form of persecution is understood as being embedded in a context of complex legacies of the formation, transition to and expansion of capitalist, patriarchal and racialized social orders (Federici, 2014; Celi et al, 2022). Here, criminalization is a tool used in efforts to accumulate capital, and dilute, control and eliminate dissenting voices that advocate for marginalized and exploited communities standing in the way of capitalist appropriation typically disguised as 'progress' and 'modernization'. Others have examined criminalization as a systemic state response to collective mobilization in the context of retrenching established civil and political rights and as a way of delegitimizing activists, paving the way for gross human rights violations (Doran, 2017). Analysing the growing criminalization of activism is crucial for understanding violent relations and the state of democracy in Latin America.

There is a body of literature about relations between the state and civil society in Latin America that sets the scene for the current political situation. This has sometimes shed light on what these relations mean for democracy, with an emphasis on participatory democratic politics as a symptom of deeper democracy and more civil society involvement (Avritzer, 2002, 2006). The expansion of the persecution of activists and dissenting voices indicates a reversal of prior attempts to promote participatory democracy (Avritzer, 2002, 2006). An increasing number of studies of these relationships indicate that 'new laws and measures are transforming the peaceful and normal actions of citizens in a democratic context into crimes subject to punishment' (Doran, 2017: 185).

Criminalization is facilitating human rights violations against mobilizing populations, including disappearances, arbitrary detention and assassination. As a process, it works to legitimize repression by constructing community members as public enemies, who are accused and defined as violent or delinquent (Doran, 2017). Criminalization is a strategy to intimidate, inhibit and delegitimize struggles, utilized alongside other forms of repression, including assassinations of human rights activists and environmental defenders (Alcázar, 2020). As a project, the criminalization of activism is a political, juridical and mediatic process that seeks to move struggles from social to penal arenas (Toledo, 2007; Palau and Corvalán, 2008; Rondón and Zambrano, 2015), while allowing for exploitation and capital expansion through the intensification of extractive projects and the dispossession of Indigenous, Black and *campesino* communities and territories (Navarro and Pineda, 2009; Bran-Guzmán, 2017). In this context, activism and protests are framed and persecuted through diverse 'new' legal categories in the region, including anti-terrorism laws in Chile (Toledo, 2007), Ecuador (Solís and Pérez, 2014), El Salvador (Girón, 2009), Brazil (Amaral et al, 2017; Almeida et al, 2020), Colombia (Rodriguez, 2015); and drug trafficking legislation in Mexico (Cedano, 2008; Dorbecker, 2010) and Bolivia (Veltzé and Tudela, 2010).

This chapter draws on studies written chiefly, albeit not exclusively, from Latin America, and makes a claim for the importance of shedding light on competing voices and discourses from which we can draw wider lessons. In light of the recent mobilizations such as 'Kill the Bill' in response to attempts to expand policing powers and constrain protesters in the UK (Cavalcanti et al, 2021), it has become clear that these lessons certainly have significance beyond Latin America. Writing and thinking with activists from the margins, we attempt to offer a modest contribution to a 'criminology from the margins' (Zaffaroni, 1988). This contribution builds on previous work by Southern (Connell, 2007; Carrington et al, 2016; Cavalcanti, 2020), decolonial (Walsh and Mignolo, 2018; Dimou, 2021) and counter-colonial scholars (Agozino, 2003) by elucidating research done by colleagues in Latin America and challenging the legacy of imperialism and its effects on unequal social relations.

Notwithstanding their criticisms and points of disjuncture (Moosavi, 2019; Ciocchini and Greener, 2021; Dimou, 2021), all these paradigms and frameworks recognize diverse histories, politics, cultures, socioeconomic contexts and practices that have been marginalized. They point to the ways in which Southern experiences have been dismissed, but yet remain central to understanding our world. This is not a claim that experiences are universal or generalizable but rather that dialogue with, and lessons from, these experiences and other knowledges enrich our understanding of the social world. As Carrington and colleagues have put it in relation to criminology, a Southern perspective is

> inclusive of scholars from both North and South and seeks to work with and complement—to Southernize—other established and emerging fields. ... It seeks to introduce a perspective based on the analysis of historical and contemporary relationships linking South and North that have been constitutive of forms of life and thought in both, but which have been obscured by the metropolitan hegemony over criminological knowledge. (Carrington et al, 2018: 11)

The chapter starts by briefly examining the history of repression and authoritarianism which shapes contemporary criminalization today. Then it sheds some light on the state of mobilization in Latin America, before examining examples of three cases: Brazil, Ecuador and Mexico.

Historical context

The repression affecting dissenting voices today has colonial foundations. As Chies (2020) explained, colonizers utilized militarized practices and strategies to facilitate appropriation, subjugation and slavery. This process is entangled with the Jesuit missions, which served the Portuguese and Spanish crowns. For over three centuries, 'as many as five million Africans were enslaved and transported to Brazil, mostly to be put to work on sugar plantations, many of which were owned by Jesuits' (Darke and Khan, 2021: 6). Flag planters or '*bandeirantes*' as they are known in Portuguese, began to form an emerging militarized population since colonization and the emergence of wars over the creation and defence of borders. This historical process of expropriation and repression utilized racism as an ideology and rationale for exploitation, persecution and criminalization. Institutions of servitude and exploitation were created with the aim of dividing the Indigenous population and apparently 'civilizing' them, converting them to Christianity. Both *encomendados*[2] and those enslaved were subjected to brutal forms of violence, kept captive and inherited or transferred as if they were property (Chies, 2020; Darke and Khan, 2021). Slaves provided labour and some were also used as soldiers with the promise of freedom. Militarization, colonialism and slavery are foundations of current social and power relations in Latin America, from which criminalization and the birth of criminal justice systems cannot be separated.

Pinheiro (1991) developed the concept of a 'socially implanted authoritarianism' that has continuity and longevity, first emerging when Brazil was a colony of the Portuguese Empire, persisting after independence in 1822 and even after Brazil's periods of transition to democracy in the 20th century. Chiefly, this is because authoritarian culture and politics are embedded in multiple spheres of power, the body, social relations and even internalized. However, authoritarian politics are not representative of a monolithic culture, as illustrated by heterogenous forms of organizing and resisting the longevity of these issues (Figure 14.1).

Figure 14.1: Protests led by women in October 2018, Recife, Brazil, against the presidential campaign of Jair Bolsonaro

Source: Photo by Társio Alves

As the Peruvian scholar Quijano (2007) explained, a hierarchical and racialized social order has had continuity in Latin America through forms of power that can be understood through the concept of coloniality. While domination through colonialism has been defeated in many formal senses, Quijano argues that coloniality as a power structure, that is, the 'specific colonial structure of power produced the specific social discriminations which later were codified as "racial", "ethnic", "anthropological" or "national", according to the times, agents, and populations involved' (Quijano, 2007: 168) has persisted. 'This power structure was, and still is, the framework within which operate the other social relations of classes or estates' (Quijano, 2007: 168).

The authoritarianism that persists through coloniality is not limited to the institutions of violence. The institutions of violence reflect social and power relations that remain unequal and hierarchical. These institutions have, as a foundation, relations of domination, they are able to remain arbitrary despite political transitions, despite the re-establishment of direct democracy and voting rights. They are institutions that are able to continue negating citizenship and fundamental rights to the 'masses'. According to Fominaya and Wood (2011) the 'global war on terror' has generated more tools for repression through anti-terrorism legislation that has been used to quash dissent and to criminalize political activists. The mere threat of terrorism charges has spread rapidly, affecting human rights activists across Latin America who are facing these charges.

Brazil

In the Brazilian case, the attempt at 'monopolizing violence' by the state during the dictatorship (1964–1985) paved the way for militarization and the formation of death squads, militias and violence that exists not as a state of exception, but which is normalized (Pinheiro, 1991; Huggins, 1998; Cavalcanti and Garmany, 2020). This is violence as the rule, not the exception (Pinheiro, 1991). For Almeida et al (2020) the discussion of the criminalization of protests and activists goes beyond formal juridical processes by shedding light on the very definition of crime, showing that what is conceived as a legitimate political act is an object of contestation. As they argue, criminalization results from disputes among diverse social actors – militants, the police, lawyers, judges, prosecutors, the media – around juridical classifications that can frame acts as legitimate forms of protest or crimes. For example, Brazil's new anti-terrorism law (Law n. 13.260/2016, from project n. 2.016/2015) was originally rationalized and justified by the government as necessary to deal with potential threats associated with mega-events (the Football World Cup and the Olympics in Brazil), but the passing of this law threatened the right to protest and increased the powers of the criminal justice system to persecute social movements (Almeida et al, 2020). But this is not the only new law being used to limit what is considered politically legitimate. Brazil also passed the Law of Criminal Organizations (Law n. 12.850/2013, from project n. 6.578/2009), which activists perceived as posing a threat to collective political action (Law n. 12.850/2013, from project n. 6.578/2009). These examples show a trend towards punitive criminal justice approaches that are increasingly being used to control political dissent.

The process of criminalization of political activists and social movements is enabled through rhetorical strategies and criminal justice methods to delegitimize and prosecute activists. For example, members of groups such as the movement for free transport (Movimento Passe Livre) have been affected by extrajudicial and semi-juridical discourses in juridical processes incriminating them (Almeida, 2020). As Almeida explains, these discourses seek to distinguish and generate a hierarchy between different modalities of protest (peaceful/violent, legitimate/illegitimate), and between citizens (peaceful/vandals, workers/protesters). Within the lenses of the criminal justice system, a citizen 'worker' is the only political subject deserving of the state's protection. These distinctions thus limit the space and actions that can be considered politically legitimate, giving way to processes of criminalization that reproduce social inequalities, forms of physical and symbolic violence that constrain public and democratic deliberation (Almeida, 2020).

Fon Filho (2008) argues that, often, the outcome of such interventions by the law and institutions of the state is the negation of the exercise of democracy, where the state moves to restrict the activities of social movements. The examples of persecution, stigmatization and criminalization of the Landless Movement (Movimento Sem Terra or MST) epitomize his point. The MST proposes collective responses to dispossession by occupying unused land, developing its own schools through methods of liberation education, collective food crops, and a complex structure to deliver health provision, transport and communication. Yet, the MST is routinely stigmatized in the media, accused of being against 'progress and development', and presented as violent, bandits, organized criminals or terrorists (Fon Filho, 2008). The state response to movements and their mobilizations has increasingly been to target leadership members with heavy fines and to permit private security firms to exercise methods of surveillance and repression against activists (Fon Filho, 2008). The outcome of these approaches is that the state operates in the service of elite, private and corporate interests.

In response to criminalization, Almeida (2020) argues that activists are developing strategies of resistance including, first, the inversion of accusations of violence, for instance by pointing to the violations and crimes committed by the state and private sector. Second, refusing to accept discourses of violence in criminal justice processes. Third, refuting accusations of violence and criminality. Fourth, acknowledging acts of violence by certain groups (for example, those who adopt the *black bloc* tactic, using masks and directing violence at property and financial institutions such as banks), but distancing their own movements rhetorically from those involved in *black bloc* tactics.

Explaining repression in Ecuador

The political elites in Ecuador have inherited colonial traditions of government through an authoritarian presidential regime, and the permanent resort to governments of experts who seek to impose neoliberal reforms based on the conditions of international financial agencies, without listening to the demands of activists, social movements or the wider public (Walton and Ragin, 1990; Silva, 2009; Acemoglu and Robinson, 2019).

Since the return to democracy in 1979, Ecuador has experienced four waves of resistance to neoliberal policies that were repressed to varying degrees by each government in power, shaped by the economic, political and social circumstances of each phase. The powerful Ecuadorian Indigenous movement has played a major role in each wave of resistance (Guerrero, 1993; North, 2004; Silva, 2009; Ponce et al, 2020). At the same time, outside the great waves of neoliberal resistance, social activists have experienced state criminalization, especially in the field of anti-mining resistance (Amnesty International, 2012; Bowen, 2015; Celi et al, 2022).

In this section, we will focus our analysis on the fourth wave of resistance to neoliberalism that Ecuador has been experiencing since 2019. That year, President Lenin Moreno issued Decree 883, ordering the elimination of fuel subsidies, to comply with his commitments to the International Monetary Fund. This was considered a draconian measure for the popular economy. The elimination of fuel subsidies aggravated the situation of the vulnerable population, generating an immediate increase in the prices of basic goods and public transportation (Ponce et al, 2020).

In response to Moreno's decree, the transport sector was paralysed on 4 October 2019, and numerous social organizations in the country announced large mobilizations in the direction of Quito to demand the repeal of Decree 883. The mobilization was led by Confederación de Nacionalidades Indígenas del Ecuador (CONAIE), following the same path of previous revolts since the 1990s: the blockading of streets, and the mobilization of thousands of Indigenous families (including women and children), from the Andean communities to Quito, the capital city of Ecuador (Guerrero, 1993; Yashar, 2005).

The government, with support from Congress and hegemonic media, rejected dialogue with the revolt's leaders and ordered immediate repression through the police and the Ecuadorian army (Ramírez, 2020). Repression was systematic. According to the report of the Special Commission for Truth and Justice in Ecuador, there is evidence of at least 123 violations of the right to personal integrity, 38 violations of the right to liberty personnel, six extrajudicial executions, 22 attacks against the right to life, three cases of sexual violence and 20 eye injuries (Defensoría del Pueblo del Ecuador, 2021).

Faced with widespread repression, Indigenous movements and their urban allies, including thousands of students and young Indigenous people living in cities, participated in protests and confrontations that lasted 14 days, ending in deaths that are attributed exclusively to police forces (Ponce et al, 2020; Defensoría del Pueblo del Ecuador, 2021). Ecuador experienced in this way 'crazy moments' (Tarrow, 2002) that were surprising, even for the leaders of CONAIE who have difficulties representing people on the streets. Indigenous leaders did not anticipate such a repressive response from the state. After all, in previous occasions of neoliberal resistance, governments had accepted negotiations with the powerful Indigenous movement (Silva, 2009). As Luisa Lozano, the main leader of CONAIE, explained:

'There has been total repression, not only our people said that, the Inter-American Court of Human Rights and Amnesty International say the same thing. There is clear evidence that the state wanted to exterminate us and silence us only with repression. At the same time, the first intention was to talk, to talk. ... When we saw that tremendous repression and that many people had died in the fight, the people rose even more; they became more indignant. They came from the north, from Imbabura, from Cayambe, and even from Chimborazo.' (Interview with Israel Celi, April 2020)

The hegemonic media avoid broadcasting protests and state repression. Instead, in coordination with the government, they demonized Indigenous leaders, referring to them as communist, internal enemies and *correístas* (Iza Salazar et al, 2020). During and after the revolt of October 2019, the Ecuadorian state also released national security speeches that identify internal enemies among the social movements (Ramírez, 2020). The Truth and Justice Commission led by the Ecuadorian ombudsman, which investigated the events of October 2019, reported evidence of the discursive justification of repression articulated by Moreno's government. Repression was legitimized through the idea that democracy was under attack by international communism and the followers of the former president Rafael Correa (Defensoría del Pueblo del Ecuador, 2021: 238–239).

The current government of Guillermo Lasso in Ecuador is also spreading national security ideologies, in conjunction with right-wing governments in

Latin America and Spain, as evidenced by 'Carta de Madrid', a neocolonial ideological declaration, signed by legislators and ex-government agents of Ecuador and other countries (Carta de Madrid, 2021). The economic crisis occasioned by the current pandemic has been compounded by the entrenchment of practices of the free market, budget austerity and extractivism. The continuation of radical protests remains highly probable (Ponce et al, 2020). The Indigenous movement has confronted neoliberal reforms and the extractive model of economic development since the 1990s and is the only social movement that has important veto powers over public policies in Ecuador (Mejía Acosta et al, 2011). The veto powers of the Indigenous movement could lead to radical confrontations with authoritarian leaders and neoliberal elites that can employ surveillance, the criminalization of protest and the militarization of democracy to assure the economic agenda of neoliberalism and extractivism (Grandin, 2007; Iza Salazar et al, 2020).

If social movements adopt a radical strategy to street protests, this could lead to worse outcomes for Indigenous activists' rights. Peaceful protests are also possible after the traumatic events of October 2019. This is an option for important sectors of the Indigenous movement. As presidential candidate Yaku Pérez Guartambel noted in a recent interview:

'I remember that when they committed fraud against us, they wanted to go out and burn the ballot boxes and take over the Electoral Tribunal. I called for a peaceful protest. They accused me of resisting through little flowers and doves of peace. I prefer to be told that, but I will not resort to violence. I believe in peace. Violence leads us nowhere. … But peace without content is the same as nothing. There is no peace without social justice. Young people must be called so that they do not lose their irreverence and rebellion, but without falling into vandalism and violence.' (Interview with Israel Celi, June 2021)

Mexico

As in many other countries in Latin America, Mexico has experienced high levels of criminalization of activists in the last two decades. In the Mexican case, one must highlight the secondary effects of the War on Drugs launched by former president Felipe Calderon, which reorganized criminal activities in the country and impacted on the human rights of journalists and activists. This 'War' is known to have caused thousands of disappearances, murders and persecutions to – although not exclusively – human rights activists. Dorbecker (2010) argues that at the same time neoliberal reforms have reduced public spending while prompting growing participation in protests in the country. The criminal law has been regularly used against social movements, especially unionists and peasants. According to Cedano

(2008), there is no novelty in the criminalization of social protest in recent years, because the country has been experiencing these trends since the governments of Partido Revolucionario Institucional (PRI), between 1929 to 2000, and from 2012 to 2018. However, those conditions accelerated the human rights abuses that have occurred in the years of 'transition to democracy', from 2000 onwards. The criminalization of protest in recent years takes place in a context of significant militarization taking place under the veil of legitimacy provided by the War on Drugs.

Several examples in the last two decades have shown the increasing criminalization of protest and activists, in its different forms, in the country. Cortez (2008) documents that since 2007, more cases provide evidence of such practices, for example a protest in Yucatan, southern Mexico, where, in March 2007, a number of young people demonstrating against George Bush's visit were arrested for a month with no right to bail for taking part in the demonstration. In May that same year, in San Luis Potosí, demonstrators were arrested for protesting against a mining enterprise, being accused of property damage, riot and criminal association. Accordingly, many activists have been prosecuted with similar charges since the 2000s for protesting (Morales, 2008). Doran (2017) notes that in 2013 alone, according to the National Network for Human Rights Defenders in Mexico, 242 assaults against female human rights defenders and female journalists in Mexico were documented, and that 'female human rights defenders and journalists prefer not to report the assaults and threats that they receive' (Doran, 2017: 201).

Cedano's (2008) research reveals how women and Indigenous populations are specifically targeted by government repression agencies. The case of the struggle in San Salvador Atenco, in 2006, exemplifies that, when women were arrested, some were sexually abused by police agents while being transferred to prison. To add to these issues, a law known as 'Atenco Law' was passed in March 2016 in the state of Mexico to regulate the use of public force, empowering state police to intervene when they consider any demonstration illegal (Mendoza, 2016).

Particularly severe were the repression laws to address protests that arose in Mexico between 2012 and 2014, beginning in 2012 with #Yosoy132, which demanded the democratization of communication, following teachers' movements protests in 2013 and their activism around educational reform. Then the Aytozinapa protests, motivated by the murder of six students and the disappearance of 43 others from the Rural Normal Isidro Burgos of Ayotzinapa, Guerrero, Mexico, led to mass demonstrations between the months of October and December 2014. That particular cycle of protests was followed by the approval of several state 'anti-protest' laws in Mexico, according to the Control of Public Space Report, in 2014, in Quintana Roo, Chiapas, Federal District and Puebla (Frente por La Libertad de Expresion y Protest Social, 2015).

These examples reveal that activism has been heavily penalized through new laws that passed in the 21st century in Mexico, in order to criminalize peaceful protest, hunger strikes, civil disobedience and other forms of dissent, with the claim that they pose a threat to security and stability. As in other Latin American countries, new legislation has created a favourable environment for criminalization, frequently supported by judicial institutions in reaction to mass mobilizations such as recent student protests (Doran, 2017). Nonetheless, some organizations have emerged to shine a light on this phenomenon, such as Article XIX, Comité Cerezo México, Global Witness, Frente Nacional Contra la Represión, Liga Mexicana de Derechos Humanos, Red Nacional de Organismos Civiles de Derechos Humanos, the 'Protesting is a right, not a crime' campaign and many others (Morales, 2008).

While in Brazil the legal accusation of 'gang formation' has been systematically used since 2013 to frame activists, in Mexico the constitutional reform of 2008 has paved the way for the transformation of practices of legitimate demand for civil rights into criminal acts. For example, 'the occupation of politicians' offices (*plantón*) is now considered criminal confinement, and participants are subject to heavy prison sentences' (Doran, 2017: 192). Aside from criminalization, the country faces a severe challenge with the prosecution, disappearance and killing of its activists. According to a report by Global Witness (2021), in 2020 in Mexico, there were 30 lethal attacks against land and environmental defenders, a 67 per cent increase from 2019. Half of all the attacks in the country were directed against Indigenous communities and impunity for such crimes against defenders remains high.

Conclusion

Blaming victims of social injustices and criminalizing them are familiar strategies for justifying and legitimizing repression (Doran, 2017). Latin American governments repress the poorest and most mobilized populations while constructing them as dangerous 'because they are bearers of demands for social change' (Lessa, 2011, cited in Doran, 2017: 198). Criminalization is intertwined with limited versions of democracy, the legacy of authoritarianism and the intensification of punitiveness and securitization (Doran, 2017; Cavalcanti, 2020).

Our findings reveal that the overall escalation of violence in Latin America, accompanied by increasing levels of punitiveness and criminal justice responses against acts perceived as 'criminal', have also produced a system for punishing, criminalizing and persecuting political opponents and social justice activists. Socioeconomic factors, such as high levels of inequality and an imposed model of neoliberal reforms and austerity economics that generates yet more divisions and inequalities in the continent (and worldwide), continue to create and maintain interlocking systems of oppression that result in resistance, protests, demonstrations and diverse forms of social justice activism. The result is a continent permeated by struggles and contested politics, experiencing diverse forms of resistance amid escalating violence and criminalization.

Notes

1. As Domi describes (2019: 8), 'stronger types of pepper and tear gas are being added to their inventory, stronger corrosive chemicals to the water sprayed by the *guanaco* (water cannon), and various types of pellets and supposed rubber bullets are being shot at anyone who should, intentionally or inopportunely, get too close'.
2. *Encomienda* means 'commission'. It was an exploitative system (close to slavery) used during colonialism to give the 'right' to control the labour of and collect tribute from colonized populations, granting colonizers rewards for service to the Spanish crown. The native inhabitants, known as *encomendado* (meaning 'commended') to the Spaniards, were expected to pay tribute and work for colonizers, for example in fields and mines.

References

Acemoglu, D. and Robinson, J. (2019) *The Narrow Corridor: States, Societies, and the Fate of Liberty*. New York: Penguin.

Agozino, B. (2003) *Counter-Colonial Criminology: A Critique of Imperialist Reason*. London: Pluto Press.

Alcázar, A.A. (2020) La criminalización de la protesta social: Un estado de la cuestión. *Rev. Rupturas*, 10(1): 25–43.

Almeida, F. de (2020) 'Vândalos', 'Trabalhadores' e 'Cidadãos': Sujeição Criminal e Legitimidade Política na Criminalização dos Protestos de Junho de 2013. *DADOS*, 63(4): 7–35.

Almeida, F. de, Monteiro, F.J. and Smiderle, A. (2020) A criminalização dos protestos do movimento passe livre em São Paulo (2013–2015). *Revista Brasileira de Ciências Sociais*, 35(102): 1–24.

Amaral, A.J., Fiedler, C.Z., Pilau, L. and Medina, R. (2017) As Forças Policiais nas 'Jornadas de Junho' de 2013: Um Estudo sobre a Criminalização das Manifestações em Porto Alegre/RS. *Revista InSURgência*, 3(2): 208–237.

Amnesty International (2012) *'So that No One Can Demand Anything': Criminalizing the Right to Protest in Ecuador*. London: Amnesty.

Avritzer, L. (2002) *Democracy and the Public Space in Latin America*. Princeton: Princeton University Press.

Avritzer, L. (2006) New public spheres in Brazil: Local democracy and deliberative politics. *International Journal of Urban and Regional Research*, 30(3): 623–637.

Bowen, J.D. (2015) Rethinking democratic governance: State building, autonomy, and accountability in Correa's Ecuador. *Journal of Politics in Latin America*, 7(1): 83–110.

Bran-Guzmán, E. (2017) Conflictividad socioambiental en Centroamérica. Una década de rearticulación y movilización social y política. *Argumentos*, 30(83): 43–68.

Buhl, K. and Korol, C. (2008) Criminalización de los Movimentos Sociales, in K. Buhl and C. Korol (eds) *Criminalización de la protesta y de los movimientos sociales*. São Paulo: Fundación Rosa Luxemburgo, pp 10–15. Available from: https://www.rosalux.org.mx/sites/default/files/pdf/criminalizacion_protesta.pdf [Accessed 18 October 2021].

Carrington, K., Hogg, R. and Sozzo, M. (2016) Southern criminology. *The British Journal of Criminology*, 56 (1): 1–20. https://doi.org/10.1093/bjc/azv083

Carrington, K., Hogg, R., Scott, J. and Sozzo, M. (2018) Criminology, southern theory and cognitive justice, in K. Carrington, R. Hogg, J. Scott and M. Sozzo (eds) *The Palgrave Handbook of Criminology and the Global South*. Basingstoke: Palgrave, pp 3–17.

Carta de Madrid (2021) En Defensa de La Libertad y La Democracia en La Iberosfera. *Foro Madrid*. Available from: https://fundaciondisenso.org/wp-content/uploads/2021/04/FD-Carta-Madrid-AAFF-V24.pdf [Accessed 18 October 2021].

Cavalcanti, R.P. (2020) *A Southern Criminology of Violence, Youth and Policing: Governing Insecurity in Urban Brazil*. London and New York: Routledge.

Cavalcanti, R.P. and Garmany, J. (2020) The politics of crime and militarised policing in Brazil. *International Journal for Crime, Justice and Social Democracy*, 9(2): 102–118.

Cavalcanti, R.P., Dadusc, D., Schlembach, R. and Fatsis, L. (2021) Silencing the streets: From covid exceptions to police crackdowns. *The British Society of Criminology*, 7 April. Available from: https://thebscblog.wordpress.com/2021/04/07/silencing-the-streets-from-covid-exceptions-to-police-crackdowns/ [Accessed 13 October 2021].

Cedano, P.R. (2008) La Criminalización de la Protesta Social en México, in K. Buhl and C. Korol (eds) *Criminalización de la protesta y de los movimientos sociales*. São Paulo: Fundación Rosa Luxemburgo, pp 136–180. Available from: https://www.rosalux.org.mx/sites/default/files/pdf/criminalizacion_protesta.pdf [Accessed 13 October 2021].

Celi, I., Cavalcanti, R.P. and Souza, G.I. (2022) An analysis of the criminalisation of socio-environmental activism and resistance in contemporary Latin America, in V. Vegh Weis (ed) *Criminalization of Activism: Historical, Present and Future Perspectives*. London: Routledge, pp 191–200.

Chies, L.A.B. (2020) Militarismo, racismo e sensibilidades bárbaras: Sociogênese do autoritarismo do controle social e punitivo no Cone Sul. Paper presented at ANPOCS, 7 December 2020.

Ciocchini, P. and Greener, J. (2021) Mapping the pains of neo-colonialism: A critical elaboration of southern criminology. *The British Journal of Criminology*, 61(6): 1612–1629.

Connell, R. (2007) *Southern Theory: The Global Dynamics of Knowledge in Social Science*. Cambridge: Polity.

Darke, S. and Khan, O.P. (2021) Coloniality, just war & carceral injustice in Brazil. *Punishment and Society*, 23(5): 723–740.

Defensoría del Pueblo del Ecuador (2021) *Informe de la Comisión Especial para la Verdad y la Justicia respecto de los hechos ocurridos en Ecuador entre el 3 y el 16 de octubre de 2019*. Quito: Defensoría del Pueblo.

Dimou, E. (2021) Decolonizing southern criminology: What can the 'decolonial option' tell us about challenging the modern/colonial foundations of criminology? *Critical Criminology*, 29: 431–450.

Domi, B. (2019) Chile despertó: Momentary impressions from the revolt. *Interface: A Journal For and About Social Movements*, 11(2): 5–10.

Doran, M.-C. (2017) The hidden face of violence in Latin America: Assessing the criminalization of protest in comparative perspective. *Latin American Perspectives*, 44(5): 183–206. doi: 10.1177/0094582X17719258.

Dorbecker, M.R. (2010) La criminalización de la protesta social como forma de restricción de la libertad de expresión en México: movimientos sociales en el centro de la llamada 'lucha contra la delincuencia organizada', in E. Bertoni (ed) *¿Es legítima la criminalización de la protesta social? Derecho penal y libertad de expresión en América Latina*. Buenos Aires: Universidad de Palermo, pp 145–161.

Federici, S. (2014) *Caliban and the Witch: Women, the Body and Primitive Accumulation*. New York: Autonomedia.

Fominaya, C.F. and Wood, L. (2011) Repression and social movements. *Interface: A Journal For and About Social Movements*, 3(1): 1–11.

Fon Filho, A. (2008) Criminalización de los Movimientos Sociales: Democracia y Represión de los Derechos Humanos, in K. Buhl and C. Korol (eds) *Criminalización de la protesta y de los movimientos sociales*. São Paulo: Fundación Rosa Luxemburgo, pp 75–107. Available from: https://www.rosalux.org.mx/sites/default/files/pdf/criminalizacion_protesta.pdf [Accessed 13 October 2021].

Frente por La Libertad de Expresion y Protest Social (2015) Control del espacio público 3.0. Informe sobre retrocesos en las libertades de expresión y reunión en el actual gobierno, 1a Edición, México, D.F. Available from: https://libertadyprotesta.org/wp-content/uploads/2018/05/control_espacio_publico_3_fleps_2015.pdf [Accessed 22 November 2022].

Girón, J.H. (2009) *La criminalización de la protesta pública en El Salvador, una forma de violación a derechos fundamentales*. El Salvador: Instituto Americano de Educación Superior.

Global Witness (2021) Last line of defense: The industries causing the climate crisis and attacks against land and environmental defenders. Available from: https://www.globalwitness.org/en/campaigns/environmental-activists/last-line-defence/ [Accessed 18 October 2021].

Grandin, G. (2007) *Empire's Workshop: Latin America, the United States and the Rise of the New Imperialism*. New York: Owl Books.

Guerrero, A (1993) De sujetos indios a ciudadanos étnicos: de la manifestación de 1961 al levantamiento indígena de 1990, in A. Adrianzén, J.-M. Blanquer, R. Ortega, C.I. Degregori, P. Gilhodes, A. Guerrero, P. Husson and J.-P. Lavaud (eds) *Democracia, etnicidad y violencia política en los países andinos*. Lima: IEP Ediciones y Instituto Frances de Estudios Andinos, pp 83–101.

Huggins, M.K. (1998) *Political Policing: The United States and Latin America*. Durham, NC: Duke University Press.

Iza Salazar, L., Tapia Arias, A. and Madrid Tamayo, A. (2020) *Estallido. La rebelión de Octubre en Ecuador*. Quito: Ediciones Red Kapari.

Mejía Acosta, A., Araujo, M.C., Pérez-Liñán, A. and Saiegh, S. (2011) Jugadores de veto, instituciones volubles y políticas de baja calidad: el juego político en Ecuador, in C. Scartascini, P.T. Spiller, E.H. Stein and M. Tommasi (eds) *El juego político en América Latina. ¿Cómo se deciden las políticas públicas?* Bogotá: Banco Interamericano de Desarrollo, pp 245–295. Available from: https://publications.iadb.org/publications/spanish/document/El-juego-pol%C3%ADtico-en-Am%C3%A9rica-Latina-%C2%BFC%C3%B3mo-se-deciden-las-pol%C3%ADticas-p%C3%BAblicas.pdf [Accessed 18 October 2021].

Mendoza, V. (2016) Aprueban 'ley Atenco' en Edomex; faculta uso de la fuerza pública en protestas, *Revista Proceso*, 17 March. Available from: www.proceso.com.mx/433880/aprueban-ley-atenco-faculta-uso-la-fuerza-publica-en-protestas-en-edomex [Accessed 22 November 2022].

Moosavi, L. (2019) A friendly critique of 'Asian criminology' and 'southern criminology'. *The British Journal of Criminology*, 59(2): 257–275. https://doi.org/10.1093/bjc/azy045

Morales, E.C. (2008) Criminalización de la protesta social en México. *El Cotidiano*, 23(150): 73–76.

Navarro, M.L.T. and Pineda, C.E.R. (2009) Luchas socioambientales en América Latina y México. Nuevas subjetividades y radicalidades en movimiento. *Revista Bajo El Volcán*, 8(14): 81–104.

North, L. (2004) State building, state dismantling, and financial crises in Ecuador, in J.-M. Burt and P. Mauceri (eds) *Politics in the Andes: Identity, Conflict, Reform*. Pittsburgh: University of Pittsburgh Press, pp 187–206.

Palau, M. and Corvalán, R. (2008) Criminalización de movimientos sociales en Paraguay: algunos elementos para comprender su magnitud, in K. Buhl and C. Korol (eds) *Criminalización de la protesta y de los movimientos sociales*. São Paulo: Fundación Rosa Luxemburgo. Available from: https://www.rosalux.org.mx/sites/default/files/pdf/criminalizacion_protesta.pdf [Accessed 13 October 2021].

Pinheiro, P.S.R. (1991) Autoritarismo e transição. *Revista USP*, 9: 45–56.

Ponce, K., Vasquez, A., Vivanco, P. and Munck R. (2020) The October 2019 and citizens uprising in Ecuador. *Latin American Perspectives*, 47(5): 9–19. doi:10.1177/0094582X20931113

Quijano, A. (2007) Coloniality and modernity/rationality. *Cultural Studies*, 21(2–3): 168–178. DOI: 10.1080/09502380601164353

Rábago Dorbecker, M. (2010) La criminalización de la protesta social como forma de restricción de la libertad de expresión en México: movimientos sociales en el centro de la llamada 'lucha contra la delincuencia organizada', in E. Bertoni (ed) *Es legítima la criminalización de la protesta social*. Buenos Aires: Universidad de Palermo, CELE, pp 145–161.

Ramírez, F. (2020) Paro plurinacional, movilización del cuidado y lucha política. Los signos abiertos de Octubre, in F. Ramírez (ed) *Octubre y el derecho a la resistencia: revuelta popular y neoliberalismo autoritario en Ecuador*. Buenos Aires: CLACSO, pp 11–44.

Rodriguez, E.C. (2015) El derecho a la protesta social en Colombia. *Pensamiento Jurídico*, 42: 47–69.

Rondón, D.V. and Zambrano, R.Q. (2015) *La criminalización de la protesta y el caso Majaz*. Perú: OXFAM.

Silva, E. (2009) *Challenging Neoliberalism in Latin America*. New York: Cambridge University Press.

Solís, F. and Pérez, C. (2014) Territorio, resistencia y criminalización de la protesta, in J. Cuvi (ed) *La Restauración Conservadora del Correísmo*. Quito: Montecristi Vive, pp 1–17.

Tarrow, S. (2002) Ciclos de acción colectiva: entre los momentos de locura y el repertorio de contestación, in M. Traugott (ed) *La protesta social*. Barcelona: Hacer Editorial, pp 70–110.

Toledo, V. (2007) Prima ratio. Movilización mapuche y política penal. Los marcos de la política indígena en Chile 1990–2007. *OSAL*, 22: 253–275.

Veltzé, E.R. and Tudela, F.L.R. (2010) Criminalización y derecho a la protesta, in E. Bertoni (ed) *¿Es legítima la criminalización de la protesta social? Derecho penal y libertad de expresión en América Latina*. Buenos Aires: Universidad de Palermo, pp 17–45.

Walsh, C. and Mignolo, W. (2018) *On Decoloniality: Concepts, Analytics, Praxis*. Durham, NC and London: Duke University Press.

Walton, J. and Ragin, C. (1990) Global and national sources of political protest: Third world responses to the debt crisis. *American Sociological Review*, 55(6): 876–890. doi:10.2307/2095752

Yashar, D. (2005) *Contesting Citizenship in Latin America: The Rise of Indigenous Movements and the Postliberal Challenge*. Cambridge: Cambridge University Press.

Zaffaroni, E.R. (1988) *Criminologia: aproximacion desde un margen*. Bogotá: Temis.

15

Framing Human Insecurity between Dispossession and Difference

Guilherme Benzaquen and Pedro Borba

Introduction

The expression 'security' is surrounded by a conservative atmosphere. Concerns about stability, security and order have been largely raised by those who intended to preserve things from change. National security, in particular, is still a restricted subject, prone to unaccountable state decisions, policies and regimes. The close links between security studies, national security and military expertise kept the field apart from cross-cutting political controversies over the desirable aims and standards for a political community (Waever, 2015). In this context, the meanings of (in)security unavoidably restated an attachment to stasis and equilibrium, or to the absence of credible threats.

In its classical sense, security is understood in Hobbesian terms as the neutralization of threats assured by a well-functioning sovereign state (Morgenthau, 1948; Waltz, 1979; see also Muhammad and Riyanto, 2021). Insecurity, hence, is an unstable and unpredictable condition of absence of state authority, that is, civil war. What defines modern states is the provision of protection within their borders, which means controlling physical violence inside and threats from outside. What follows from that is the differentiation and inner specialization of the personnel responsible for security as a public policy. There is a nationally bounded circuit that shapes security as ostensive protection in the interaction between rulers and ruled.

More recently, critical perspectives emerged around two overlapping issues. First, who defines what security means in practice? That leads us to underscore how power relations shape decision-making and how 'security concerns' remain an open path for exceptional measures of government. In other terms, specialized security establishments do not simply deal with a given set of risks, rather, they control the means to define what is a threat, whether it shall be a foreign state, the labour movement, the immigrants or undercover terrorism. The analysis of political boundary setting and the discursive constitution of threats and risks are fundamental for a critical appraisal on security studies. The second issue that paved the way for this critical renewal could be phrased as such: what should security be able to encompass? If one recognizes that people are subject to food insecurity, energy insecurity, health insecurity and so on (sometimes expressed as broadly 'human security issues'), the corresponding view of security should encompass dimensions beyond armed conflict and violent death (Sen, 2000b; King and Murray, 2002). In complex societies, human beings face dangers and risks that are not narrowly military in scope, and an adequate concept of their secure living must be correspondingly inclusive.

These two broad questions offered multiple ways of re-evaluating the relation between state and security, and among those stand postcolonial perspectives. The wording here is flexible since there is no single, coherent theory that unifies the heterogeneous body of scholarship labelled as postcolonial or decolonial. Instead of broadening disputes, our proposal in this chapter is to explore critical insights on security and insecurity, building upon a dialogue between Marxism and postcolonialism. In particular, we are interested in how categories like empire and imperialism, once a building block for radical appraisal of world politics, could be reinterpreted and reassessed in a historical context where formal empires largely ceased to exist. The imperial formation of modernity is a major issue for postcolonialists, while the capitalist drive for imperialism remains the ground for a long debate among Marxists. Our main argument profits from both. We suggest empires should not be analytically understood only by their formal political institutions, but also by the articulation they have historically produced between the colonial difference and accumulation by dispossession. The examination of the long-term consequences of this articulation might be a step to sharpen the contribution of postcolonialism to security analysis.

The chapter is divided into three sections, apart from this introduction and the final remarks. First, we outline the basic features of critical security studies and its project for establishing a comprehensive notion of security, as well as its tendency to embrace liberal cosmopolitanism (Gowan, 2001). The second section, in contrast, presents the categories of capitalist dispossession and colonial difference as cornerstones for contemporary critical theory. Specifically, we intend to show how modern empire-building formed long-standing connections and affinities between dispossession and difference, in a way that shaped societies. For a broad conception of security that is concerned with socioeconomic inequalities, segregation, environmental damage and food supply, as well as multiple forms of political violence, we suggest that unveiling the entanglements between dispossession and difference might be a promising path. The third section describes empirical instances in which such entanglements can be observed, detailing how human insecurity arises in concrete situations.

The frontiers of security and the frontiers of critique

The emergence of critical security studies in the 1980s and 1990s created a counter-current to the restricted way in which the field was shaped during the Cold War, as a form of 'expert system' applied to war-making (Buzan, 1991; Krause and Williams, 1997). In this context, critical studies incorporated much of the contestatory atmosphere of the social movements for disarmament and denuclearization in Europe, which challenged the statist assumptions of national security. The so-called 'new social movements' brought new concerns (ecological, feminist, cultural) to the security agenda, which shifted its emphasis from discernible threats to a comprehensive provision of welfare, protection and equality. An epitome of this heterodoxy was the lecture 'Security and Emancipation' delivered by Ken Booth in 1990, which positioned a universalist and progressive perspective for the field (Booth, 1991; Krause and Williams, 1997). This critical turn in security studies was quickly institutionalized and served as the basis for the 1994 UNDP report on Human Security, which defines as its normative parameter 'freedom from fear and freedom from want'. Thus, the guarantee of security would be a result of a society composed of individuals free from the threats of violence and poverty, that is, living in dignified conditions (Peoples and Vaughan-Williams, 2010).

There is, therefore, a priority shift from security of the frontiers to the frontiers of security itself, making it an open, interdisciplinary and progressive concept. Instead of a binary schema, the term security moves on to include a notion of development, in a sense analogous to what Amartya Sen had proposed for the idea of freedom (Sen, 2000a). In a lecture in 2000, Sen himself recognized the affinity of the concept of human security with a global justice paradigm (Sen, 2000b). Thus, as security is no longer simply survival and stability per se, there is a reform programme to be conducted on a global scale to enable people to achieve self-realization in their lives. Correspondingly, the reference point of the analysis shifts. Instead of strategic calculation, where a positional logic prevails, the emphasis is on egalitarian universal values, which regulate practices through a transcendental referent (Villa, 2008). Security studies could no longer be restricted to the ethnocentric bias intrinsic to national interest and its operations (Krause and Williams, 1997). The critique of 'methodological nationalism', which analytically subdues 'society' to the state, is overlaid with a critique of what we could describe as a 'nationalist methodology', a departure point guided by the particularism of the threat spectrum defined by a state or coalition of states.

It is worth looking at the arguments separately. 'Methodological nationalism' is conceived in social theory as a naturalization of existing states as a framework for the analysis of any social phenomena. As Tilly (1984: 21) stated, 'sociologists usually began with existing national states and defined society residually'. In other terms, each society is a set of explanatory vectors delimited at the scale of its sovereign territory. The experience of (in)security, therefore, must be a phenomenon intelligible from the geopolitical position of the state that protects – or should protect – and its rivals. By conflating nation, state and society, methodological nationalism elides the inadequacy, the conflicts and even the opacity that cross, from a historical and normative point of view, the conjunctions between these poles (Chernilo, 2005).

The 'nationalist methodology', in turn, corresponds to a positionality bias in which the reasoning on security issues is, directly or indirectly, engaged with the decision-making of a specific nation state. What effectively matters, in this case, is not security in general, but the protection of a state, its territory and its citizens. While the friend–foe opposition provides the building block for strategic studies, a national-based point of view informs the fundamental cultural values of scientific activity. From a critical perspective, if the circuit between threats and protection is circumscribed by national parameters, its understanding will always be one-sided and policy-oriented.

This fissure in the link between methodological nationalism and nationalist methodology is essential to unveiling the potentialities of a postcolonial perspective for security analysis. But this is only half the story. Thus, we need to re-examine what is critical for critical security studies by foregrounding the global hierarchy between North and South. There are two basic directions in which this is relevant. First, there is a clear Eurocentric component in the way critical security studies established itself as a vanguard for the renewal of the field. In the 1960s and 1970s, Third World political movements, notably the Non-Aligned Movement and its vindication for a New International Economic Order, had as their central demand the overcoming of militarism and classical geopolitics in international affairs, articulating an alternative agenda around development and decolonization. At the heart of this agenda there were inequality, racism and self-determination of peoples as a counterpoint to the Cold War arms race. When the revision of security parameters became institutionalized in the 1990s, it already incorporated a distinct ideological context, also rendering its anti-colonial precedents invisible.

Second, the individual-centred (or liberal cosmopolitan) approach to security has not been able to extricate itself from liberal reasoning about the sovereignty of the personal sphere. Deprivation, environmental risk and violence are framed as empirical obstacles to the full development of individual trajectories that, by aggregation, compose all human societies. Security is a precondition for the potency of individuals, while insecurity is a set of global deficiencies to be addressed. In the effort to defy traditional statism, a cosmopolitan individualism is on the way. Instead of thinking of one's own security in the face of an enemy, security is designed from above, against threatening circumstances without specific causes. In this way, 'human security' is institutionalized as a foundation for an ambitious global governmentality, as the UNDP report makes clear when it envisages 'a United Nations human development umbrella' of international organizations (UNDP, 1994: 83–89). The West is expected to take the initiative in 'emancipation' as the achievement of human security (Barkawi and Laffey, 2006: 350), reproducing a language peculiar to the old colonial bureaucracies (Duffield, 2009). In the extreme, such security management leaves open the space for direct interventionism by powerful states on the pretext of the 'responsibility to protect' individuals from their violent surroundings.

We need to go a step further in order to explore elements of a critical and postcolonial perspective on insecurity. In the following, we aim to demonstrate that the critique of 'methodological nationalism' does not necessarily imply a cosmopolitan point of view, abstracted from power relations between states, cultures and individuals. In the same way, it is necessary to validate the critique of the 'nationalist methodology' without blurring its politics. Insecurity, vulnerabilities and real threats are not 'global challenges' to be managed by the 'international community', but contexts of actual dispute involving incompatible values and interests. One cannot revise the normative concept of security without a critical revision of its opposite, without treating 'threats' and 'risks' as something beyond a collection of empirical incidents. A conceptual framework is needed that can link the mechanisms that generate human insecurity to social theory.

In the critical tradition stemming from Marxism, this function was mainly performed by the concept of imperialism, which connected the phenomenon of interstate war to the socio-spatial expansion of capitalism (for a review, see Brewer, 1990). The systemic imperatives of accumulation were operating behind the power politics that moved states, armies and colonial enterprises. Today this kind of causal imputation is being challenged as analytically reductionist (Arrighi, 1978, 2009; Harvey, 2003; Gonçalves and Costa, 2020). Meanwhile the use of the term imperialism has become trivial as a codename for the actions of the great powers abroad, especially US militarism, losing much of its sociological density. The emptying of the concept of imperialism has left a crucial gap in what distinguishes critical perspectives on security from liberal cosmopolitanism. How, then, to rethink the generative mechanisms of (in)security when the links between capitalism and violence do not literally imply empire-building? Or, again, how to explore a critical perspective on security that does not reinstate reductionism?

Dispossession, difference and violence

In this section, we seek to establish a dialogue between the contemporary renewal of Marxist theory of imperialism and a postcolonial approach to difference. Both of them share the goal of not merely understanding historical empire-building, but also refining concepts for a critique of present-day post-imperial societies. On the one hand, the central theme of Marxist discussion has been dispossession and extractivism as overarching concepts to deal with the exercise of state power to foster capitalist accumulation globally. On the other hand, the central theme of postcolonial critique is to demonstrate how modern European empires have historically instituted, modulated and institutionalized colonial difference as a technique of government, which subsists even after the process of formal decolonization (see Fatsis, this volume, and Trafford, 2021).

It is possible to locate a bifurcation in the contemporary use of the concepts of imperialism and empire. Marxism has moved towards an analysis of imperialism that mostly abstracts empires as such, encompassing in their place militarism and interventionism in a broader sense (Magdoff, 1969; Galtung, 1971; Amin, 1977). Meanwhile, historical analysis of empires has taken its scope of observation beyond the 19th-century Western imperial forms, inasmuch as it increasingly set aside imperialism as a concept rooted in capitalist industrialization (Bayly, 2004; Cooper, 2005; Esherick et al, 2006; Darwin, 2008). The two fields apparently seem to deal with different problems using their own languages. The attempt to rethink the place of state and violence in critical theory needs to re-evaluate this gap, unveiling the entanglements between dispossession and difference in post-imperial societies. Let us first outline the context of each of the terms in order to illuminate their connections.

According to Marx, the emergence of a global system marked by a cleavage between the possessors of the means of production and the possessors of labour power was made possible by extremely violent processes in the Old and the New Worlds. The states in formation were central actors in the process, using techniques such as the enclosure of communal lands, the criminalization of vagrancy, the forced creation of new markets and the financing of colonial and slave enterprises. Although there are specific passages in Marx that enable a different reading, the consolidated interpretation argues there is a main problem in the formulations about 'primitive accumulation' as the foundation of 'capitalist accumulation': the implicit argument is that this would be an outdated or transitory phase. It is in dialogue with this problem that a growing effort in critical theory to reformulate this analysis has become popular. What would be, in Marx, an original violent act based on dispossession and responsible for founding the possibilities of reproduction of capital, is transformed, in these new theorizations, into a necessary process for the constant reproduction of capitalism. Although there is no consensus on the deployment of the analysis, a basic understanding is that there are in capitalism processes of accumulation external to the circuit of expanded reproduction, which appeal regularly to state agency and its violence (Harvey, 2003; Sanyal, 2007; Dörre, 2009; Singh, 2016; Walker, 2016; Gago and Mezzadra, 2017; Federici, 2019).

In this sense, 'accumulation by dispossession' (Harvey, 2003) contemplates different initiatives through which capital valorization appeals to direct spoliation, circumventing voluntary market exchange thanks to political power, thus subsidizing expanded reproduction with surplus and new frontiers of accumulation. Capitalism persists with a constant movement of expropriation of the non-capitalist, that is, there is a constant process of exploitation and commodification because of the capitalist need for expanded accumulation (Dörre, 2009). This internal/external dialectic, this shifting of boundaries, is a constant movement of capital, but it must be stressed that it necessarily depends on state intervention, partly through its armed corporations, but more broadly through the exercise of administrative power.

Luxemburg (2003) had already identified this expansive vector, explaining it as an imperialist impetus that would seek and impose consumption on non-capitalist social formations. When addressing the 'method of violence', the author reveals an important aspect of the production of insecurity: the fact that political violence and economic processes are 'organically interlinked', since expanded reproduction requires dispossession. As is known, violence was conceived by Marx (1977) as the secret of primitive accumulation. If we claim the continuity of this type of accumulation through dispossession, we claim that violence remains the secret of the functioning of capitalism. This becomes clear in the example provided by the collective Midnight Notes (1990): Filipinos evicted from land to be used as 'free enterprise zones' are the condition of falling wages and unemployment in the United States.

As in the case of 'primitive accumulation', contemporary dispossession often occurs through enclosure. This is a 'structural component of class struggle' (Midnight Notes, 1990: 1) and a unifying feature of the global proletariat because it is from numerous uprootings that all have entered (and are entering) capitalism. This process has an important political aspect, which is the displacement of workers from spaces and relations in which they were familiar enough to organize and resist. This is a relevant aspect because 'class war does not happen on an abstract board toting up profit and loss, it is a war that needs a terrain' (Midnight Notes, 1990: 6).

The postcolonial discussion of difference, on the other hand, keeps imperial government and its forms in modern history at the centre of the problem.

In doing so, they recognize a productive dimension to political power: the colonial experience is not equivalent to the violent repression of conquered peoples but constitutes in its core specific forms of subjectification. In this way, modern colonialism has not only formed large multinational political entities, but has fertilized diverse branches of knowledge about peoples, social practices and the resulting sociocultural differences. To some extent, Edward Said's (1978) seminal study of *Orientalism* described how a Western-centred 'imaginary geography' organized the world on the premise of colonial difference. In this context, the use of violence by colonial armies and administrators is not a strategic or purely cruel act, but rather the result of a representation of Eastern peoples that leaves no alternative. Violence does not start where reason and knowledge end, but it is through them that it becomes intelligible. In the first place, then, the colonial difference constitutes a language in which the use of exceptional measures becomes not only possible, but somehow unavoidable.

In the 1990s, Latin American critical thought reconstructed the genealogy of the colonial difference to the European invasion of America. On colonial contact in America, a representation of the world is founded that divides the full individualities defined within the perimeter of European civilization from the American peoples defined by otherness (or alterity). This otherness is a reflexive, partial, immature condition. It is through the formation of a stratified colonial society that the first codes and practices are developed to institutionalize linguistic, cultural, racial and economic differences. This form of social classification develops what has become known as the coloniality of power, whose implications go far beyond the Latin American colonial context (Quijano, 2000). With colonial independence, the formation of a racialized national ideology, with dependent economies, implies a form of 'rearticulation of the coloniality of power upon new bases' (Quijano, 2000: 228). In the logic by which political elites conceive their tasks, this can take the form of a wilderness to be tamed or even a people to be exterminated (Lindqvist, 2018), an emptiness to be fulfilled, or a 'bruteness' to be policed, educated and 'civilized' according to universal values. If violence is required, its exercise is channelled through the spaces, peoples and cultures that are perceived to require disciplinary development, and therefore represent a form of modernizing intervention over 'backwardness'.

From the 16th century onwards, European empires were political organizations based on the classification and segmentation of the populations under their rule. What historiography has shown is that the homogeneous image of the national state overshadowed the importance of these composite political forms in institutional and spatial terms. Imperial spaces have thus become a privileged spot to observe how universal concepts about the human person are refracted, split and modulated according to circumstance.

Modern colonialism is founded on European universalism while at the same time denying it. For Partha Chatterjee (1993, 2011), this modulation corresponds to the rule of colonial difference. The social context of the colony requires that immediate considerations of risk and possible outcomes shape the application of universal principles, interposing a calculus of political expediency. This modulation does not invalidate the universal character of the principles. This is because there are conditions observed among peoples and local cultures that invalidate the general assumptions that Western philosophy has established for the human person.

Thus, an administrative logic of managing these populations prevails, whether to control and subdue them, or to foster change from outside. The rule of colonial difference simply informs concrete decisions in circumstances where there is a refraction of the premises of rationality, self-determination or morality. By establishing the institutional forms in which *otherness will become the exception*, this rule also preserves the self-referred universalism of colonial enterprise as a whole. In sum, the colonial difference is not the same as racial, linguistic, religious or cultural discrimination, but it is a kind of template by which to successfully mobilize any of these criteria for managing populations. In the contemporary world, it allows us to grapple with 'global practices of boundary-making and border controls that mimic in explicit detail practices of colonial cartography, based as they were on white supremacist ideals' (Anievas et al, 2014: 10).

At this point, it is understandable why a disassociation arose between the Marxist debate on imperialism and the postcolonial critique of difference. While it is true that both use modern empire-building as a reference for theorizing, the ways in which they do so point in different directions. On the one hand, we have a Marxist re-reading of imperialism that emphasizes how processes of dispossession are recreated in contemporary capitalism, bypassing the regulated circuit of surplus value extraction. On the other hand, we have a postcolonial reading of difference that indicates how political power organizes the exception based on markers engendered by governance of imperial spaces. It is unreasonable to expect that one argument can be simply reduced to the other. Our claim is slightly different. We believe that formal political empires can be understood as 'vanishing mediators' (compare Jameson, 1973) that shaped historical affinities and entanglements between capitalist dispossession and colonial difference, creating reciprocal stimulation and institutionalization. For instance, a conventional procedure of capitalist dispossession, like chattel slavery in the Americas, rests on a whole cultural and institutional complex of segregation within imperial spaces. Likewise, a full-fledged expression of the rule of colonial difference, like the representation of Indigenous territories in the Americas as empty 'wilderness' or unruly chaos, serves as a building block for genocide, violent eviction and commodification.

Therefore, the long-term institutionalization of imperial rule in the world-system bounded together forms of dispossession and difference in a catalytic effect. As a matter of fact, neither all forms of colonial difference were operative to capital, nor all forms of dispossession were strictly marked by difference. The point is not to lump them into the same concept. The key argument is that, channelled through historical empires, dispossession and difference enlarged their affinities and connections: state-propelled dispossession usually found a fast track when it followed up existing representations of otherness, while colonial social hierarchies were reinforced by material inequalities shaped by capitalist forms of dispossession. In other words, one cannot properly frame a concept such as 'accumulation by dispossession' without considering how it mingles with 'different disciplinary regimes producing an accumulation of "differences" and hierarchies' (Federici, 2019: 16). Meanwhile, it is unrealistic to represent cultural or racial stratification as a mere discursive or psychological operation, neglecting its encroachment on daily dynamics of routine lived experiences.

The mediation is evanescent precisely because such affinities develop an autonomous logic beyond the institutional framework of formal Western empires. Once they faded from the historical scene in the 19th and 20th centuries, the entanglements they welded between capitalism, exception and governmentality were not cancelled, but remained somehow available to be triggered in the postcolonial world. Certainly there is no single pattern for this to happen, since both difference and dispossession are concepts shaped by their context of actualization. Generally speaking, we state that the interplay between colonial difference and capitalist dispossession is the ground on which Marxist and postcolonial traditions might converge to explain contemporary forms of broadly 'neo-imperialist' practices. Moreover, it is the same ground where we place the generative mechanisms for human insecurity, as it moulds an 'active management of spatiotemporal zones of insecurity and existential threat' (Singh, 2016: 39).

The production of human insecurity: illustrations

Dispossession and difference are not abstract philosophical entities, so we shall explore in this section three illustrative cases from contemporary Latin America.

Maceió is a large city of over one million inhabitants on the northeastern coast of Brazil, capital of the state of Alagoas. Since 1975, a Brazilian petrochemical company called Braskem has conducted the intensive extraction of rock salt in its powerplant in Maceió, encouraged by the policy of heavy industrialization of the Brazilian civil-military dictatorship (1964–1985). There were many objections to this extraction activity in a very populated urban area. However, relying on both state support and regulatory omissions, including from environmental inspection agencies, Braskem maintained its activities with 35 mines until it destabilized underground cavities causing soil subsidence and cracks (Serviço Geológico do Brasil, 2019). There were already some signs of the process, but in 2018, these intensified after heavy rains and a seismic tremor of 2.4 on the Richter scale. In four neighbourhoods around Braskem power plant, about 55,000 people live at risk or have been removed from their homes. Today, the area consists of blocked streets, abandoned buildings and a few residents who resist despite the risks. Former residents' accounts are full of mentions of unemployment, illness and suicides. Those who still resist in the region report the many dangers they face: the high degree of vulnerability to urban violence and the uncertainty of new tremors, cracks and subsidence (Pronzato, 2021).

The second case takes us to Campeche, Mexico. There the Ka' Kuxtal Much Meyaj organization brings together Mayan *campesinos* who have been resisting daily under the slogan '*protejamos nuestras semillas*' ('protect our seeds'). One of their main proposals is to take back control of food systems through the distribution of native seeds (Tzec-Caamal, 2018). Therefore, they resist planting techniques that have put at risk the possibility of reproducing life in their 17 communities. The region has suffered from the use of genetically modified seeds that rely heavily on agrochemicals for cultivation. Bayer is mentioned as one of the major companies responsible for threats to food security in the region (Akerson, 2021). Since the purchase of Monsanto, the German multinational has occupied a prominent position among the global seed corporations that have, in recent years, advanced rapidly in building a technical, economic and legal monopoly of seeds. In a process that has affected agricultural production around the world, seed corporations manipulate seed genes and, with the complicity of the state, impose economic and legal restrictions on traditional crops. The result is that seeds cease to be a property deriving from the previous harvest, as there is an ongoing effort to separate the farmer from his capacity for self-provisioning. This has been signified as the loss of a 'seed sovereignty', a process that has its origins in 1930 but has accelerated in recent decades (Kloppenburg, 2010; Cáceres, 2014).

Finally, there is the case of soy production in Paraguay. The country is the world's fourth largest exporter of soy. The sector is composed of latifundia with highly complex machinery and biotechnology, located mainly in the east of the country. Soy currently occupies three-quarters of the arable land in Paraguay, which has the most concentrated land ownership structure in the world. The Gini index of rural property reaches 0.93 (Guereña and Rojas Villalba, 2016). There is a close link between landowners and institutional politics, forged especially during the military dictatorship of Alfredo Stroessner (1954–1989). According to the Truth and Justice Commission, about 7,800 hectares were granted irregularly by the Stroessner regime to politicians, military personnel and businessmen, who enjoyed government subsidies for the expansion of the soybean frontier. For decades, supported by the use of official and paramilitary violence, this expansion has advanced over Indigenous territories and peasant settlements. Notwithstanding the protests of the rural social movement, there is extensive complicity of control institutions with the illegalities of the soy agribusiness. The expansion of soy evicted rural populations and led Indigenous communities to proletarianization and impoverishment, weakening the country's food sovereignty while deepening environmental conflicts in the countryside. From 1990 to 2019, 519 land occupations by peasants were reported, in some cases lasting for years (Kretschemer et al, 2019).

In all three cases we are facing differential processes of dispossession, typical of contemporary capitalism, which depend on and entail insecurity. These cases are paradigmatic of what, in the words of critical security studies, is formulated as a concern about violent threats and deprivations arising from poverty (Peoples and Vaughan-Williams, 2010). We propose, therefore, to look at these cases of articulation between legal and extra-legal threats according to what was discussed in the previous sections.

First, let us look at how exploitation and dispossession complement each other in all three cases. In all of them, commodity production is possible only with the forced insertion of territories, workers and raw materials into global circuits of capital accumulation. Moreover, this forced insertion takes place under the sign of the exception, underpinning the promotion of insecurity. For example, even though technical opinions advised against the exploitation of rock salt in urban territory, the construction of 35 mines was necessary for Braskem to become the largest producer of polyvinyl chloride (PVC) in the Americas. Over decades, the subsoil of four neighbourhoods served as a mainstay for extended accumulation. This was done without the recommended distance between mines, something that made decades of huge profits possible but was evidently unsustainable in the long term. After the socio-environmental disaster, the result was immediately unfavourable to the company, which was forced to terminate its activities in the region and pay compensation to those affected. Even so, it is important to note that the eviction of the population was quickly reinserted into the normal circuit of capital. The compensation paid to the former residents led to the transfer of ownership of the abandoned territory to Braskem. If the soil subsidence is solved, this area surrounding a large lagoon in the city will be re-evaluated with significant gains for the company (Pronzato, 2021). In the face of a productive and environmental crisis, direct spoliation subsidizes expanded reproduction with new frontiers of capital expansion based on a 'spatio-temporal fix' (Harvey, 2003), which means, in this case, population displacement and future real estate speculation. Thus, the 'narrow sphere of productive relations' depends on a 'more expansive sphere of appropriation' (Singh, 2016: 40) that operates in a territory of difference.

As already noted, this is only possible on account of and by generating violence through the double action of capital and the state. Coincidentally, two of the three cases presented have their turning points in dictatorial periods. These are, perhaps, only extreme examples of processes that do not depend on dictatorships, because they constitute the norm of contemporary capitalism. Soybean production in Paraguay shows how, after the broad support given by the military dictatorship, a series of legal and extra-legal coercions is still in place. The state forces and private security companies act jointly in carrying out intimidation and violence against peasants, whose most expressive actions are evictions, arrests and murders (Kretschmer et al, 2019). Thus, state action to promote insecurity is violent, administrative and legal. Something similar occurs in southern Mexico, which is experiencing a series of developmentalist state interventions without the consent and consultation of the affected peoples. The Mayan Train, for example, is one of the projects launched by the current government of López Obrador that seeks to promote tourism, energy production and commercial agriculture in the region. This economic venture requires dumping and causes serious environmental risks for the sustainability of the region. This is only possible through the institution of difference, or, as the Zapatistas have already pointed out, by transforming the local population and nature into objects to be consumed and by constituting a specific alterity to the Mayan peoples that subsumes their heterogeneous identities (Walsh, 2021).

This concept of development from above is, as we have seen, also characteristic of the dispute over land in Paraguay. In effect, the directive of the Colorado Party was to erect a national mythology of Hispanic-Guarani fusion, while erasing the Indigenous and peasant population actually existing in the country. The official thinking of the dictatorship in the 1970s conceived the countryside as a still uncultivated wilderness. Under the influence of geopolitical theories of the period, the Stroessner regime stated unfulfilled tasks of national integration, since, in the words of two official intellectuals, 'the Power of the State … is encompassing within its political actions only a territorial limit far behind the real frontiers of the Nation-State' (quoted in Lima, 2018: 64). Accordingly, mechanized agriculture is a vector for subduing space to 'progress' and 'civilization', which are taken forward essentially by foreign capital, including Brazilian landowners and transnational corporations for machinery, shipping and agricultural inputs. The main task the Paraguayan political elites set for themselves was to organize and manage the internal colonization of the country.

Moreover, there is a clear articulation between natural extractivism in a stricter sense and the global networks of financial capital. As is well known, in Latin America, many cases similar to those presented here have been interpreted based on the notion of extractivism or neo-extractivism. Building upon this extensive and heterogeneous debate, Gago and Mezzadra (2017) propose a wider notion of extraction, that has three main characteristics: (1) it is not restricted to operations of commodification of raw materials; (2) it assumes a certain exteriority to the natural circuit of capital; and (3) it is not associated solely with the rural. The authors propose a link between exploration and extraction to rethink how social reproduction continually depends on extractive practices. This applies to the cases we briefly described in this chapter. For instance, while the seeds commercialized by Bayer are employed in a rural context, the company is a key player in the financialization of agricultural inputs. Like other economic sectors, global seed corporations make part of their earnings from financial transactions, often in the stock market or in providing agricultural credit. One of the effects of this intertwining between finance and food production has been the intensification of the exploitation of food workers and small farmers as a means of realizing shareholder value (Isakson, 2014).

Hence, the entanglements between dispossession and difference offer a template to analyse violence and insecurity, acknowledging security as an omnilateral social and environmental condition. The concrete forms of these entanglements should not be presumed theoretically, but assessed in empirical research. In doing so, they frame insecurity on a global scale without sticking to liberal assumptions of cosmopolitanism. The affinity between dispossession and difference certainly does not dismiss classical themes for the theories of imperialism: the US War on Terror after 2001, for instance, is about oil, extractivism and military Keynesianism as much as it is about orientalist myths of unruliness, political decay and the Western civilizing mission. From large-scale war-making to daily practices of eviction, racism, extraction and legal exceptionalism, one could trace back how difference and dispossession mingle to engender spatiotemporal zones of insecurity.

Conclusion

Our aim in the present chapter was to present a critical approach to the production of insecurity based on the thesis that there are a myriad of violent processes that can be traced to the intertwinings of colonial difference and capitalist dispossession. We argue that the formal empires operated historically as vanishing mediators of this articulation in a way that subsisted even after the dismantling of imperial spaces in 19th and 20th centuries. Thus, dispossession becomes incomprehensible under the prism of an abstract universal subject, since it is based on and promotes differentiation. Moreover, colonial difference does not stem from a narrative of historical immobility, but from the ways in which coloniality is reinstituted as a relational form. Apart from older colonial forms of expropriation and slavery, the articulation between capitalist dispossession and colonial difference resurges, enmeshed in contemporary forms of extractivism and human displacement, in military interventionism in the global South, in migrant, informal or coerced forms of labour, as well as in many other instances of human insecurity. Much research could be done on its specific contexts, but our purpose was to show how coloniality does not reside in the remote past or in the outer peripheries; it is constituted as a historical dynamic of the world-system. By acknowledging it, one finds a promising resource for understanding enduring hierarchies embedded in the imperial formation of modernity.

References

Akerson, L. (2021) *Maya Activist Groups Fight to Protect Indigenous Territorial Rights*. Available from: https://nacla.org/maya-activist-groups-fight-protect-indigenous-territorial-rights [Accessed 27 October 2021].

Amin, S. (1977) *Imperialism and Unequal Development*. New York: Monthly Review Press.

Anievas, A., Manchanda, N. and Shilliam, R. (2014) Introduction, in A. Anievas, N. Manchanda and R. Shilliam (eds) *Race and Racism in International Relations: Confronting the Global Color Line*. London and New York: Routledge, pp 1–15.

Arrighi, G. (1978) *The Geometry of Imperialism: The Limits of Hobson's Paradigm*. London: New Left Books.

Arrighi, G. (2009) *Long Twentieth Century: Money, Power and the Origins of Our Time*. New York and London: Verso.

Barkawi, T. and Laffey, M. (2006) The postcolonial moment in security studies. *Review of International Studies*, 32(2): 329–352.

Bayly, C. (2004) *The Birth of Modern World (1780–1914): Global Connections and Comparisons*. Oxford: Blackwell.

Booth, K. (1991) Security and emancipation. *Review of International Studies*, 17(4): 313–326.

Brewer, A. (1990) *Marxist Theories of Imperialism: A Critical Survey*. London: Routledge.

Buzan, B. (1991) *People, States and Fear*. Boulder: Lynne Rienner.

Cáceres, D. (2014) Accumulation by dispossession and socio-environmental conflicts caused by the expansion of agribusiness in Argentina. *Journal of Agrarian Change*, 15(1): 116–147.

Chatterjee, P. (1993) *The Nation and its Fragments: Colonial and Postcolonial Histories*. Princeton: Princeton University Press.

Chatterjee, P. (2011) *Lineages of Political Society: Studies in Postcolonial Democracy*. New York: Columbia University Press.

Chernilo, D. (2005) *Social Theory of the Nation State: The Political Forms of Modernity beyond Methodological Nationalism*. London: Routledge.

Cooper, F. (2005) *Colonialism in Question: Theory, Knowledge, History*. Berkeley and Los Angeles: University of California Press.

Darwin, J. (2008) *After Tamerlane: The Global History of Empire since 1405*. London: Bloomsbury.

Dörre, K. (2009) The new Landnahme: Dynamics and limits of financial market capitalism, in K. Dörre, S. Lessenich and H. Rosa (eds) *Sociology, Capitalism, Critique*. London: Verso, pp 11–66.

Duffield, M. (2009) Liberal interventionism & the fragile state: Linked by design?, in M. Duffield and V. Hewitt (eds) *Empire, Development & Colonialism*, Woodbridge: Boydell & Brewer, pp 116–129.

Esherick, J., Kayali, H. and Van Young, E. (eds) (2006) *Empire to Nation: Historical Perspectives on the Making of the Modern World*. Lanham and Boulder: Rowman & Littlefield.

Federici, S. (2019) *Re-enchanting the World: Feminism and the Politics of the Commons*. Oakland: PM Press.

Gago, V. and Mezzadra, S. (2017) A critique of the extractive operations of capital: Toward an expanded concept of extractivism. *Rethinking Marxism*, 29(4): 574–591.

Galtung, J. (1971) A structural theory of imperialism. *Journal of Peace Research*, 8(2): 81–117.

Gonçalves, G. and Costa, S. (2020) From primitive accumulation to entangled accumulation: Decentring Marxist theory of capitalist expansion. *European Journal of Social Theory*, 23(2): 146–164.

Gowan, P. (2001) Neoliberal cosmopolitanism. *New Left Review*, 11: 79–93.

Guereña, A. and Rojas Villalba, L. (2016) *Yvy Jara: los Dueños de la Tierra en Paraguay*. Asunción: OXFAM/Paraguay.

Harvey, D. (2003) *The New Imperialism*. New York: Oxford University Press.

Isakson, S. (2014) Food and finance: The financial transformation of agro-food supply chains. *The Journal of Peasant Studies*, 41(5): 749–775.

Jameson, F. (1973) The vanishing mediator: Narrative structure in Max Weber. *New German Critique*, 1: 52–89.

King, G. and Murray, C.J.L. (2002) Rethinking human security. *Political Science Quarterly*, 116(4): 585–610.

Kloppenburg, J. (2010) Impeding dispossession, enabling repossession: Biological open source and the recovery of seed sovereignty. *Journal of Agrarian Change*, 10(3): 367–388.

Krause, K. and Williams, M. (1997) From strategy to security: Foundations of critical security studies, in K. Krause and M. Williams (eds), *Critical Security Studies: Concepts and Cases*. London: UCL Press, pp 33–61.

Kretschemer, R., Irala, A. and Palau, M. (2019) *Ocupaciones de tierra: marcas del conflicto rural (1990–2019)*. Asunción: Base Is.

Lima, L. (2018) *Stroessner: Biografia, História e Propaganda (1972–1979)*. Foz do Iguaçu: UNILA.

Lindqvist, S. (2018) *Exterminate all the Brutes*. London: Granta.
Luxemburg, R. (2003) *The Accumulation of Capital*. London: Routledge.
Magdoff, H. (1969) *The Age of Imperialism: The Economics of US Foreign Policy*. New York: New York University Press.
Marx, K. (1977) *Capital*, vol 1. New York: Vintage Books.
Midnight Notes (1990) The new enclosures. *Midnight Notes*, 10: 1–9.
Morgenthau, H. (1948) *Politics among Nations: The Struggle for Power and Peace*. New York: Alfred Knopf.
Muhammad, A. and Riyanto, S. (2021) International security studies: Origins, development and contending approaches. *Brazilian Journal of Strategy & International Relations*, 10(20): 230–249.
Peoples, C. and Vaughan-Williams, N. (2010) *Critical Security Studies: An Introduction*. London and New York: Routledge
Pronzato, C. (2021) *A Braskem passou por aqui: A catástrofe de Maceió*. Available from: https://www.youtube.com/watch?v=zBOJbOGcBwo [Accessed 27 October 2021].
Quijano, A. (2000) Coloniality of power and Eurocentrism in Latin America. *International Sociology*, 15(2): 215–232.
Said, E. (1978) *Orientalism: Western Concepts of the Orient*. New York: Pantheon.
Sanyal, K. (2007) *Rethinking Capitalist Development: Primitive Accumulation, Governmentality and Post-colonial Capitalism*. New Delhi: Routledge.
Sen, A. (2000a) *Development as Freedom*. New York: Alfred A. Knopf/Borzoi Books.
Sen, A. (2000b) Why human security? *International Symposium on Human Security*, Tokyo, July 2000, pp 1–12.
Serviço Geológico do Brasil (2019) *Estudos sobre a instabilidade do terreno nos bairros Pinheiro, Mutange e Bebedouro, Maceió (AL): Ação emergencial no bairro Pinheiro*. Available from: https://rigeo.cprm.gov.br/jspui/bitstream/doc/21133/1/relatoriosintese.pdf. [Accessed 27 October 2021].
Singh, N. (2016) On race, violence, and so-called primitive accumulation. *Social Text*, 34(3): 27–50.
Tilly, C. (1984) *Big Structures, Large Processes, Huge Comparisons*. New York: Russell Sage Foundation.
Trafford, J. (2021) *The Empire at Home: Internal Colonies and the End of Britain*. London: Pluto Press.
Tzec-Caamal, N. (2018) Las Fiestas de Semillas Nativas en Campeche, in L. Lönnquist (ed) *Morral de Experiencias para la Seguridad y Soberanía Alimentarias: Aprendizajes de organizaciones civiles en el sureste mexicano*. San Cristóbal de las Casas: El Colegio de la Frontera Sur, pp 158–163.
UNDP (United Nations Development Program) (1994) *Human Development Report*. Oxford: Oxford University Press.

Waever, O. (2015) The history and social structure of security studies as a practico-academic field, in T. Berling and C. Bueger (eds) *Security Expertise: Practice, Power, Responsibility*. London: Routledge, pp 76–107.

Walker, G. (2016) *The Sublime Perversion of Capital: Marxist Theory and the Politics of History in Modern Japan*. Durham, NC: Duke University Press.

Walsh, C. (2021) Decolonial praxis: Sowing existence-life in times of dehumanities. *International Academy of Practical Theology*, São Leopoldo, April 2019, pp 4–12.

Waltz, K. (1979) *Theory of International Politics*. Reading, MA: Addison-Wesley.

Villa, R. (2008) Segurança internacional e normatividade: é o liberalismo o elo perdido dos critical securities studies? *Lua Nova*, 73: 75–122.

16

Private Military Force in the Global South: Mozambique and Southern Africa

John Lea

The return of private military force

The development of warfare and armed conflict since the Second World War has seen a gradual return of the use of private military force. Armed force organized and deployed by non-state private companies or mercenaries usually, though not always, acting in the service of states has, until recently, involved small-scale conflicts predominantly located in the global South. The first manifestation of this was shortly after the Second World War, particularly in Africa. In an international context generally supportive of colonial independence the direct repression of struggles against colonialism was widespread but unpopular. The use of mercenaries enabled elements within former colonial powers to deny direct involvement in repression while in the shadows agents recruited 'newly discharged soldiers from the metropolitan states to crush, sabotage, frustrate or delay the aspirations for self-determination' (Musah and Fayemi, 1999: 20; see also Miller, 2020). This use of mercenaries came to a head in the mid-1970s in the anti-colonial struggle and civil war in Angola. Mercenary intervention was a disaster and the majority were captured and tried, given long prison sentences or executed (Wrigley, 1999). The United Nations (UN) banned mercenaries in 1995 but increasingly tolerates and indeed makes use of what are now known as private military companies (PMCs).

The transition from mercenaries to PMCs was partly a change in nomenclature and, crucially, a change in legitimacy. Whereas the term mercenary had come to connote illegal armed force deployed for dubious purpose, PMCs were increasingly employed by governments or international organizations, including the UN, as necessary and legitimate components of military missions. The role of the private company Executive Outcomes during the civil war in Sierra Leone during the 1990s is often seen as a key factor in the transition to legitimacy. The company was initially regarded by the UN as a disruptive mercenary force but subsequently came to be seen as an agent of stability and support for the legitimate government (see Fitzgibbon and Lea, 2020: 55ff).

The widespread employment of large PMCs such as Blackwater, DynCorp and Aegis by the US military in Iraq and Afghanistan in the early 2000s illustrated another element of the move away from the mercenary model. These entities, increasingly known as 'contractors', are 'more like heavily armed multinational corporations' (McFate, 2019: 2), and in Afghanistan and Iraq were deployed predominantly in areas other than direct combat. These included logistics, intelligence analysis, training, guarding US embassies and facilities and VIP close protection. Behind this deployment lay the idea of a new division of labour in which the diversity of skills and technology required to support the operations of a modern military is more effectively bought in from the private sector while the military itself concentrates on its 'core competences' of front-line combat. So the image was that although 'today, America can no longer go to war without the private sector' (McFate, 2016), contractor-PMCs are relegated to non-combatant roles and firmly subordinated to the military chain of command.

This division of labour unravelled in spectacular fashion in Afghanistan and Iraq for the simple reason that the United States was fighting a new type of war. In Iraq, for example, following the initial defeat of the Iraqi army, the enemy were mainly local insurgents, some morphing into international terrorist groups, deploying hit-and-run asymmetric warfare, dressed identically to and effectively hiding within the local civilian population. In such a context not only did the regular US military commit a large number of human rights violations against civilians but also the contractors frequently found themselves in heavy combat situations and acted similarly. The notorious Nisour square massacre in Baghdad in 2007 in which employees of the American PMC Blackwater opened fire on a crowd of Iraqi civilians killing 17 and wounding many more (Glanz and Rubin, 2007) obliterated in a few minutes the distinction between modern PMCs and the old-fashioned 'gunslinger' mercenaries of an earlier period.

As experience further south in the Sahel and sub-Saharan Africa showed, neither had those more traditional mercenaries gone away. There were still plenty of smaller 'PMCs' of less respectable repute led by White ex-military from the former colonial regimes of Rhodesia and apartheid-era South Africa. And even the larger, more 'respectable' PMCs working with the US military were themselves recruiting largely ex-military special forces. The real difference was, and is, the context in which the private military were working (see McFate in Mullin, 2020). Contractors working for the US military in Afghanistan and Iraq sheltered under an umbrella of legitimacy while very similar organizations hiring their services to weaker militaries in African states would be more exposed, like their employers, to accusations of brutality and human rights violations. In other words, an understanding of the role of private military force today requires an understanding of the scenarios in which it is deployed rather than how large or supposedly 'legitimate' are the commercial organizations providing it.

But what all these conflicts in the global South involving various combinations of mercenaries and PMCs have in common is that they are predominantly involved in asymmetric warfare: low intensity (overwhelmingly small arms), engagements of short duration over a small battlespace against opponents with limited resources. By contrast, in the global North, tensions between Russia and the former Soviet state of Ukraine whose governments have since 2014 aspired to membership of 'the West', broke into open warfare with the Russian incursion into Ukraine beginning in February 2022. This action, ostensibly in support of the Donbas provinces of eastern Ukraine wishing to break away from the Kiev government and retain close ties with Russia, has returned Europe to the type of 'industrialized warfare' last seen in 1945. In sharp contrast to the armed conflicts of the global South, the high intensity, large scale, combined arms (aviation, artillery, armour and infantry) mobile engagements over a wide battle front would seem to provide little opportunity for private sector involvement in combat-related activities.

Volunteers, many with previous military experience, from a variety of states – including France, Poland, Canada, the United States and United Kingdom, have joined the Ukrainian armed forces, but as individuals rather than organized mercenary or PMCs (Soufan Center, 2022). Casualty rates have been high and many have returned home after facing unexpectedly intensive Russian artillery barrages. Many were 'western military veterans who either have never deployed into combat previously or have experienced only asymmetrical insurgencies – not this type of war, with contested airspace, unrelenting rocket bombardment, and swarms of drones with sophisticated thermal targeting technology' (Horton et al, 2022).

Such comments, although referring to individual volunteers, imply that the type of mercenary or PMC organizations characteristic of global South conflicts would require considerable adaption in equipment and training to survive in Ukraine. But an example of precisely such adaption may be evident in the activity of the hitherto shadowy Russian PMC, the Wagner Group, which, as we shall see, is playing an increasing role in both types of armed conflict.

Returning our focus to the global South, and particularly to sub-Saharan Africa, we find some states seriously weakened through internal war. Such low intensity, asymmetric conflicts may also prompt UN peacekeeping intervention as for example in the Democratic Republic of the Congo since 1999 (see Murphy, 2016). UN forces in such situations employ PMCs, though very much in the 'rear areas' model, to guard refugee camps, aid supply dumps and convoys and the personnel of non-governmental organizations (NGOs) operating under UN auspices. The legitimacy of UN peacekeeping operations is heavily dependent on the visible neutrality of UN armed contingents and this is an added incentive to keep private sector involvement away from conflict zones, though this is not always possible (Fitzgibbon and Lea, 2020: 59). Alternatively governments of such states may themselves employ mercenaries in an attempt to strengthen their position against insurgents. This characterized the Sierra Leone civil war, noted earlier, and, as we shall discuss presently, has occurred in Nigeria and Mozambique.

The governance assemblage in postcolonial states

An important characteristic of many postcolonial states in the global South debilitated by 'structural adjustment' and other policies imposed by the imperialist powers of the global North is the presence on the national terrain of powerful non-state actors capable of neutralizing or effectively substituting for the state particularly in areas related to security. Apart from mercenary/PMCs and other private security organizations supplementing the state through provision of additional armed force, there is a likely presence of at least two other powerful non-state actors. Local insurgents with links to powerful globally organized jihadi networks such as Islamic State (ISIS) may be attempting to replace the state entirely and in the territory they control may impose alternative, and brutal, forms of governance. Finally, transnational corporations (TNCs), particularly those involved in extractive industries such as oil or precious metals, may attempt to either divert the resources of the state to prioritize the protection of their own assets or directly employ private security for this purpose.

Insurgents

The 2011 Arab uprisings and the overthrow of the Gaddafi regime in Libya, combined with the defeats suffered by ISIS in Syria and Iraq, has increased the prominence of the group in the Sahel and sub-Saharan Africa more generally. A recent report for the UN Security Council summarized the situation:

> The most striking development of the period under review was the emergence of Africa as the region most affected by terrorism. ... Several of the most successful affiliates of ISIL (its Central Africa and West Africa Province) and Al-Qaida (in Somalia and the Sahel region) are located in the continent, where they are spreading their influence

and activities, including across national borders. Instances of contagion from Mali into Burkina Faso, Côte d'Ivoire, the Niger and Senegal and incursions from Nigeria into Cameroon, Chad and the Niger, from Somalia into Kenya and from Mozambique into the United Republic of Tanzania are all concerning. One of the most troubling events of early 2021 was the deterioration of the security situation in Cabo Delgado Province in northern Mozambique, where the local ISIL affiliate stormed and briefly held a strategic port near the border with the United Republic of Tanzania before withdrawing with spoils, positioning it for future raids in the area. (UNSC, 2021: 5–6)

The events in Mozambique will be discussed in detail presently. Here it should be emphasized that the growing strength of ISIS in the region is its ability to link with and impose its trademark on local conflicts and grievances. Where states have difficulty in meeting the basic security needs of the population, and even more where the population believes the state to be prioritizing the needs of visiting TNCs, then ISIS has a real basis for growth (Munshi, 2021). However, despite cashing in on local resentments there is little evidence that ISIS has done much to directly meet the needs of the local population in terms of efforts to organize food production. Rather there is a tendency to rely on income from smuggling precious metals and drugs (Lister, 2021).

Transnational corporations

Foreign TNCs have a variety of assets such as mining encampments and oil and gas extraction facilities and pursue a variety of strategies to protect them. They are likely, like any business corporation, to employ private security companies to provide guarding and access control. More elaborate strategies involve agreements with the state, to divert police and military resources to specific protection of company assets. In return TNCs may directly finance sections of the state police and military. They may also contribute to social stability via 'outreach work' benefiting local communities or via exemplary adherence to international human rights norms (Abrahamsen and Williams, 2017), though such beneficence may not extend far beyond the immediate hinterland of the TNC locations (Hönke, 2013).

Such measures have conflicting results. On the one hand financial investment in security and social development might be seen to be welcomed. On the other the skewing of resource distribution away from the needs of the general population and towards the particular security requirements of TNCs may end up further weakening the state and creating opportunities for the insurgents. Alternatively, on occasion TNCs have been alleged to enter directly into covert agreements with insurgents. An important case was in Nigeria during the 1990s where the Shell oil company was alleged to have financed both state military and criminal gangs to suppress popular resistance to community destruction through oil pollution (see Amunwa and Minio, 2011; Amnesty International, 2017).

Mercenaries and militaries

States besieged by insurgencies may request military assistance. Such assistance may come from three sources. First, neighbouring states who may share an interest in containing ISIS-linked insurgencies. Second, that interest may also be shared by major states of the global North, some of whom are former colonial powers. For example, the containment of an ISIS-led resurgence in the Sahel and sub-Saharan Africa in general 'is now the priority area for French external counter-terrorism operations and is rising rapidly in importance to the US' (Reeve and Pelter, 2014: 2). A large French special forces presence in Mali and other former French colonies in the Sahel region began in 2014 and US special forces were also involved. Finally, mercenaries or PMCs may be hired in an attempt to augment the state military. In all these cases there arises the problem of the degree of actual control over the actual conduct of the 'visitors' both in relation to human rights compliance and the conduct of the conflict. Visiting forces, moreover, may have other agendas than simply assisting the host state to defeat the insurgency. In the Sierra Leone civil war, for example, the PMC/mercenary organization Executive Outcomes achieved considerable leeway in deciding the conduct and duration of the conflict. The company was said to have had its own agenda relating to agreements with various diamond and oil TNCs operating in the region and was able to guarantee the protection of its clients' interests, even determining the duration of the conflict in this respect (see O'Brien, 1999; Keen, 2012).

Nevertheless the 'request for assistance' has given a new lease of life to the traditional role of mercenaries as front-line combat military for hire, rather than as 'contractors' concerned mainly with training and logistics – though they may also fulfil this role. This was illustrated by Nigeria's employment of South African mercenaries in the fight against the Boko Haram Islamist insurgency during 2015–2016. This employment 'has essentially been a return to the position of Executive Outcomes of the late 80's and 90's. Specifically, it is alleged that many of the mercenaries are former soldiers of the South African Defence Force, from the pre-apartheid era' (Gough, 2017: 152). Similarly, Sean McFate – former mercenary now an academic – comparing the Nigerian situation to Afghanistan and Iraq, commented that:

> [T]his was a more full-blooded mercenary operation than the sort that we are used to of late. These were real, hardcore mercenaries. This

was very different from the ways PMCs were used by the coalition in Iraq, say, where they did convoy protection, defence of buildings or people. This was pure offense, and they did a great job. Well ... an effective job, at least. (Quoted in Bayley, 2016)

These 'real, hardcore mercenaries' were allegedly employed by a PMC called Specialised Tasks, Training, Equipment and Protection International (see Pfotenhauer, 2016). As we shall see, similar arrangements were made by the government of Mozambique a few years later. South African mercenaries have a reputation for effectiveness and have been involved in a number of conflicts in the region in both combat and training. In the latter role they were also involved in Iraq and Afghanistan (Varin, 2015).

Assemblages and states

Private military and security, TNCs and insurgents, all occupying the same national terrain as the state's own assets, sustains the view that governance can be understood as the interaction between different components of an 'assemblage' of state and non-state actors. However, it would be incorrect to see the state as simply one security provider among several which, depending on the balance of forces between different components of the assemblage, 'might be differently assembled in different places' (Abrahamsen and Williams, 2017: 19). This could be read as neo-colonialist ideology: the idea that the weakness and corruption of the local state could be compensated by powerful visitors: private military and security or TNCs both with strong human rights-compliance derived from their organization base in the global North.

Such a standpoint easily becomes an updated version of the colonialist 'civilizing mission' in which morally and technically superior Western TNCs and PMCs come to the rescue of debilitated former colonial states unable to guarantee security to their citizens. Such a view certainly takes a rather blinkered view of the actual conduct of 'visitors', in particular foreign mercenary forces. More profoundly, it fails to see the connection between the very presence of visiting Western TNCs as part of a neoliberal global imperialism enforced through agencies such as the World Bank and International Monetary Fund (IMF), and the latter's policies of enforced privatization and 'structural adjustment'. These policies are arguably designed to maintain the subservience of former colonial states to global financial interests – that is, the maintenance of precisely their postcolonial status.

In this context the state remains the only potential vehicle for democratic expression by the mass of the population against such interests. Its corruption and debilitation through penetration by other components of the assemblage – TNCs in particular – deprives the masses of effective representation, Achille

Mbembe described the impact of the fragmentation of state sovereignty into a labyrinth 'assemblage' of corruption and clientelism under conditions of armed conflict as a system of 'indirect private government' in which:

> the violence of war and control of the means of coercion weigh decisively today in the organization of postcolonial societies. Where it happens, war provokes a rearrangement of the ways territory and people are administered, as well as a transformation of the ways resources are tapped and distributed, of the framework in which disputes are settled. These new forms of more or less total control not only blur the supposed relationship between citizenship and democracy; they in fact incapacitate whole sections of the population politically. (Mbembe, 2001: 232)

He might well have been referring to recent events in Mozambique to which we now turn as graphic illustration of the themes already outlined.

Mozambique

Mozambique secured independence from Portugal in 1975 after a long armed struggle led by the Frente de Libertação de Moçambique (FRELIMO) – Mozambique Liberation Front . But a decade-long civil war (1982–1992) was funded by South Africa on behalf of imperialist interests. Although FRELIMO won the war the economy was devastated and Mozambique was forced to join the IMF and World Bank and undergo the 'shock therapy' of 'structural adjustment', a rapid shift from state-managed to free market economy, cuts in public spending and massive privatization of state assets including key banks. As in the Yeltsin years (1990s) in Russia following the collapse of the USSR, this enabled some members of the political elite to transform themselves into wealthy capitalist 'oligarchs' largely subservient to foreign imperialist interests (see Hanlon, 2021a).

The early 2000s saw the discovery of mineral deposits, including rubies, various precious metals, coal and natural gas. In 2010 the second largest natural gas deposits in Africa were discovered off the coast of the northernmost Mozambique province of Cabo Delgado. This attracted the attention of global oil corporations like Exxon-Mobil but specifically the French TNC TotalEnergies. The hope was that Mozambique would become 'Africa's Kuwait'. Gas would not only enrich the elite but prosperity would 'trickle down' to the masses. The onshore gas liquification plants were established on the Afungi peninsula a few miles from the town of Palma in Cabo Delgado. However, continuous delay in expected income streams from the gas extraction meant no serious new government revenue and little increased employment for locals (Hanlon, 2021b). The poor waited in vain for benefits from gas extraction and other extraction activities (for example, gold and rubies) financed by Western companies. Instead they experienced land dispossession – on behalf of the mining companies – and a failure of the central government to compensate with investment in social development (Ahmed, 2020; Matsinhe, 2020).

From 2017 onwards, undoubtedly fuelled by unfulfilled expectations and a sense of political exclusion, an increasingly serious insurgency began in Cabo Delgado, led by a local Islamist group Al-Shabaab (unrelated to the Somalian group of the same name) believed to have links to ISIS. In August 2020 insurgents occupied the TotalEnergies liquified natural gas (LNG) refinery at the port of Mocímboa da Praia in Cabo Delgado. Another important episode was the attack on the town of Palma, just to the north of the gas refineries, beginning on 24 March 2021. The 'battle of Palma' was a microcosm of the wider conflict that has engulfed much of Southern Africa.

The battle of Palma: March 2021

Al-Shabaab rebels besieged Palma and on 24 March they ransacked banks, government offices, food storage warehouses and the local military base and killed dozens of local people. Many locals escaped south towards the TotalEnergies compound where both Mozambique military and private security were located. Thousands of civilians fled from the area (see Lister, 2021; Warner et al, 2021). Over the period since the insurgency began in 2017 and up to March 2021 it is estimated that 2,500 people were killed and nearly 700,000 internally displaced (Vines, 2021).

By 28 March the insurgents had departed. The attack illustrated both the increasing strength and military sophistication of the insurgents and the weakness of the Mozambique military. As Lister noted: 'no reinforcements were dispatched to defend Palma despite there being a capable force guarding the Afungi complex—about 10–15 kilometers away' (Lister, 2021: 21). That is to say, the state military in the area were concentrated at the TotalEnergies LNG plant and seemed apparently reluctant to move quickly to the defence of the local civilian population and it was not until four days later (28 March) that an effective counter-attack was launched. In this the Mozambique government forces were heavily dependent on the participation of private military, notably a small South African mercenary group, the Dyck Advisory Group (DAG) (of which more presently) and another well-established PMC, Control Risks, which also provided security services to the gas extraction TNCs (Mosse, 2021). TotalEnergies also evacuated most of its staff from the Afungi facilities, effectively calling a halt to the whole gas operation (Hill et al, 2021) with severe consequences for the economy of the whole country. There was indeed speculation that TotalEnergies would shift activities to South Africa (Lister, 2021: 25).

The fragmenting assemblage

The particular conflict in Mozambique in March 2021, although part of a wider ongoing regional conflict evident since 2017, illustrates how different parts of the 'assemblage' pull in different directions largely to the detriment of the mass of the population. 'Private security companies protect the gas installations, mercenaries back the government, and Islamist militants back the insurgents – turning this into a war in which wealthy individuals and institutions are protected, and the poor suffer even more' (Hanlon, 2020).

TotalEnergies

To begin with the French TNC TotalEnergies. The company was naturally anxious to guarantee the security of its LNG extraction assets. The company, together with other extraction TNCs operating in the locality, deployed a variety of private security companies to protect its premises (Feller, 2021). But for defence against the mounting ISIS-inspired Al-Shabaab insurgency it looked naturally in the first instance to the Mozambique government which had invited it to develop LNG extraction in Cabo Delgado. The company was concerned about the weakness of the state military in terms of adequacy of equipment and training in the face of the insurgency. Lister quoted an expert at the time of the March 2021 incident, saying it was 'stunning that the security forces were not better prepared for such an attack and that their capabilities have not improved despite the insurgency being in its fourth year' (Lister, 2021: 21–22).

TotalEnergies sought to remedy the situation by funding the state military. In August 2020 the company signed a memorandum of understanding with the FRELIMO government concerning security for onshore and offshore LNG development which, according to the company website, 'provides that a Joint Task Force shall ensure the security of Mozambique LNG (TotalEnergies' local operation), project activities in Afungi site and across the broader area of operations of the project. Mozambique LNG shall provide logistic support to the Joint Task Force' (TotalEnergies, 2020). The result was that while 'the government units protecting Afungi are well supplied and undergo additional training' (Vines, 2021), in the opinion of several commentators national military security became skewed in the direction of TotalEnergies to the detriment of the general population. Piers Pigou of the International Crisis Group called the agreement 'a defining moment' in the 'Iraqification' of the conflict, which highlighted 'the dangers of a security approach that ironclads the green zone [i.e. the LNG facilities] and does very little for the rest of the country' (quoted by Cotterill, 2020). The Mozambique human rights NGO, Democracy and Development, said:

> [W]hen the government allows the deployment of military personnel for the protection of 'private interests in exchange for payments', it is 'privatising' the services of the defence and security forces ... even if the defence and security policy talks about the need for protection of vital interests, this should not happen in a commercial logic where the Mozambique LNG project remunerates the defence forces as if they were a private company. (Frey, 2020)

TotalEnergies claimed that the agreement provided security benefits to local communities. The problem was illustrated during the March 2021 incident where workers who had taken refuge in Palma from the insurgents were relatively ignored – the army took some time to arrive in Palma – having been presumably defending the TNC facilities. A researcher for Human Rights Watch commented that 'it is simply not fair that people who built these towns [for the gas mining companies in Cabo Delgado] see themselves ignored because the priority is to defend these big investments' (quoted in Cotterill, 2020).

The mercenaries

The inefficiency of the government military in the face of the Al-Shabaab insurgency, together with the effective diversion of the better trained elements to the specific needs of the TNC, left the state with the police as its main agency for general security provision for the population as a whole. The government had been reluctant to call direct military assistance from other states – either regional or global – fearing that this would portray Mozambique as a 'failed state' (see Cotterill, 2021). Nevertheless it was clear that a 'request for assistance' from outside Mozambique was necessary. As with Nigeria and the fight against Boko Haram a few years earlier, Mozambique fought the Al-Shabaab insurgency during 2021 with the help of White-led South African mercenaries. In 2019, as the insurgency intensified, the FRELIMO government had initially turned to the shadowy Russian Wagner PMC, which has substantial interventions in Africa. But the PMC proved to be a spectacular failure at the type of bush guerrilla warfare characteristic of the region and did not collaborate well with local Mozambique military (Sauer, 2019; Balestrieri, 2020). So Mozambique repeated the Nigerian strategy and turned to mercenaries whose origins lay in apartheid-era South Africa and Rhodesia.

The main subcontractor was the DAG, a South African organization led by Lionel Dyck, a veteran of Rhodesian special forces who, unlike many White military, had stayed with the new Zimbabwe army as a paratroop officer. DAG was originally a shoestring operation with three helicopters and 30 men armed mainly with sniper rifles (Thornycroft, 2020). There were also issues concerning the legality of DAG under recent South African legislation such as the Prohibition of Mercenary Activities Act of 2006. Nevertheless in 2020 the operation was expanded.

There are two issues arising from the activities of DAG. The first is human rights violations. Amnesty International, in an investigation of the conduct of the various parties to the conflict in 2021, reported that:

> [L]ocal residents said they personally observed DAG helicopters and light aircraft direct machine gun fire at civilian infrastructure, including hospitals, schools, and homes made of mud and thatch. ... In a broad pattern reflected in multiple engagements, witnesses consistently said the helicopters fired indiscriminately into crowds, or dropped ordnance, without distinguishing between combatants and civilians. (Amnesty International, 2021: 17)

DAG did agree to employ independent lawyers to investigate the allegations (Reuters, 2021). Nevertheless the employment of mercenaries in a front-line combat role, particularly if not integrated firmly into the state military chain of command, involves a lack of control over their conduct of hostilities. DAG's behaviour may also of course be a result of a lack of concern with the protection of the civilian population, a throwback to the colonial apartheid-era origins of this particular mercenary group. However, brutal human rights violations and war crimes were documented by the same Amnesty report also in the case of the Mozambique military. These included 'attempted beheading, torture and other ill-treatment of prisoners; the dismemberment of alleged Al-Shabaab fighters; possible extrajudicial executions; and the transport and discarding of a large number of corpses into apparent mass graves' (Amnesty International, 2021: 14). Indeed, there may also have been, as in Iraq and Afghanistan, a mutual reinforcement process whereby 'the military leads the way and lays down the parameters of acceptable behaviour in similar situations for the private sector' (Fitzgibbon and Lea, 2020: 69).

The second issue is the increasingly 'geriatric' character of the apartheid-era White-led mercenary organizations, at least as regards their leadership. Even during the earlier deployments in Nigeria, commentators were questioning the continued relevance of this type of old-fashioned mercenary 'soldiers of fortune' in future conflicts in the region (Smith, 2016). If private military force is to continue to operate in the region then it will be provided by others.

Finally, it comes as no surprise that the insurgents themselves, Al-Shabaab, inspired by and with links to ISIS, should engage in widespread violations of human rights and international humanitarian law. The treatment of the local civilian population by the insurgents was brutal and clearly amounted to a war crime. It included, according to Amnesty International, 'that those civilian men who fought back against Al-Shabaab were "beheaded" and "chopped"

'... the first being a simple decapitation, the second imitating the quartering of an animal during butchering' (Amnesty International, 2021: 12).

The future of private warfare

Following the Palma events the Mozambique government came to accept that it needed to 'look beyond private contractors for effective counterinsurgency operations' (Vines, 2021). But dispensing with the private sector was difficult for a number of reasons. First, an important characteristic of the White-led mercenary outfits was their competence as front-line combatants familiar with the warfare and terrain of the region. External military assistance was forthcoming in 2021 taking the form of special forces from official South African and major Western militaries – US, UK, and Portugal – later joined by the EU as a whole. However, these contingents have mainly restricted themselves to training activities (EURACTIV/AFP, 2021). Similar training contributions have been provided by more conventional PMCs (that is, not involved directly in combat) such as Paramount and Burnham Global (Zitamar News, 2021). Some of this activity is being financed by TotalEnergies.

Furthermore, there are obstacles to increasing military aid, particularly from major states of the global North. While there is certainly concern about the spread of ISIS-led insurgencies in the Sahel and further south, a reluctance to provide military assistance, beyond the supply of equipment, training and advice, is attributable to the state of public opinion. In the receiving African countries there is a degree of public sensitivity concerning former colonial powers, such as France and Portugal, sending large contingents of front-line troops to the region (see Pilling, 2021). Meanwhile there is considerable public reluctance in both the United States and the European former colonial powers to support open-ended military commitments which produce casualties but little discernible progress. Sufficient war-weariness on the part of the American public prompted US president Biden's precipitate withdrawal from Afghanistan in August 2021 – already presaged by the policies of his predecessor, Trump. Shortly afterwards, in September, France announced the withdrawal of half its force of 5,000 troops which had been in Mali since 2013 as part of 'Operation Barkhane', against local ISIS-linked insurgents. These withdrawals of combat troops and downgrading to training missions left two alternatives for Mali, Mozambique and other African states fighting ISIS-inspired insurgencies.

The first option was assistance from those African states with strong military forces. For Mozambique, significant aid came in the form of 1,000 soldiers and paramilitary police from Rwanda who, during August 2021, 'achieved in weeks what Mozambican and other forces had been unable to do in years' (Schipani, 2021). The Al-Shabaab insurgency is, for the moment, contained and there is hope that TotalEnergies will resume LNG extraction operations.

Meanwhile in Mali, following the French downsizing, a second alternative has emerged with the government reportedly in the process of negotiating (as of September 2021) a contract with the Wagner PMC (Nichols, 2021). Despite its earlier problems in Mozambique, noted earlier, Wagner is one of the largest PMCs operating in Africa and is reportedly active in around 20 African states (Scorpio, 2019) as well as the Middle East. Owned by Yevgeny Prigozhin, a close friend of Vladimir Putin, Wagner is arguably the most modern iteration of the mercenary/PMC in that, in the African context, it straddles the division between the apartheid-era mercenaries of dubious provenance but skilled at front-line combat, and the 'legitimate' PMCs employed by Western militaries, particularly in Iraq and Afghanistan, oriented more to logistics and guarding. It is a complete private army which can substitute effectively for a state military – which is why there is a suspicion that this is precisely what it is – the Russian army by any other name (see Marten, 2020). Indeed, in December 2021 key EU states, including Germany, 'deeply regretted' the contract signed by Mali with Wagner and placed a question mark over their own military training missions in Mali (Kurmayer, 2022). Meanwhile Sean McFate reports an encounter between US regular military and Wagner forces in Syria where 'it took America's most elite troops and advanced aircraft four hours to repel 500 mercenaries. What happens when non-elite troops must face 1000? 5000? More? Annihilation, most likely' (McFate, 2020: 4).

Although writing well before the Ukraine conflict erupted into open warfare in 2022 McFate in effect underlines the capacity of Wagner to act effectively in a diversity of scenarios. On the one hand, with 'the world's most powerful nations ... once again competing for the control of the abundant natural resources of the African continent' (Adam, 2018), the future of private military seems assured. It enables competing states to keep their military interventions at a 'deniable distance'. Meanwhile African governments in receipt of such assistance can avoid appearing as the direct vassals of one or other of the major powers. In this context the 'Wagner model' has much in its favour. It is, as we have argued, becoming a key state military resource in conflicts in sub-Saharan Africa. At the same time Wagner seems equally at home in the industrial warfare of the global North. Recent reports from the Ukraine, with all the admitted limitations of front-line journalism, indicate Wager mercenaries are well integrated into Russian military front-line operations, much in the manner of classic mercenary deployment in European wars of past centuries (BBC, 2022; Kim, 2022).

References

Abrahamsen, R. and Williams, M.C. (2017) Golden assemblages: Security and development in Tanzania's gold mines, in P. Higate and M. Utas (eds) *Private Security in Africa: From the Global Assemblage to the Everyday. Africa Now*. London: Zed Books, pp 15–31.

Adam, A. (2018) Are we witnessing a 'new scramble for Africa'? *Al Jazeera*, 27 March. Available from: www.aljazeera.com/opinions/2018/3/27/are-we-witnessing-a-new-scramble-for-africa [Accessed 17 October 2021].

Ahmed, K. (2020) How did a 'cocktail of violence' engulf Mozambique's gemstone El Dorado? *Guardian*, 18 September.

Amnesty International (2017) *Nigeria: A Criminal Enterprise? Shell's Involvement in Human Rights Violations in Nigeria in the 1990s*. London: Amnesty International.

Amnesty International (2021) *'What I Saw Is Death': War Crimes in Mozambique's Forgotten Cape*. London: Amnesty International.

Amunwa, B. and Minio, M. (2011) *Counting the Cost: Corporations and Human Rights Abuses in the Niger Delta*. London: Platform.

Balestrieri, S. (2020) Wagner Group: Russian mercenaries still foundering in Africa. Available from: sofrep.com/news/wagner-group-russian-mercenaries-still-foundering-in-africa/ [Accessed 12 October 2021].

Bayley, B. (2016) What does Nigeria's use of private military companies against Boko Haram mean for the world? *Vice*. Available at: www.vice.com/en_us/article/exqe9z/nigeria-pmcs-boko-harem [Accessed 6 December 2017].

BBC (2022) What is Russia's Wagner Group of mercenaries in Ukraine? *BBC News*, 5 April. Available from: www.bbc.co.uk/news/world-60947877 [Accessed 3 June 2022].

Cotterill, J. (2020) French oil group Total steps up security co-operation with Mozambique. *Financial Times*, 3 September.

Cotterill, J. (2021) Mozambique looks to private sector in war against Islamists. *Financial Times*, 15 March.

EURACTIV/AFP (2021) EU begins military training against Mozambique insurgency. Available from: www.euractiv.com/section/global-europe/news/eu-begins-military-training-against-mozambique-insurgency/ [Accessed 11 November 2021].

Feller, G. (2021) An overview of foreign security involvement in Mozambique. *Defense Web*. Available from: www.defenceweb.co.za/featured/an-overview-of-foreign-security-involvement-in-mozambique/ [Accessed 4 September 2021].

Fitzgibbon, W. and Lea, J. (2020) *Privatising Justice: The Security Industry, War and Crime Control*. London: Pluto.

Frey, A. (2020) Mozambique: NGO criticises 'privatisation of sovereignty' in government accord. *Club of Mozambique*. Available from: clubofmozambique.com/news/mozambique-ngo-criticises-privatisation-of-sovereignty-in-government-accord-170019/ [Accessed 31 March 2021].

Glanz, J. and Rubin, A.J. (2007) From errand to fatal shot to hail of fire to 17 deaths. *New York Times*, 3 October.

Gough, D.J. (2017) *The Privatisation of Violence: An Examination of Private Military and Security Contractors and Their Effect on Sovereignty and Fundamental Rights in a Globalised World*. Birmingham City University, Birmingham. Available from: www.open-access.bcu.ac.uk/6976/1/GOUGH D.J. PhD Thesis.pdf [Accessed 1 October 2022].

Hanlon, J. (2020) Mozambique: Are the drums of war silencing any hope of peace? *All Africa*, 27 July. Available from: https://allafrica.com/stories/202007270606.html [Accessed 21 November 2022].

Hanlon, J. (2021a) Imperialism and Mozambique, in I. Ness and Z. Cope (eds) *The Palgrave Encyclopedia of Imperialism and Anti-Imperialism* (2nd edition). Cham: Palgrave Macmillan, pp 1879–1888.

Hanlon, J. (2021b) Mozambique's Frelimo gambled everything on gas – and lost. *Daily Maverick*, 8 April

Hill, M., Nhamire, B. and de Beaupuy, F. (2021) Rebel attack leads Total to evacuate Mozambique LNG staff. Available from: www.worldoil.com/news/2021/3/29/rebel-attack-leads-total-to-evacuate-mozambique-lng-staff [Accessed 7 September 2021].

Hönke, J. (2013) *Transnational Companies and Security Governance: Hybrid Practices in a Postcolonial World*. Abingdon: Routledge.

Horton, A., Nakhlawi, R. and Mekhennet, S. (2022) Ukraine war volunteers are coming home, reckoning with difficult fight. *Washington Post*, 28 May.

Keen, D. (2012) *Useful Enemies: When Waging Wars Is More Important than Winning Them*. New Haven: Yale University Press.

Kim, V. (2022) What is the Wagner Group? *New York Times*, 31 March.

Kurmayer, N. (2022) Germany mulls aborting military operations in Mali. *Euractiv*. Available from: www.euractiv.com/section/politics/short_news/germany-mulls-aborting-military-operations-in-mali/ [Accessed 15 January 2022].

Lister, T. (2021) The March 2021 Palma attack and the evolving jihadi terror threat to Mozambique. *CTC Sentinel*, 14(4): 19–27.

Marten, K. (2020) *The GRU, Yevgeny Prigozhin, and Russia's Wagner Group: Malign Russian Actors and Possible U.S. Responses*. Washington, DC: US Congress.

Matsinhe, D. (2020) OP-ED: Mozambique: The forgotten people of Cabo Delgado. *Daily Maverick*, 28 May.

Mbembe, A. (2001) *On the Postcolony: Studies on the History of Society and Culture 41*. Berkeley: University of California Press.

McFate, S. (2016) America's addiction to mercenaries. *The Atlantic*. Available from: www.theatlantic.com/international/archive/2016/08/iraq-afghanistan-contractor-pentagon-obama/495731/ [Accessed 13 November 2021].

McFate, S. (2019) *Mercenaries and War: Understanding Private Armies Today*. Washington, DC: National Defense University Press.

McFate, S. (2020) *Mercenaries and Privatized Warfare Current Trends and Developments*. Geneva: The United Nations Working Group on the Use of Mercenaries.

Miller, P. (2020) *Keenie Meenie: The British Mercenaries Who Got Away with War Crimes*. London: Pluto Books.

Mosse, M. (2021) Palma almost liberated … but terrorists received reinforcements and there is again fighting in the vicinity of the town. *Carta de Moçambique*. Available from: clubofmozambique.com/news/palma-almost-liberated-but-terrorists-received-reinforcements-and-there-is-again-fighting-in-the-vicinity-of-the-town-carta-de-mocambique-188034/ [Accessed 7 September 2021].

Mullin, E. (2020) What role will mercenaries play in future warfare? An interview with Dr. Sean McFate. *NAOC*. Available from: natoassociation.ca/what-role-will-mercenaries-play-in-future-warfare-an-interview-with-dr-sean-mcfate/ [Accessed 12 October 2021].

Munshi, N. (2021) Instability in the Sahel: How a jihadi gold rush is fuelling violence in Africa. *Financial Times*, 27 June.

Murphy, R. (2016) UN peacekeeping in the Democratic Republic of the Congo and the protection of civilians. *Journal of Conflict and Security Law*, 21(2): 209–246.

Musah, A.-F. and Fayemi, K. (1999) Africa in search of security: Mercenaries and conflicts – an overview, in A.-F. Musah and K. Fayemi (eds) *Mercenaries: An African Security Dilemma*. London: Pluto Press, pp 13–42.

Nichols, M. (2021) Lavrov says Mali asked private Russian military company for help. *Reuters*, 26 September. Available from: www.reuters.com/world/africa/mali-asked-private-russian-military-firm-help-against-insurgents-ifx-2021-09-25/ [Accessed 11 November 2021].

O'Brien, K. (1999) Private military companies and African security 1990–98, in A.-F. Musah and K. Fayemi (eds) *Mercenaries: An African Security Dilemma*. London: Pluto Press, pp 43–75.

Pfotenhauer, D. (2016) The case for private contractors in northern Nigeria. *African Defence Review*. Available from: www.africandefence.net/case-for-pmcs-in-nigeria/ [Accessed 6 December 2017].

Pilling, D. (2021) Africa has quietly become the epicentre of the Islamist threat. *Financial Times*, 2 September.

Reeve, R. and Pelter, Z. (2014) *From New Frontier to New Normal: Counter-Terrorism Operations in the Sahel-Sahara*. London: Remote Control Project.

Reuters (2021) Dyck Advisory Group to investigate after Amnesty says it shot at civilians in Mozambique. *DefenceWeb*. Available from: www.defenceweb.co.za/security/national-security/south-african-company-to-investigate-after-amnesty-says-it-shot-at-civilians-in-mozambique/ [Accessed 10 September 2021].

Sauer, P. (2019) In push for Africa, Russia's Wagner mercenaries are 'out of their depth' in Mozambique. *The Moscow Times*, 19 November.

Schipani, A. (2021) Rwanda flexes muscles in fight against terror in Mozambique. *Financial Times*, 3 October.

Scorpio (2019) Russia's shadow presence in Africa: Wagner group mercenaries in at least 20 countries aim to turn continent into strategic hub. *Daily Maverick*, 15 November.

Smith, M. (2016) *Boko Haram: Inside Nigeria's UnHoly War*. London: I.B. Tauris.

Soufan Center (2022) *Foreign Fighters, Volunteers, and Mercenaries: Non-State Actors and Narratives in Ukraine*. New York: Soufan Center.

Thornycroft, P. (2020) Anti-poaching squad drives insurgents out of northern Mozambique with snipers and helicopters. *The Telegraph*, 9 June.

TotalEnergies (2020) Total signs agreement with the government of Mozambique regarding the security of Mozambique lng project. Available from: www.total.com/media/news/press-releases/total-signs-agreement-government-mozambique-regarding-security-mozambique [Accessed 31 March 2021].

UNSC (2021) Twenty-eighth report of the Analytical Support and Sanctions Monitoring Team submitted pursuant to resolution 2368 (2017) concerning ISIL (Da'esh), Al-Qaida and associated individuals and entities. S/2021/655. United Nations Security Council. Available from: https://www.securitycouncilreport.org/atf/cf/%7B65BFCF9B-6D27-4E9C-8CD3-CF6E4FF96FF9%7D/S_2021_655_E.pdf [Accessed 21 November 2022].

Varin, C. (2015) Why Nigeria is turning to South African mercenaries to help fight Boko Haram. *The Conversation*. Available from: theconversation.com/why-nigeria-is-turning-to-south-african-mercenaries-to-help-fight-boko-haram-38948 [Accessed 16 October 2021].

Vines, A. (2021) Lessons from Palma attack: What next for the insurgency in Cabo Delgado? *The Mail & Guardian*, 4 April.

Warner, J., Cummings, R. and O'Farrell, R. (2021) *The Islamic State in Africa: The Emergence, Evolution, and Future of the Next Jihadist Battlefront*. London: Hurst & Co.

Wrigley, C. (1999) *The Privatisation of Violence: New Mercenaries and the State*. London: Campaign Against Arms Trade. Available from: www.caat.org.uk/resources/publications/government/mercenaries-1999 [Accessed 7 March 2020].

Zitamar News (2021) DAG mercenaries to leave Cabo Delgado in April as Mozambique's military takes over. *Zitmar News*. Available from: zitamar.com/dag-mercenaries-to-leave-cabo-delgado-in-april-as-mozambiques-military-takes-over/ [Accessed 10 September 2021].

17

Distant Conflicts, Southern Deaths: The Trials of Neoliberal Internationalism in 'Southern Nowhere'

Peter Squires

Introduction

> We're God knows where, out in the desert, in the middle of fucking nowhere ... rattling around in the back of our Warrior as the RPGs and machine gun fire rattle in. (Wood, 2019: 3)

Discussing the wars in Iraq and Afghanistan, Derek Gregory (2004: 11) assesses the imperial legacy they embody. He suggests that the 'War on Terror' marks 'a violent return of the colonial past, with its split geographies of "us" and "them", "civilisation" and "barbarism", "good" and "evil"'. Such categories invoke the distancing that 'otherness' has facilitated, empowering the deployment of righteous violence against those who were neither assumed to know, nor presumed to deserve, any better. Where once this violence was orchestrated by gentlemen wearing red tunics, jodhpurs and pith helmets (cited in Sanghera, 2021), more recently it arrives with camouflaged 'Dusty Warriors' scrambling from the back of armoured personnel carriers (Holmes, 2007). One may be tempted to suggest that, in other respects, little has changed since these very same regions were contested in the 19th and early 20th centuries as empires fought over territories, drew lines in the sand (Barr, 2012) and the British, in particular, sought to protect overland routes (and, later, oil – Barr, 2019) from Russian and Turkish incursion, to India, the supposed 'jewel' in its imperial crown (Satia, 2008). For indeed, as we have seen in earlier chapters in this collection, and as a host of revisionist historical scholarship has confirmed, violence and conflict – either the military violence of warfare, genocide or massacre, or the economic violence of dispossession, enslavement and exploitation – were irretrievably enmeshed within the experience of empire (Walter, 2017). This might be the initial violence of discovery and conquest (Callwell, 1896/1996; Gott, 2011), the normalization of imperial expansion and daily rule (Dwyer and Nettelbeck, 2018; Muschalek, 2019) or the bloody struggles of withdrawal and emancipation (Elkins, 2005; Thomas, 2012).

And yet, as has been argued (see Chapter 2, this volume) the ruling narrative story is also one of increasing regulation, sometimes referred to as the 'liberal paradox of empire' (Dwyer and Nettelbeck, 2018; Andrews, 2021) or even of 'liberal militarism'. This argument reflects what Neocleous refers to as 'one of liberalism's major myths ... that capitalism and peace go hand in hand, that law and the state exist in order to realize this "liberal peace" within society, and that international law exists to ensure peace between states' (Neocleous, 2014: 7). On this view, crime, conflict and violence are represented as something *outside* of liberal order, threats to be contained or eliminated. As is clear, only a profound forgetfulness about the violent origins of empire (playing much the same role as the myth of 'social contract') can sustain this viewpoint. The 'liberal paradox' poses the issue that, even if the early years of colonial expansion were driven by imperatives of conquest and exploitation – including slavery – imperialism eventually conferred many, some might say, *compensatory*, benefits. 'Civilization' and Christianity may have been among the earliest, but also education, law, railways, an expansion of trade, rising living standards, even democracy. These issues are hotly contested, however, and although not directly the chief focus of this chapter, empiricist-minded critics, pointing to the continued poverty, inequality and economic underdevelopment of many former colonized states and regions, have argued that the benefits of colonization have often been rather thinly and selectively spread, tending to compound and intensify inequalities and racialized hierarchies. At other times where colonized societies were incorporated into globalized trading networks, it was often under only extremely unfavourable terms. Countries and regions were exploited for raw materials, their economies distorted and dominated by 'primitive accumulation' practices and primary extractive industries (mining, logging, food production), the commercialization of agriculture (see Chapter 15, this volume) and by the dispossession of peasants and small farmers. Their economies are often weighed down by servicing huge debts while employment opportunities tend to be restricted to semi- and unskilled work in the aforementioned sectors with few opportunities for advancement. Opportunities for women are often even more restricted except in sectors and regions where a low-paid, seemingly pliable and dispensable, workforce is required – the *maquiladora* assembly plants in Mexico and other parts of

Central America (favoured by lower tariffs and duties, in this case the North American Free Trade Agreement [NAFTA], permitting the relocation of production in order to drive down labour costs (Broughton, 2015) are perhaps among the better known examples (Vulliamy, 2011).

Marikana: primitive accumulation and political violence

More critical commentators make the point that the economic exploitation of both peoples and national resources (via dispossession, forced migration and restrictive laws governing trade unions and Indigenous activism) are themselves a form of structural violence frequently aided by tough paramilitary policing, and severe clampdowns on protest and opposition (see Chapter 14, this volume). An incident, on 16 August 2012, illustrates this point. At the Marikana platinum mine in South Africa, the scene of an 'unofficial' wildcat strike by miners, 34 miners were shot dead (and 78 injured) by the South African Police Service (SAPS). A wave of strikes protesting about pay, health and safety and working conditions had broken out earlier in the year although the mining company (Lonmin) had declined to meet with *non-recognized* rival union negotiators. The shooting was the most lethal police confrontation since the ending of apartheid with unfavourable comparisons drawn with the Soweto (1976 – up to 700 feared killed, many of them children) and Sharpeville (1960 – 69 killed) police mass shootings. Brogden and Shearing (1993) have argued that, for many years under apartheid the South African police force had largely deluded itself that it 'successfully managed situations of conflict ... with minimum use of force' (De Witt, cited in Brogden and Shearing, 1993: 17). By contrast, they argue, in public order management incidents, the SAPS has quickly 'resorted to the type of weaponry characteristic of military rather than police action, often against essentially unarmed or retreating crowds ... [and] there has rarely been effective judicial condemnation' (Brogden and Shearing, 1993: 18).

Nevertheless, opinions were divided following the 2016 publication of the Report of the Commission of Inquiry into the Marikana shootings (Marikana Commission of Inquiry, 2016). While the report criticized the actions of the company, apparently colluding with the police to break the strike, it criticized the strikers themselves for confronting the police with a variety of weapons. However, contrary to evidence suggesting that the police were primarily responsible for the deaths (AMCU, 2014), the Commission produced a narrative judgement, distributing responsibility around the various parties involved. The police were found to have failed on a number of fronts: succumbing to political and company pressure in adopting inappropriately confrontational tactics, lacking a plan for the incident, and lacking clear public order management capacity or effective leadership. A later review of the case by the Institute for Security Studies argued that:

> [T]he critical factor was that senior leaders of the SAPS were *partisan* in relation to the conflict. [But] … they did not know that [politicians] had put pressure on Lonmin not to reach a compromise with the strikers … the senior leaders of the SAPS had started coming under political pressure to deal with the conflict at Marikana in a *decisive* way. (Bruce, 2016: 49, emphasis added)

The Commission noted that 'the measures at the disposal of Public Order Policing are completely inadequate for the purposes of dealing with crowds, armed as they were, with sharp weapons and firearms' (2016: 547). However, it continued, 'automatic rifles like the R5 have no place in public order policing … military assault weapons have no place in law enforcement'. An immediate withdrawal of the R5 assault rifle was recommended, with the proviso that 'any replacement weapon system should not be capable of "automatic fire" mode' (Commission of Inquiry, 2016: 547). Ultimately, the Commission's findings fell short of holding the SAPS wholly responsible for the shootings and it then passed responsibility to the Director of Public Prosecutions 'with a view to ascertaining criminal liability on the part of all members of the South African Police Services who were involved' (2016: 546). Of the police killings, themselves, the report noted that 'members of the South African Police Services … firing shots at the strikers, may have exceeded the bounds of self and private defence and [delayed] in conveying medical assistance', while senior officers had been lacking in their incident management. However, as of August 2020, no prosecutions had begun concerning the 34 killings on 16 August, although nine police officers had faced prosecutions relating to a series of deaths and related offences in the earlier days of the strike. Furthermore, the government had still not published a 2018 report by the Panel of Experts on Policing and Crowd Management established following recommendations of the original Commission of Inquiry (Fekethe, 2020). At the time of writing, several cases running into 2022 had still not been concluded (Khumalo, 2022).

The Marikana incident, in many respects, provides a useful illustration of the Marxist critique of the reformist 'liberal empire' thesis. The continuity with earlier police massacres under the apartheid regime suggests a policing system still deeply rooted in its racist colonial past. The complicity between government politicians, mining company chiefs and police leaders indicate that policing goals and tactics were selected to prioritize a series of economic and political interests, irrespective of law and accountability, culminating in the illegal use of excessive force (Bruce, 2016). Despite police reform and the overwhelmingly African makeup of the attending police, the SAPS were performing precisely the same role they always had – performing it in near identical ways, safeguarding 'security, order and accumulation' (Neocleous, 2014: 13). Neocleous' argument sees warfare and policing as seamlessly interlinked activities, the military arm securing population conquest and the incorporation of territory – or colonialism – and the policing arm achieving continued 'pacification' of Indigenous peoples. What Neocleous calls 'war power' and 'police power' are formed of the same imperatives and a capacity for violence was essential to both: 'we need to think of war and police as processes working in conjunction as state power' (Neocleous, 2014: 13). Yet just as differing regimes of accumulation have their own characteristics and modes of being, feudalism replaced by capitalism and private property, slavery overtaken by free labour markets, welfare capitalism by liquid, neoliberal international finance, inefficient production by more efficient (profitable, economic) systems, so policing – or more broadly *legal regulation* – adapts accordingly.

Regulating empire: towards a methodology

Criminal justice historian Martin Wiener provides an intriguing illustration of the evolution of law and policing in his study of mixed race murder adjudications around the British Empire between 1870 and 1935 (Wiener, 2009). His study takes in India, Queensland, Australia, Fiji, Trinidad and the Bahamas, Kenya and British Honduras and proceeds to explore what we have already encountered as a profound contradiction of empire. While the empire came to be justified as 'a benevolent liberating mission to many millions of Asians, Africans, and other non-Europeans enslaved by ignorance, oppressive traditions, and misrule, it depended at the same time upon the subordination of these millions to the authority of the small ruling British elite' (Wiener, 2009: 1). And while 'the single most important exemplar of the claimed beneficence of the Empire was its system of laws', in particular the 'equality of individuals' before the law and the entitlement of all to its protection, in many of the distant outposts of Empire this principle was routinely overlooked in practice. The 'most basic working principle of Empire' was inequality and next came violence. 'White on "coloured" violence was ingrained in the everyday life of Empire' (Wiener, 2009: 7). White elites and settlers could abuse and maltreat their servants and employees, punish, whip, rape and rob them, sometimes killing Indigenous persons with apparent impunity or quite realistic expectations of acquittal or leniency (Wiener, 2009: 1–2). 'Beating of servants was frequent and unremarkable, only reaching the courts (and not always even then) if a victim died' (Wiener, 2009: 7), it was not uncommon for small fines only to be levied against those guilty of employee homicide (Wiener, 2009: 145), while 'the charge of rape was almost never brought against Europeans' even though compensation might sometimes be paid to families or husbands (Wiener, 2009: 165). Settlers were often the worst (although soldiers often presented particular problems of drunkenness, violence and indiscipline, especially in India [Wiener, 2009: 138–139]). Settlers were typically the lowest of the colonial White 'elite' and often the closest associates of Indigenous people who they forcibly employed and exploited, frequently abused and overworked, and whose lands they coveted and sometimes stole and yet, from whom, instant deference was expected. In such colonial contexts riven by deep divisions of class and race, interracial murder trials provided a fascinating test case of the entanglements of culture, context and law.

Over the period covered by Wiener's study, the Colonial Office in London sought to encourage due process and adherence to principles of justice in matters of legal administration, despatching reforming Attorney Generals and Judges to distant parts of the empire, only to receive complaints and petitions from colonists and settlers where they reached verdicts disapproved of by local White interests, curbing the excesses of White brutality, or rendered verdicts which were thought to impinge upon the economic profitability of the colony – for instance, banning the flogging of female employees or conspiring in the de facto reintroduction of slavery or forced labour. Judges regarded as sympathetic to native rights sometimes had to be removed after vociferous protests filtered back to London. Settlers frequently demanded such concessions to assist in their presumed prerogative to run their affairs as they saw fit, treat their natives as they thought best or secure help from the army in order to summarily remove Indigenous peoples from good quality land so that settlers might expand their farms and plantations (or at least that the military not interfere to stop them doing this) (Wiener, 2009: 206). Back in London, Wiener cites evidence to suggest that Colonial Office officials and London politicians often considered settlers 'agents of their own misfortune', their belligerent attitudes fostering discontent and resistance among Indigenous peoples and thereby demanding larger police and security establishments (Wiener, 2009: 196n9). Elsewhere, it was noted that 'it is quite impossible to rule an English colony on upright principles' (Wiener, 2009: 125).

In many ways, Wiener's detailed historical study bears out the conquest/pacification sequence of empire building described by Neocleous (2014), the deft slippage between war power and police power. As Wiener notes: 'The frontier war had to be won before the law could operate throughout the colony, [only] in the wake of the establishment of "order", "law" could come into its own' (2009: 43, 69–70). Later, as the British (and other European powers) began to disengage from empire, often in the face of local resistance and developing insurgency movements, rising levels of violent conflict prompted a profound militarization of colonial police departments, new tactics and equipment (water-cannon, armoured vehicles, specialist riot squads) and new divisions of responsibility between the civil and military authorities (Anderson and Killingray, 1992; Elkins, 2005; Thomas, 2012). Alongside these there emerged a new police-military security doctrine, 'low intensity operations' (Kitson, 1971), a doctrine subsequently deployed in Northern Ireland (Burke, 2021). Although Kitson's strategies were lauded by empire loyalists and military authorities alike, Arquilla's judgement appears the more enduring. 'Kitson's many campaigns, taken together, seem to constitute a mad Arthurian quest to shore up a tottering empire' (Arquilla, 2011: 225), characterized more by violence and disorder than the rule of law, he argued.

As Wiener and many others have argued, violence was routine and endemic to the daily life of empire (see Chapter 2, this volume, for a wider literature). The phases of conquest and withdrawal, beginnings and endings, often coincided with the most appalling massacres (Hale, 2013). Gott (2011) and Newsinger (2006) catalogue many such incidents where, rather than police 'minimum force' and 'peace-keeping', notions such as 'punitive expeditions', 'search and destroy' missions or 'exemplary punitive force' better account for the actions which targeted entire populations (Bennett, 2014: 90). Given the troubled colonial context of conflict, economic pressures, racial divisions and consolidated animosities cultivated over many years, colonized societies could be exceedingly fractious. A collective experience of daily slights, indignities, inequalities and abuses invariably magnified by the arrogant disdain with which White elites often viewed 'natives', compounded by the overwhelming power and authority of the latter, implied that violence was never far from the surface. Accordingly, history throws up many examples of neocolonial injustice involving atrocities occasioned when 'pacification' warped into unreasonable and lethal force against civilians in conflict settings. In addition to those already referred to in this chapter, examples might include Wounded Knee (South Dakota, USA, 1890), Amritsar (India, 1919), the Tulsa Race massacre (Oklahoma, USA, 1921), Batang Kali (Malaysia, 1948), Mueda (Mozambique, 1960), My Lai (Vietnam, 1968) and Derry (Northern Ireland, 1972), among the most well known.

Yet even more recently, during the military 'peacekeeping' operations in Afghanistan and Iraq there have likewise been a large number of abuse allegations, including several major investigations and inquiries into alleged unjustified killings and human rights abuses by deployed military personnel. In the remainder of this chapter, pursuant to our concern with Southern violence in neoliberal imperialist 'peacekeeping operations', the deployment of war power as state strategy (Neocleous, 2014), or 'policing wars' and the practice of *policing* military conduct (Holmqvist, 2014), these incidents will now be our focus.

Combat as a crime scene? Regulating the ethical battlefield

In reviewing these events our aim is certainly not to re-try the ways in which incidents have been resolved or concluded. Extensive inquiries, running to many thousands of pages or prolonged court cases, often followed by appeals, have already settled many of the issues, although often only after many years of arguing, lobbying and pressure for the release of 'restricted' official documents – some of which never have been released. On the other hand, the very nature of the wars in Iraq and Afghanistan, with journalists 'embedded' with military units, a political strategy in itself (Pfau et al, 2005a, 2005b), and saturation media coverage in 24-hour, non-stop rolling new bulletins have meant that these conflicts have been more exposed to media audiences than any previous conflicts. Nor are we aiming to judge or second-guess the actions of soldiers under live-firing, life-threatening battlefield situations. Soldiers facing legal questioning in the wake of abuse allegations have sometimes described the disconcerting experience of having to recall and justify decisions taken many years earlier, sometimes in the midst of fire-fights.

> An infantry soldier is trained to close with and destroy the enemy ... these were enemy fighters we were dealing with. ... In the situation you don't mess about, your body is filled with adrenaline, you feel totally pumped. And when you are fighting for your life you'll do what it takes to make sure you stay alive. The situation ... was one of chaos ... we did our best in circumstances that were chaotic and messy. That should be enough, you shouldn't have your split second life or death decisions picked apart. (Wood, 2019: 227–229)

Yet in some of the cases which we will discuss in what follows it is equally apparent that many of the targeted victims were manifestly *not* enemy combatants, as military spokespersons will often claim, but innocent civilians, including women and children.[1] And finally, as we shall see, there were issues of memory and post-traumatic stress disorder (PTSD), questions about strategy and tactics, training and equipment, misgivings about the supportiveness of military hierarchies, and personal issues to contend with (Lorenzo, 2014). Rather than castigate individuals, however (although in some cases this may have been an entirely legitimate response), our aim is to reflect upon the attempted regulation of (unwarranted) military violence deployed in both warfare and peacekeeping operations, all the time recognizing that the combination of both 'empire' and 'wartime' have, throughout history, proven to be exceptionally crimogenic contexts (DiPietro, 2016; McGarry and Walklate, 2019).

In 2005 in Haditha, Iraq, US marines killed 24 unarmed Iraqi civilians. Women and children were among those killed, many shot at close range. Although the military initially attributed the killings to shrapnel from a roadside bomb, this attempted cover up quickly collapsed when the bodies were examined. No shrapnel was found; the deaths all resulted from rifle fire. A nine-year-old Iraqi girl, Eman, witnessed the killings and was interviewed by *Time* magazine:

> 'A big noise woke us all up, then we heard a lot of shooting [then] the marines entered the house, shouting in English ... they went into my father's room and we heard shots.' The marines then entered the living room. 'I couldn't see their faces very well – only their guns sticking into the doorway. I watched them shoot my grandfather, first in the chest and then in the head. Then they killed my granny.' [Next] the troops started firing toward the corner of the room where she and her younger brother were hiding; other adults shielded the children from the bullets but died in the process. Eman says her leg was hit by a piece of metal and her brother was shot near his shoulder. (Goldenberg, 2006)

Eight marines were subsequently charged in relation to the incident and three officers were accused of failing to conduct a proper investigation into the incident, but in due course all the more serious charges were dropped. Only one marine eventually had to face court martial for 'negligent dereliction of duty', and his penalty involved reduction in rank and a pay cut. In the wake of the incident, the US military leaders announced that troop commanders had been instructed 'to conduct core warrior values training, highlighting the importance of adhering to legal, moral and ethical standards on the battlefield' (Coker, 2007: 133). Whether this represents 'rearguard ethics' or a further step towards the ethical battlefield remains to be seen. Military researchers have often reported symptoms of combat euphoria and joy in killing – or maybe just survival. Troops in basic training were routinely encouraged to psych themselves up to kill and show their 'screaming war face', while bayonet drill especially was designed to put steel in the soul of the soldier (Bourke, 2015). How effective the new ethical training was might be gleaned from the following incidents.

In March the following year, five American soldiers took part in a home invasion near the town of Al-Mahmudiyah in which four members of an Iraqi family were killed. The 14-year-old daughter of the household was first raped by three of the men and then killed. The soldiers attempted to cover up their crimes by setting fire to the bodies, but this drew the attention of neighbours who found the bodies and reported the incident. However, the crimes only became known to US military authorities three months later when a colleague of the four men effectively became a whistleblower and, risking retribution from his colleagues, reported what he had overheard. The four men who perpetrated the killings were later convicted and given long sentences in Fort Leavenworth. The alleged ringleader, Steven Green, died following a suicide attempt in 2014. Something of the closed and toxic military culture was exposed when an interview with Green was published in the *Washington Post*:

> I came over here because I wanted to kill people. ... [But] the truth is, it wasn't all I thought it was cracked up to be. I mean, I thought killing somebody would be this life-changing experience. And then I did it, and I was like, 'All right, whatever.' I shot a guy who wouldn't stop when we were out at a traffic checkpoint and it was like nothing. Over here, killing people is like squashing an ant. I mean, you kill somebody and it's like 'All right, let's go get some pizza'. (Quoted in Tilghman, 2006)

Many of Green's fellow soldiers knew of his violent and sexual inclinations, and a number were disciplined and discharged for helping him conceal evidence. American military attitudes and behaviour strikingly similar to those expressed by Green have been reported elsewhere and in earlier times. Fitzgibbon and Lea (2020: 69) cite Ethan McCord, an Iraq veteran, who described a new standard operating procedure (SOP) advocated by his battalion commander:

> 'We had a pretty gung-ho commander, he decided that because we were getting hit by IEDs [improvised explosive devices] a lot, there would be a new battalion SOP. He goes, "If someone in your line gets hit with an IED, 360 rotational fire. You kill every motherfucker on the street." McCord went on to remark that 'a lot of other soldiers were just sitting there looking at each other like, "Are you kidding me? You want us to kill women and children on the street?" And you couldn't just disobey orders to shoot, because they could just make your life hell in Iraq. So like with myself, I would shoot up into the roof of a building instead of down on the ground toward civilians. But I've seen it many times, where people are just walking down the street and an IED goes off and the troops open fire and kill them.' (Lopez, 2010: np)

A mere three days following the home invasion, US troops were accused of rounding up Iraqi citizens in Ishaqi, a town just north of Baghdad, first handcuffing them and then shooting them in the head. Victims included five children and four women and, in order to conceal their crimes, the soldiers then called in an airstrike to destroy the house. US military authorities first denied the incident, but later were forced to investigate when information about the incident was discovered in State Department communications published by WikiLeaks (BBC News, 2006; Elliott, 2011).

The aforementioned incidents perpetrated by US coalition troops in Iraq and Afghanistan, were it not for the ensuing cover-ups and obfuscation attempts, might conceivably be attributed to rogue and undisciplined individuals and groups – in other words, 'bad apples'. Unfortunately, the analysis we have been pursuing so far has focused upon the potent combination of military culture, armed masculine power, the impunity of conquering empire and a racialized disrespect for 'natives' or civilians. This tends to bring the practice of violent human rights abuse closer to the terrain of institutional policy, and de facto standard practice, than occasional aberration. A series of air strikes during 2004 and 2008, in Mukaradeeb, Iraq, and the Nangarhar and Kandahar Provinces, in Afghanistan, during which a number of wedding parties or processions were hit, rather confirm an official reluctance to differentiate between insurgent and civilian targets. One hundred and fifty two people, in total, were killed, including a large number of women and children although, following an inquiry, only *one* of the targets was said to contain insurgent militia fighters (Farmer, 2008; Sturcke, 2008). The treatment of civilian casualties as mere *collateral damage* forcefully confirms Neocleous' point about the essential transformation brought to war power *as policing* by the use of air attacks and drone strikes. For despite talk of precision-targeting and 'surgical strikes', drone warfare 'looks rather like colonial warfare of the 1920s'; air force implies that there are no longer civilians, 'the distinction between the combatant ... on which the entire notion of "humanity in warfare" rests, became meaningless once air power was created' (Neocleous, 2014: 155–160). Taking the argument one step further, and reflecting upon US military responses to drone-strike massacre claims in Iraq and Afghanistan, he argues that, with the advent of seemingly indiscriminate air strike targeting in the war on terror, where anyone may be construed to be a legitimate target, the only way to reclaim civilian status is *retrospectively*, on death (Neocleous, 2014: 160–161).

A final area of concern regarding American force abuses of power concerns the roles, actions and missions of the many private military companies (PMCs) and contractors working in conjunction with coalition forces in Iraq and Afghanistan. Many PMC employees are former military and 'special forces' trained operatives. Lea (Chapter 16, this volume) describes the recent regrowth of this form of military deployment, raising issues of accountability and control (Singer, 2008 [2003]; Fitzgibbon and Lea, 2020). The significant role played by mercenaries and privateers in the early days of imperial expansion is acknowledged, in the late 18th century, when the East India Company's armed force outnumbered the British army. 'Expanding European armies relied substantially (and in some cases primarily) on forces that were neither national nor public' (Abrahamson and Williams, 2011: 11). In Iraq, one PMC, Blackwater (since 2014, renamed Constellis Holdings) gained notoriety after its personnel opened fire on unarmed Iraqi civilians in Nisour Square, Baghdad, in September, 2007, killing 17 people and seriously injuring 20 more (Scahill, 2007). The shooting started as a Blackwater convoy, carrying VIPs (the company's role was to provide close VIP protection and transport), encountered other traffic considered to be 'close and threatening'. Not unlike airstrike 'collateral killings' it is difficult to avoid the conclusion that what Newsinger calls Blackwater's 'shoot first and drive off culture' (Newsinger, 2016: 96) was a function of policy, or, perhaps more accurately, its *commercial contract*. Thus:

> [A] case can be made that its readiness to shoot at Iraqis on suspicion was in fact a commercial decision that was put into effect by means of an aggressive military culture. Clients were reassured by the knowledge that they would be protected whatever the collateral damage inflicted on the Iraqi people. (Newsinger, 2016: 96)

Fitzsimmons (2016: 5) has similarly argued that 'Blackwater's military culture motivated its personnel to fire upon suspected threats more quickly, at greater range and with a greater number of bullets. ... [Blackwater gunmen] inflicted a great deal of harm, much of this upon non-insurgents who posed little or no threat to the firm or its clients'. Following the Nisour Square shootings, the Iraqi government revoked the company's licence to operate although this was later reinstated by the Central Intelligence Agency. Congressional hearings and further civil cases followed and eventually three Blackwater employees were convicted on 14 manslaughter charges in the United States, although in 2020 they were pardoned by President Trump.

Singer has concluded that some of the 'darkest episodes of the Iraq war all involved privatized military firms', including 'allegations of overbilling and other forms of war profiteering', killings, mutilations, torture and disappearances and not forgetting the long-running Abu Ghraib prison abuse scandal 'where private military employees were reported ... to have been an integral part of the pattern of abuse' (Singer, 2008 [2003]: 248). In many ways, such routine military abuse seems broadly consistent with the violence and inhumane treatment characteristic of the end of (British) empire days in India, Malaya, Kenya, Yemen and elsewhere (Elkins, 2005, 2022; Newsinger, 2006; Wiener, 2009) although not overlooking the British Army's own serial mistreatment of detainees in Iraq and Afghanistan, even before the Baha Mousa death in custody revelations surfaced (Williams, 2012: 174, 191). As Whyte (2007) has argued, a central aspect of neoliberal hegemony building has typically entailed 'the subjugation of the norms of international law to the norms and values of the "free" market', although it is arguable that 'the institutionalisation of corruption in the Iraqi reconstruction economy' is not so much a challenge to the new neoliberal order as a key manifestation of it (Whyte, 2007: 189, 191).

While the US involvement in Iraq and Afghan 'peace-building' throws up many instances of violence, abuse and corruption, those referred to earlier being some of the better known, other coalition forces, Britain and Australia, in particular, have also had their own abuse issues. Lacking perhaps the scale and audacity of US military abuses, British and Australian cases nevertheless reveal a series of pressures and processes bringing greater regulative scrutiny and accountability to bear upon military hierarchy, the conduct of war and battlefield practices. None of the cases which follow developed without controversy as they began to subject what Wood (2019) has termed the messy chaos of combat to precise legal and ethical reflection, evidence assessment, courtroom challenge, legal testing and forensic examination.

A first case involved the death, in 2003, in a temporary military detention facility near Basra, Iraq, of a 26-year-old hotel receptionist named Baha Mousa. Along with several other men he was held for 48 hours, during which time the detainees were repeatedly tortured, beaten and interrogated in 50 degree temperatures and forced to adopt painful stress positions while hooded and handcuffed – interrogation techniques which had been prohibited since 1972 (Newbery, 2016; Bates, 2019). A post-mortem on the body found 93 separate external injuries, including ligature marks on Mousa's neck. Further internal injuries then became apparent. The pathologist confirmed that a sustained beating, 'persistent, intense, cruel and intentional', had taken place but that death had occurred as a result of positional asphyxia, a consequence of Mousa, 'weakened by the unrelenting battering, [being] forced into a posture that would have compressed his lungs to the point where he could no longer breathe, suffocating him' (Williams, 2012: 8). Four years later, the soldier chiefly responsible for inflicting the injuries and indirectly causing the death, the first British soldier ever to be convicted of a war crime, was dismissed from the army and jailed for a year. Apparently the soldier's favourite 'trick' was to beat the detainees in turn, an abuse he called 'conducting the choir' as his victims screamed in pain (Morris, 2007). Several other soldiers also on trial, including a senior officer of colonel rank, were acquitted although the trial judge had critical words for the delay in bringing the case, the 'closing of ranks' which had impeded the investigation (Gage, 2011: 1), and the non-existent supervision of the soldiers responsible for the detainees. For his part, the convicted soldier claimed that in beating the detainees he was simply maintaining the 'shock of capture', effectively 'conditioning' detainees for interrogation, which was what his superiors wanted. He felt he had been let down and scapegoated by the army and indicated that he would be willing to reveal who else had been involved in the violence.

Following the trial the army conducted its own investigation into *Cases of Deliberate Abuse and Unlawful Killing in Iraq* (Aitken, 2008). In addition to the Mousa case, it considered five other incidents, running to only 37 pages. Akam (2021: 453) suggests that the report was 'not a whitewash' but it did include the following summary observation:

> We can be assured that the great majority of officers and soldiers who have served in Iraq have done so to the highest standards of the army under extraordinarily testing conditions. There is no evidence of fundamental flaws in the army's approach to preparing for or conducting operations: we remain the envy of our allies for the professionalism of our conduct. (Aitken, 2008: 25)

Based on evidence we have addressed, so far, of American excesses, that might now seem a rather low threshold by which to judge ourselves. But worse was to come.

Later in the year, the Baha Mousa Inquiry was established under the 2005 Inquiries Act. Chaired by Sir William Gage, a former High Court judge, the Inquiry's report was published three years later in 2011; it comprised three volumes and ran to over 1,300 pages. The Inquiry considered several aspects of the evolution of military interrogation strategy, including the evolution of 'five techniques', which, supposedly banned in 1972, 'resurfaced in Iraq, thirty years later'. It looked at the specifics of Mousa's experience, explored policy, doctrine and the training of military interrogators, going on to make 73 recommendations (Bennett, 2014: 214). The inquiry uncovered relatively routine usage of racist language directed at Mousa, but rejected the notion that the violence was 'racially motivated' (Gage, 2011: 408), it argued that while the abuse was 'not an isolated incident', neither was it entrenched as a 'culture of violence' within the Battlegroup (Gage, 2011: 409). Bennett remarked, however, that there was no room for complacency that the military would learn the appropriate lessons, noting that 'the army is prone to making serious mistakes at the outset of its counter-insurgency campaigns, having to re-learn the basic principles of its own doctrine' (Bennett, 2014: 222). Based on a stream of further abuse allegations he predicted that other public inquiries would follow.

The Al Sweady Inquiry was launched in 2009, and in different respects it was both more, although, perhaps ultimately, less controversial than its predecessor, and for a while the two inquiries ran concurrently. Al Sweady was more controversial given that the allegations which emerged followed a fierce battle (the Battle of 'Danny Boy'), following an attempted ambush by Iraqi militia. The complaints alleged that non-combatants had been deliberately killed, that a number of captured detainees had been executed at the army's camp, Abu Naji, and that other detainees had been abused and ill-treated there. On the other hand (albeit rather deep into the life of the Inquiry, following a late disclosure of evidence) the wrongful death complaints were withdrawn (Forbes, 2014: 69, para 103). This left only the 'ill-treatment' allegations, which, although acknowledged as potentially serious, did not have the far-reaching implications of the other complaints. In any event, as the Inquiry ran for close on five years and was the subject of TV documentaries, a film and much media reporting (Norton-Taylor, 2014), the Inquiry findings still had explosive potential. The published report ran to over 1,200 pages, comprising the verbal testimony of 282 witnesses, a forensic scrutiny of over 8,000 documents, analysis of emails and communications transcripts, and hundreds of witness statements. The chairman concluded that 'the vast majority of the allegations made against the British military (including, without exception, all the most serious allegations), were wholly and entirely without merit or justification. Very many of those baseless allegations were the product of deliberate and calculated lies on the part of those who made them' (Forbes, 2014: 973, para 5.198). However,

> [T]he conduct of various individual soldiers and some of the procedures being followed by the British military in 2004 fell below the high standards normally to be expected of the British Army. In addition ... certain aspects of the way in which the nine Iraqi detainees ... were treated by the British military, during the time they were in British custody during 2004, amounted to actual or possible ill-treatment. (Forbes, 2014: 973, para 5.196)

By the time the Inquiry report appeared, the Iraq Historic Allegations Team (IHAT), established in 2010, had begun its work, following 149 complaints made by Iraqi detainees regarding torture and abuse while in British military custody (Cobain, 2012). IHAT's path had always been a difficult one, criticized by the military and politicians when it was accused of being too zealous in its investigations and by human rights lawyers when it appeared too close to the military establishment and little more than a 'cover-up' (Bowcott, 2012). However, one of the consequences of the collapse of the 'homicide' allegations before the Al Sweady Inquiry was a sharp uptick in public and political criticism of IHAT's activities (Shackle, 2018; Williams, 2018). Many of the cases IHAT was dealing with had been referred by the lawyers now facing censure over the Al Sweady allegations and a Defence Select Committee (Defence Committee, 2017) duly recommended that IHAT be closed down. When it ceased operation in 2017, having instigated no successful prosecutions, over 3,000 outstanding cases were largely shelved. A parallel inquiry, Operation Northmoor, involved the military police investigating some 600 offences allegedly committed by troops in Afghanistan, and this investigation was also wound down in 2017. A later report of the Defence Select Committee went on to advocate protections and a statute of limitations for military personnel potentially liable to allegations of war crimes (Defence Committee, 2019), paving the way for new government legislation (Bowcott, 2020) which became the Overseas Operations (Service Personnel and Veterans) Act, 2021.

Whether such legislation would have helped resolve the case of Sergeant Alexander Blackman (*Marine A*) who, in 2013, was found guilty of deliberately shooting a wounded Taliban fighter his section had captured, in Helmand Province, Afghanistan, is unclear. The shooting occurred during a fierce fire-fight with Taliban militia. Blackman's section was contemplating retreating but were concerned that the wounded man might both restrict their retreat and also draw the attentions of their attackers. Their deliberations were all clearly captured on a fellow marine's helmet-cam. Blackman turned back to the injured man, drawing and pointing his pistol. A report in *The Times* noted how, as he pulled the trigger, 'Blackman quoted Shakespeare': not quite. Blackman's actual words were, 'there you are, shuffle off this mortal coil, you cunt. It's nothing you wouldn't do to us.' He then turned to his comrades, adding 'obviously this doesn't go anywhere, fellas. I just broke the Geneva Convention' (Akam, 2021: 387). The video evidence was compelling; Blackman was convicted of murder, and sentenced to life imprisonment. Giving evidence, one senior officer (who later resigned his commission over the case) claimed that Blackman's company was 'out of control', violent and 'gung-ho', 'treating local allies with contempt and showing little regard for the rules of engagement'. He argued that 'some marines operating in Helmand in 2011 were guilty of dehumanising the enemy … and had been too aggressive when they were supposed to be winning hearts and minds'. Blackman was not just a 'single rotten apple' the leadership and oversight of Sergeant Blackman by his commanders 'was shockingly bad, and directly causal to his conduct' (Morris, 2017).

Blackman's case attracted considerable publicity, with veterans' associations mounting a campaign, with the support of the *Daily Mail*, for a retrial or a reprieve. Senior armed forces spokesmen voiced cautious support, both concerned for the soldier but, anxious about the repercussions, also not wishing to condone his conduct (Morris, 2017). In the event, a way around the difficulties was found. An appeal hearing held that he had been suffering PTSD, combat stress and mental disorder during the incident. The murder conviction was overturned, and replaced with manslaughter on the grounds of diminished responsibility, a reduced sentence and, on the basis of 'time served', he was quickly released. Not everyone was reassured by the new verdict although it captured many important and nuanced shifts between 'old school war-fighting' and new age 'peace-keeping'; between what many individual soldiers had trained for and aspired to do, and what the military as a whole were strategically *supposed* to be doing; and between the soldier as hero and the soldier as victim.

By contrast it was the line between soldier as hero, or soldier as villain, that emerged in an Australian case bearing many similarities with the British *Marine A* incident. Ben Roberts-Smith of the Australian Special Air Service (SAS), a holder of the Victoria Cross, was cited among a number of soldiers from the Special Operations Task Group (SOTG) deployed to Afghanistan between 2005 and 2016 said to be responsible for the killing, abuse and torture of Afghan civilians. In 2020 an Inquiry report published by the Inspector General of the Australian Defence Force (IGADF, 2020) found there to be credible evidence of 23 incidents in which 39 people were killed (and others cruelly treated) by 25 members of the SOTG. The victims, it claimed, could not reasonably be regarded as combatants, but there was credible evidence that the SOTG soldiers carried 'throwdowns' (weapons, ammunition magazines and other military equipment) to place alongside bodies to convey an impression that the dead were legitimate insurgent targets (IGADF, 2020: 29–30). Declarations from whistleblowers or informants have also suggested 'Afghan civilians were used as "target practice", that a detainee was shot when there was no room for him on a helicopter, and that special forces troops operated with a sense of impunity, elitism and recklessness' (Visontay and Knaus, 2020). Journalists from Australia's ABC News similarly reported on a violent special forces culture 'out of control' (Oakes and Clark, 2017). However, the most extreme incident, sound and vision captured on helmet-cam, revealed two Australian soldiers (one a dog-handler) pursuing an unarmed man into a wheat field. The man collapsed into the wheat and lay prone as the soldiers approached. One soldier turns to the other, 'You want me to drop this cunt?' Receiving no answer, he asks his question again, the reply is inaudible, although the soldier proceeds to fire three shots into the man at almost point-blank range. All captured on camera. Incredibly, an initial investigation by the Australian Defence Force determined the shooting to be 'in self defence' and justified (Willacy, 2020). The IGADF Inquiry report recommended that the soldiers considered responsible for the full 23 incidents should be referred to the Australian Federal Police for criminal investigation and possible prosecution.

Very late in the production process of this book, new allegations surfaced against British SAS troops (already part of the 'folklore' of the modern British military [Newsinger, 1997]) regarding field executions of 54 supposed Taliban IED bomb-makers. A *Panorama* special report ('SAS Death Squads Exposed', first broadcast in July 2022) drew clear parallels between the war crimes and abuses involving Australian Special Forces and those of the SAS. It was claimed that disarmed and restrained Afghan suspects were summarily shot during SAS 'kill or capture' missions, the soldiers clearly preferring to kill. Evidence came from former soldiers (unidentified and speaking off camera), Afghan eye-witnesses and bereaved family members, crime scene analyses and 'suspicious activity' reports circulated up the military chain of command. Some senior officers were implicated in suppressing evidence and urging the termination of enquiries (such as Operation Northmoor). While the Ministry of Defence's initial reaction was to deny the claims and question the motivations of the BBC journalists and programme-makers, at the time of writing it appears that military and Ministry of Defence officials have conceded that further investigations will now be made.

Conclusion

At the conclusion of such a catalogue of war crimes and abuses, a number of things become clear. The combination of military power, a masculine propensity to violence, peer group influences, imperial culture, racial division and presumed legal immunity in the context of conquest remain a powerfully toxic combination, when the opportunity arises. This seems as true now as in the highpoint of empire, in far-flung Southern outposts. If violence was inseparably part of empire's past, it remains no less a feature of neoliberal imperialism's conflicted present. As Williams notes in his detailed interrogation of the Baha Mousa case (2013), over the 50 preceding years 'British forces had engaged in no fewer than seventeen wars around the world [and] in each one there have been illegal killings, torture and cruel treatment committed by British forces. And in every conflict the institutional response has been ambivalent if not duplicitous' (Williams, 2012: 2). As we have noted, this tendency has not been a uniquely British pathology, but more the dark side of military power itself.

In recent years mental stresses and PTSD have afforded some post-hoc rationalization, at the level of individuals, of unacceptable military behaviour. Not everyone is happy, especially given the significantly tightened legal and ethical universe in which the modern military have to operate compared with the rather more flexible, questionable or even questionably legal political rationales under which our new 'small wars' (Rubin, 2002; Forster, 2012) may be declared and conducted. Yet as Fraser (2017) has noted, 'we do the vast majority of [our] soldiers an injustice if we refuse to distinguish between those who break the law and those who do not. Everyone in Helmand was stressed. Not everyone shot their prisoners'.

Making a related point, Akam has noted that 'in the Iraq and Afghan wars, Britain developed a globally unprecedented web of accountability measures for individual malfeasance on the battlefield' (Akam, 2021: 387). Following in the tracks of Geneva Conventions, the Nuremberg tribunal, the UN Charter of 1945 and the Universal Declaration of Human Rights in 1948, the ethical and accountable combat zone came to be established. The detailed forensic deconstruction, paragraph after paragraph, of decisions, perceptions and actions on the 'Danny Boy' battlefield in Iraq throughout the Al Sweady Inquiry report represents perhaps the most meticulous version of this development, but as Akam notes, even while this was happening, no equivalent level of accountability was established 'for the high-level decision-making that led to the prosecution of two deeply troubled campaigns' in the first place (Akam, 2021: 388). Lorenzo agrees that, in the war crimes of the war on terror, 'the soldiers involved were thrashed about by social forces beyond their personal control', they worked in a 'moral and legal fog within poisoned command climates'. Furthermore, 'the social and structural conditions under which the soldiers committed actions labelled as "war crimes" were not conditions the soldiers created for themselves'. And yet, 'soldiers who are perceived as responsible for war crimes are punished while civilian and military leaders who established the conditions that made these acts possible are not' (Lorenzo, 2014: 174). The real irony of the ethical battlefield in the 'juridified' military is this seeming exoneration of the *most* powerful, and the ultimate neglect of the 'othered': the usual victims. Indeed, the passage of recent legislation, the Overseas Operations (Service Personnel and Veterans) Act, 2021, for such overtly political reasons, restricting the liability or accountability of foreign deployed troops in environments where war rapidly mutates into crime, might be a case in point. One suspects that many a military commander engaged in the pacification of Britain's southern hemisphere territories would have appreciated such a provision (though, in fact, he scarcely needed it). It marks a step back to a moral dark age, showing especially little consideration for the real *victims* of imperial violence – not the soldiers, invaders and looters, but especially the Indigenous people themselves.

Note

[1] Following Freedom of Information requests by Action on Armed Violence, the British government paid compensation to the families of at least 64 children, aged between 1 and 15, killed by British military action in Afghanistan, an investigation has found, four times higher than hitherto acknowledged (Perry, 2022). The actual figure may be double this as the ages of victims were not always given.

References

Abrahamson, R. and Williams, M.C. (2011) *Security Beyond the State: Private Security in International Politics*. Cambridge: Cambridge University Press.

Aitken, R. (2008) *Cases of Deliberate Abuse and Unlawful Killing in Iraq in 2003 and 2004*. np: The Army, Crown Copyright.

Akam, S. (2021) *The Changing of the Guard: The British Army since 9/11*. London: Scribe Publications.

AMCU (Association of Mineworkers and Construction Union) (2014) *The Marikana Commission of Inquiry: AMCU's Heads of Argument*. AMCU Counsel Chambers, 28 October.

Anderson, D.M. and Killingray, D. (eds) (1992) *Policing and Decolonisation: Nationalism, Politics and the Police 1917–65*. Manchester: Manchester University Press.

Andrews, K. (2021) *The New Age of Empire: How Racism and Colonialism Still Rule the World*. Dublin: Penguin Books.

Arquilla, J. (2011) *Insurgents, Raiders and Bandits: How Masters of Irregular Warfare Have Shaped Our World*. Chicago: Ivan R. Dee Books.

Barr, J. (2012) *A Line in the Sand: Britain, France and the Struggle that Shaped the Middle-East*. London and New York: Simon & Schuster.

Barr, J. (2019) *Lords of the Desert: Britain's Struggle with America to Dominate the Middle-East*. London and New York: Simon & Schuster.

Bates, E.S. (2019) Distorted terminology: The UK's closure of investigations into alleged torture and inhuman treatment in Iraq. *International and Comparative Law Quarterly*, 68: 719–739.

BBC News (2006) New 'Iraq massacre' tape emerges. *BBC Home* website, 2 June. Available from: news.bbc.co.uk/1/hi/world/middle-east/35039420.stm [Accessed 15 November 2022].

Bennett, H. (2014) The Baha Mousa tragedy: British Army interrogation and detention from Iraq to Afghanistan. *British Journal of Politics and International Relations*, 16(2): 211–229.

Bourke, J. (2015) *Deep Violence: Military Violence, War Play, and the Social Life of Weapons*. Berkeley: Counterpoint.

Bowcott, O. (2012) Iraq abuse inquiry was a 'cover up' whistleblower tells court. *The Guardian*, 11 December.

Bowcott, O. (2020) Bill sets five-year limit to prosecute UK armed forces who served abroad. *The Guardian*, 18 March.

Brogden, M. and Shearing, C. (1993) *Policing for a New South Africa*. London: Routledge.

Broughton, C. (2015) *Boom, Bust, Exodus: The Rust Belt, the Maquilas and a Tale of Two Cities*. Oxford: Oxford University Press.

Bruce, D. (2016) *Commissioners and Commanders: Police Leadership and the Marikana Massacre*. Pretoria: Institute for Security Studies, Monograph No. 194.

Burke, D. (2021) *Kitson's Irish War: Mastermind of the Dirty War in Ireland*. Cork: Mercier Press.

Callwell, C.F. (1896/1996) *Small Wars: Their Principles and Practice* (4th edition). Lincoln: University of Nebraska Press.

Cobain, I. (2012) Inquiry into British abuse of Iraqi prisoners faces fresh allegations. *The Guardian*, 12 October.

Coker, C. (2007) *The Warrior Ethos: Military Culture and the War on Terror*. Abingdon: Routledge.

Defence Committee (House of Commons) (2017) *Who Guards the Guardians? MOD Support for Former and Serving Personnel*. Sixth Report of Session 2016–17. HC 109, House of Commons.

Defence Committee (House of Commons) (2019) *Drawing a Line: Protecting Veterans by a Statute of Limitations*. Seventeenth Report of Session 2017–19. Sixth Report of Session 2016–17. HC 1224, House of Commons.

DiPietro, S.M. (2016) Criminology and war: Where are we going and where have we been? *Sociology Compass*, 10(4): 839–848.

Dwyer, P. and Nettelbeck, A. (eds) (2018) *Violence, Colonialism and Empire in the Modern World*. Cham: Palgrave Macmillan.

Elkins, C. (2005) *Imperial Reckoning: The Untold Story of Britain's Gulag in Kenya*. New York: Henry Holt/Owl Books.

Elkins, C. (2022) *Legacy of Violence: A History of the British Empire*. London: Bodley Head.

Elliott, J. (2011) Reporter recounts massacre revealed by WikiLeaks. *Salon*, 3 September.

Farmer, B. (2008) US warplanes bomb wedding party, Afghans claim. *Daily Telegraph*, 5 November.

Fekethe, S. (2020) No successful prosecutions for Marikana massacre, eight years later. *IOL*, 13 August. Available from: https://www.iol.co.za/news/south-africa/north-west [Accessed 15 November 2022].

Fitzgibbon, W. and Lea, J. (2020) *The Security Industry, War and Crime Control*. London: Pluto Press.

Fitzsimmons, S. (2016) *Private Security Companies during the Iraq War: Military Performance and the Use of Deadly Force*. London: Routledge.

Forbes, T. (2014) *The Report of the Al Sweady Inquiry* (2 vols), HC 818 i-ii. London: House of Commons.

Forster, A. (2012) British judicial engagement and the juridification of the armed forces. *International Affairs*, 88(2): 283–300.

Fraser, G. (2017) Marine A must not become a hero, he forgot the difference between right and wrong. *The Guardian*, 30 March.

Gage, W. (2011) *The Baha Mousa Public Inquiry Report* (3 vols), HC 1452 – i-iii. London: The Stationery Office.

Goldenberg, S. (2006) Marines may face trial over Iraq massacre. *The Guardian*, 27 May.

Gott, R. (2011) *Britain's Empire: Resistance, Repression and Revolt*. London: Verso.

Gregory, D. (2004) *The Colonial Present: Afghanistan, Palestine, Iraq*. Oxford: Blackwell.

Hale, C. (2013) *Massacre in Malaya: Exposing Britain's My Lai*. Stroud: The History Press.

Holmes, R. (2007) *Dusty Warriors*. London: Harper Perennial.

Holmqvist, C. (2014) *Policing Wars: On Military Intervention in the 21st Century*. Basingstoke: Palgrave Macmillan.

IGADF (Inspector General of the Australian Defence Force) (2020) *Afghanistan Inquiry Report*. Commonwealth of Australia.

Khumalo, Z. (2022) Marikana case: Cops back in court. *South Africa News24*, 16 February. Available from: https://www.news24.com/news24/southafrica/news/marikana-trial-cops-back-in-court [Accessed 15 November 2022].

Kitson, F. (1971) *Low Intensity Operations*. London: Faber.

Lopez, R. (2010) Soldier's shocking allegation: Troops ordered to engage in '360 rotational fire' against civilians. *Global Policy Forum*, 21 June.

Lorenzo, R. (2014) *The Puritan Culture of America's Military: US Army War Crimes in Iraq and Afghanistan*. Farnham: Ashgate.

Marikana Commission of Inquiry (2016) *Report on Matters of Public, National and International Concern Arising out of the Tragic Incidents at the Lonmin Mine in Marikana, in the North West Province*. Chairman: I.G. Farlam.

McGarry, R. and Walklate, S. (2019) *A Criminology of War?* Bristol: Bristol University Press.

Morris, S. (2007) First British soldier to be convicted of a war crime is jailed. *The Guardian*, 1 May.

Morris, S. (2017) Alexander Blackman's company was out of control, claims former comrade. *The Guardian*, 15 March.

Muschalek, M. (2019) *Violence as Usual: Policing and the Colonial State in German South-West Africa*. Ithaca, NY: Cornell University Press.

Neocleous, M. (2014) *War Power, Police Power*. Edinburgh: Edinburgh University Press.

Newbery, S. (2016) The UK, interrogation and Iraq. *Small Wars and Insurgencies*, 27(4): 659–680.

Newsinger, J. (1997) *Dangerous Men: The SAS and Popular Culture*. London: Pluto Press.

Newsinger, J. (2006) *And the Blood Never Dried: A People's History of the British Empire*. London: Bookmarks Publications.

Newsinger, J. (2016) Review of Fitzsimmons (2016). *Race & Class*, 58(2): 96–99.

Norton-Taylor, R. (2014) British soldiers 'violated Geneva conventions', al-Sweady inquiry told. *The Guardian*, 16 April.

Oakes, D. and Clark, S. (2017) The Afghan files: Defence leak exposes the deadly secrets of Australia's Special Forces. *ABC News*, 10 July. Available from: https://www.abc.net.au/news/2017-07-11/killings-of-unarmed-afghans-by-australian-special-forces [Accessed 15 November 2022].

Perry, K. (2022) Scores of Afghan children killed by British military. *The Times*, 10 November.

Pfau, M., Haigh, M.M., Logsdon, L., Perrine, C., Baldwin, J.P., Brietenfeldt, R.E., et al (2005a) Embedded reporting during the invasion and occupation of Iraq: How the embedding of journalists affects television news reports. *Journal of Broadcast Journalism & Electronic Media*, 49(4): 468–487.

Pfau, M., Wittenburg, E.M., Jackson, C., Mehringer, P., Lanier, R., Hatfield, M., et al (2005b) Embedding journalists in military combat units: How embedding alters television news stories. *Mass Communication and Society*, 8(3): 179–195.

Rubin, G. (2002) United Kingdom military law: Autonomy, civilisation, juridification. *Modern Law Review*, 65(1): 36–57.

Sanghera, S. (2021) *Empireland: How Imperialism has Shaped Modern Britain*. London: Penguin Books.

Satia, P. (2008) *Spies in Arabia: The Great War and the Cultural Foundations of Britain's Covert Empire in the Middle East*. Oxford: Oxford University Press.

Scahill, J. (2007) *Blackwater: The Rise of the World's Most Powerful Mercenary Army*. London: Serpent's Tail.

Shackle, S. (2018) Why we may never know if British troops committed war crimes in Iraq. *The Guardian*, 7 June.

Singer, P.W. (2008 [2003]) *Corporate Warriors: The Rise of the Privatized Military Industry* (updated edition). Ithaca, NY: Cornell University Press.

Sturcke, J. (2008) US air strike wiped out Afghan wedding party, inquiry finds. *The Guardian*, 11 July.

Thomas, M. (2012) *Violence and Colonial Order: Police, Workers and Protest in the European Colonial Empires, 1918–1940*. Cambridge: Cambridge University Press.

Tilghman, A. (2006) 'I came over here because I wanted to kill people'. *The Washington Post*, 30 July.

Visontay, E. and Knaus, C. (2020) Inquiry into alleged war crimes by Australian Special Forces in Afghanistan delivers final report. *The Guardian*, 6 November.

Vulliamy, E. (2011) *Amexica: War along the Border Line*. New York: Vintage Books.

Walter, D. (2017) *Colonial Violence: Colonial Empires and the Use of Force*. Oxford: Oxford University Press.

Whyte, D. (2007) The crimes of neo-liberal rule in occupied Iraq. *British Journal of Criminology*, 47: 177–195.

Wiener, M.J. (2009) *An Empire on Trial: Race, Murder and Justice under British Rule: 1870–1935*. Cambridge: Cambridge University Press.

Willacy, M. (2020) Video shows Australian SAS soldier shooting and killing unarmed man at close range in Afghanistan. ABC News Investigations & Four Corners, 16 March. Available from: www:/http.abc.net.au/news/2020-03-16/video-shows-afghan-man-shot-at-close-range-by-australian-sas/12028512 [Accessed 16 December 2022].

Williams, A. (2018) The Iraq abuse allegations and the limits of UK law. *Public Law*, 33: 461–481.

Williams, A.T. (2012) *A Very British Killing: The Death of Baha Mousa*. London: Jonathan Cape.

Wood, B. (2019) *Double Crossed: A Fighting Man under Fire*. Penguin: Random House.

18

Conclusion/Afterword

Roxana Pessoa Cavalcanti, Zoha Waseem and Peter Squires

The struggles of our contemporary moment, the deepening of social inequalities around the world, the rise of authoritarian governments, the routine violence of corporations, state institutions and state agents, as well as the contestation of these circumstances by grassroots groups and social movements – all inspired our initial symposium at the University of Brighton in 2019. Since then, the world entered the global COVID-19 pandemic, and international struggles against racism, police violence, and structural political and economic exclusions have gathered momentum, trying to disrupt the continuum of interlocking forms of oppression. More recently, new wars have started, reminding us as we move from one conjuncture to another, that this dialogue around repression and resistance is unfinished, it is a beginning, rather than an endpoint, to moments of change.

The 25 authors – thinkers, scholars and activists – who have contributed to this volume bring their situated work to name and challenge the conditions of the current moment, in attempts to collectively unsettle and address the legacies and conditions of interconnected forms of social, racial, gendered, political and economic injustices. This is an effort to transform existing social orders. We offer an admittedly value-laden contribution to current debates in the social sciences and humanities through cross-fertilization of ideas and experiences, while challenging oppression and eurocentrism. Relatedly, we demonstrate that there is much to be learned when Southern, postcolonial and decolonizing lenses are applied to criminology and criminal justice research. Their contributions must be considered, including the perspectives of Marxist, feminist, Africana and queer scholars working in Southern contexts or Southern issues. Our contributors have engaged with many of these perspectives in their respective chapters. We hope future criminological debates will continue to challenge the epistemological inequalities and hierarchies still evident as the potent legacies of colonialism, patriarchy and capitalism.

The chapters here, at their core, ask and address critical questions about 'who has the power to label another as deviant', 'who makes the rules', 'who causes the harm' and 'who collects the profits' (Agozino, 2003: 46). The aim of this task is to liberate knowledge from 'the shackles of imperialist reason' (Agozino, 2003: 245). This work urges us to address the conditions, crises and processes that are tied to specific developments in capitalism. This goes from the social processes that produce 'the human' or negate the condition of humanity to some groups, to the contemporary privatization of nature, land and institutions of repression.

The central themes of this collection have brought to the fore the importance of decolonization and abolitionist feminism. Decolonization in academic discussions often refers to three central tenets: decolonization of knowledge (for example, decolonization of the curriculum/disciplines/reading lists), decolonization of institutions (for example, acknowledgement, proportionate representation and inclusion of Indigenous, Black, Afro-descendant and diasporic scholars in universities), and, at the level of students, addressing 'attainment gaps', diversity issues and expanding access to education. Given the risk of 'Northerncentrism in the way that decolonial scholarship may ignore decolonial scholars from the global South' (Moosavi, 2020: 332), our aim has been to work in collaboration with as many authors from the global South as we could, while expanding our engagement with decolonial scholarship, the theories and knowledge produced in and from the margins. In this quest, contextualizing and bringing attention to the experiences of Indigenous peoples, Black and Afro-descendant communities, women, minorities and other marginalized groups has been one of the central themes and strengths of our collection. But decolonization also means the decolonization of the mind (Thiong'o, 1986; Mignolo, 2020), reparation and return of resources. This decolonization is not a metaphor (Tuck and Yang, 2012). As Fanon warned decades ago:

> Colonialism and imperialism have not settled their debt to us once they have withdrawn their flag and their police from our territories. For centuries the capitalists have behaved like real war criminals in the underdeveloped world. Deportation, massacres, forced labour, and slavery were the primary methods used by capitalism to increase its gold and diamond reserves, and establish its wealth and power. (Fanon, 2005 [1963]: 57)

In some ways, this project has been about opposing the violence of colonial (and postcolonial) epistemes, but our attempt here has also been to think of alternative futures by expanding our understanding of diverse experiences in contextualized and historicized material realities. It is an attempt to disrupt conventional and mainstream social science. It is an attempt to 'think otherwise' (Mignolo, 2014: 179), to understand, for example, how by looking at contemporary issues of security, policing and social order from these critical and new angles, we can challenge and understand the legacies of ideas about who counts as human, what counts as rights, and how human rights are socially and politically constructed (Mignolo, 2014). This is because the task of reintroducing 'humanity' to the world is not complete. Addressing the legacies of colonialism, empire and slavery is a 'colossal' task and agenda and requires 'European masses first to all decide to wake up, put on their thinking caps and stop playing the irresponsible game of Sleeping Beauty' (Fanon, 2005 [1963]: 62). We hope that in this text we have contributed to that project and can influence further research in this area.

When we organized the conference in Brighton, from which this book has resulted, our aims were relatively limited, in that, as explained in the Introduction, we sought to contribute to the developing project of 'Southern Criminology'. Three years on, that aspiration has clearly developed: the academic discourse of 'Southern Criminology' has evolved and has necessarily increasingly engaged with older debates on imperialism and decolonization. The #BlackLivesMatter movement has truly transcended borders, fuelling protest movements and civil society resistance against unjust regimes around the world, from the UK to Nigeria. Simultaneously, populist leaders with authoritarian tendencies have continued to curtail civil liberties, empowering law enforcement institutions to clamp down on dissent and demands for democratic rights, online and on the streets (as seen in India, Brazil, the Philippines and Pakistan). A viral pandemic has swept through the globe, intensifying inequalities of race, gender and class, and refashioning relationships between public health and social discipline while drawing upon new laws and tougher policing to protect the state and its institutions from the threat of the 'contaminated public'. Something uncannily resembling the 'pacification power' of the old global empires has resurfaced, adding impetus to a growing critique of contemporary policing theory and practice (Fatsis and Lamb, 2022). The rhetoric of 'saving lives' became the 'covid excuse' to continue re-enacting long-patterns of racialized border violence by avoiding rescuing people at the borders and letting 'othered' people die (Stierl and Dadusc, 2021). Later, as the final manuscript was being pulled together, in another echo of old empire militarism, war broke out in Europe, reawakening the nightmares of the very worst years of the 20th century (Snyder, 2011) and plunging millions into a new central European refugee crisis, only months after the humanitarian disaster of the Western exit from Afghanistan. The criminalization of immigration and the overpolicing of borders and migrants, especially after such prolonged conflicts, exacerbated processes of 'othering', creating new 'suspicious communities'.

Looking back

When the opportunity came to widen the focus of our day conference and plan this book, we tried to extend our global reach and embrace a broader range of new scholarship, even as it remained consistent with our original project of assessing the contribution of an interdisciplinary criminology to these various concerns. To this end the various chapters in this volume offer insights and commentaries from both scholars and activists in Central and Southern America, Southeast Asia, North and Southern Africa, the Middle East, the Caribbean and Oceania.

In Part I, we sought to set an imperial 'legacy context'. In so doing, we explored how colonial violence, racism and criminalization have helped establish a repressive policing template that has never been entirely eradicated and which, in moments of perceived crisis, protest, resistance, or wars on 'crime' and 'terror', resurfaces with a vengeance. In this regard, authors explored these trends by drawing upon research on the policing of creative and musical expression in Britain, the policing of dissent and sedition in Pakistan, asymmetric policing in the Middle East, and the policing of protests around the world since 2020. The chapters in this section bear out the forceful conclusion arrived at by Caroline Elkins in her recently published and much acclaimed *Legacy of Violence: A History of the British Empire* (2022):

> The same kind of control, and the dog whistles of populist racialized power that beckon it, have unfolded across the globe in various forms, whether they be in demands to go it alone, to privilege racial ethnic and religious majorities or Make America Great Again. Indeed a 'rule of law' similar to the one that underwrote ... the British Empire is clearly being deployed today in the language of 'law and order' to justify crackdowns on dissent, be they repeated protests against racial injustice in Britain, or peaceful demonstrations challenging the invocation of colonial-era laws in Modi's India, or the repression of Blacks at the hands of police forces ostensibly there to 'protect and serve' ... while deportations, crackdowns and incarcerations continue to punish society's alleged pollutants who threaten the natural order of things. (Elkins, 2022: 680)

In Part II our focus shifted to assess the potential for and extent of organizational change in a range of Southern policing and penal policy settings. The limited and problematic character of police reform in Trinidad and Tobago and in São Paulo, Brazil, are analysed from both 'top-down' and 'bottom-up' perspectives, revealing a failure to fundamentally rethink the nature of police reform and the role of the police in contemporary society (Vitale, 2017: 27). Further chapters in this part explore the unique politics of incarceration in Brazil, in their own ways detailing the character of struggles of hegemony, political economy and prison discipline in Brazil, raising questions regarding the adequacy of Northern 'political economy of imprisonment' perspectives in explaining penal politics in the global South.

Part III shifts focus, somewhat, seeking to understand Indigenous perspectives on historical processes of conflict, resistance and culture-making. Where Parts I and II focused upon the violent legacies of policing and struggles around authority in the penal system, Part III considers the production and reproduction of a kind of liveable social order. Here, we were presented with an Indigenous narrative showing how a hundred-year-old colonial incursion eventually resulted in a resistance movement challenging the exploitation arising from mining operations in Bougainville. Although the resulting conflict claimed many lives, it facilitated a 'decolonization of knowledge' and the reclamation of cultural identity and practices. Two further chapters also participate in a political narration of *favela* culture'. In the first place, these chapters describe a kind of community activism by which certain 'community leaders' cultivate a capacity to speak for and represent their communities vis-à-vis state agencies and authorities. In a second place, we learned of the emotional politics through which communities process grief and negotiate their way through the aftermath of lethal violence. Finally, our contributors explored the ways in which postcolonial feminists working in non-governmental organizations and peacebuilding projects have sought to insert an intersectional gender perspective into developing debates about peace and human security.

Our focus shifts once again in Part IV, where we engage with a number of the harms associated with the policies, interventions and practices of modern states, their institutions and their corporate surrogates, especially including police and military agencies. In some locations this involves the criminalization (*over-criminalization*) of democratic protest and in other contexts exploitative forms of extractivism (primitive accumulation), coerced and informal labour, and the forced displacement of Indigenous peoples from new commercial enclosures. Going further into the realm of corporate harm and privatization of security, we explored the role of new private security and private military companies (mercenaries) found to be undertaking the coercive dirty work of states and corporations. Similarly, a final chapter explored the sudden deaths, torture and inhuman treatment that has so often accompanied the military adventures of Northern states and coalitions, the dark side of a renewed neoliberal imperialism.

Throughout this collection, we have argued from and prioritized the integrity and coherence of distinctly 'Southern' and 'postcolonial' perspectives, with new and, often silenced, Indigenous voices enriching criminology through the pursuit of justice, security and the furtherance of human rights. At times this has entailed exposing criminalizing processes, abuses and harms and pointing out the limits of Northern or 'imperial' vision. But in sharp contrast to the hegemony of neoliberal imperialism, this does not imply any new totalizing vision, rather it is offered as a critique – a corrective – perhaps a 'pedagogy of the oppressed' (Freire, 1970) and a critique of 'imperialist reason' as Agozino (2003) put it. In this book we hope we have contributed to liberatory and humanizing aims.

Pathways for further research

In conclusion, this collection looked at the margins, at and from the periphery, as places not of absence with simply a legacy of pain, as decolonial feminists Lelia Gonzalez (2020 [1988]) and Djamila Ribeiro (2019) propose, thinking of these as spaces of struggle and resistance, spaces of 'potencia' (Gago, 2020), where communities organize and struggle for justice. This is an attempt to create radical alternative futures with better access to education, health, housing, employment opportunities, that challenge the oppression and criminalization of marginalized groups.

Moving forward, Southern and postcolonial research within criminology, and of course more interdisciplinary work that connects to this discipline, should further this important agenda. In doing so, we ask researchers to consider several important questions and concerns. In the first instance, what should be the methodological and ethical concerns guiding Southern and postcolonial criminology? Brown (2021) wrote about the importance of conducting ethical research, such that does not use Southern citizens and subjects as a 'means' to knowledge production, but rather, as we have sought to do here, gives their perspectives, voices and narratives the space they deserve, and the epistemological power they have not yet held.

Second, in taking up the idea of pacification (as discussed by Squires in Chapter 2 of this volume, and Neocleous elsewhere), as well as the harmful subjugation and subservience of certain communities, classes and races, both in Southern spheres but also in Northern (and Western) spaces, the discipline will benefit from developing intersectional approaches to crime, insecurity and global harms, considering not just the social markers of race, class and gender, but also ethnicity, religion, caste and age. Relatedly, empirical inquiries on Southern and postcolonial perspectives will also benefit from the way critical criminology investigates the role of the state in the commission of crimes and harms. How can the state, and its institutions and actors, be brought more critically into our conversations? The study of state crimes is still a developing area (Green and Ward, 2004; Stanley and McCulloch, 2013; Lasslett, 2014), but no doubt challenges a range of capitalist and neocolonial discourses, especially in how it connects to the sheer range of atrocities committed by the elite, the powerful, the protected – environmental crime, conflict-induced crime, financial and corporate crime, even state terrorism. While some of our contributions have touched upon these varieties of injustices, we hope this volume will influence further empirical and theoretical inquiries into these areas and expand the ambit of Southern and postcolonial criminology.

And lastly, how can Southern and postcolonial perspectives inform our understanding when it comes to knowledge production pertaining to transformative and policy-driven initiatives? Penal and prison reforms in the global South have often uncritically adopted and tried to implement donor-funded, Western-centric reform agendas and strategies, largely unsuccessfully (such as the idea of 'community policing'). What would an Indigenous approach to such reform strategies and change look like? Again, some of our contributors have attempted to pave the way for such thinking and debates, and we hope these will be developed and expanded in subsequent scholarship on Southern, postcolonial and critical perspectives on crime, justice, punishment and social order to yield tangible results for human security, liberty and freedom.

References

Agozino, B. (2003) *Counter-Cultural Criminology: A Critique of Imperialist Reason*. London: Pluto Press.

Brown, M. (2021) Truth and method in southern criminology. *Critical Criminology*, 29: 451–467.

Elkins, C. (2022) *Legacy of Violence: A History of the British Empire*. London: Bodley Head.

Fanon, F. (2005 [1963]) *The Wretched of the Earth*. New York: Grove Press.

Fatsis, L. and Lamb, M. (2022) *Policing the Pandemic: How Public Health becomes Public Order*. Bristol: Bristol University Press.

Freire, P. (1970) *Pedagogy of the Oppressed*. New York: Continuum Books.

Gago, V. (2020) *Feminist International: How to Change Everything*. London: Verso Books.

Gonzalez, L. (2020 [1988]) Por Um Feminism Afro-Latino-Americano, in H.B. De Hollanda (ed) *Pensamento Feminista Hoje: Perspectivas Decoloniais*. Rio De Janeiro: Bazar Do Tempo, pp 12–20.

Green, P. and Ward, T. (2004) *State Crime: Governments, Violence and Corruption*. London: Pluto Press.

Lasslett, K. (2014) *State Crime on the Margins of Empire: Rio Tinto, the War on Bougainville and Resistance to Mining*. London: Pluto Press.

Mignolo, W. (2014) From 'human rights' to 'life rights', in C. Douzinas and C. Gearty (eds) *The Meanings of Rights: The Philosophy and Social Theory of Human Rights*. Cambridge: Cambridge University Press, pp 161–180.

Mignolo, W.D. (2020) On decoloniality: Second thoughts. *Postcolonial Studies*, 23(4): 612–618.

Moosavi, L. (2020) The decolonial bandwagon and the dangers of intellectual decolonisation. *International Review of Sociology*, 30(2): 332–354. DOI: 10.1080/03906701.2020.1776919

Ribeiro, D. (2019) *Quem Tem Medo do Feminismo Negro?* São Paulo: Compahia das Letras.

Snyder, T. (2011) *Bloodlands: Europe between Hitler and Stalin*. London: Vintage Books.

Stanley, K. and McCulloch, J. (eds) (2013) *State Crime and Resistance*. London: Routledge.

Stierl, M. and Dadusc, D. (2021) The 'Covid excuse': European border violence in the Mediterranean Sea. *Ethnic and Racial Studies*. DOI: 10.1080/01419870.2021.1977367

Thiong'o, N.W. (1986) *Decolonising the Mind: The Politics of Language in African Literature*. London: James Currey.

Tuck, E. and Yang, K.W. (2012) Decolonization is not a metaphor. *Decolonization: Indigeneity, Education & Society*, 1(1): 1–40.

Vitale, A. (2017) *The End of Policing*. London: Verso.

Index

References to figures appear in *italic* type; those in **bold** type refer to tables.
References to endnotes show both the page number and the note number (54n3).

'21st century policing model' 112–113

A

ABG (Autonomous Bougainville Government) 201, 206, 207
ableism 63
Aboriginal people, Australia 27
Abramson, R. 332–333
Abu Ghraib prison 333
Abuelas de Plaza de Mayo (Grandmothers of the Plaza de Mayo), Argentina 237
abuses and war crimes, Iraq and Afghanistan 15, 322, 328–339, 350
activism
  criminalization of 4, 14–15, 269–271, 349, 350
  Brazil 273–285
  Ecuador 275–277
  historical context 271–273, *272*
  Mexico 277–279, 279–280
  Palácio *favela*, Rio de Janeiro 5, 14, 211–227
  policing of political protest 33–38
Aden (Yemen) 36
Adivasi people, India 63, 71
Adorno, S. 144–145, 161, 177
Aegis 305
aerial warfare 34–37, 332
Afghanistan
  abuses and war crimes 15, 322, 328–339
  'police bombing' 34–35
  US use of PMCs (private military companies) 305, 306, 317
  US withdrawal from 316
Africa
  colonial banning of African music and cultural expression 49
  colonial origins of policing 66
  COVID-19 pandemic and police violence 64
  mercenaries 304, 305–306

African-Americans
  police violence 11, 12, 33, 69–70
  see also Black people
Afro-diasporic music culture (drill music) 9, 13, 45–48, 50–51, 349
  colonial context of 48–51
  and decolonization of criminology 45–46, 51–53
Agozino, B. 1, 347, 351
Aguirre, C. 173
'air control' 34–37
Aitken, R. 335
Akam, S. 335, 339–340
Al Sweady Inquiry 335–336, 340
ALER (Human Rights Commission of the State of Rio de Janeiro) 238
Aliverti, A. 87
Al-Mahmudiyah, Iraq 330–331
Almeida, F. de 273, 274–275
Al-Qaida 307–308
Al-Shabaab 312, 313, 314, 315–316
Amnesty International 111, 315–316
Amritsar/Jallianwala Bagh massacre, India 1919 7, 34, 90, 238
Anderson, D.M. 30–31, 34
Anievas, A. 294
anti-police protest movements, and police violence 13, 62–65, 69–77
  colonial roots of policing 67–69
  shared themes in 65–67
Anti-Terrorism Act (ATA) (1975), Pakistan 85, 94
anti-terrorism legislation 273
  Latin America 270
Aotearoa-New Zealand
  anti-police protests 65, 66
  colonial origins of policing 66
  police killings of Black and Indigenous people 65
Arendt, H. 32

INDEX

Argentina 237–238
arms trade/arms control 6, 7–8, 9, 27–28
Arms Trade Treaty, UN 6
Arquilla, J. 328
Article XIX 279
Association of Caribbean Commissioners of Police 111
asymmetric warfare 305, 306
ATA (Anti-Terrorism Act) (1975), Pakistan 85, 94
'Atenco Law,' Mexico 278
Australia
  anti-police protests 65, 66, 69
  and Bougainville 192–193, 198, 200–201, 204
  military abuses and war crimes, Iraq and Afghanistan 15, 322, 338
  police killings of Black and Indigenous people 11, 65, 70, 72
Australian Defence Force 338
Autonomous Bougainville Government (ABG) 201, 206, 207

B

Bakhle, J. 85, 99
Balbus, I.D. 29
Baloch people, Pakistan 87
Banks, Joseph 27
Basu, Soumita 260
Bayer 296, 299
Bayley, B. 309–310
BCL (Bougainville Copper Ltd.) 192, 201, 202, 203, 207
Behlendorf, B. 96
Belgian Congo 32
Bell, E. 23
Belur, J. 11
Benard, Cheryl 252
Bennett, H. 335
Birmingham, UK, firearms production 25–26
black bloc tactics 275
Black epistemology 51–53
Black music *see* Afro-diasporic music culture (drill music)
Black people 11, 13, 347
  see also African-Americans
Blackman, Alexander 337–338
Blackwater 305, 333
Blanchard, E. 32, 36, 68
BLM (Black Lives Matter) movement 11, 30, 45, 64–65, 348
'blowback' 9, 11
Bodezan, S.J. 147
Boin, A. 144
Boko Haram 309
Bolivia 270
Bolsonaro, Jair 257
'boomerang effects' 8–13

Booth, Ken 288
Bosnia 254, 259
Bougainville 4, 14, 192–194, 350
  colonial period 197–200
  crisis and cultural renewal 192–194, 200–208
  pre-colonization period 194–197
Bougainville Copper Ltd. (BCL) 192, 201, 202, 203, 207
BRA (Bougainville Revolutionary Army) 192, 203–204
Bradford, B. 129, 131
Braskem petrochemical company, Maceió, Brazil 295–296, 297–298
Bratton, William 113
Brazil 3, 65, 135, 176, *272*
  anti-terrorism laws 270, 273–274
  Braskem petrochemical company, Maceió 295–296, 297–298
  Carandiru prison massacre, 1992 176
  criminal justice system 274
  criminalization of activists 273–275
  democratic period (1983 -) 123, 135, 179
  democratic policing 14, 128–129, *130*, 131, **131**, *132*, 133–136, **136–139**
  gender relations 262
  GINI index 175–176
  historical development and structure of policing 2–3, 12, 120–125
  industrialization 172, 175, 179–180
  killings of police officers 120–121
  mass incarceration 171–172, 180, 350
  military dictatorship period (1964–1985) 120, 122–123, 179, 273
  PC (civil police) 121–122, 123, 131, 133
  Penal Code 1830 174
  Penal Code 1930 174
  penal policy 3
  penal system 152–153
  PM (military police) 121–122, 122–123, 124–125, 131, 133, 134–135, 238
  police violence and killings 11, 65, 72, 120–121, 178–179
  young victims in São Paulo 14, 232–248
  Political Economy of Punishment (PEofP) 14, 169–170
  imprisonment rates and employment rates 170–173, 180
  labour conditions 179–180
  less eligibility principle 170, 175–176, 178, 181
  prison and state violence 176–179, 181
  productive relations 170, 173–175
  prison riots 14, 143–144, 160–164, 238
  2013–2015 surge in 155–160, *157*, 161
  Guarapuava penitentiary riot 151–155
  PCE (Penitenciaria Central de Estado/ Central Penitentiary of the State) riot, 2010 147–151, 160, 161

prison torture 176–177
slavery 173–175, 181, 271–272
state enlargement and modernization 172
and the UN WPS (Women, Peace and Security) Agenda 256–257
urbanization 172, 174
violence of society 178–179
war on drugs, and police violence 70–71
see also Rio de Janeiro; São Paulo
Britain *see* UK (United Kingdom)
Brogden, M. 114, 324
Brown, M. 351
Burnham Global 316
Bush, George W. 13, 278
Butler, Judith 261, 262

C

Cabral, Amilcar 194
Calderon, Felipe 277
calypso music, policing of 49–50, 51
Canada
  anti-police protests 65
  police killings of Black and Indigenous people 65, 70, 73
  police leaders in Trinidad and Tobago 112–113
  police violence against women and girls 74
capitalist accumulation 291–292
capitalist dispossession *see* dispossession
carceral state 63, 75
Caribbean
  anti-police protests 65
  colonial banning of African music and cultural expression 48–49
  decolonization and policing 34
  Carnival celebrations, policing of 49–50
Carrabine, E. 164
Carrington, K. 1, 2, 3, 5, 10, 11, 12, 87, 271
'Carta de Madrid' 277
Casanova. M.R. 258
caste, and police violence 75
CDHS (Centre for Defence of Human Rights) 241
Cedano, P.R. 277–278
CEM (Centre for Metropolitan Studies), USP (São Paulo University) 234
Central Armed Police Forces, India 71
Charleston Police Department, US 32
Chatterjee, P. 212, 294
Chevigny, P. 11
Chew, E. 26
Chies, L.A.B. 271
Chile 269, 270
China 34
Churchill, W. 7, 35
citizenship status, and police violence 69
civil police (PC), Brazil 121–122, 123, 131, 133

civil unrest
  decolonization and policing and policing 33–37
  see also activists, criminalization of; public order policing
class 63
  and police violence 69, 73, 75
Clayton, A. 35
climate change, and migration 6
Coelho, E.C. 177
'coercive instrumentation of freedom' 261, 262
Coker, C. 330
Cole, B. 24
Colombia 270
  and the UN WPS (Women, Peace and Security) Agenda 257–258
colonial difference *see* difference
Colonial Office, London 327
Colonial Police Force 31
colonial policing practices 23–24
  and Black culture and music 45–46, 48–51
  and decolonization 13, 33–37
  'Irish' or 'Ulster' model 30–31
  labour force control 32–33
  public order control 29
coloniality 62, 63, 74
  Latin America 273
colonization, benefits of 323
Colorado Party 298
Comaroff, J. 23, 24
Comaroff, J.L. 23, 24
Comité Cerezo México 279
Committee of the Restructuring of the Police Service (CRPS), Trinidad and Tobago 108
community policing initiatives, Trinidad and Tobago 111–115
CONAIE (Confederación de Nacionalidades Indígenas del Ecuador) 275–277
Connell, R. 5
Consolidated Act 1787 49
Constabulary Ordinance 1905 (Trinidad and Tobago) 108
Constellis Holdings 333
'contractors' *see* PMCs (private military companies)
Control Risks 312
Conzinc Rio Tinto of Australia (CRA) 200–201, 202
counter-colonial criminology 86–89
counterinsurgency doctrine 8
counterterrorism, and sedition laws 84, 85, 94
COVID-19 pandemic 10, 65, 346, 348
  and police violence 64, 66, 72–73
Cozzi, Eugenia 246
CRA (Conzinc Rio Tinto of Australia) 200–201, 202

INDEX

cria 219
Criminal Behaviour Orders 47, 50–51
criminology, decolonization of 45–46,
   51–53, 86–89, 99
Crown Prosecution Service, UK 47
CRPS (Committee of the Restructuring
   of the Police Service), Trinidad and
   Tobago 108
cultural renewal, Bougainville 193–194
Cunneen, C. 4, 88
Curtice, T.B. 96

D

DAG (Dyck Advisory Group) 312, 314–315
Dalit people, India 71
Danish Greenland 32
Darke, S. 271
Dasgupta, R. 98
De Giorgi, A. 169, 170
decolonial feminism 75
decolonization 7, 69, 347
   and colonial policing practices 13, 23–24,
      33–37
   of criminology 45–46, 51–53, 86–89, 99
   of institutions 66, 347
   of knowledge 191, 347, 350
   of the mind 347–348
   of university curricula 45
Defence Select Committee, UK 336–337
DeKeseredy, W. 10–11
Democracy and Development 313–314
democracy, wars for 9
democratic policing 119–120, 126–128
   Brazil 128–129, *130*, 131, **131**, *132*,
      133–136, **136–139**
Democratic Republic of the Congo 307
denuclearization movement 288
'developing countries' terminology 226
Dias, C.N. 177
difference 287, 288, 291–295, 297, 299–300
Digga D 50
disabilities, people with 63
   and police violence 65, 69, 73, 75
disarmament movement 288
dispossession 287, 288, 291–295, 297,
   299–300, 312
distributive justice 129, 133
domestic violence, by police officers 74
Domi, B. 269
Doran, M.-C. 278
Dorbecker, M.R. 277
Dresden 37
drill music *see* Afro-diasporic music culture
   (drill music)
Drill Music Translation Cadre, Metropolitan
   Police 47
drone warfare 332
drug trafficking legislation, Latin
   America 270

Dunbar-Ortiz, R. 27
Dwyer, P. 29–30
Dyck Advisory Group (DAG) 312, 314–315
DynCorp 305

E

East India Company 332
Ecuador
   anti-terrorism laws 270
   criminalization of activists 275–277
   Special Commission for Truth and
      Justice 276
Egypt 34, 36
El Salvador 253, 270
Elkins, Caroline 34, 38, 349
emotional abuse and coercive control 10
emotional language 234
empire, as a concept 287, 291
enclosure 292
   see also dispossession
England and Wales
   deaths in police custody 70, 72, 73
   see also UK (United Kingdom)
equity, in democratic policing 126
Estalonho, murder victim in Santana,
   São Paulo 245, 246, 248
ethical combat zone 339–340
Evans, J. 3
Ewatski, Jack 112–113
Executive Outcomes 305, 309
extractivism 277, 291, 298–299, 300, 350

F

'failed/failing' states 7, 8
'Families of *gatillo fácil* victims,' Argentina 238
Fanon, Franz 7, 31, 194, 347, 348
FARC-EP (Revolutionary Armed Forces of
   Colombia - People's Army) 257–258
Farias, J. 241
favelas, Brazil 176
   community activism in Palácio *favela*,
      Rio de Janeiro 5, 14, 211–227
   subaltern integration of 215–216
Fayemi, K. 304
femicide 10, 12
feminism 11
   abolitionist 347
   decolonial 75
   postcolonial 253, 262, 263, 350
Fernandez-Bessa, C. 88
firearms, proliferation of 24–28
First Nations people 66
   see also Indigenous people
Fitzgibbon, W. 331
Fitzsimmons, S. 333
Floyd, George 64, 65, 66, 72
   see also anti-police protest movements,
      and police violence; BLM (Black Lives
      Matter) movement

Fominaya, C.F. 273
Fon Filho, A. 274
food security
 Paraguay 297
 'seed sovereignty,' Mexico 296, 299
Forbes, T. 336
Forest Department, India 71
Foucault, M. 9
France
 anti-police protests 65, 69
 colonial police 31, 68
 military assistance by 309–310, 316
Franco, M.S. 178
Fraser, G. 339
FRELIMO (Frente de Libertação de Moçambique/Mozambique Liberation Front) 311, 313, 314
French Algeria 32
French, D. 34
'French' model of policing 122
Frente de Libertação de Moçambique/Mozambique Liberation Front (FRELIMO) 311, 313, 314
Frente Nacional Contra la Represión 279
Frey, A. 314
Frontier Crimes Ordinance, Pakistan 95
'frontier' masculinity 12

G

Gage, William 335
Gago, V. 299
Gandhi, Mohandas 90
gangs
 gang surveillance 10
 policing of 'gang' cultures 29, 46–48
 and prison riots 144–145
Garner, Eric 72
gas extraction, Mozambique 311–316
gender 63
 balancing and mainstreaming in UN WPS Agenda 254, 256
 failure to protect against gender-based violence 73–74
 and police violence 69, 73, 75
 see also women
General Police Intendancy, Brazil 122
genetically modified seeds 296
Geneva Conventions 9, 339
Geneva disarmament conference, 1933
 and 'police bombing' 36–38
genital mutilation 10
George Mason University, US 111
German South-West Africa 27, 32
Germany 65
Germany New Guinea (Bougainville) 193, 198
Ghana 64, 67, 68
Gibbs, Dwayne 112–113
Giuliani, Rudy 113

Gizelis, T.-I. 260
Global Homicide Report (UNODC) 25
'global South' 2, 23
 as a moving border 212, 226
Global Witness 279
Gonzalez, Leila 351
Gott, R. 34, 328
Goveia, E.V. 49
Gramsci, A. 146, 162, 163, 164
Grandmothers of the Plaza de Mayo (Abuelas de Plaza de Mayo), Argentina 237
Grech, S. 75
Green, Steven 331
Gregory, Derek 322
Grenier, J. 27
Griffith, Gary 110
Guarapuava penitentiary riot, Brazil 151–155
Guernica 37
Guyana 13

H

Haditha, Iraq 330
Haiti, sexual abuse by the UN Peacekeeping Mission 259
Hall-Sanchez, A. 10–11
Hamshi, Javed 91
Harrington, C. 260
Hashim, A. 84
Hawkins, R. 30
Headrick, D.R. 25
'hearts and minds' strategies 6, 10, 28, 224, 337
hegemony, and prison riots 143, 146, 155, 160–164
high policing 12–13
Hill, R.S. 29
Hillyard, P. 9
Hiroshima 37
Holmqvist, C. 8
Honduras 13
honesty, in PJT (procedural justice theory) 126, 127
Hong Kong 64, 82
honour killings 10
Horton, A. 306
Human Rights Commission of the State of Rio de Janeiro (ALER) 238
hyper-incarceration 63

I

IGADF (Inspector General of the Australian Defence Force) 338
IHAT (Iraq Historic Allegations Team) 336
IMF (International Monetary Fund) 207, 275, 310, 311
immigration 6, 9, 348
 and police violence 69
Immigration Removal Centres 6
imperial policing, liberal myth of 28–33

INDEX

imperialism 287, 290–291, 294, 299
imprisonment 10, 63
  see also Brazil
India 34
  anti-police protests 64, 66
  counterterrorism laws 85
  'police bombing' 35
  police violence 64–65, 66
    against women 74
  sedition laws and dissent 82, 84, 85, 89–91
Indian Army 71
Indian Imperial Police 31
Indian Penal Code 82, 89
indigeneity 4
Indigenous people 3, 4, 29, 347, 350
  Ecuador 275–277
  and firearms proliferation 26
  gender-based violence against 74
  mixed race murder adjudications in the British Empire, 1870–1935 326–327
  and police violence 11, 65, 68, 69, 75
  'scalp-hunting' 27
  see also dispossession
Indochina 68
industrial disputes, policing of 29, 68
industrialization, and firearms proliferation 26
information, in democratic policing 126
Inspector General of the Australian Defence Force (IGADF) 338
Institute for Security Studies 325
institutional racism 11
institutions, decolonization of 66, 347
insurgents, and PMCs (private military companies) 307–308
International Crisis Group 313
international law 9, 10
International Monetary Fund (IMF) 207, 275, 310, 311
international order, enemies of 10
International Violence Against Women Survey (IVAWS) 73–74
internment 9
inter-racial murders 29
interrogation practices 9, 10
intimate partner violence 10, 12
Iraq
  abuses and war crimes 15, 322, 328–339
  'police bombing' 34–35, 36
  US invasion of 261, 262
  US use of PMCs (private military companies) 305, 306, 317
Iraq Historic Allegations Team (IHAT) 336
'Irish' model of colonial policing 30–31
Iruinu, Chief Blaise 4, 192, 193, 194–200, 201–208
Ishaqi, Iraq 331–332
ISIS (Islamic State) 307–308, 316
Israel 262

Italy 35
IVAWS (International Violence Against Women Survey) 73–74

J

Jamaica 49, 65
Japan 64
Jasper, J. 235
Jauregui, B. 11
Jefferies, C. 107
Jimeno, Myriam 234
Jones, K. 26, 27
Jones, T. 126

K

Ka' Kuxtal Much Meyaj, Mexico 296
Karp, A. 25
Kenya 4, 9, 11, 34, 64
  anti-police protests 64, 66
Khan, O.P. 271
Kiernan, V.G. 37
Killingray, D. 30–31, 34, 67
Kimball, P. 143–144, 160
Kirchheimer, O. 169, 170, 171, 172, 181
Kitson, F. 328
KKK (Ku Klux Klan) 33
Knife Crime Prevention Orders 47
knowledge, decolonization of 191, 347, 350
Koerner, A. 173
Koram, K. 7, 8
Korea 64
KRS-One 53
Kumar, Kanhaiya 98
Kumar, R. 29

L

labour unrest 33–34
Lasso, Guillermo 276–277
Latin America
  anti-police protests 65
  coloniality and social order 273
  criminalization of activists 269–280
  critical thought 293
  mass incarceration 171
  'socially implanted authoritarianism' in 272
  state-society relations 270
Law of Criminal Organizations, Brazil 274
'lawfare' 83–84
Lea, J. 331, 332
legal penal system 46, 47, 54n5
Lehning, J.R. 31
LGBTQI communities 65–66, 259
liberal cosmopolitanism 287, 289–290, 299
'liberal empire' thesis 10, 325–326
'liberal militarism' 323
'liberal paradox of empire' 323
Libya 35
Liga Mexicana de Derechos Humanos 279
Lindqvist, S. 36

Lloyd George, D. 7, 37
Loader, I. 30
London Blitz 37
Loperena, C.A. 13
Lopez, R. 331
López Obrador, Andrés Manuel 298
Lorenzo. R. 340
'low intensity operations' 328
low policing 12
Lozano, Luisa 276
Lusophone (Portuguese) Empire 29
Luxemburg, R. 292
lynching
  Brazil 178
  US 33

M

Mães de Luto (Mothers in Mourning) 241
Mães de Maio (Mothers of May) 238, 241
Maguire, E.G. 111
Maintenance of Public Order Ordinate (MPO, 1960), Pakistan 85, 94
Malaysia 64, 82
Mali 309, 316, 317
Malik, H. 86
Manuel, M. 88
marginalization 62
Marikana police massacre, South Africa 324–326
Mars, J.R. 13
martial law 31
Martin, Trayvon 11
Marxist theory 287, 290, 291–292, 294–295, 325
masculinity
  and gun ownership 27
  'Southern masculinity' 12
Mastrofski, S. 111
matrilineal society, Bougainville 202
Mayan peoples 298
Mayan Train, Mexico 298
Mbembe, Achille 310–311
McClintock, A. 262
McCord, D.J. 48
McCord, Ethan 331
McFate, Sean 305, 309–310, 317
McKittrick, K. 53
McLaughlin, E. 121
Melossi, D. 171, 178
memory writings 235
mercenaries 8, 304, 305, 307, 309–310, 332–333
  Mozambique 311–316
  see also PMCs (private military companies)
'methodological nationalism' 288–289, 290
metropolitan centres, and colonial policing practices 68–69
Metropolitan Police
  Drill Music Translation Cadre 47
  institutional racism 11

Mexican Revolution, women's role in 252
Mexico 298
  anti-protest laws 278–279
  criminalization of activists 277–279
  drug trafficking legislation 270
  dual policing system 12
  'seed sovereignty' 296, 299
  violence to women 12
  War on Drugs 277–278
Mezzadra, S. 299
Middle East 35
Midnight Notes 292
Mignolo, W. 62, 63, 76, 348
military abuses and war crimes, Iraq and Afghanistan 15, 322, 328–339
military police (PM), Brazil 121–122, 122–123, 124–125, 131, 133, 134–135, 238
Mills, C. 52
mind, the, decolonization of 347–348
'minimum force' 38
mining, in Bougainville 192, 193, 194, 198, 200–201, 202, 207
Ministry of Defence, UK 339
Misse, M. 178
MNU-CDR (Unified Black Movement Against Racial Discrimination), Brazil 71
modernity 62, 287
Mohanty, C. 262
Moisés, murder victim in Santana, São Paulo 243–245, *244*, 248
Monsanto 296
Moosavi, L. 347
'moral effect' of air policing 34, 36
moral shock 235
Moreno, Lenin 275
Mothers of May (Mães de Maio) 238, 241
Mothers in Mourning (Mães de Luto) 241
Mousa, Baha 333, 334–335, 339
Movimento Passe Livre, Brazil 273
Movimento Sem Terra/Landless Movement (MST) 274
Mozambique 4
  mercenaries 307, 310, 311–316
MST (Movimento Sem Terra/Landless Movement) 274
Musah, A.-F. 304
Muschalek, M. 31–32
Musharraf, Pervez 91
Muslim immigration 261, 262–263
Muslim people, India 63, 71

N

Nagasaki 37
Namaliu, Rabbie 203, 204
NAP (National Plans of Action), UN WPS Agenda 256
Nath, Kedar 90
National Campaign Against Torture (NCAT), India 71, 74

National Congress of British West Africa 7
National Human Rights Commission 64, 71, 74
National Network for Human Rights Defenders, Mexico 278
National Plans of Action (NAP), UN WPS Agenda 256
national security 286
nationalism, sedition laws and dissent 89–91
'nationalist methodology' 289, 290
native Americans, police shootings 11–12
NCAT (National Campaign Against Torture), India 71, 74
Neocleous, M. 9–10, 12–13, 34, 35–36, 37, 63, 323, 326, 327, 332, 351
neocolonialism 310
neoliberal imperialism 4, 14, 15, 339, 350–351
neoliberal internationalism 9–10
neoliberalism 170, 171, 260
Nettelbeck, A. 29–30
Network of Communities and Movements against Violence (Rede de Comunidades e Movimentos contra Violência), Brazil 238
neutrality, in PJT (procedural justice theory) 126, 127
New International Economic Order 289
'new social movements' 288
New Zealand *see* Aotearoa-New Zealand
Newsinger, J. 29, 34, 328, 333
NGOs (non-governmental organizations), Trinidad and Tobago 112, 115
Nicaragua 145
Nigeria 34
  anti-police protests 64, 66
  extrajudicial killings and excessive us of police force 11, 64
  mercenaries 307, 309
  sedition laws and dissent 82, 89
  Shell's use of PMCs 306
Nisour Square, Iraq 333
Niterói *see* Palácio *favela*, Rio de Janeiro, community activism in
Non-Aligned Movement 289
Northern Ireland 9
  'low intensity operations' 328
  police reforms 111
Nuremburg tribunal 339

O

'Occidentosis' of criminology 46
O'Dod, D.J. 108
Omissi, D.E. 35, 36
Ona, Francis 202–203
Operation Northmoor 336, 339
O'Reilly, C. 29
organizational justice 129, 133

organized crime perspective on prison riots 144–145
Orwell, George 38
Otto, Dianne 261
Overseas Operations (Service Personnel and Veterans) Act 2021, UK 337, 340

P

pacification 13, 15, 35, 38, 326, 327, 328, 340, 348, 351
Pakistan
  corruption 72
  dual policing system 12, 96–97
  racialized violence towards minorities 87, 97
  sedition laws and dissent 13–14, 82–86, 88–91, 95–99, 349
    PTM (Pashtun Tahafuz Movement) 92–93, 93–95, 95–96, 97
    SSM (Student Solidarity March), 2019 91–93, 97, 98
Pakistan Electronic Crimes Act 2016 93, 99
Pakistan Penal Code (PPC) 85
Pakistan Tehreek-e-Insaaf government 85–86
Palácio *favela*, Rio de Janeiro, community activism in 5, 14, 211–227
Palestine 34, 262
Panel of Experts on Policing and Crowd Management, South Africa 325
Panguma Landowners' Association (PLA) 201
Panguna mine, Bougainville 192, 193, 198, 200–201, 202, 207
Papua New Guinea (PNG) *see* PNG (Papua New Guinea)
Paraguay, soy production 296–297, 298–299
Paramount 316
Paraná, Brazil *see* Brazil, prison riots
Paranaense group 149–151
parole 63
participation
  in democratic policing 126
  in PJT (procedural justice theory) 126, 127
Partido Revolucionario Institucional (PRI), Mexico 278
Pashtun people, Pakistan 87
Pashtun Tahafuz Movement (PTM) 92–93, 93–95, 95–96, 97
patriarchy 11
PC (civil police), Brazil 121–122, 123, 131, 133
PCC (Primeiro Comando da Capital) 145, 146, 148, 149–151, 152, 153, 161, 165, 177–178, 238
PCE (Penitenciaria Central de Estado/Central Penitentiary of the State) riot, 2010, Brazil 147–151, 160, 161
'Peelian Principles' of policing 30, 107

Pelter, Z. 309
Penitenciaria Central de Estado/Central Penitentiary of the State (PCE) riot, 2010, Brazil 147–151, 160, 161
Pérez Guartambel, Yaku 277
Philippines 64, 68, 70
Pigou, Piers 313
Pinheiro, P.S.R. 272
Pino, N.W. 112, 115
Pita, María Victoria 246–247
PJT (procedural justice theory) 121, 126–127
  democratic policing in Brazil 128–129, *130*, 131, **131**, *132*, 133–136, **136–139**
  see also democratic policing
PLA (Panguma Landowners' Association) 201
PM (military police), Brazil 121–122, 122–123, 124–125, 131, 133, 134–135, 238
PMCs (private military companies) 8, 15, 304–307, 309–310, 350
  abuses of power by 332–333
  assemblages of states and non-state actors 310–311
  future of 316–317
  and insurgents 307–308
  see also mercenaries
PNG (Papua New Guinea) 199–200
  and Bougainville 192–193, 203–204, 205, 207
  Westminster parliamentary system 199–200
PNGDF (Papua New Guinea Defence Force) 192, 203–204
police abolition 45
'police bombing' 34–37
police corruption, Trinidad and Tobago 108–109
Police, Crime, Sentencing and Courts Bill, UK 38, 47
police reform 3, 105–106
  Brazil 3
  and decolonization 33–34
  Northern Ireland 111
  SIDS (small-island developing states) 105–106
  Trinidad and Tobago 14, 106–115, 349
police torture
  Bangladesh 71
  India 63, 64–65, 71
  Pakistan 71–72
police violence
  colonial roots of policing 67–69
  shared themes in 65–67
  see also anti-police protest movements, and police violence
policing
  colonial roots of 66, 67–69
  cultural and political dimensions of 46, 48–53
  and military power/militarization 8, 12–13, 33, 63
  and penal power 63
  'policing by consent' 30, 38, 67

'Policing for People' model 111
Political Economy of Punishment (PEofP), Brazil 3, 14, 169–170
  imprisonment rates and employment rates 170–173, 180
  labour conditions 179–180
  less eligibility principle 170, 175–176, 178, 181
  prison and state violence 176–179, 181
  productive relations 170, 173–175
political protest see activism
politicians
  Palácio *favela*, Rio de Janeiro 216–217, 222, 224–226
postcolonial feminism 253, 262, 263, 350
postcolonial theory 287, 291, 292–293, 294, 295, 350, 351, 352
post-Fordism 170
post-traumatic stress disorder (PTSD) 329, 339
PPC (Pakistan Penal Code) 85
pre-trial detention 63
Prevention of Terrorism Act 2002, India 85
PRI (Partido Revolucionario Institucional), Mexico 278
Prigozhin, Yevgeny 317
Primeiro Comando da Capital (PCC) 145, 146, 148, 149–151, 152, 153, 161, 165, 177–178, 238
private military companies (PMCs) see PM (military police), Brazil
procedural justice theory (PJT) see PJT (procedural justice theory)
Progressive Students Collective, Pakistan 91
Prohibition of Mercenary Activities Act 2006, South Africa 315
protest, criminalization of see activism, criminalization of
PTM (Pashtun Tahafuz Movement) 72, 92–93, 93–95, 95–96, 97
PTSD (post-traumatic stress disorder) 329, 339
public order management 9, 33–37
public order policing, South Africa 324–326

Q

Quevedo, R. 50, 51
Quijano, A. 273
Quinton, P. 129, 131

R

race 63
  in British criminology 87
  and gun ownership 27
  and police violence 65, 69–70, 72–73, 75
'racial contract' 52
racial profiling 69
RAF (Royal Air Force)
  'police bombing' 34–37
rape 10, 12, 326–327
  in Brazilian prisons 177–178

INDEX

Rattray, W.A.R. 144
Razack, S.H. 11–12
RCADIC (Royal Commission into Aboriginal Deaths in Custody), Australia 65, 70
React or Die (Reaja ou Será Mortx), Brazil 71
rebranding *see* police reform
Red Nacional de Organismos Civiles de Derechos Humanos 279
Rede de Comunidades e Movimentos contra Violência (Network of Communities and Movements against Violence), Brazil 238
redress, in democratic policing 126
Reeve, R. 309
'regime change,' wars for 9
religion, and police violence 69, 75
rendition practices 10
Renfrew, B. 37
reparations, for police killings 238–239
Report of the Commission of Inquiry into the Marikana shootings 324–325
respect, in PJT (procedural justice theory) 126, 127
responsiveness, in democratic policing 126
Revolutionary Armed Forces of Colombia – People's Army (FARC-EP) 257–258
Rhodesia, ex-military mercenaries from 305, 314–315
Ribeiro, Djamila 351
right-realist perspective on prison riots 143–144, 145
Rio de Janeiro 70
  community activism in Palácio *favela* 5, 14, 211–227
  House of Correction 173
Rio Tinto 192
Roberts-Smith, Ben 338
Robson *see* Palácio *favela*, Rio de Janeiro, community activism in
Rodney, Walter 194
Rogério, murder victim in Santana, São Paulo 232–233, 234, 239, 240–241, 248
Roussef, Dilma 256
Royal Commission into Aboriginal Deaths in Custody (RCADIC), Australia 65, 70
Royal Irish Constabulary 31
  and policing in Trinidad and Tobago 107
Royal Police Guard, Brazil 122
RUC (Royal Ulster Constabulary), and policing in Trinidad and Tobago 107–108
Rusche, G. 169, 170, 171, 172, 181
Russia 311
  invasion of Ukraine 2022 306, 317
Rwanda 254
  genocide 237

S

Sahel 305–306, 307–308
Said, Edward 293
Salla, F. 143, 144–145, 161
Sankara, Thomas 194
Santana, São Paulo, Brazil, young victims of violence 14, 232–248
Santos, Juan Manuel 257
Santos, T.D. 179
São Paulo, Brazil
  democratic policing 128–129, *130*, 131, **131**, *132*, 133–136, **136–139**, 349
  young victims of violence 14, 232–248
SAPS (South Africa Police Service) 324–326
SARS (Special Anti-Robbery Squad), Nigeria 64
Satia, P. 25–26, 35, 36, 191
'scalp-hunting' 27
Scott, Gavin/Scott Drug Report 108–109
security 286–288
  critical security studies 287, 288–291
sedition laws and dissent 82
  Pakistan 13–14, 82–86, 88–91, 95–99
    PTM (Pashtun Tahafuz Movement) 92–93, 93–95, 95–96
    SSM (Student Solidarity March), 2019 91–93, 97, 98
'seed sovereignty,' Mexico 296, 299
Sen, Amartya 288
Serero, Perpetua 203
Serious Violence Reduction Orders 47
settler communities
  and firearms proliferation 26
  mixed race murder adjudications in the British Empire, 1870–1935 326–327
sexual orientation, and police violence 69, 73, 75
sexual trafficking 10
sexual violence 73–74
  in Brazilian prisons 177–178
  against men and boys 259
  by police officers 74
  UN WPS (Women, Peace and Security) Agenda 256
  in war and conflict 252, 253, 259–260
Sharpeville police massacre, South Africa 324
Shear, K. 27
Shearing, C. 324
Shell oil company 306
SIDS (small-island developing states), police reform 105–106
Sierra Leone, PMCs (private military companies) 305, 307, 309
Simmel, Georg 219
Singer, P.W. 333
Singh, A. 84, 89
Singh, Bhagat 90
Singh, M. 98
Skjelsbaeck, Inger 253
'slave patrol' policing 32–33, 48
slavery 5
  Brazil 173–175, 181, 271–272

colonial banning of African music and
    cultural expression 48–49
  and firearms 25–26
Small Arms Survey, UNODC 24
social regulation model 121
'socially implanted authoritarianism,' in Latin
    America 272
Somalia 34–35, 36
Somare, Michael 200
South Africa 34
  anti-police protests 64, 66
  ex-military mercenaries from 305, 309, 310
    DAG (Dyck Advisory Group) 312, 314–315
  firearms proliferation 26, 27
  police killings 324–326
  violence to women 12
South Africa Police Service (SAPS) 324–326
South Asia 11
  South Asian criminology 87–88
'Southern criminology' 86, 348, 351
'Southern masculinity' 12
'Southern perspectives' 86–89, 271, 350, 352
  concept and terminology 2, 62–63
'Southern Perspectives' research seminar,
    University of Brighton 2019 1, 346, 348
'Southern' policing practices 23–24
Soweto massacre, South Africa 324
soy production, Paraguay 296–297, 298–299
Spanish Civil War, women's role in 251
Special Anti-Robbery Squad (SARS),
    Nigeria 64
Special Commission for Truth and Justice,
    Ecuador 276
Specialised Tasks, Training, Equipment and
    Protection International 310
SSM (Student Solidarity March), 2019 91–93,
    97, 98
state violence
  global movement against 64–67
  see also police violence
Stavrianakis, Anna 7–8, 27–28
Stevenson, B. 12
stop-and-search practices 47, 69
Storey, W.K. 26
'strangers' 219
'structural adjustment' policies 307, 310, 311
Student Solidarity March (SSM), 2019 91–93,
    97, 98
Students Action Committee, Pakistan 91
sub-Saharan Africa
  insurgents and PMCs 307–308
  mercenaries 305–306
  UN peacekeeping forces and PMCs 307
Sudan 36
Suppression of Terrorist Activities Act 1975,
    Pakistan 85
surveillance practices 9, 33
'sustainable peace' 255, 256
Sykes, G.M. 145

T

Taiwan 64
Tankebe, J. 67, 68
Tauri, J. 4
tax havens 10
Theatre and Dance Hall Ordinance, Trinidad
    1934 50
'third world' terminology 226
Thomas, M. 31, 32, 33, 38
Tilghman, A. 331
Tilly, C. 289
TNC (transnational corporations) 310–311
  use of PMCs 307, 308–309
Toroama, Ishmael 193
TotalEnergies 311–312, 313–314, 316
trade unions
  decolonization and policing and
    policing 33–34
transformative justice 193
Transjordan 36
transnational corporations (TNC) see TNC
    (transnational corporations)
Trinidad and Tobago 2, 65
  colonial banning of African music and
    cultural expression 49, 50, 51
  deaths in police custody 111
  illegal drug trade 108–109
  police reform 14, 106, 349
    adoption foreign policing
      models 110–115
    colonial history and legacies 106–110
    political disruption 109–110
Trouillot, M.-R. 4, 5
Truth and Justice Commission,
    Paraguay 296–297
Tyler, Tom 121

U

UFF (Universidade Federal Fluminense),
    Brazil 212
UK (United Kingdom)
  anti-police protests 65, 69
  British overseas territories, as tax havens 10
  Carnival celebrations 49–50
  colonial mixed race murder adjudications,
    1870–1935 326–328
  'Kill the Bill' protests 270
  military abuses and war crimes, Iraq and
    Afghanistan 15, 322, 334–340
  'Peelian Principles' of policing 30, 107
  'police bombing' 34–37
  police violence, Black and racially
    minoritized people 72–73
  'policing by consent' 30
  policing practices 23–24
  sedition laws 84
Ukraine, Russian invasion of, 2022 306, 317
'Ulster' model of colonial policing 30–31

INDEX

UN (United Nations)
  Arms Trade Treaty 6
  ban on mercenaries 304
  Charter, 1945 339
  Committee against Torture 71
  High Commissioner for Human Rights 70
  Minimum Rules for the Treatment of Prisoners 147
  Observer Mission, Bougainville 204–205
  peacekeeping forces
    sexual abuse by 254, 259–260, 263
    use of PMCs 307
  UN WPS (Women, Peace and Security) Agenda 253–255, 261–263, 350
    critical views on 258–261
    in Latin America and the Caribbean 255–258
  World Food Programme 176
UNDP (United Nations Development Programme), Human Security report 288, 290
UNGA (United Nations General Assembly), Resolution 70/262/2016 255
UNHRC (United Nations Human Rights Council) 257
Unified Black Movement Against Racial Discrimination (MNU-CDR), Brazil 71
Universal Declaration of Human Rights, 1948 339
Universidade Federal Fluminense (UFF), Brazil 212
university curricula, decolonization of 45
Unlawful Activities Prevention Act (1967), India 85
UNODC (United Nations Office of Drugs and Crime) 24, 25
UNSC (United Nations Security Council) 307–308
  Resolutions 255, 260
  Resolution 1325/2000 254–255, 259, 260, 261
US (United States)
  anti-police protests 69
  colonial policing 68
  military abuses and war crimes, Iraq and Afghanistan 15, 322, 328–333
  military assistance by 309–310
  PMCs (private military companies) 305, 317
  police violence 11–12, 69–70, 72
  policing of African music and cultural expression 48
  policing of race riots, 1960s 29
  prison riots 143–144
  'scalp-hunting' 27
  slave patrols 32–33, 48
  and the UN WPS (Women, Peace and Security) Agenda 257
  withdrawal from Afghanistan 316
  women's role in Civil War 252
Useem, B. 143–144, 160

V

Van Craen, M. 127
Vianna, A. 241
Vietnam 37, 253
violence
  everyday violence in colonies 31–32, 326–328
  see also police violence
'virginity testing' of South Asian migrant women 10

W

Wacquant, L. 170–171
Wagner Group 306, 314, 317
Walter, D. 8
Waqar, A. 98
War on Drugs, Mexico 277–278
'war on terror' 8, 13, 273, 299, 322
Waseem, Z. 72
waste dumping 3
Watt, Steve 112–113
Wazir, Alamgir 92, 93, 97, 98
Wazir, Ali 94–95, 97
weaponization 24–28
Weegels, J. 145
Weiner, Martin 29, 326–328
Weis, V.V. 88
'welfare checks,' and police violence 73
Welzer, H. 6
West Africa 49
West, H.G. 4
Westminster parliamentary system
  PNG (Papua New Guinea) 199–200
  Trinidad and Tobago 109–110
White vigilantes, 'slave patrols' 32–33
Whiteness terminology 54n3
Whyte, B. 333, 334
Williams, A. 339
Williams, M.C. 332–333
Williams, Stephen 112
Willis, G.B. 11
women 347
  abuse by police in Mexico 278
  and conflict 14, 251–253
    UN WPS (Women, Peace and Security) Agenda 253–263, 350
  defining the category of 262
  economic impacts of colonization 323–324
  and police violence 65, 75
  role in Second World War 251
  in TTPS (Trinidad and Tobago Police Service) 113
  violence against 10–11
    failure to protect 73–74
Wood, B. 329, 334
Wood, L. 273
World Bank 200, 207, 310

World Conference on Women, Beijing, 1995 254
World Health Organization 73

Y

Yonucu, D. 88
#Yosoy132 protest, Mexico 278
Young, J. 2
young victims of police violence in São Paulo 232–235
  emotions and affect 234, 235–237
  legal defence 239, 243, 245, 246, 247–248
  recognition, tributes and memorialization 235, 237–239, 242–245, *244*, 246–248
  support for victim's families 239–240, 241–242
Yugoslavia 253, 254

Z

Zapatistas 298

www.ingramcontent.com/pod-product-compliance
Lightning Source LLC
Chambersburg PA
CBHW051524020426
42333CB00016B/1761